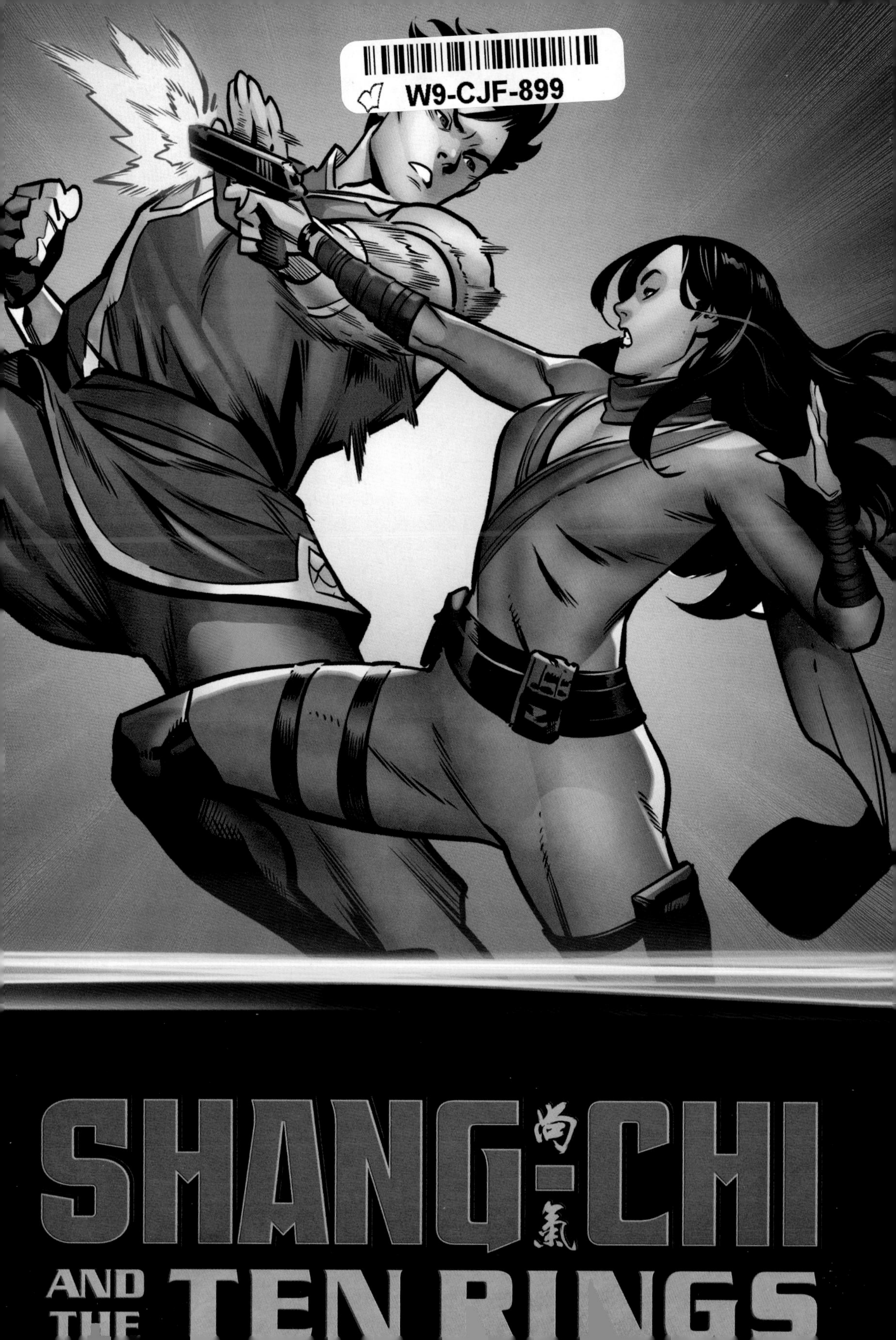

SHANG-CHI 尚氣

AND THE TEN RINGS

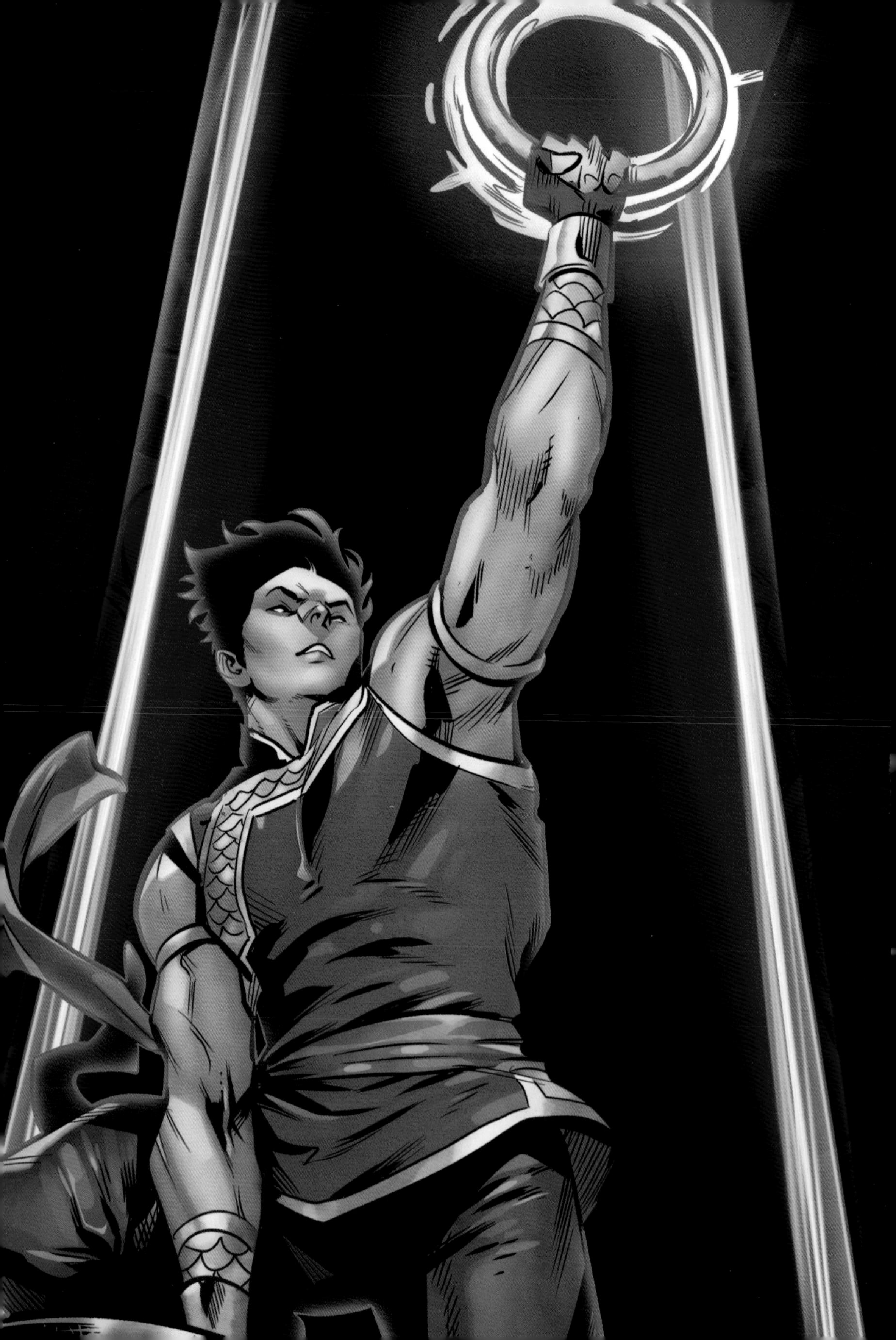

FROM THE DAY HE WAS BORN, HIS EVIL FATHER TRAINED HIM TO BE A LIVING WEAPON. HIS MIND, BODY AND SPIRIT HONED TO A RAZOR'S EDGE, HE NOW USES HIS ABILITIES TO STRIKE DOWN INJUSTICE AND ATONE FOR HIS FAMILY'S MISDEEDS. HE IS...

SHANG-CHI 尚氣
AND THE TEN RINGS

SHANG-CHI HAS RECENTLY TAKEN OVER HIS FATHER'S ORGANIZATION, THE FIVE WEAPONS SOCIETY. IT HASN'T BEEN EASY AS HE STRUGGLES TO TURN A FORCE OF EVIL INTO AN INSTRUMENT FOR GOOD.

BUT THAT ISN'T THE ONLY PROBLEM — SHANG-CHI HAS ALSO INHERITED A DEADLY WEAPON FROM ANOTHER DIMENSION: THE TEN RINGS! AND SUCH POWER DOES NOT GO UNNOTICED BY OTHERS...

WRITER **GENE LUEN YANG**

ARTIST **MARCUS TO**

COLOR ARTIST **ERICK ARCINIEGA**

LETTERER VC's **TRAVIS LANHAM**

COVER ART **DIKE RUAN** & **MATTHEW WILSON**

SHANG-CHI: MASTER OF THE TEN RINGS

WRITER **GENE LUEN YANG**   ARTIST **MICHAEL YG**

COLOR ARTISTS **ERICK ARCINIEGA** WITH PROTOBUNKER'S **FER SIFUENTES-SUJO**

LETTERER VC's **TRAVIS LANHAM**   COVER ART **JIM CHEUNG** & **ROMULO FAJARDO JR.**

ASSISTANT EDITOR: **KAT GREGOROWICZ**   EDITOR: **DARREN SHAN**   SPECIAL THANKS TO **TOM BREVOORT**

COLLECTION EDITOR JENNIFER GRÜNWALD
ASSISTANT EDITOR DANIEL KIRCHHOFFER
ASSISTANT MANAGING EDITOR MAIA LOY
ASSOCIATE MANAGER, TALENT RELATIONS LISA MONTALBANO

JEFF YOUNGQUIST VP PRODUCTION & SPECIAL PROJECTS
RODOLFO MURAGUCHI WITH SALENA MAHINA BOOK DESIGNERS
ADAM DEL RE SENIOR DESIGNER
DAVID GABRIEL SVP PRINT, SALES & MARKETING
C.B. CEBULSKI EDITOR IN CHIEF

SHANG-CHI AND THE TEN RINGS. Contains material originally published in magazine form as SHANG-CHI AND THE TEN RINGS (2022) #1-6 and SHANG-CHI: MASTER OF THE TEN RINGS (2023) #1. First printing 2023. ISBN 978-1-302-94835-1. Published by MARVEL WORLDWIDE, INC., a subsidiary of MARVEL ENTERTAINMENT, LLC. OFFICE OF PUBLICATION: 1290 Avenue of the Americas, New York, NY 10104. © 2023 MARVEL. No similarity between any of the names, characters, persons, and/or institutions in this book with those of any living or dead person or institution is intended, and any such similarity which may exist is purely coincidental. Printed in the U.S.A. KEVIN FEIGE, Chief Creative Officer; DAN BUCKLEY, President, Marvel Entertainment; DAVID BOGART, Associate Publisher & SVP of Talent Affairs; TOM BREVOORT, VP, Executive Editor; NICK LOWE, Executive Editor; VP of Content, Digital Publishing; DAVID GABRIEL, VP of Print & Digital Publishing; SVEN LARSEN, VP of Licensed Publishing; MARK ANNUNZIATO, VP of Planning & Forecasting; JEFF YOUNGQUIST, VP of Production & Special Projects; ALEX MORALES, Director of Publishing Operations; DAN EDINGTON, Director of Editorial Operations; RICKEY PURDIN, Director of Talent Relations; JENNIFER GRÜNWALD, Director of Production & Special Projects; SUSAN CRESPI, Production Manager; STAN LEE, Chairman Emeritus. For information regarding advertising in Marvel Comics or on Marvel.com, please contact Vit DeBellis, Custom Solutions & Integrated Advertising Manager, at vdebellis@marvel.com. For Marvel subscription inquiries, please call 888-511-5480. Manufactured between 1/27/2023 and 2/28/2023 by SEAWAY PRINTING, GREEN BAY, WI, USA.

0 9 8 7 6 5 4 3 2 1

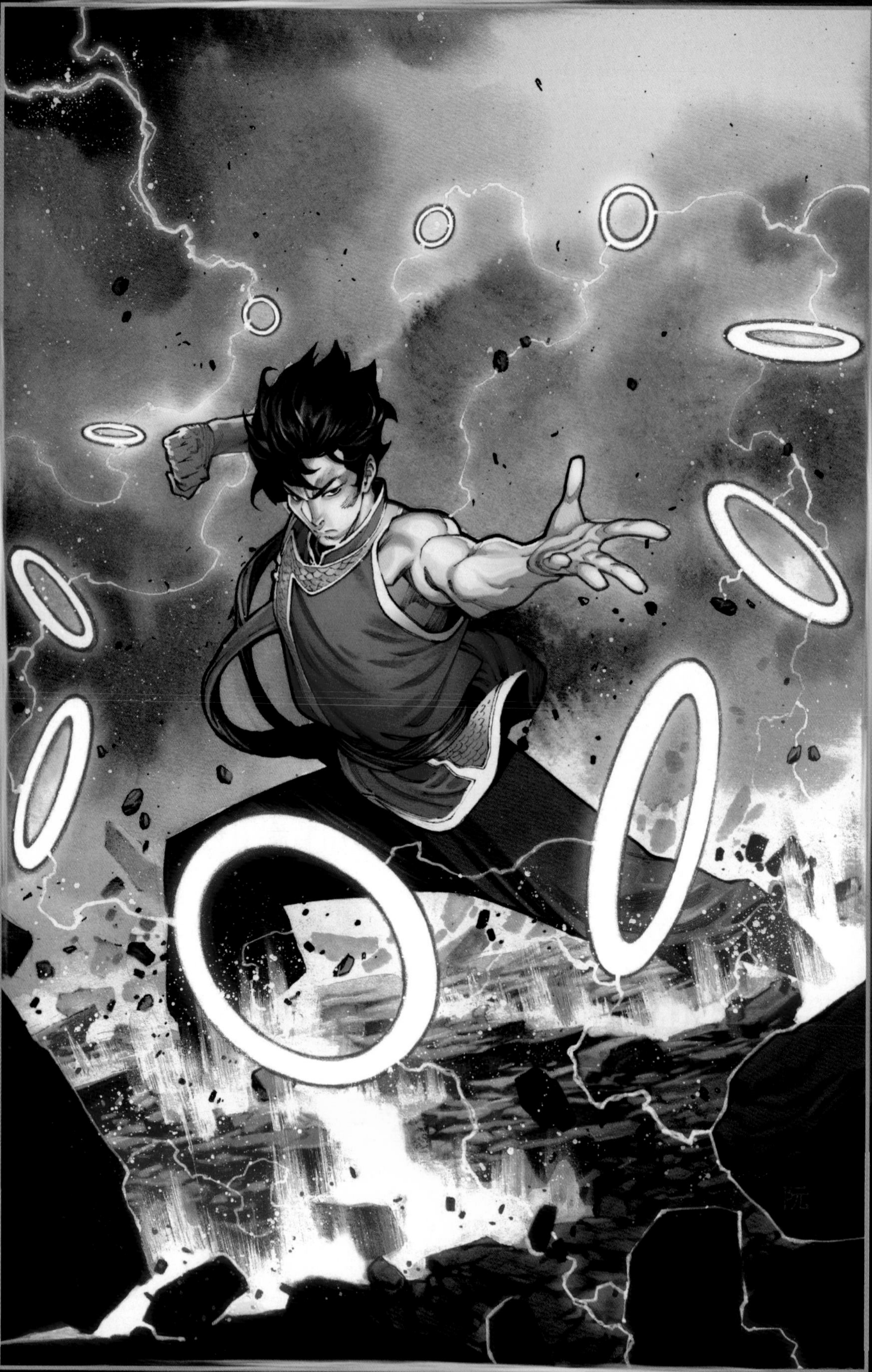

ONE

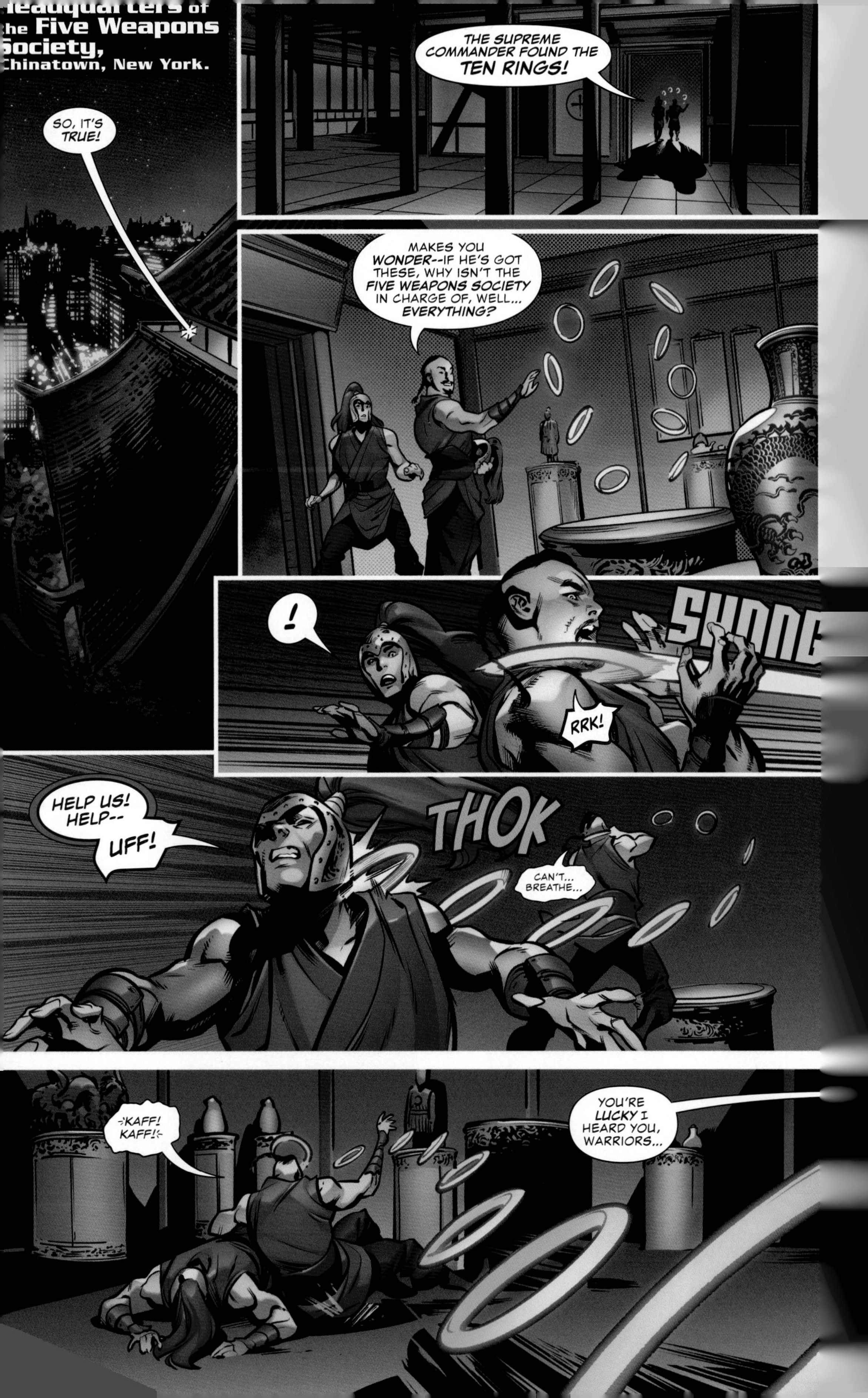
Headquarters of the Five Weapons Society, Chinatown, New York.
SO, IT'S TRUE!
THE SUPREME COMMANDER FOUND THE TEN RINGS!
MAKES YOU WONDER--IF HE'S GOT THESE, WHY ISN'T THE FIVE WEAPONS SOCIETY IN CHARGE OF, WELL... EVERYTHING?
!
RRK!
HELP US! HELP-- UFF!
THOK
CAN'T... BREATHE...
KAFF! KAFF!
YOU'RE LUCKY I HEARD YOU, WARRIORS...

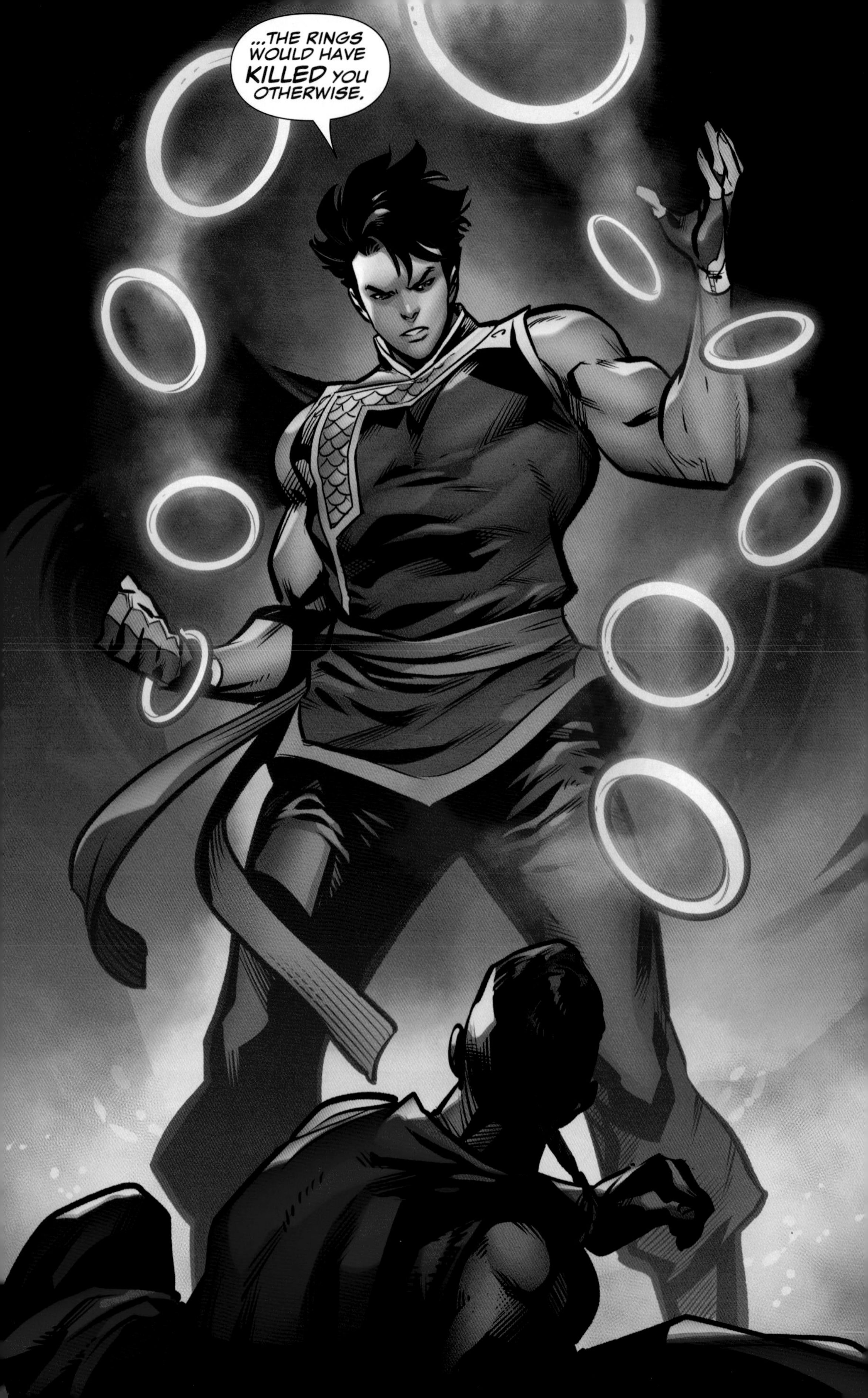
...THE RINGS WOULD HAVE KILLED YOU OTHERWISE.

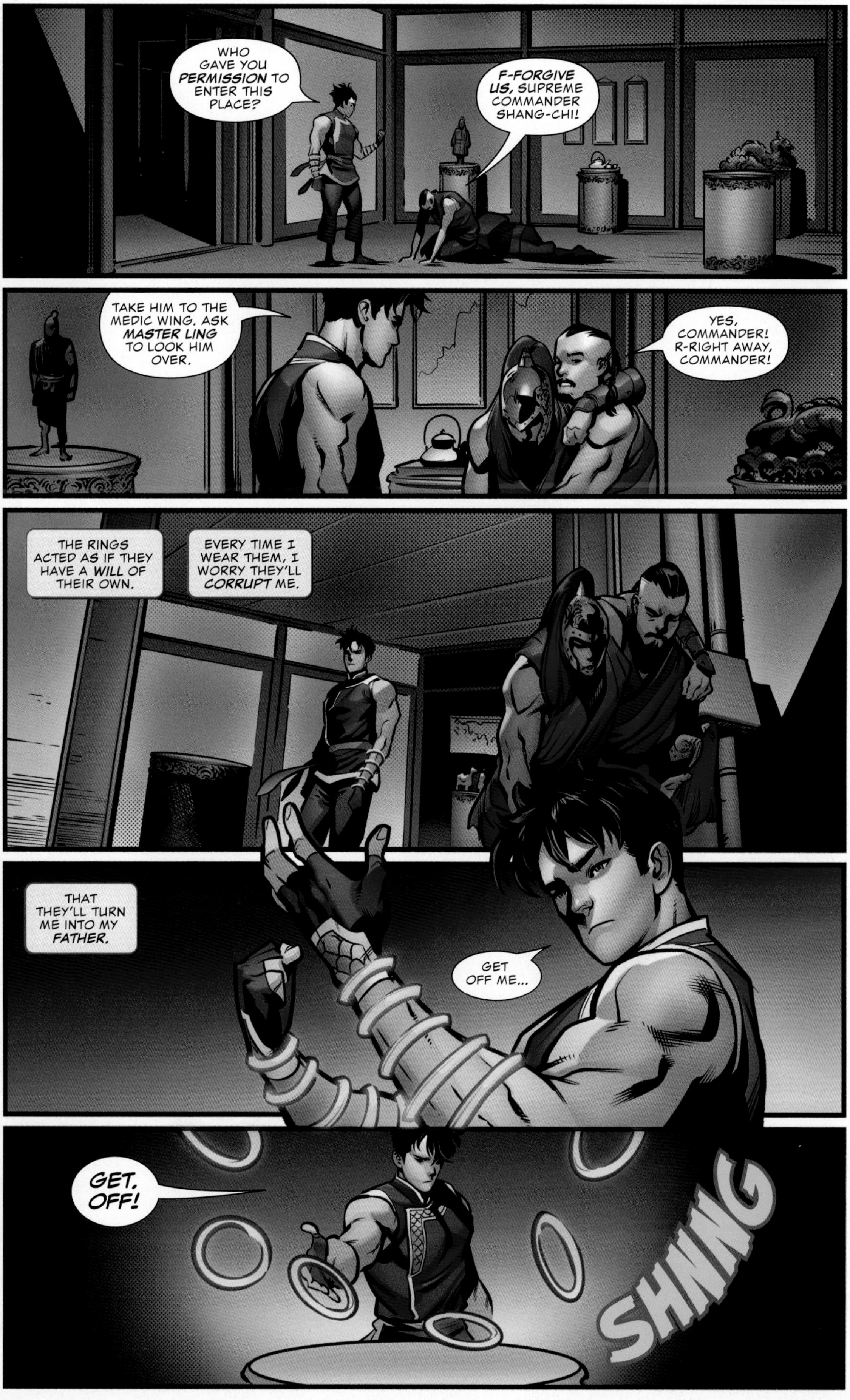
WHO GAVE YOU PERMISSION TO ENTER THIS PLACE?
F-FORGIVE US, SUPREME COMMANDER SHANG-CHI!
TAKE HIM TO THE MEDIC WING. ASK MASTER LING TO LOOK HIM OVER.
YES, COMMANDER! R-RIGHT AWAY, COMMANDER!
THE RINGS ACTED AS IF THEY HAVE A WILL OF THEIR OWN.
EVERY TIME I WEAR THEM, I WORRY THEY'LL CORRUPT ME.
THAT THEY'LL TURN ME INTO MY FATHER.
GET OFF ME...
GET. OFF!
SHNNG

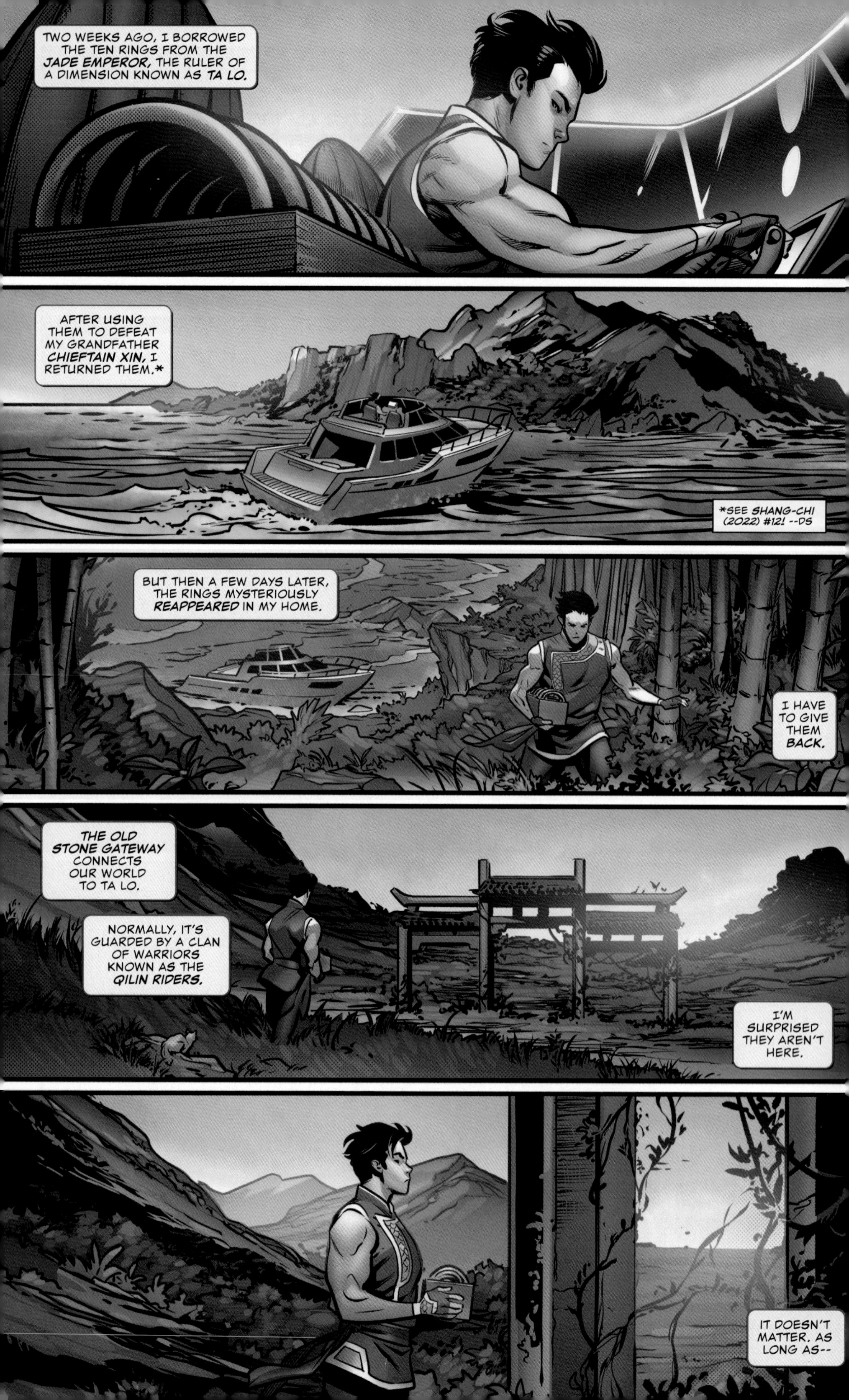

TWO WEEKS AGO, I BORROWED THE TEN RINGS FROM THE JADE EMPEROR, THE RULER OF A DIMENSION KNOWN AS TA LO.
AFTER USING THEM TO DEFEAT MY GRANDFATHER CHIEFTAIN XIN, I RETURNED THEM.*
*SEE SHANG-CHI (2022) #12! --DS
BUT THEN A FEW DAYS LATER, THE RINGS MYSTERIOUSLY REAPPEARED IN MY HOME.
I HAVE TO GIVE THEM BACK.
THE OLD STONE GATEWAY CONNECTS OUR WORLD TO TA LO.
NORMALLY, IT'S GUARDED BY A CLAN OF WARRIORS KNOWN AS THE QILIN RIDERS.
I'M SURPRISED THEY AREN'T HERE.
IT DOESN'T MATTER, AS LONG AS--

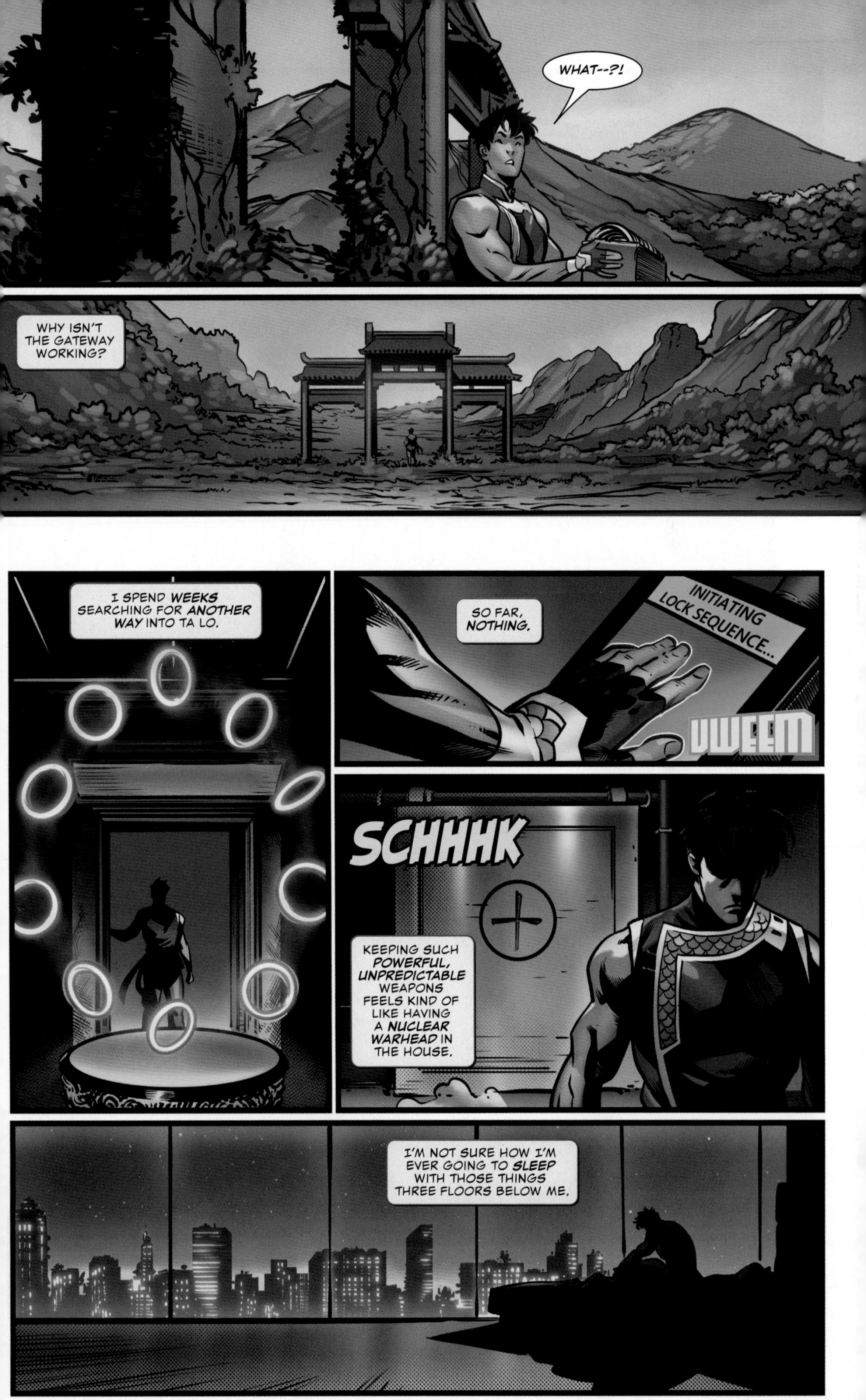
WHAT--?!
WHY ISN'T THE GATEWAY WORKING?
I SPEND WEEKS SEARCHING FOR ANOTHER WAY INTO TA LO.
SO FAR, NOTHING.
INITIATING LOCK SEQUENCE...
VWEEM
SCHHHK
KEEPING SUCH POWERFUL, UNPREDICTABLE WEAPONS FEELS KIND OF LIKE HAVING A NUCLEAR WARHEAD IN THE HOUSE.
I'M NOT SURE HOW I'M EVER GOING TO SLEEP WITH THOSE THINGS THREE FLOORS BELOW ME.

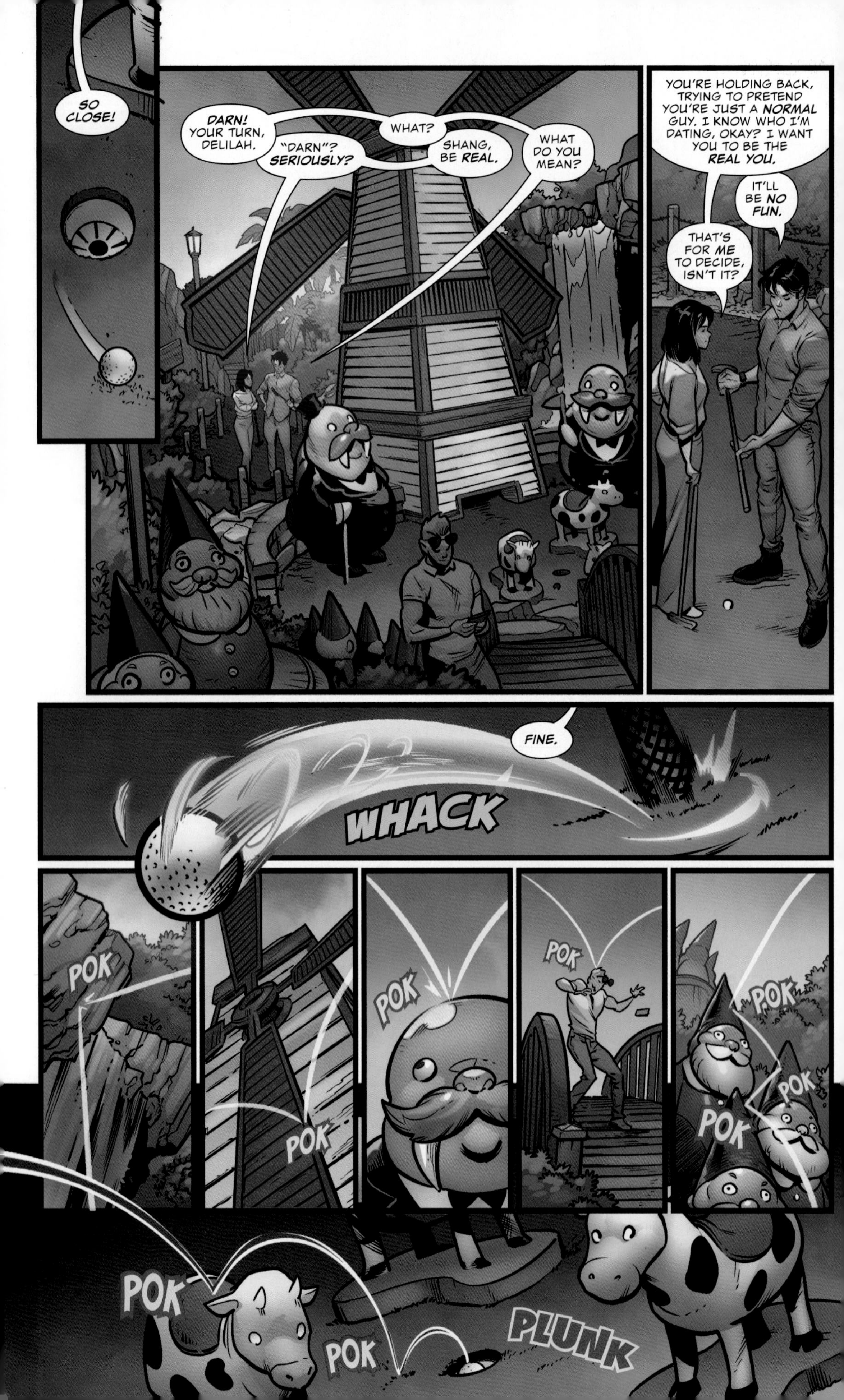
SO CLOSE!
DARN! YOUR TURN, DELILAH.
"DARN"? SERIOUSLY?
WHAT?
SHANG, BE REAL.
WHAT DO YOU MEAN?
YOU'RE HOLDING BACK, TRYING TO PRETEND YOU'RE JUST A NORMAL GUY. I KNOW WHO I'M DATING, OKAY? I WANT YOU TO BE THE REAL YOU.
IT'LL BE NO FUN.
THAT'S FOR ME TO DECIDE, ISN'T IT?
FINE.
WHACK
POK
POK
POK
POK
POK
POK
POK
POK
POK
PLUNK

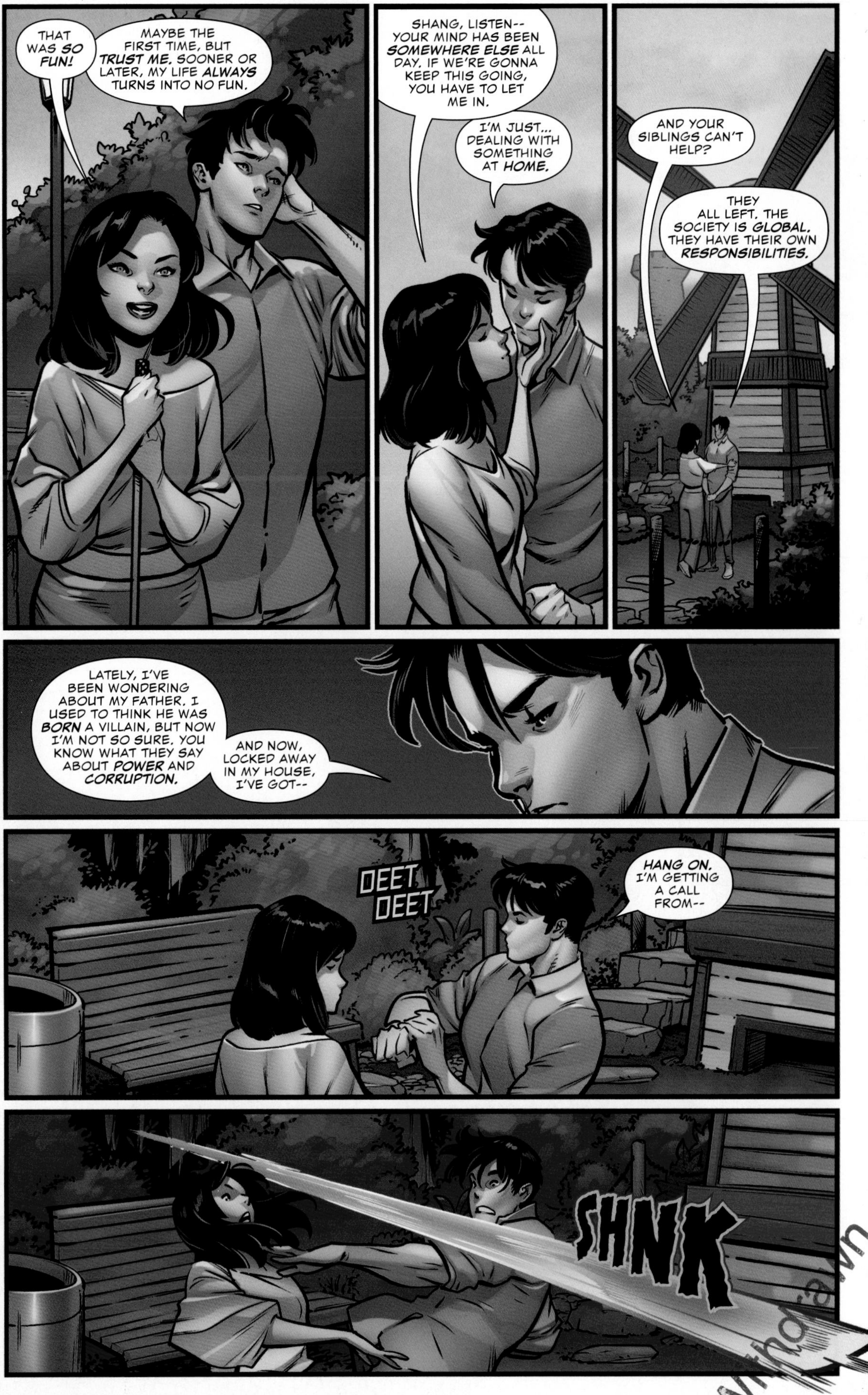
THAT WAS SO FUN!
MAYBE THE FIRST TIME, BUT TRUST ME. SOONER OR LATER, MY LIFE ALWAYS TURNS INTO NO FUN.
SHANG, LISTEN-- YOUR MIND HAS BEEN SOMEWHERE ELSE ALL DAY. IF WE'RE GONNA KEEP THIS GOING, YOU HAVE TO LET ME IN.
I'M JUST... DEALING WITH SOMETHING AT HOME.
AND YOUR SIBLINGS CAN'T HELP?
THEY ALL LEFT. THE SOCIETY IS GLOBAL. THEY HAVE THEIR OWN RESPONSIBILITIES.
LATELY, I'VE BEEN WONDERING ABOUT MY FATHER. I USED TO THINK HE WAS BORN A VILLAIN, BUT NOW I'M NOT SO SURE. YOU KNOW WHAT THEY SAY ABOUT POWER AND CORRUPTION.
AND NOW, LOCKED AWAY IN MY HOUSE, I'VE GOT--
DEET DEET
HANG ON. I'M GETTING A CALL FROM--
SHNK

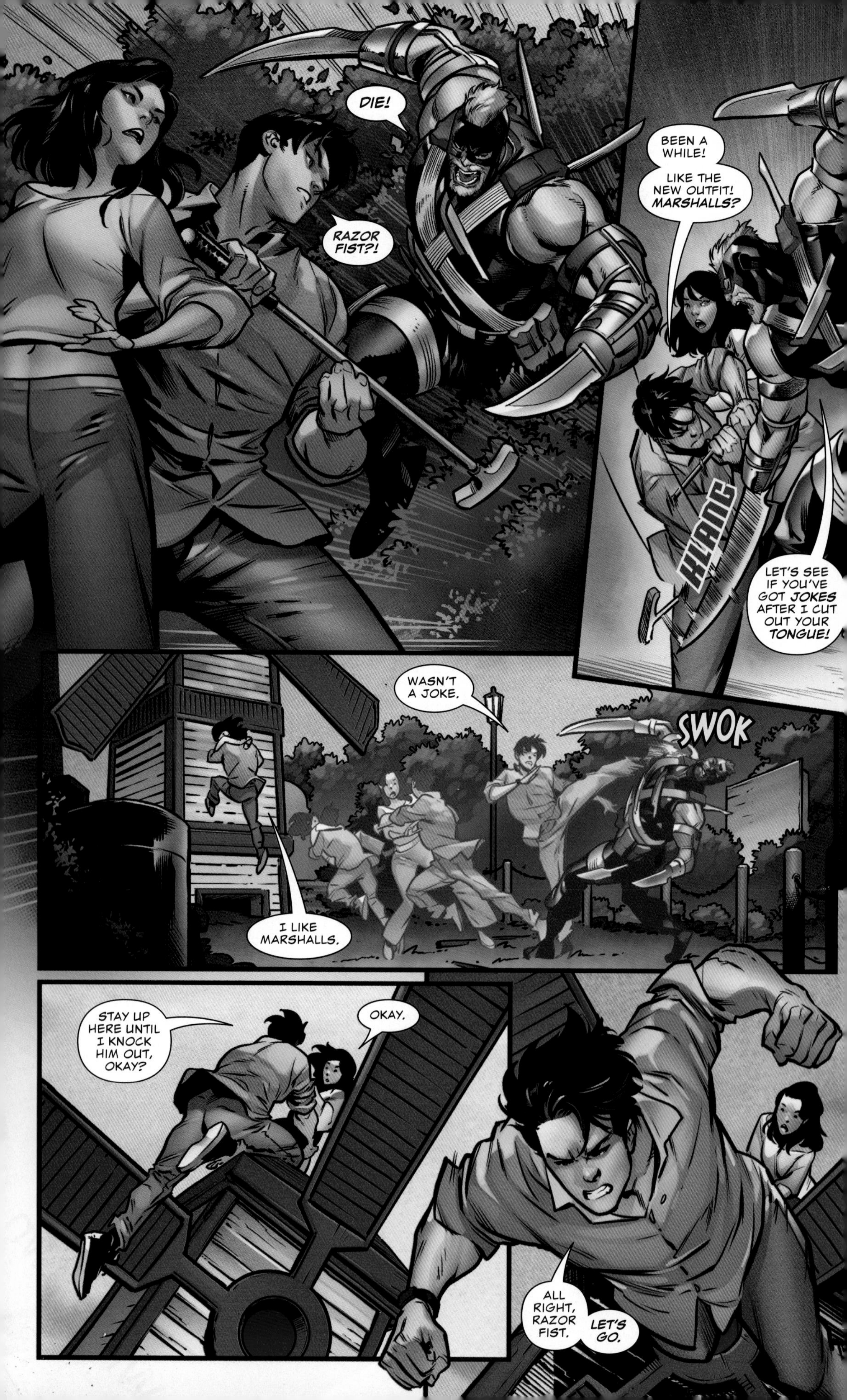
DIE!
RAZOR FIST?!
BEEN A WHILE!
LIKE THE NEW OUTFIT! MARSHALLS?
KLANG
LET'S SEE IF YOU'VE GOT JOKES AFTER I CUT OUT YOUR TONGUE!
WASN'T A JOKE.
SWOK
I LIKE MARSHALLS.
STAY UP HERE UNTIL I KNOCK HIM OUT, OKAY?
OKAY.
ALL RIGHT, RAZOR FIST.
LET'S GO.

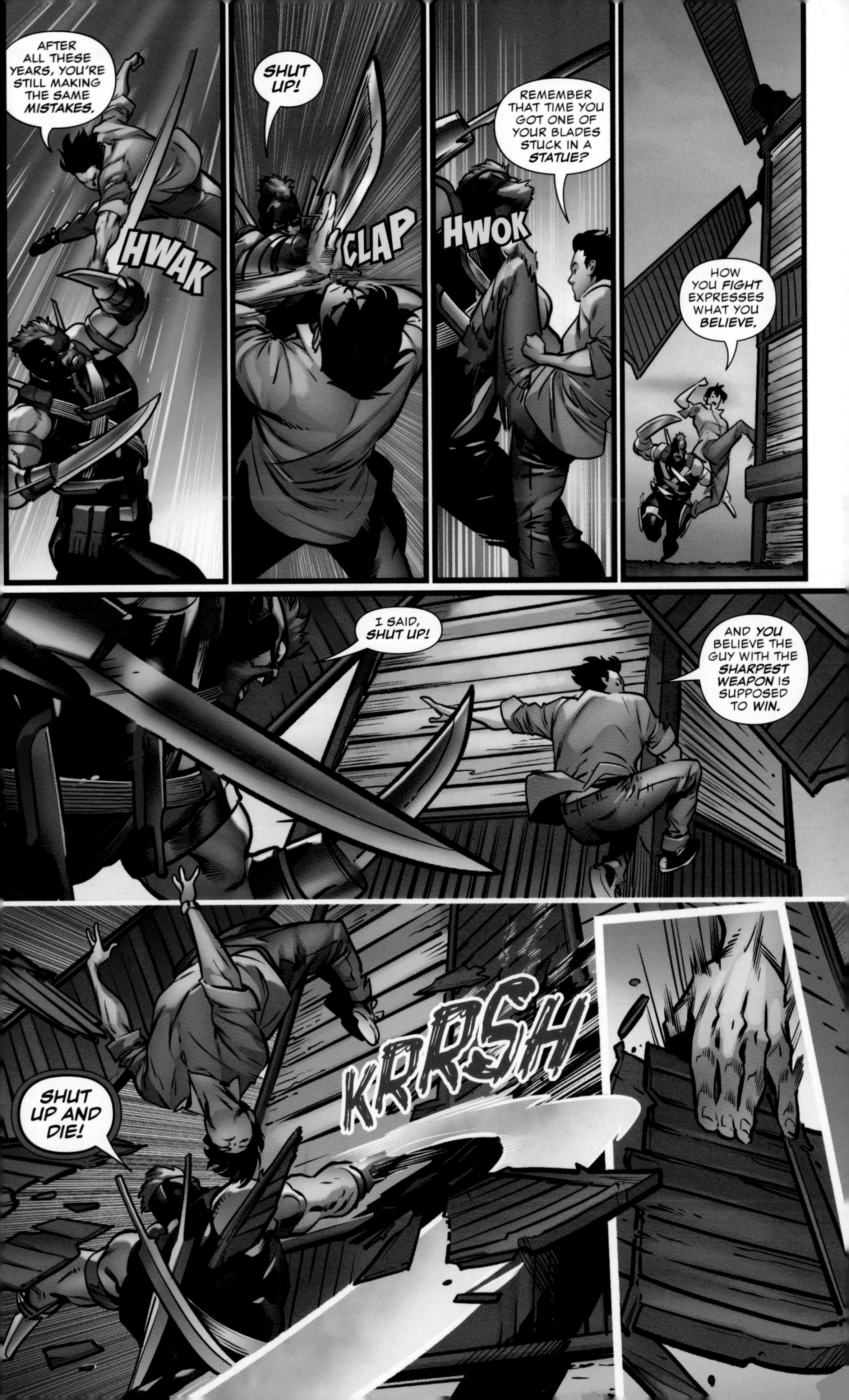
AFTER ALL THESE YEARS, YOU'RE STILL MAKING THE SAME MISTAKES.
HWAK
SHUT UP!
CLAP
HWOK
REMEMBER THAT TIME YOU GOT ONE OF YOUR BLADES STUCK IN A STATUE?
HOW YOU FIGHT EXPRESSES WHAT YOU BELIEVE.
I SAID, SHUT UP!
AND YOU BELIEVE THE GUY WITH THE SHARPEST WEAPON IS SUPPOSED TO WIN.
SHUT UP AND DIE!
KRRSH

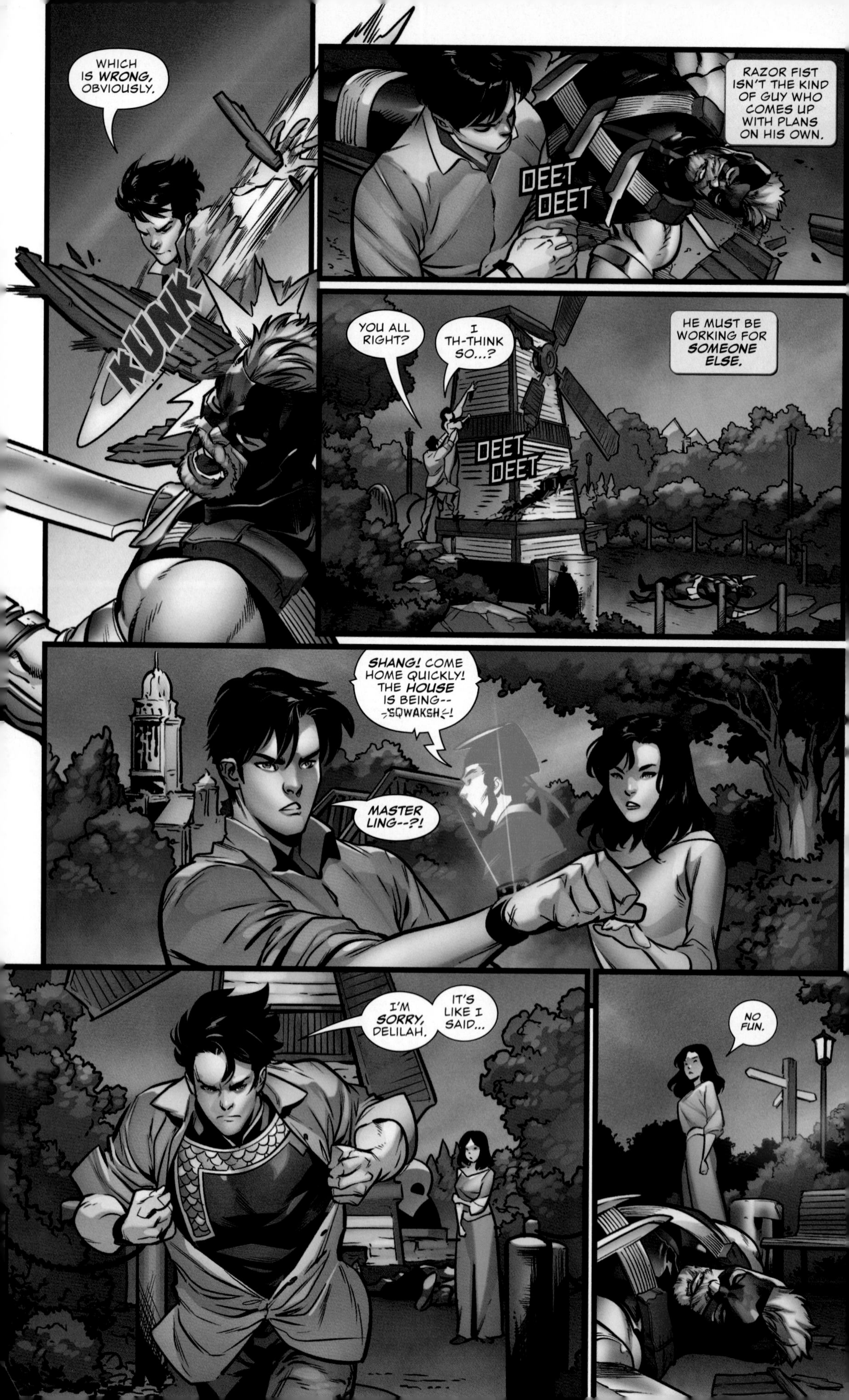
WHICH IS WRONG, OBVIOUSLY.
KUNK
RAZOR FIST ISN'T THE KIND OF GUY WHO COMES UP WITH PLANS ON HIS OWN.
DEET DEET
YOU ALL RIGHT?
I TH-THINK SO...?
HE MUST BE WORKING FOR SOMEONE ELSE.
DEET DEET
SHANG! COME HOME QUICKLY! THE HOUSE IS BEING-- SQWAKSH!
MASTER LING--?!
I'M SORRY, DELILAH.
IT'S LIKE I SAID...
NO FUN.

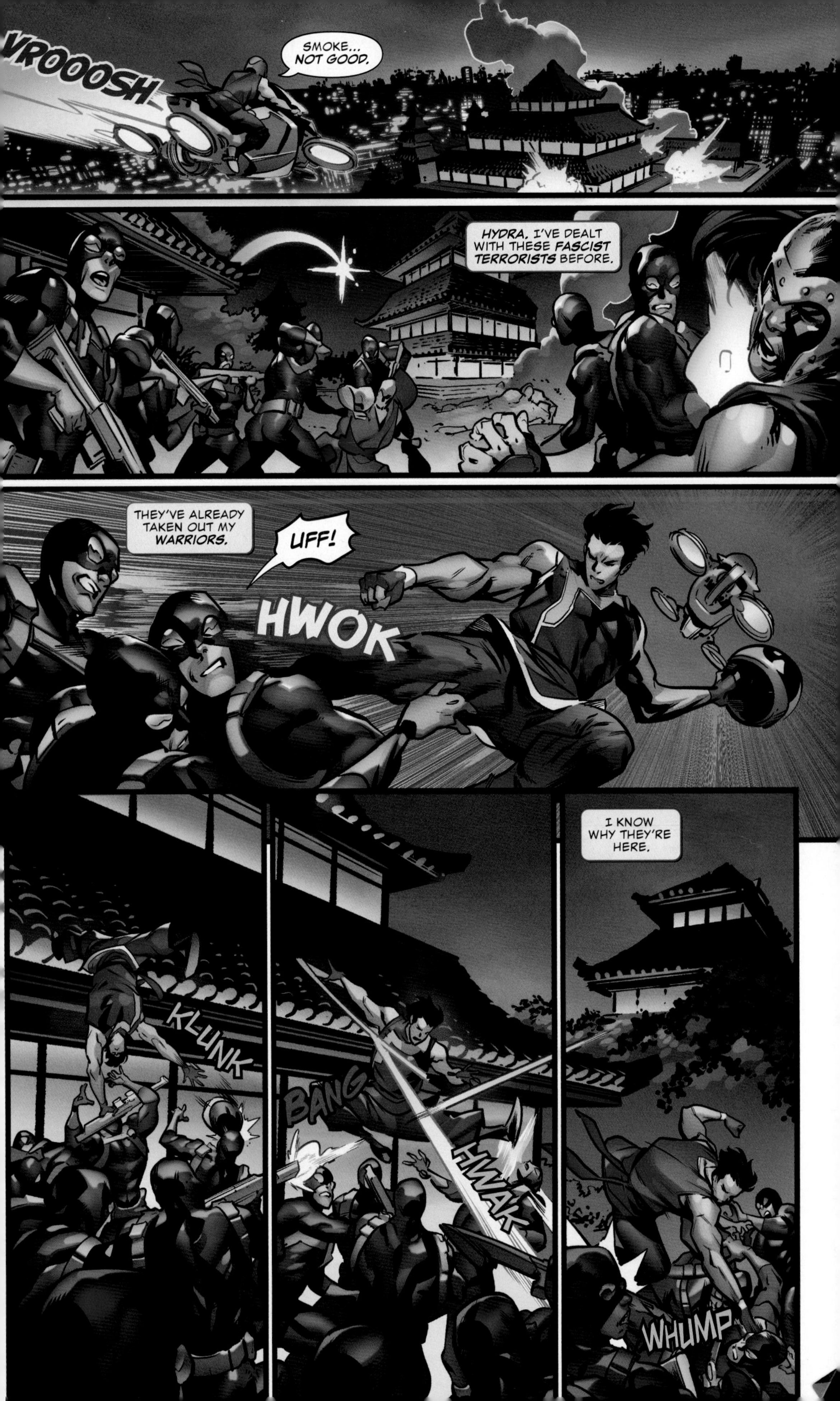

VROOOSH
SMOKE... NOT GOOD.
HYDRA. I'VE DEALT WITH THESE FASCIST TERRORISTS BEFORE.
THEY'VE ALREADY TAKEN OUT MY WARRIORS.
UFF!
HWOK
KLUNK
BANG
HWAK
I KNOW WHY THEY'RE HERE.
WHUMP

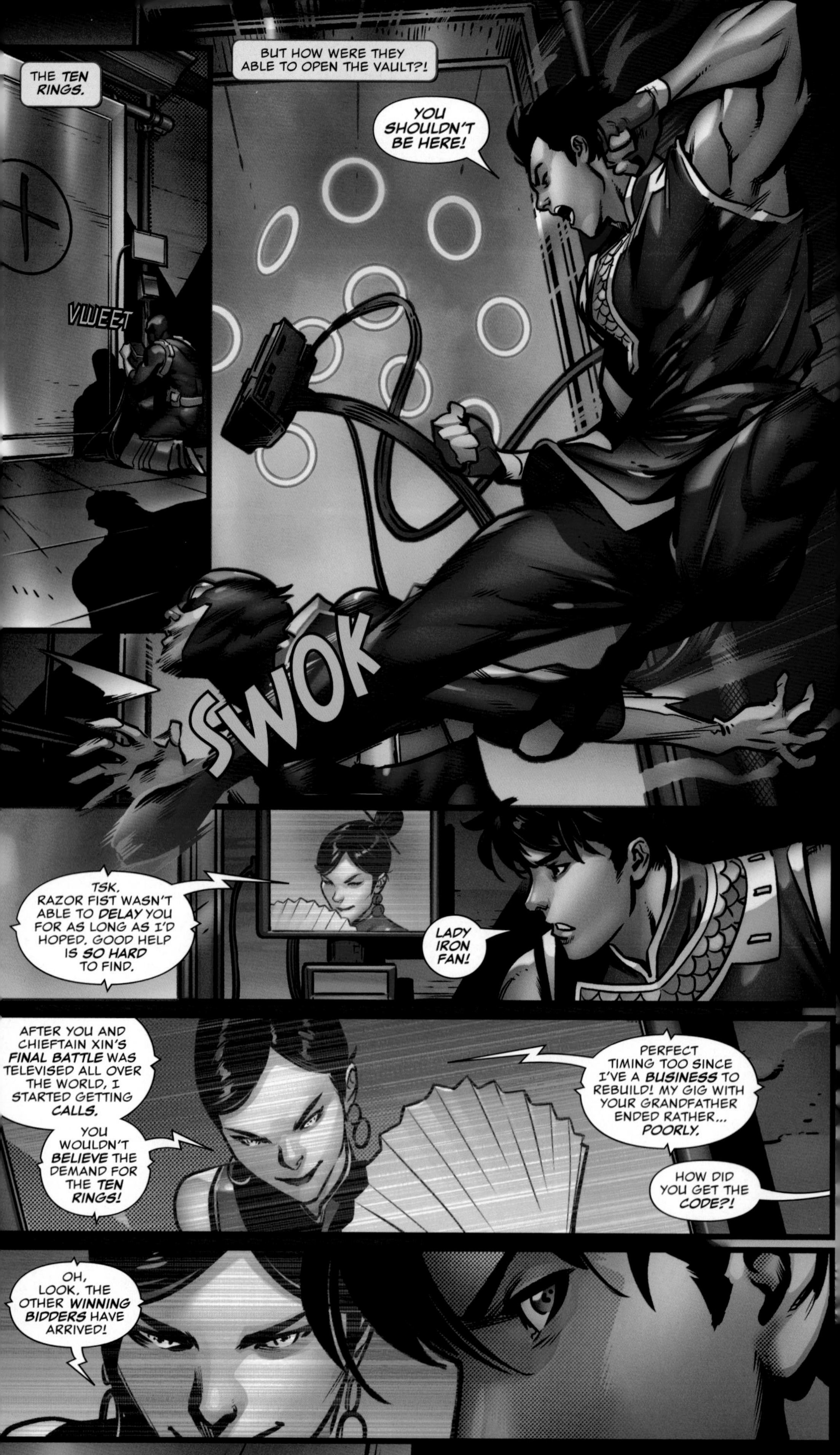

THE TEN RINGS.
BUT HOW WERE THEY ABLE TO OPEN THE VAULT?!
VWEET
YOU SHOULDN'T BE HERE!
SWOK
TSK. RAZOR FIST WASN'T ABLE TO DELAY YOU FOR AS LONG AS I'D HOPED. GOOD HELP IS SO HARD TO FIND.
LADY IRON FAN!
AFTER YOU AND CHIEFTAIN XIN'S FINAL BATTLE WAS TELEVISED ALL OVER THE WORLD, I STARTED GETTING CALLS.
YOU WOULDN'T BELIEVE THE DEMAND FOR THE TEN RINGS!
PERFECT TIMING TOO SINCE I'VE A BUSINESS TO REBUILD! MY GIG WITH YOUR GRANDFATHER ENDED RATHER... POORLY.
HOW DID YOU GET THE CODE?!
OH, LOOK, THE OTHER WINNING BIDDERS HAVE ARRIVED!

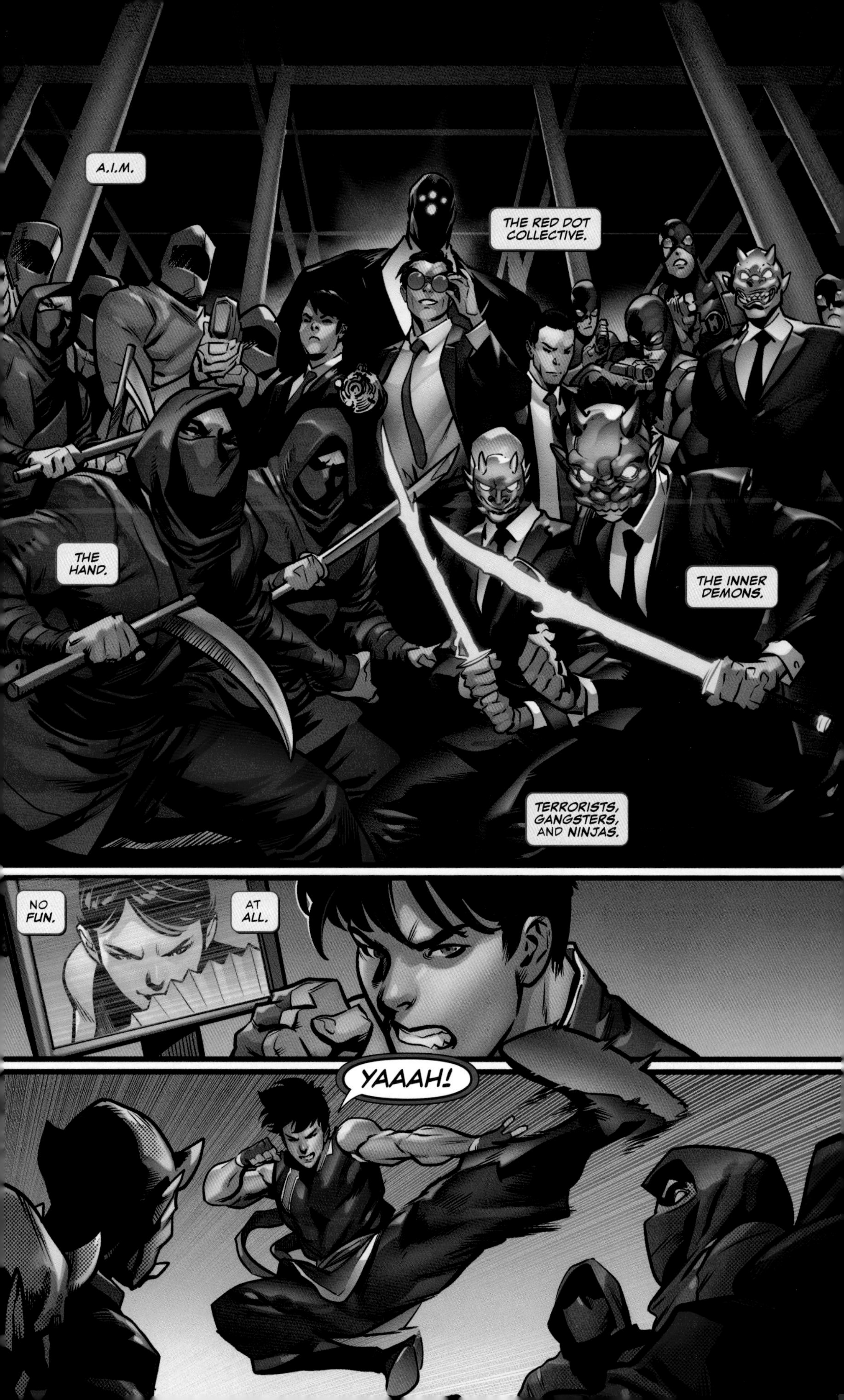
A.I.M.
THE RED DOT COLLECTIVE.
THE HAND.
THE INNER DEMONS.
TERRORISTS, GANGSTERS, AND NINJAS.
NO FUN.
AT ALL.
YAAAH!

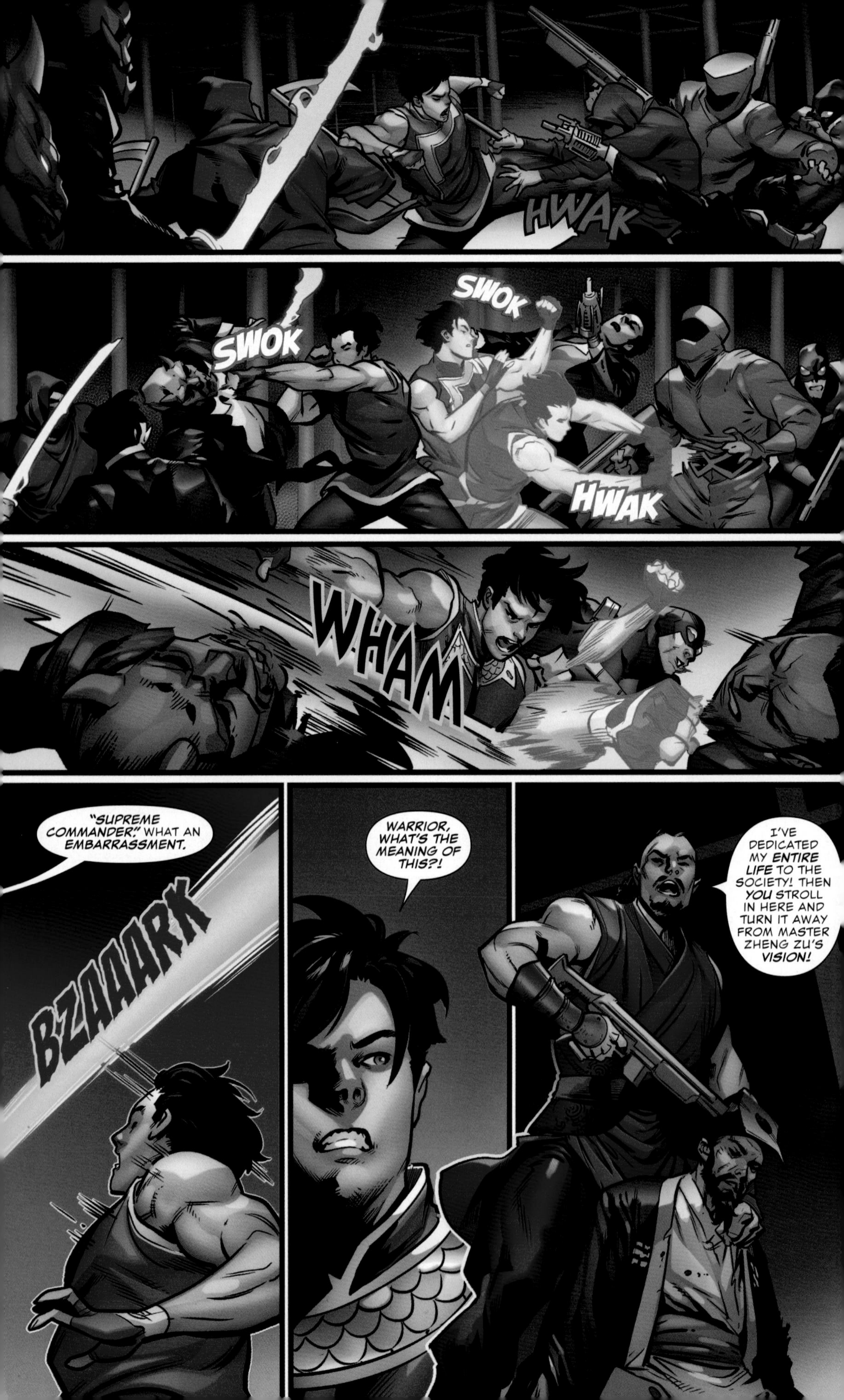
HWAK
SWOK
SWOK
HWAK
WHAM
"SUPREME COMMANDER," WHAT AN EMBARRASSMENT.
BZAAARK
WARRIOR, WHAT'S THE MEANING OF THIS?!
I'VE DEDICATED MY ENTIRE LIFE TO THE SOCIETY! THEN YOU STROLL IN HERE AND TURN IT AWAY FROM MASTER ZHENG ZU'S VISION!

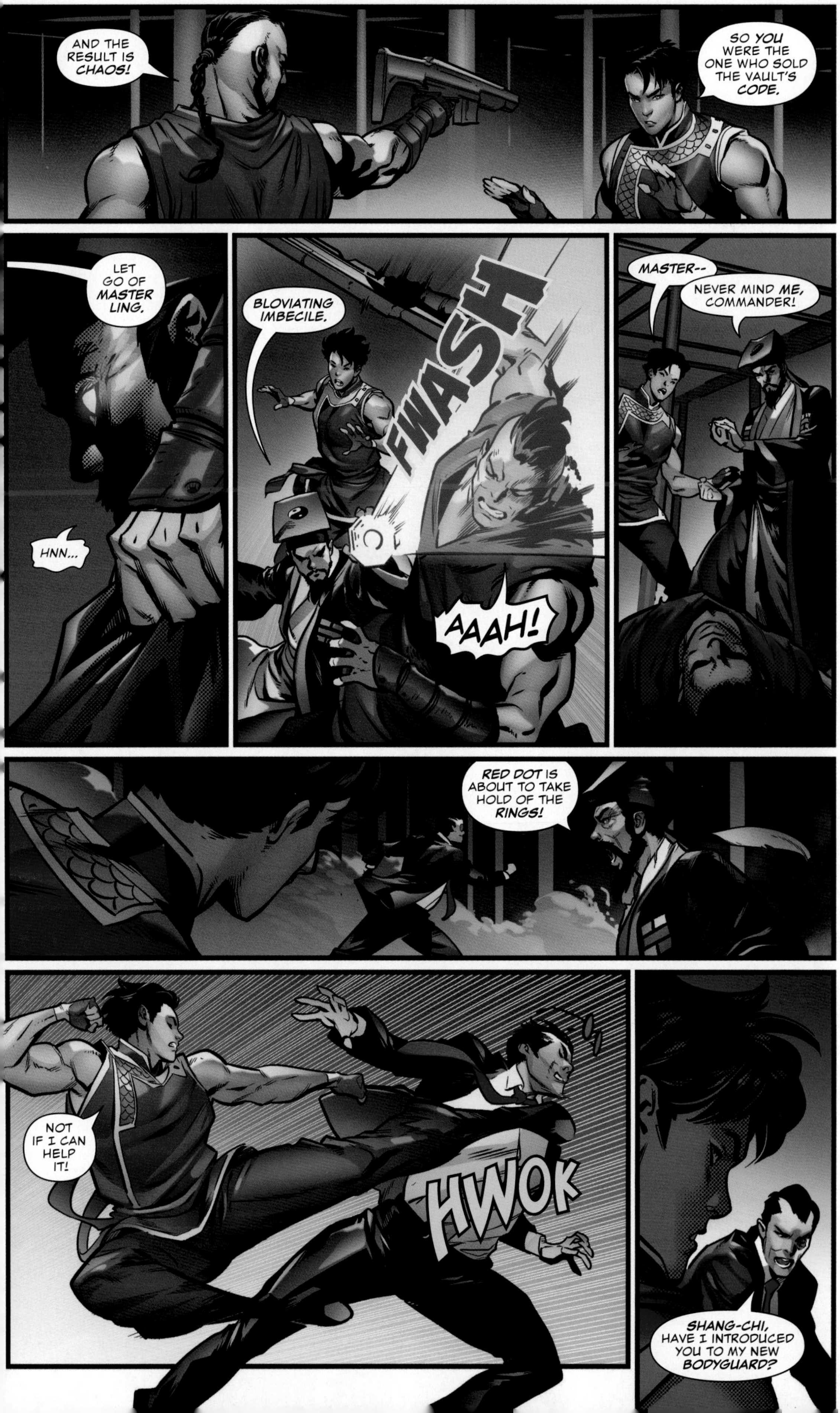

AND THE RESULT IS CHAOS!
SO YOU WERE THE ONE WHO SOLD THE VAULT'S CODE.
LET GO OF MASTER LING.
HNN...
BLOVIATING IMBECILE.
FWASH
AAAH!
MASTER--
NEVER MIND ME, COMMANDER!
RED DOT IS ABOUT TO TAKE HOLD OF THE RINGS!
NOT IF I CAN HELP IT!
HWOK
SHANG-CHI, HAVE I INTRODUCED YOU TO MY NEW BODYGUARD?

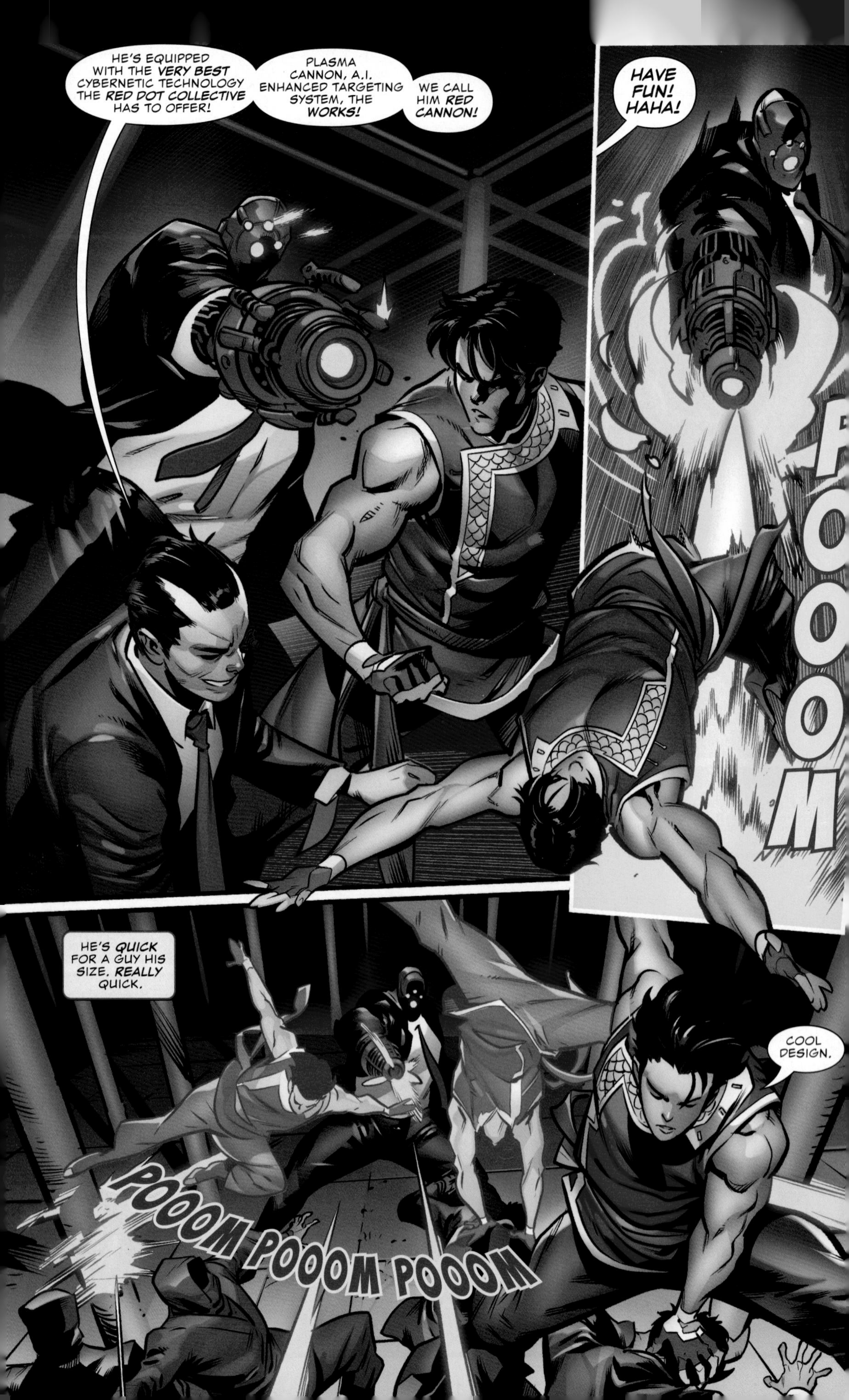

HE'S EQUIPPED WITH THE VERY BEST CYBERNETIC TECHNOLOGY THE RED DOT COLLECTIVE HAS TO OFFER!
PLASMA CANNON, A.I. ENHANCED TARGETING SYSTEM, THE WORKS!
WE CALL HIM RED CANNON!
HAVE FUN! HAHA!
POOOM
HE'S QUICK FOR A GUY HIS SIZE. REALLY QUICK.
COOL DESIGN.
POOOM POOOM POOOM

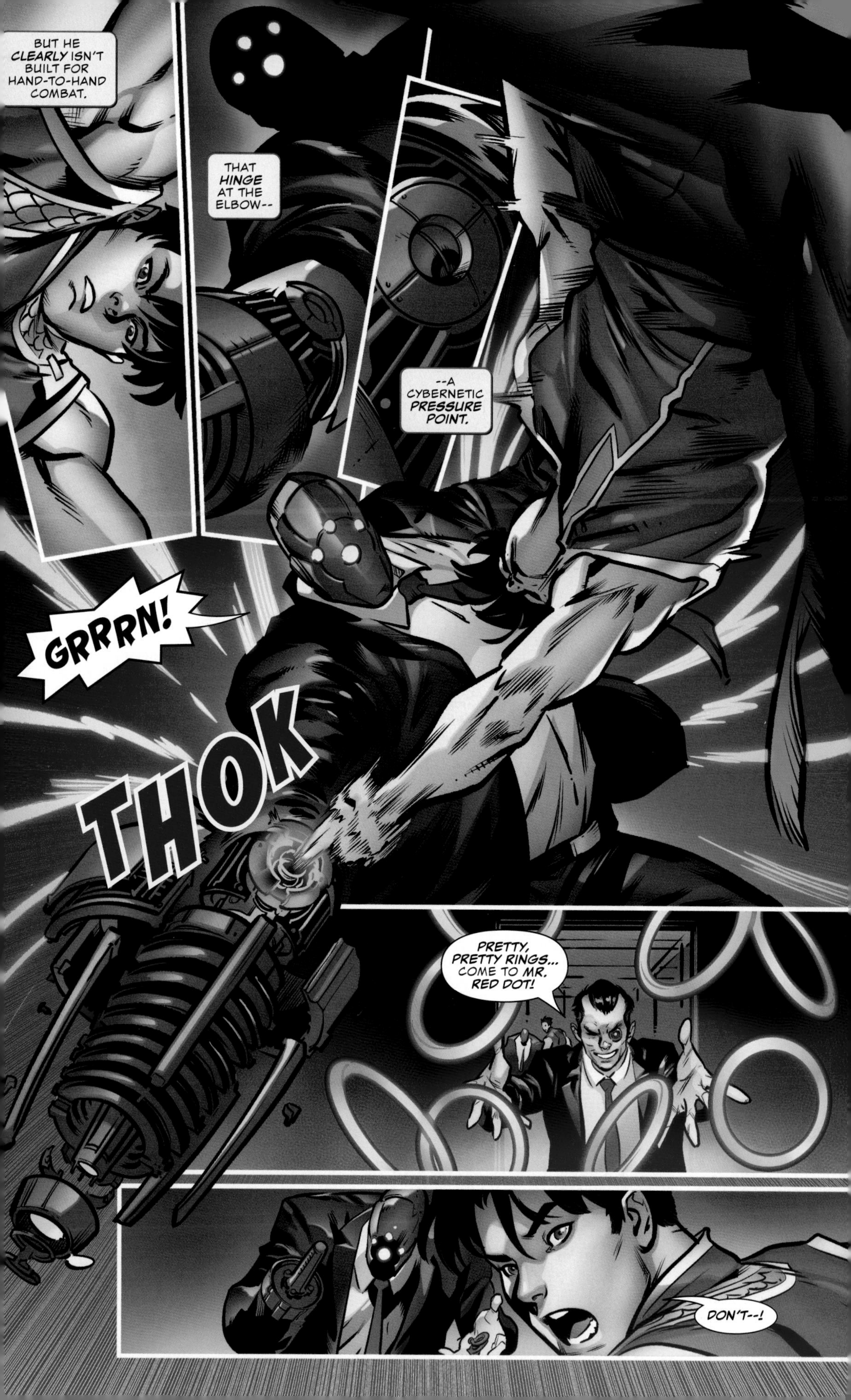
BUT HE CLEARLY ISN'T BUILT FOR HAND-TO-HAND COMBAT.
THAT HINGE AT THE ELBOW--
--A CYBERNETIC PRESSURE POINT.
GRRRN!
THOK
PRETTY, PRETTY RINGS... COME TO MR. RED DOT!
DON'T--!

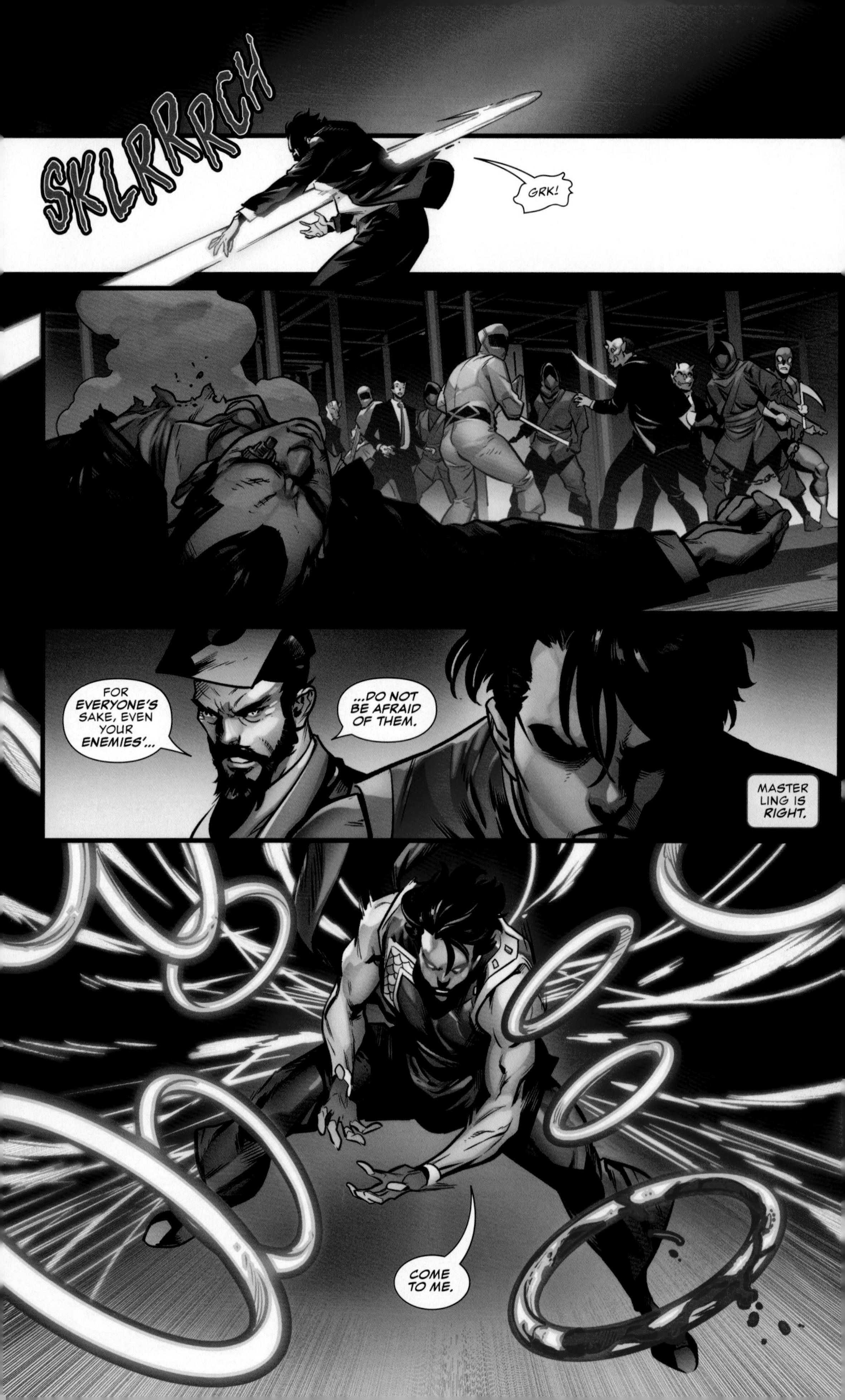
SKLRRRCH
GRK!
FOR EVERYONE'S SAKE, EVEN YOUR ENEMIES'...
...DO NOT BE AFRAID OF THEM.
MASTER LING IS RIGHT.
COME TO ME.

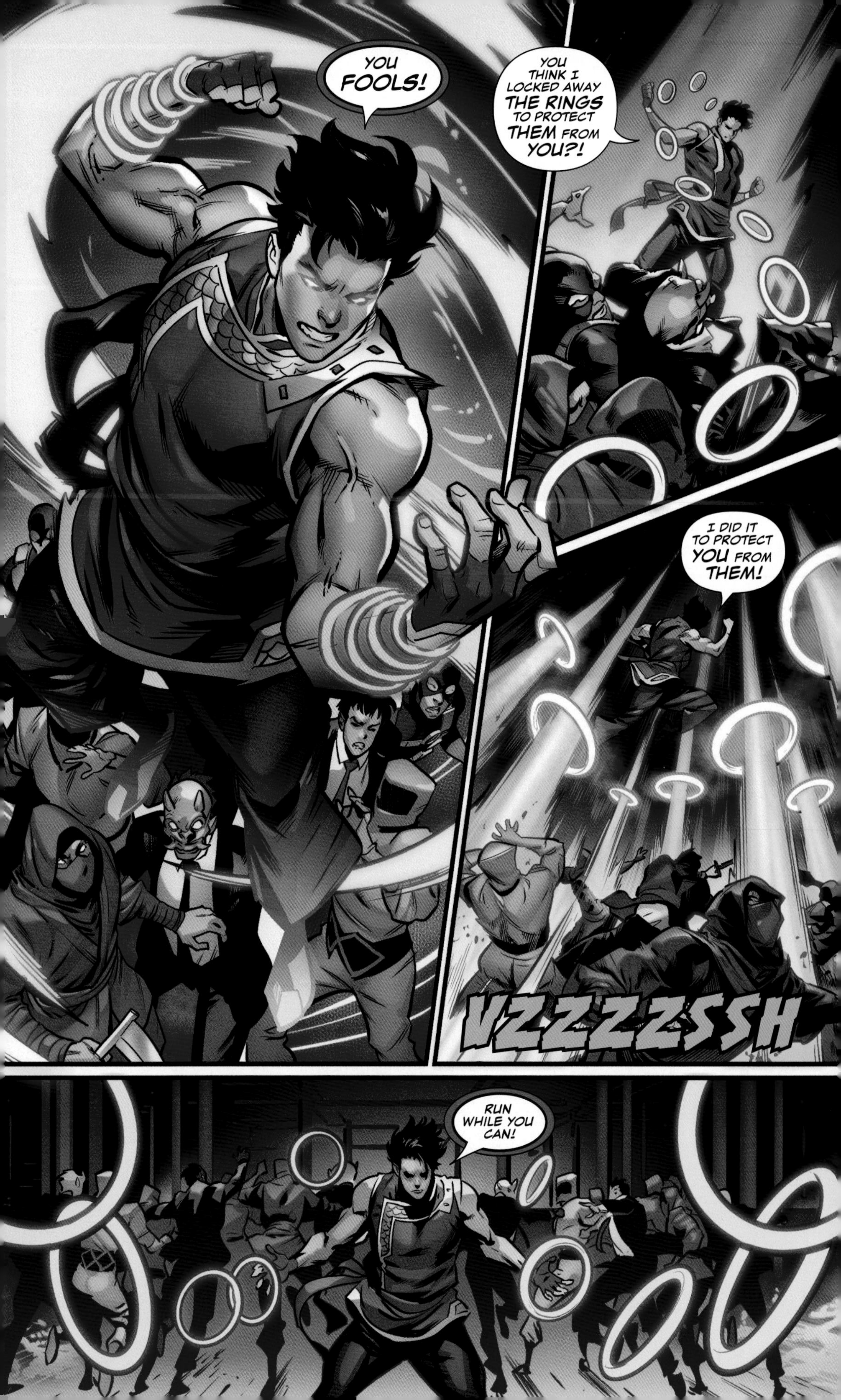
YOU FOOLS!
YOU THINK I LOCKED AWAY THE RINGS TO PROTECT THEM FROM YOU?!
I DID IT TO PROTECT YOU FROM THEM!
VZZZZZSSH
RUN WHILE YOU CAN!

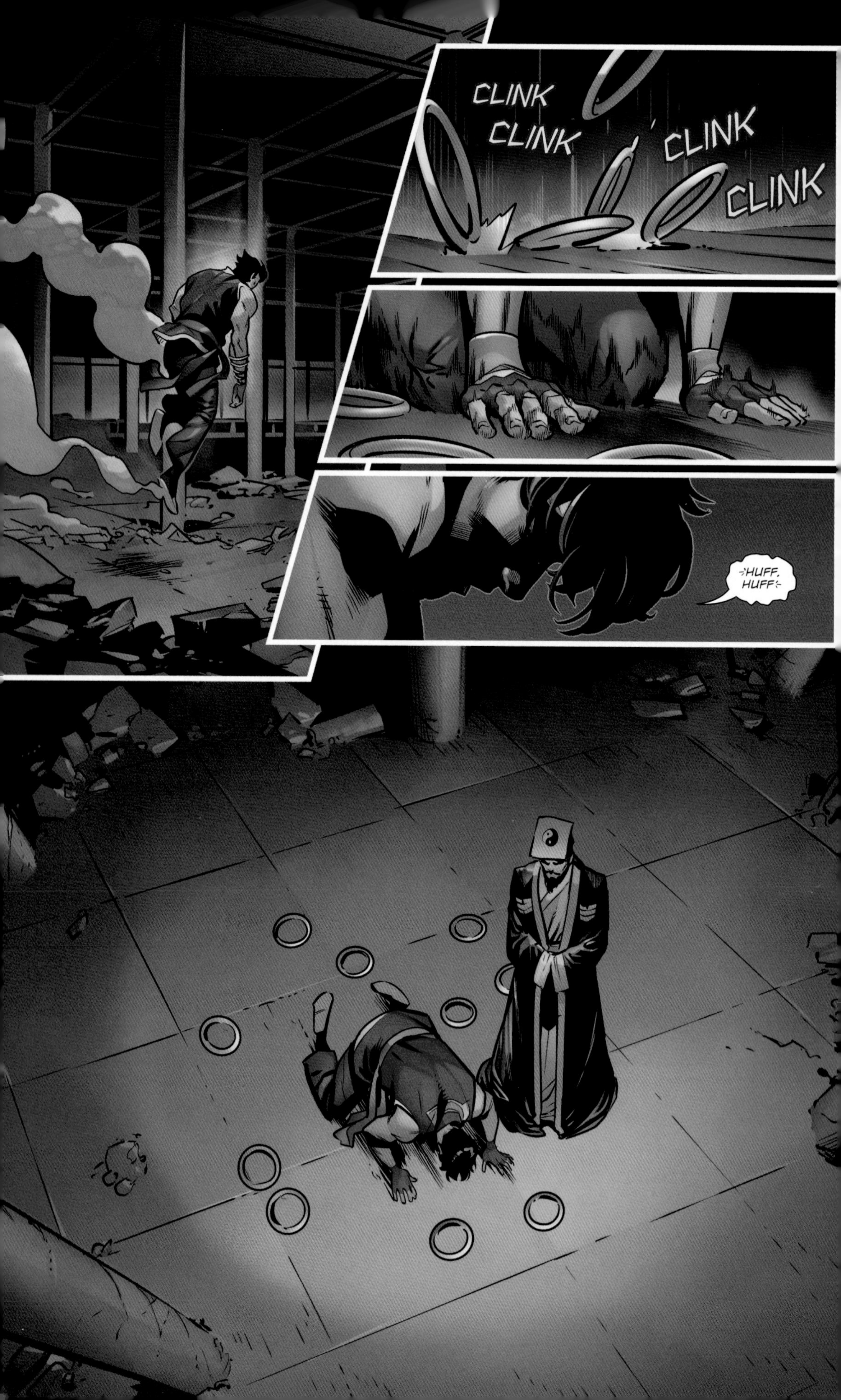
CLINK
CLINK
CLINK
CLINK
HUFF, HUFF

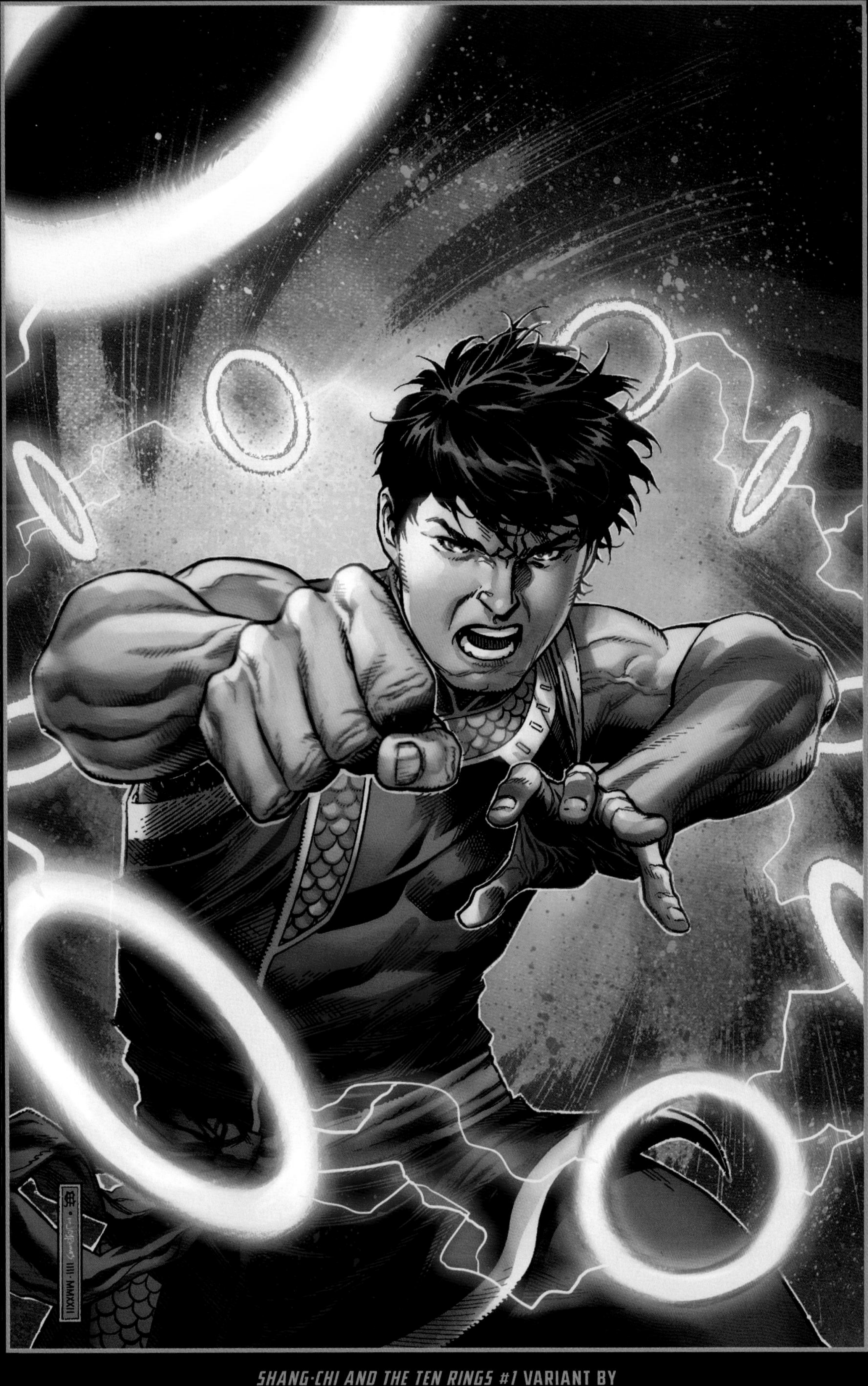

SHANG-CHI AND THE TEN RINGS #1 VARIANT BY

JIM CHEUNG & JAY DAVID RAMOS

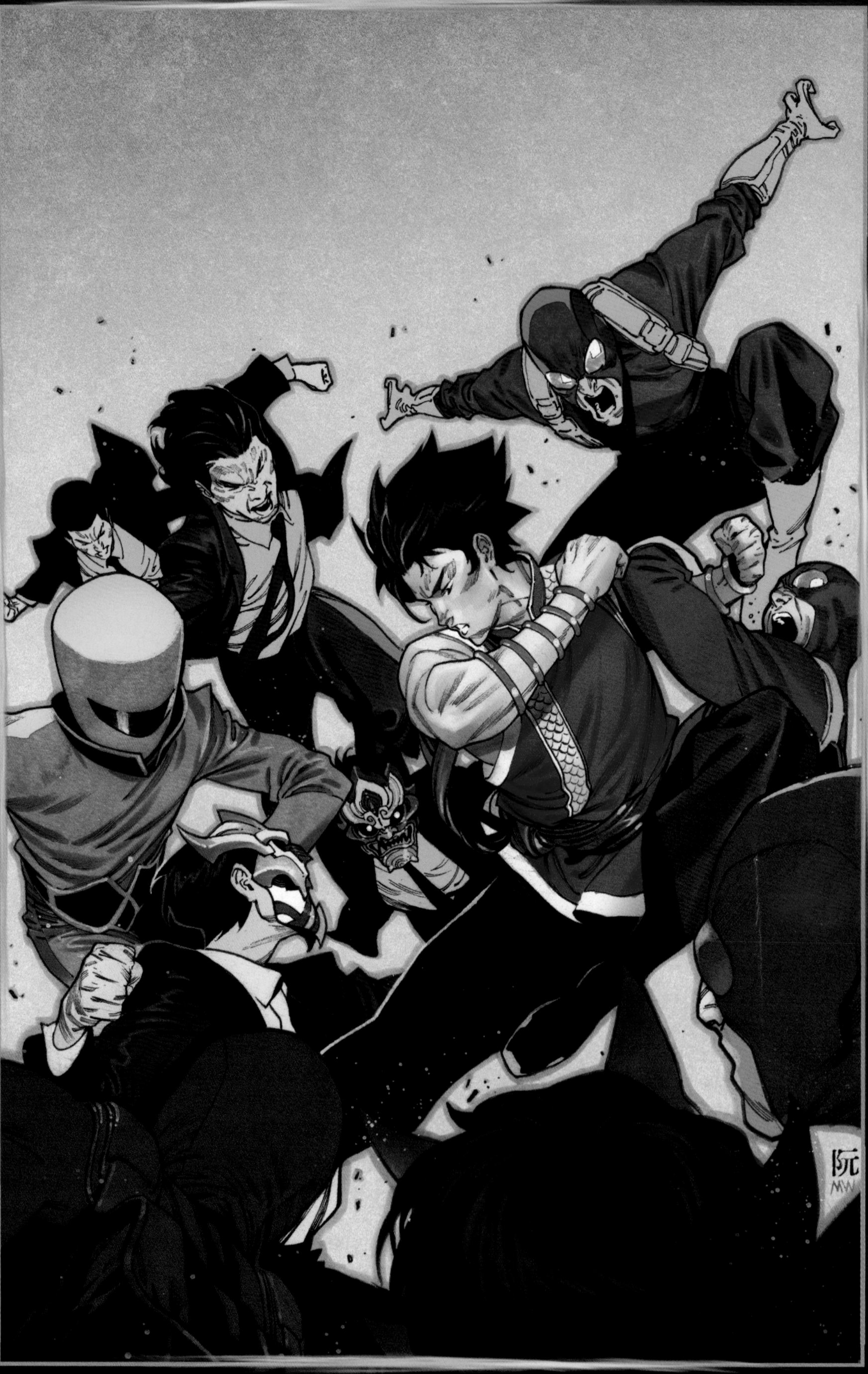

TWO

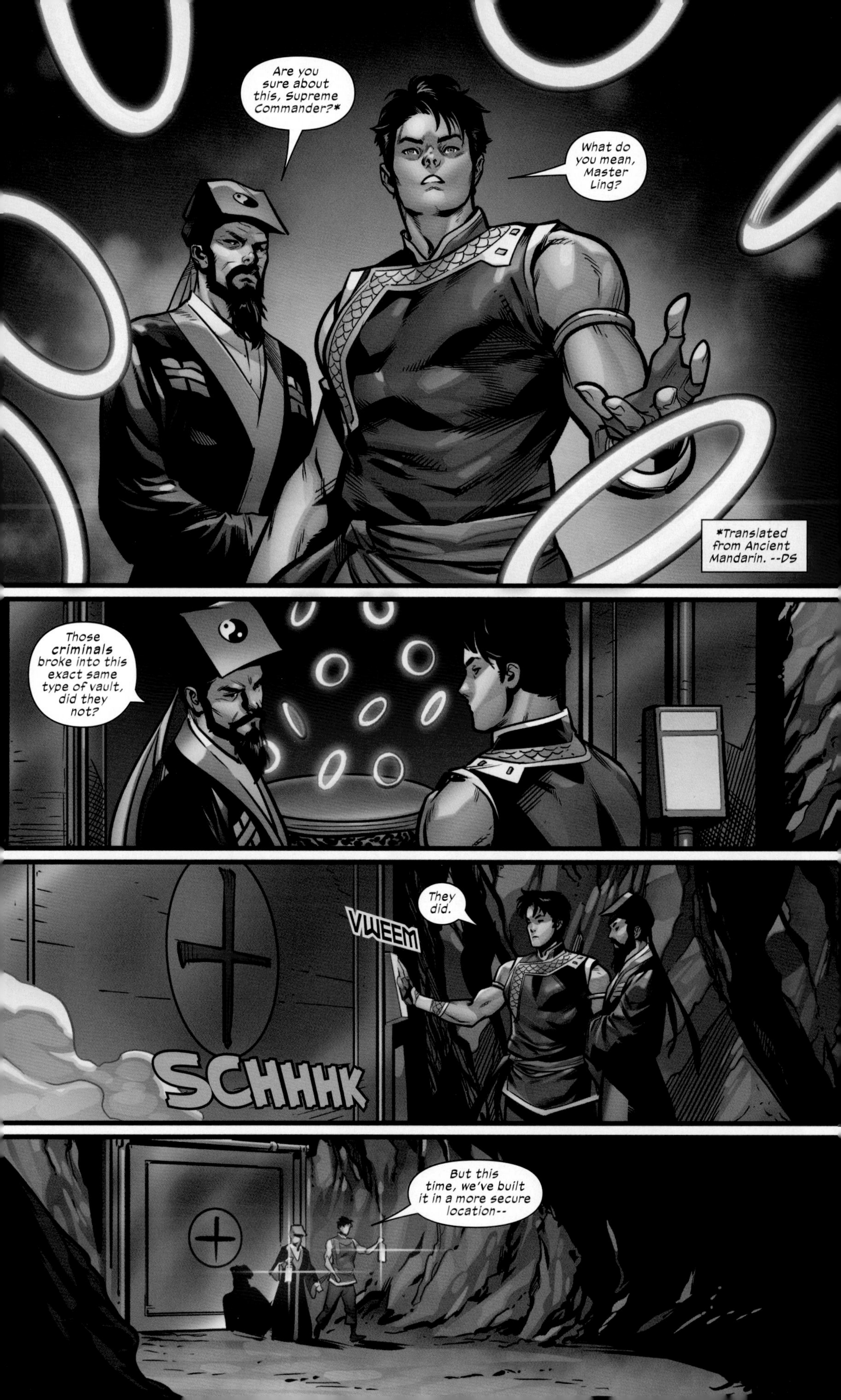

Are you sure about this, Supreme Commander?*
What do you mean, Master Ling?
*Translated from Ancient Mandarin. --DS
Those **criminals** broke into this exact same type of vault, did they not?
They did.
VWEEM
SCHHHK
But this time, we've built it in a more secure location--

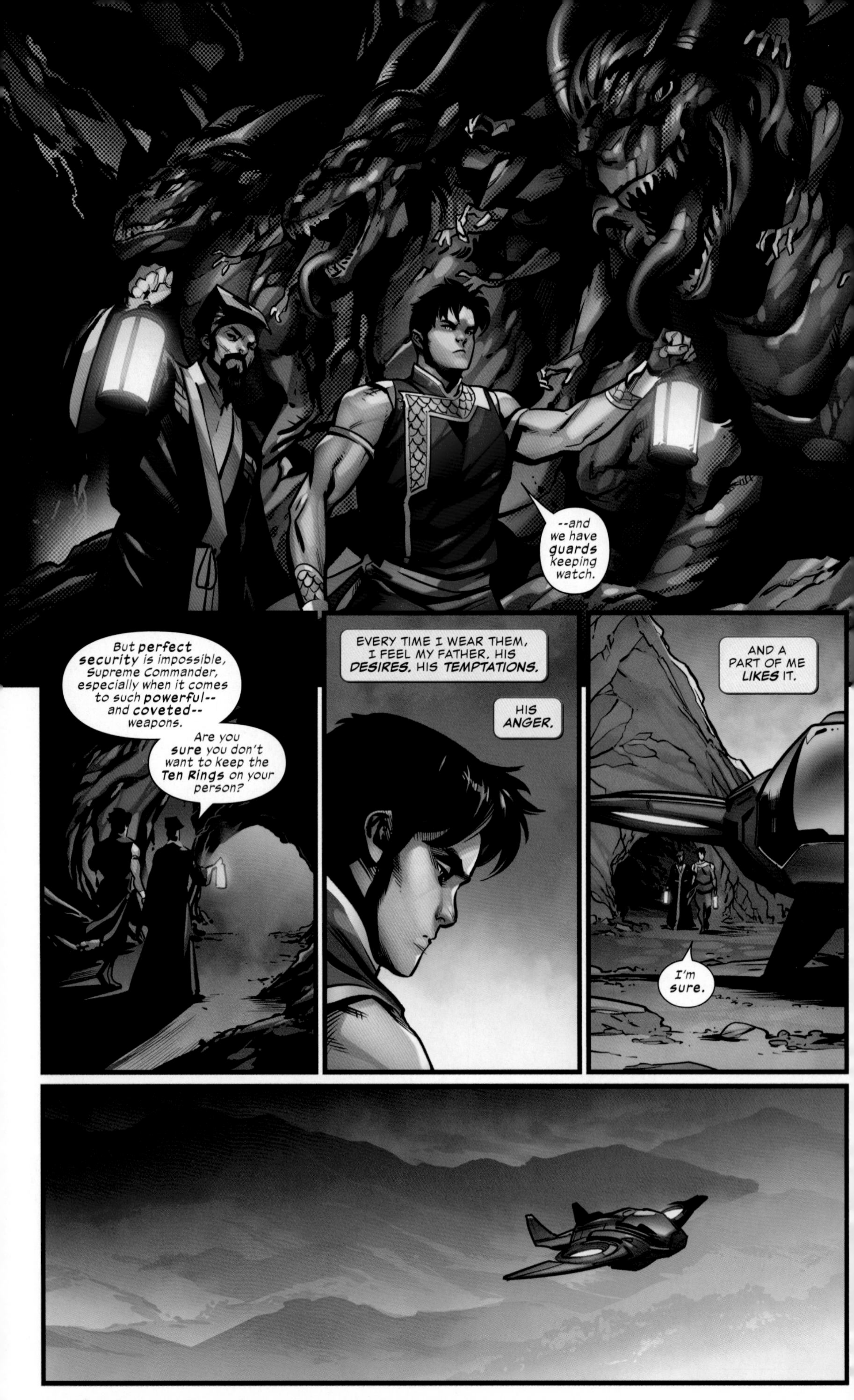
--and we have guards keeping watch.
But perfect security is impossible, Supreme Commander, especially when it comes to such powerful--and coveted--weapons.
Are you sure you don't want to keep the Ten Rings on your person?
EVERY TIME I WEAR THEM, I FEEL MY FATHER. HIS DESIRES. HIS TEMPTATIONS.
HIS ANGER.
AND A PART OF ME LIKES IT.
I'm sure.

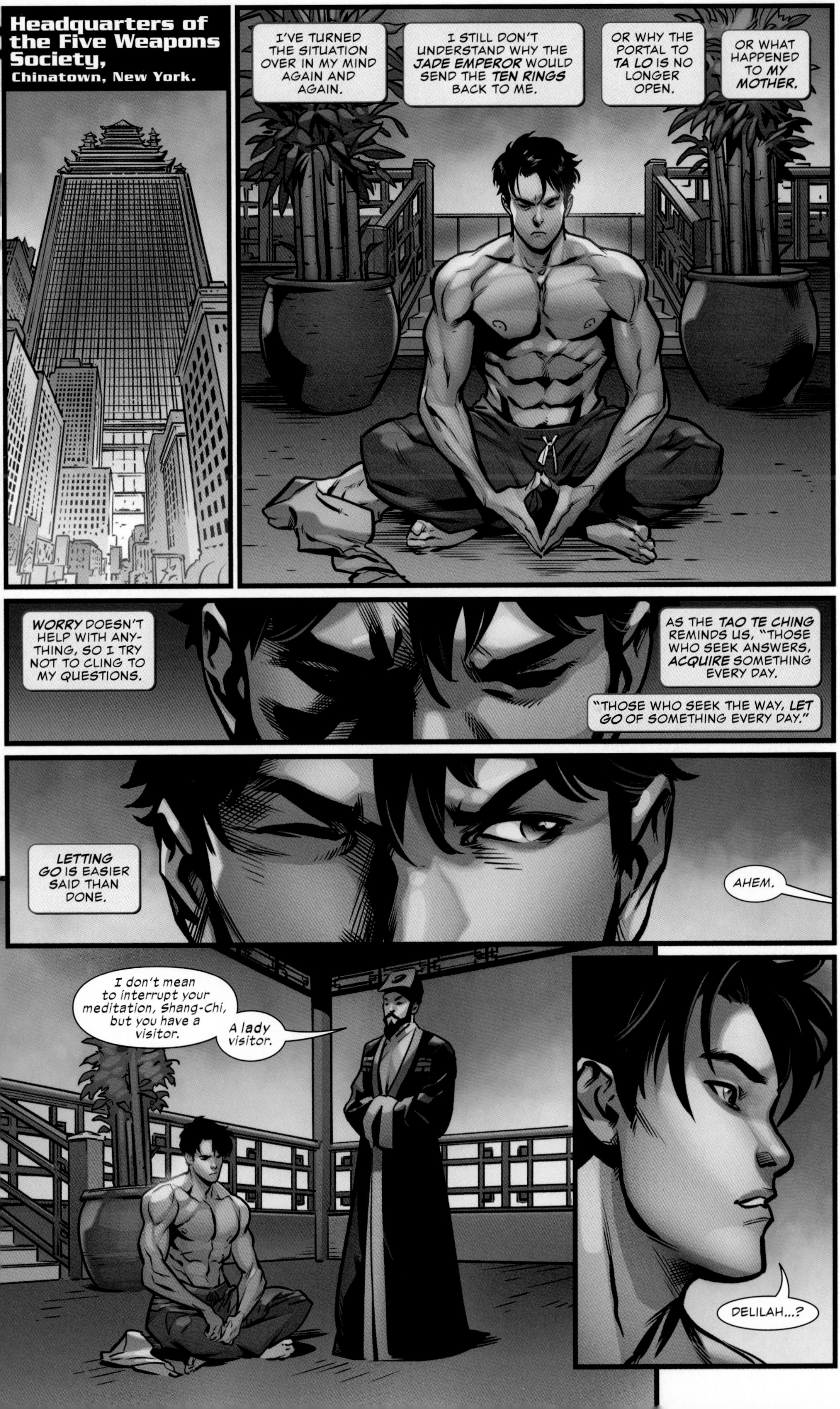
Headquarters of the Five Weapons Society,
Chinatown, New York.
I'VE TURNED THE SITUATION OVER IN MY MIND AGAIN AND AGAIN.
I STILL DON'T UNDERSTAND WHY THE JADE EMPEROR WOULD SEND THE TEN RINGS BACK TO ME.
OR WHY THE PORTAL TO TA LO IS NO LONGER OPEN.
OR WHAT HAPPENED TO MY MOTHER.
WORRY DOESN'T HELP WITH ANY-THING, SO I TRY NOT TO CLING TO MY QUESTIONS.
AS THE TAO TE CHING REMINDS US, "THOSE WHO SEEK ANSWERS, ACQUIRE SOMETHING EVERY DAY.
"THOSE WHO SEEK THE WAY, LET GO OF SOMETHING EVERY DAY."
LETTING GO IS EASIER SAID THAN DONE.
AHEM.
I don't mean to interrupt your meditation, Shang-Chi, but you have a visitor.
A lady visitor.
DELILAH...?

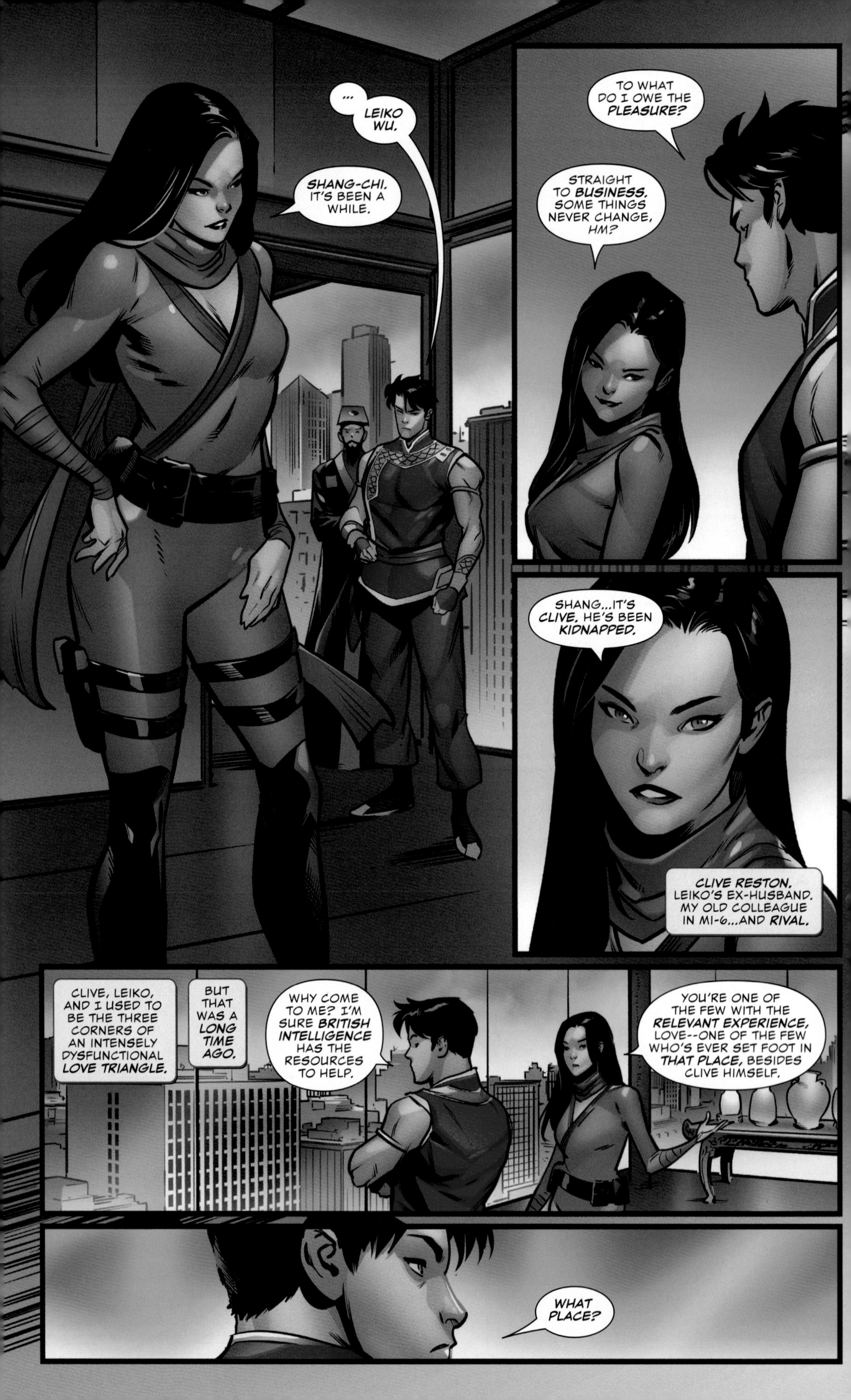
SHANG-CHI. IT'S BEEN A WHILE.
... LEIKO WU.
TO WHAT DO I OWE THE PLEASURE?
STRAIGHT TO BUSINESS. SOME THINGS NEVER CHANGE, HM?
SHANG...IT'S CLIVE. HE'S BEEN KIDNAPPED.
CLIVE RESTON. LEIKO'S EX-HUSBAND. MY OLD COLLEAGUE IN MI-6...AND RIVAL.
CLIVE, LEIKO, AND I USED TO BE THE THREE CORNERS OF AN INTENSELY DYSFUNCTIONAL LOVE TRIANGLE.
BUT THAT WAS A LONG TIME AGO.
WHY COME TO ME? I'M SURE BRITISH INTELLIGENCE HAS THE RESOURCES TO HELP.
YOU'RE ONE OF THE FEW WITH THE RELEVANT EXPERIENCE, LOVE--ONE OF THE FEW WHO'S EVER SET FOOT IN THAT PLACE, BESIDES CLIVE HIMSELF.
WHAT PLACE?

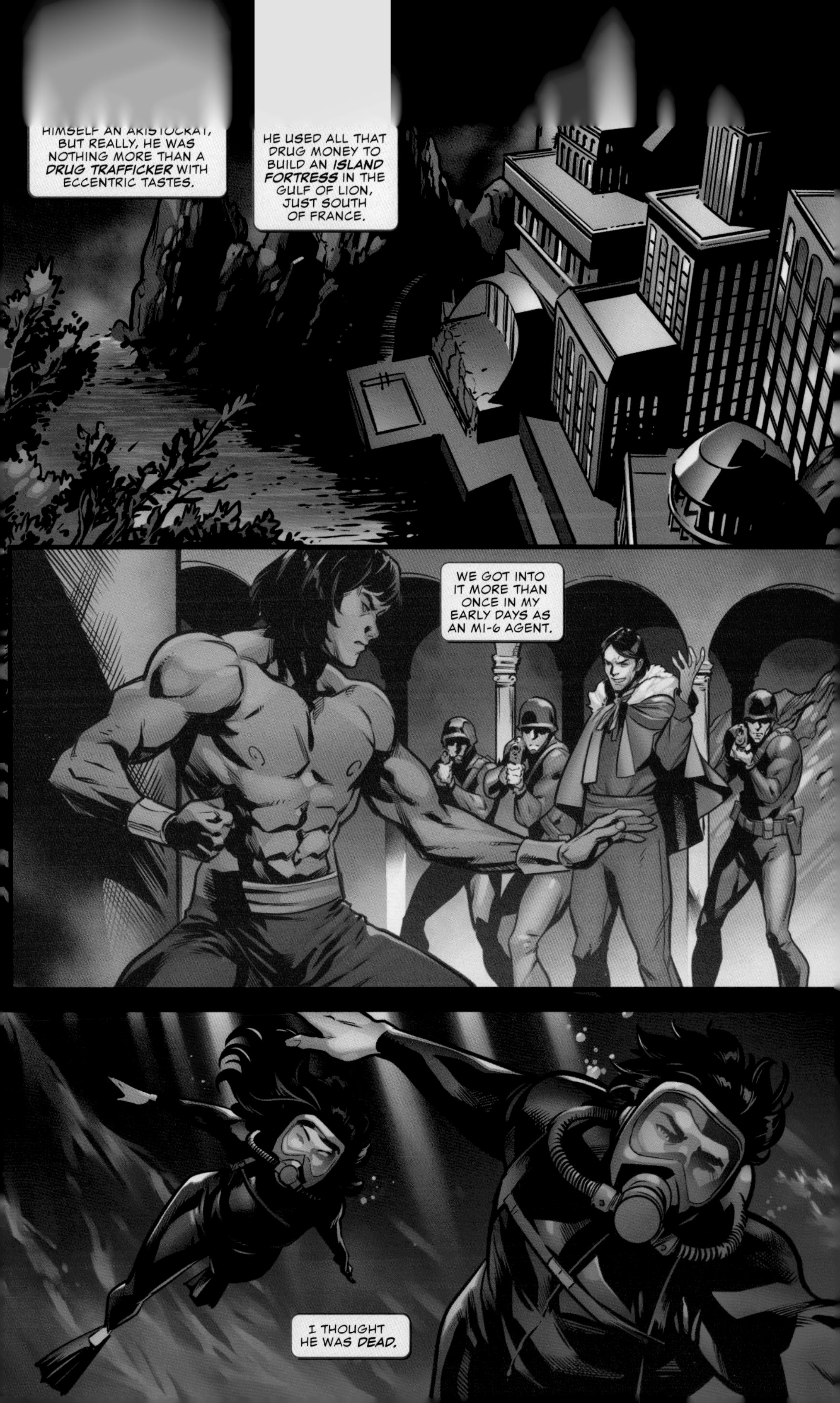
HIMSELF AN ARISTOCRAT, BUT REALLY, HE WAS NOTHING MORE THAN A DRUG TRAFFICKER WITH ECCENTRIC TASTES.
HE USED ALL THAT DRUG MONEY TO BUILD AN ISLAND FORTRESS IN THE GULF OF LION, JUST SOUTH OF FRANCE.
WE GOT INTO IT MORE THAN ONCE IN MY EARLY DAYS AS AN MI-6 AGENT.
I THOUGHT HE WAS DEAD.

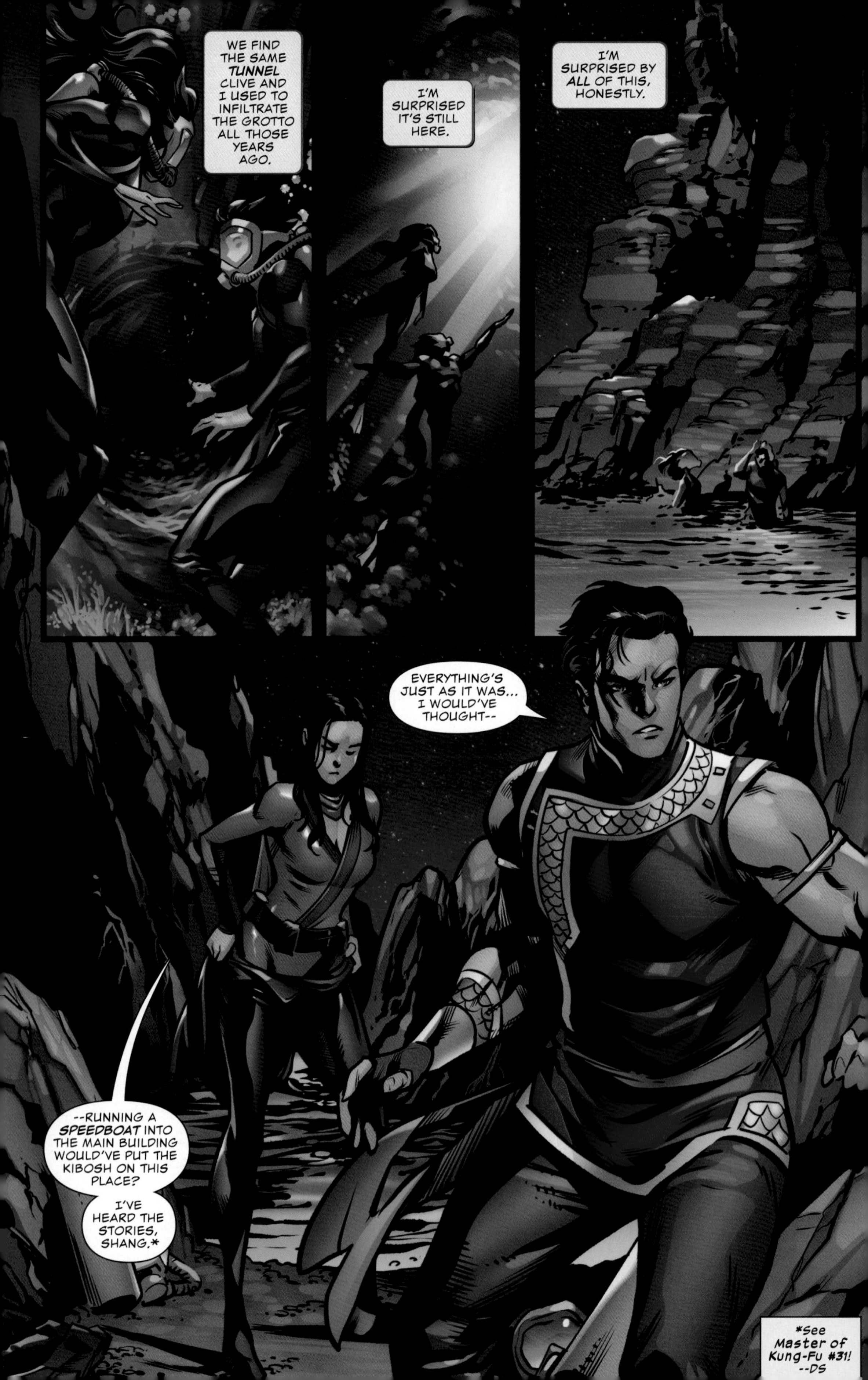
WE FIND THE SAME TUNNEL CLIVE AND I USED TO INFILTRATE THE GROTTO ALL THOSE YEARS AGO.
I'M SURPRISED IT'S STILL HERE.
I'M SURPRISED BY ALL OF THIS, HONESTLY.
EVERYTHING'S JUST AS IT WAS... I WOULD'VE THOUGHT--
--RUNNING A SPEEDBOAT INTO THE MAIN BUILDING WOULD'VE PUT THE KIBOSH ON THIS PLACE?
I'VE HEARD THE STORIES, SHANG.*
*See Master of Kung-Fu #31! --DS

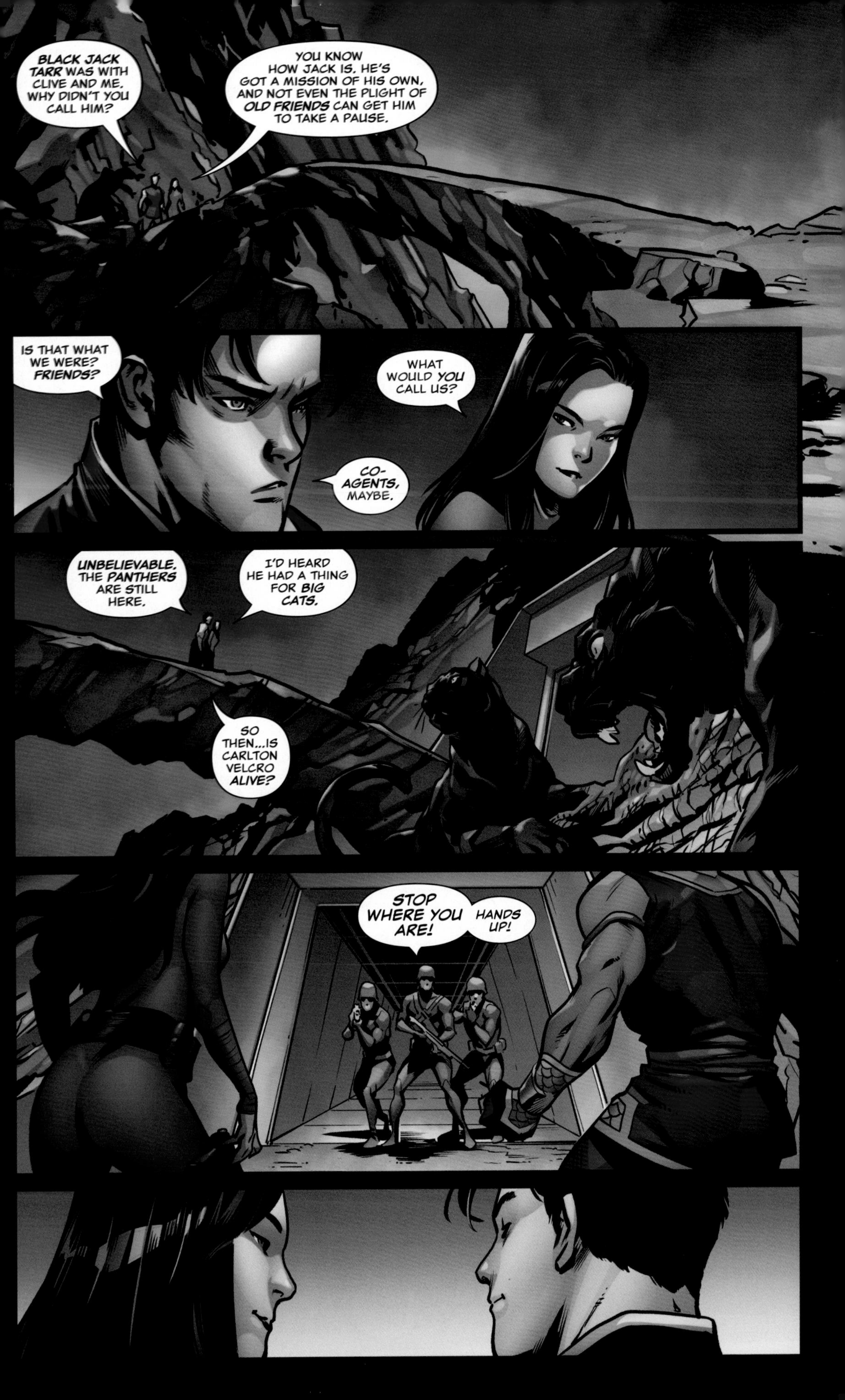
BLACK JACK TARR WAS WITH CLIVE AND ME. WHY DIDN'T YOU CALL HIM?
YOU KNOW HOW JACK IS. HE'S GOT A MISSION OF HIS OWN, AND NOT EVEN THE PLIGHT OF OLD FRIENDS CAN GET HIM TO TAKE A PAUSE.
IS THAT WHAT WE WERE? FRIENDS?
WHAT WOULD YOU CALL US?
CO-AGENTS, MAYBE.
UNBELIEVABLE. THE PANTHERS ARE STILL HERE.
I'D HEARD HE HAD A THING FOR BIG CATS.
SO THEN...IS CARLTON VELCRO ALIVE?
STOP WHERE YOU ARE!
HANDS UP!

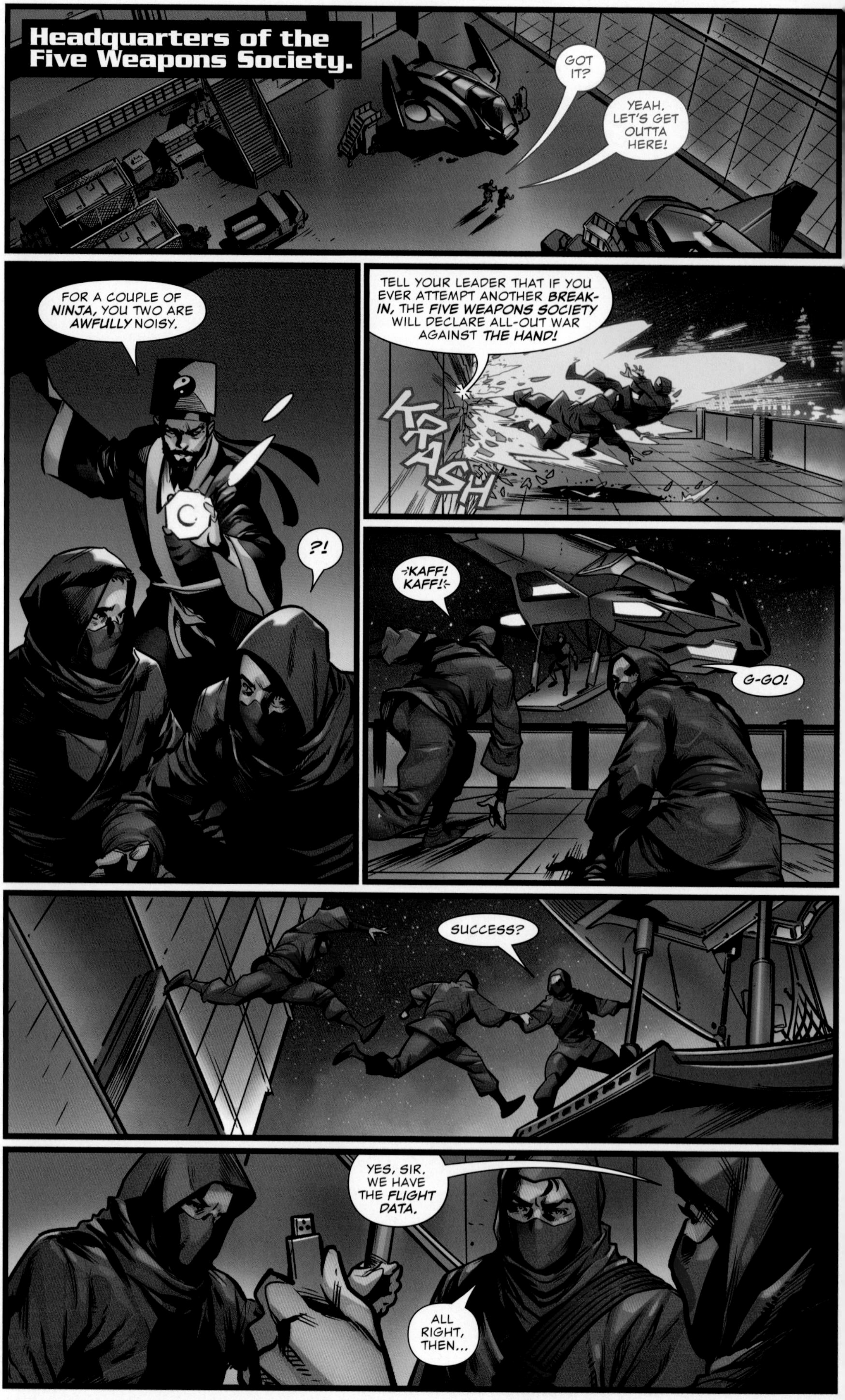
Headquarters of the Five Weapons Society.
GOT IT?
YEAH, LET'S GET OUTTA HERE!
FOR A COUPLE OF NINJA, YOU TWO ARE AWFULLY NOISY.
?!
TELL YOUR LEADER THAT IF YOU EVER ATTEMPT ANOTHER BREAK-IN, THE FIVE WEAPONS SOCIETY WILL DECLARE ALL-OUT WAR AGAINST THE HAND!
KRASH
KAFF! KAFF!
G-GO!
SUCCESS?
YES, SIR. WE HAVE THE FLIGHT DATA.
ALL RIGHT, THEN...

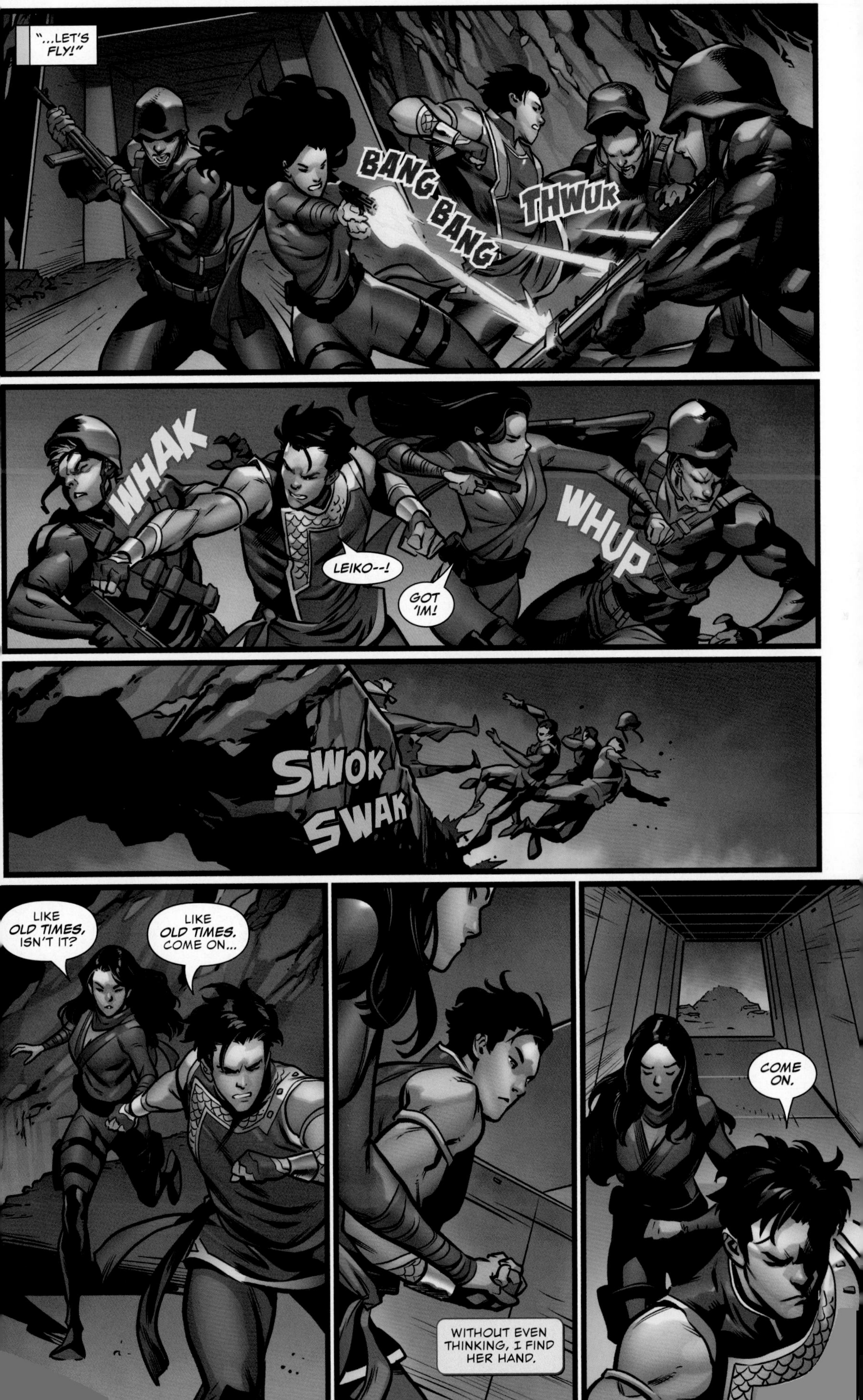
"...LET'S FLY!"
BANG BANG
THWUK
WHAK
LEIKO--!
GOT 'IM!
WHUP
SWOK
SWAK
LIKE OLD TIMES, ISN'T IT?
LIKE OLD TIMES. COME ON...
WITHOUT EVEN THINKING, I FIND HER HAND.
COME ON.

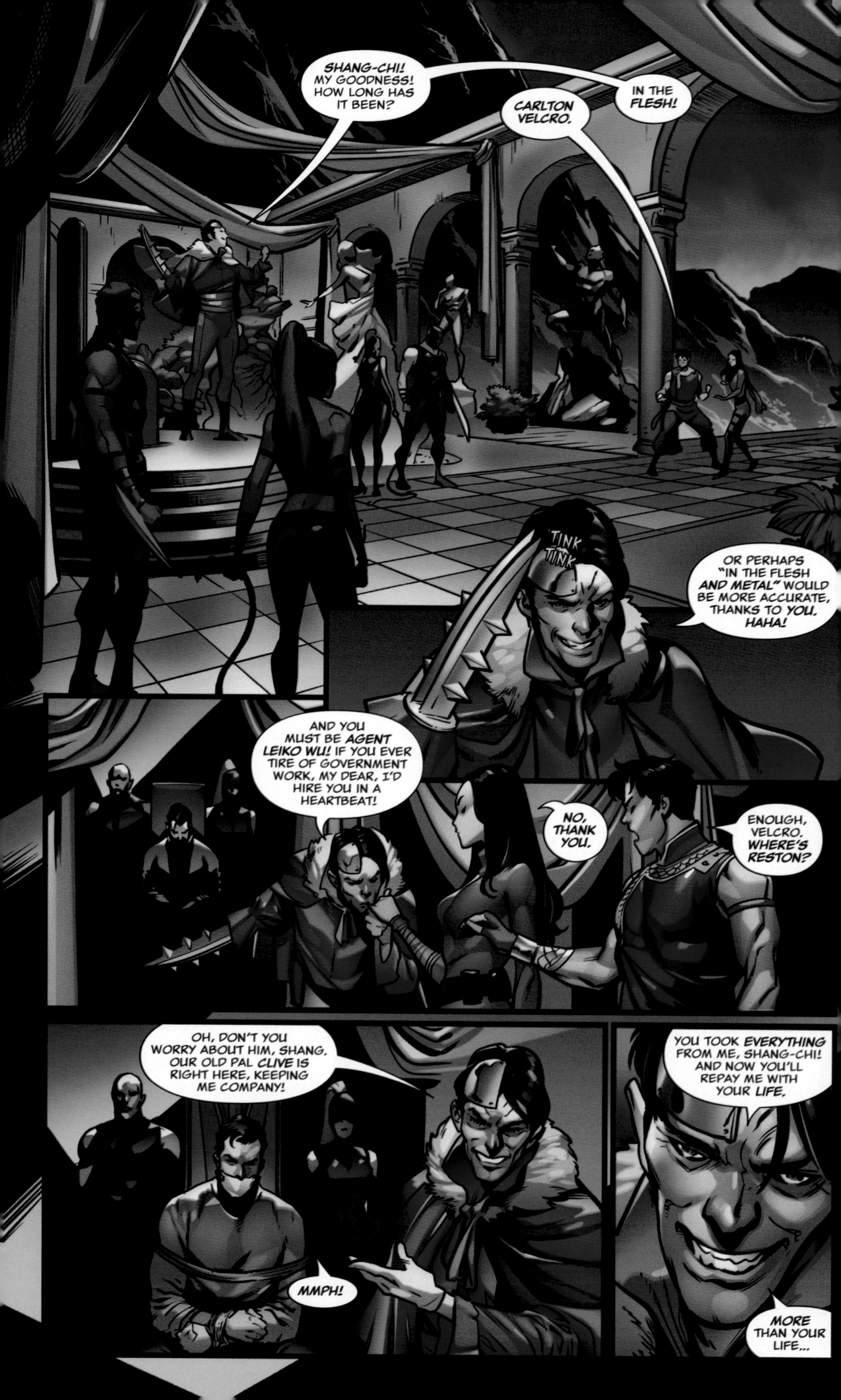
SHANG-CHI! MY GOODNESS! HOW LONG HAS IT BEEN?
CARLTON VELCRO.
IN THE FLESH!
TINK TINK
OR PERHAPS "IN THE FLESH AND METAL" WOULD BE MORE ACCURATE, THANKS TO YOU. HAHA!
AND YOU MUST BE AGENT LEIKO WU! IF YOU EVER TIRE OF GOVERNMENT WORK, MY DEAR, I'D HIRE YOU IN A HEARTBEAT!
NO, THANK YOU.
ENOUGH, VELCRO. WHERE'S RESTON?
OH, DON'T YOU WORRY ABOUT HIM, SHANG. OUR OLD PAL CLIVE IS RIGHT HERE, KEEPING ME COMPANY!
MMPH!
YOU TOOK EVERYTHING FROM ME, SHANG-CHI! AND NOW YOU'LL REPAY ME WITH YOUR LIFE.
MORE THAN YOUR LIFE...

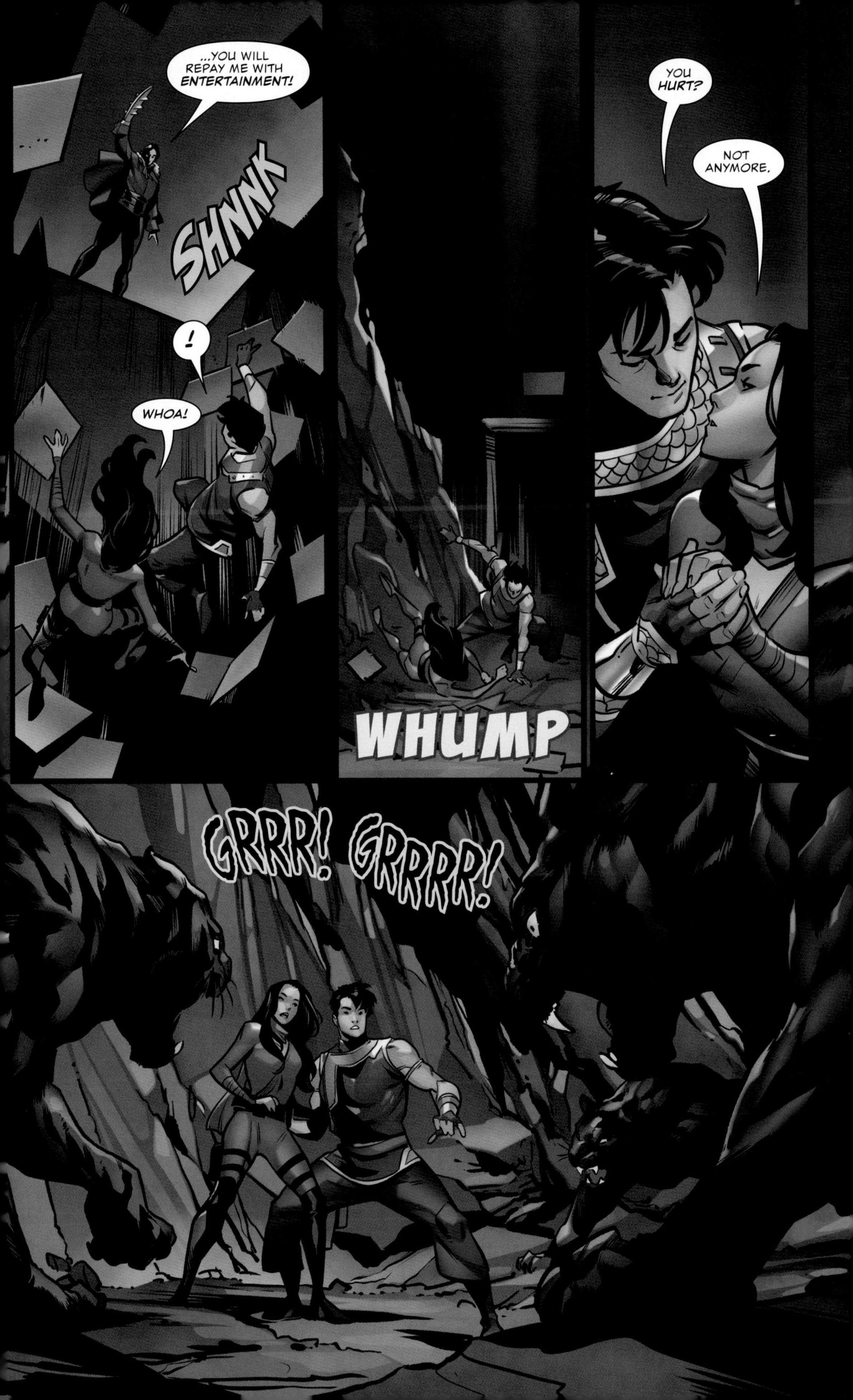
...YOU WILL REPAY ME WITH ENTERTAINMENT!
SHNNK
!
WHOA!
WHUMP
YOU HURT?
NOT ANYMORE.
GRRR! GRRRR!

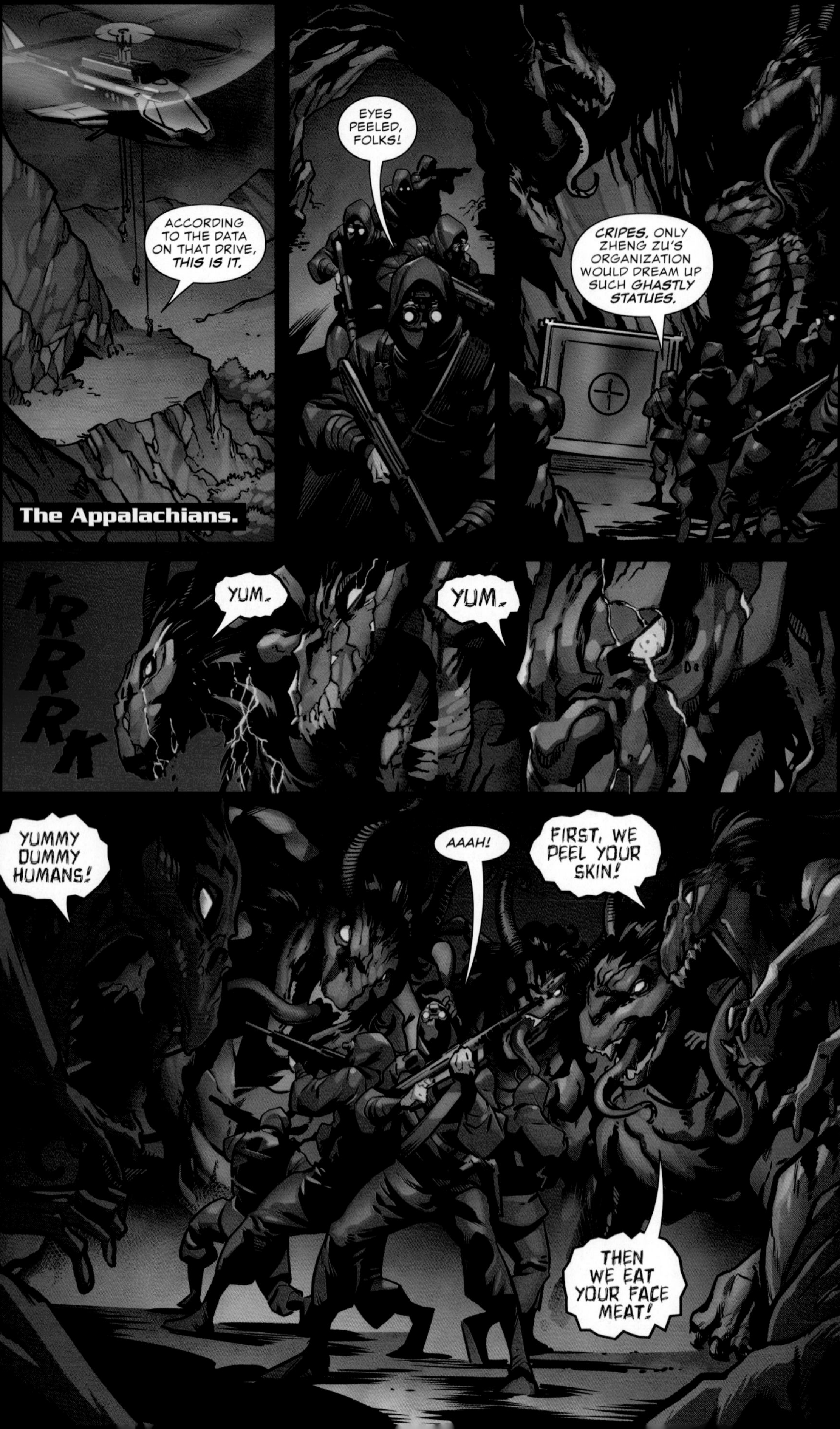
The Appalachians.
ACCORDING TO THE DATA ON THAT DRIVE, THIS IS IT.
EYES PEELED, FOLKS!
CRIPES. ONLY ZHENG ZU'S ORGANIZATION WOULD DREAM UP SUCH GHASTLY STATUES.
KRRRK
YUM.
YUM.
YUMMY DUMMY HUMANS!
AAAH!
FIRST, WE PEEL YOUR SKIN!
THEN WE EAT YOUR FACE MEAT!

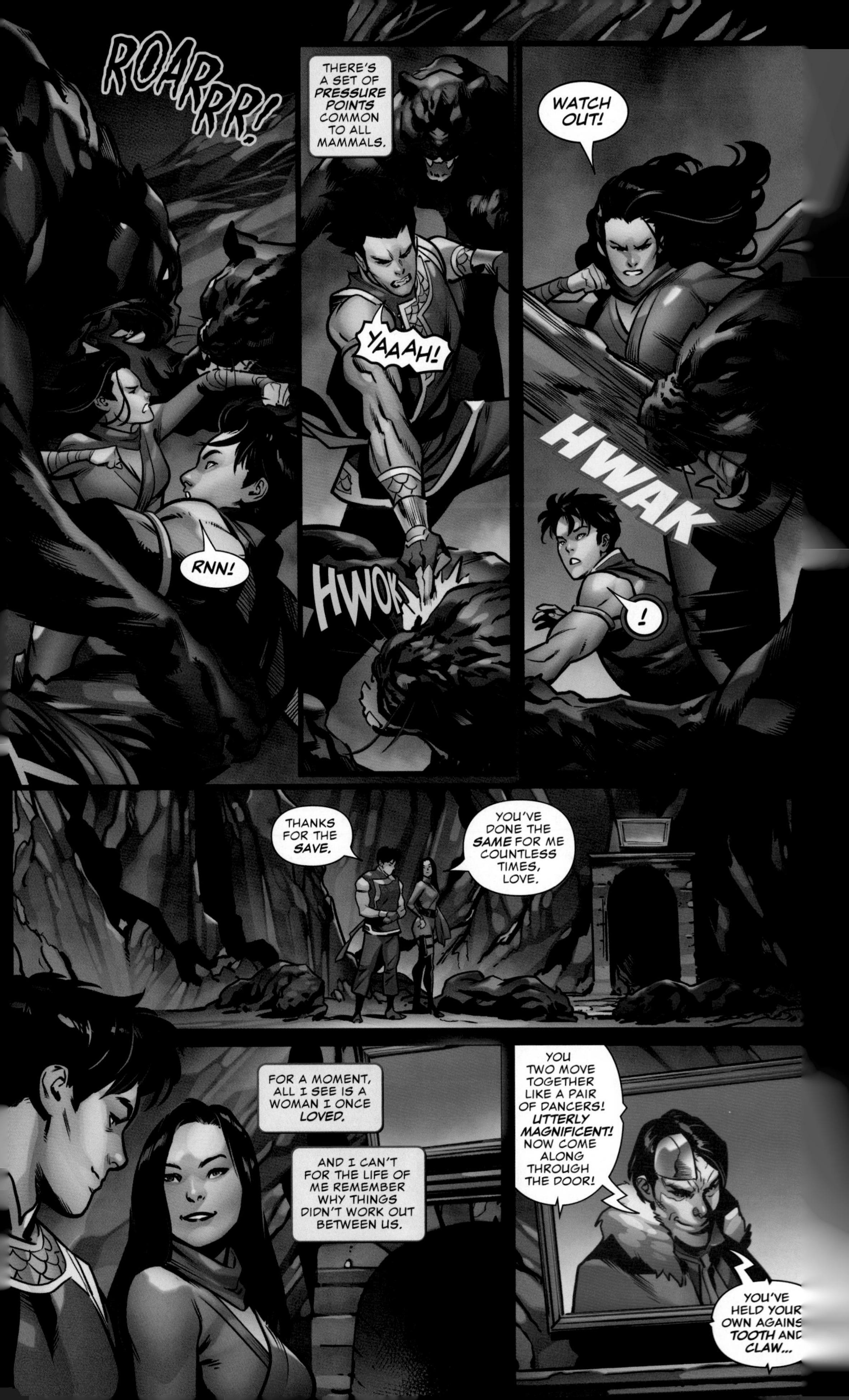
ROARRRR!
RNN!
THERE'S A SET OF PRESSURE POINTS COMMON TO ALL MAMMALS.
YAAAH!
HWOK
WATCH OUT!
HWAK
!
THANKS FOR THE SAVE.
YOU'VE DONE THE SAME FOR ME COUNTLESS TIMES, LOVE.
FOR A MOMENT, ALL I SEE IS A WOMAN I ONCE LOVED.
AND I CAN'T FOR THE LIFE OF ME REMEMBER WHY THINGS DIDN'T WORK OUT BETWEEN US.
YOU TWO MOVE TOGETHER LIKE A PAIR OF DANCERS! UTTERLY MAGNIFICENT! NOW COME ALONG THROUGH THE DOOR!
YOU'VE HELD YOUR OWN AGAINS TOOTH AND CLAW...

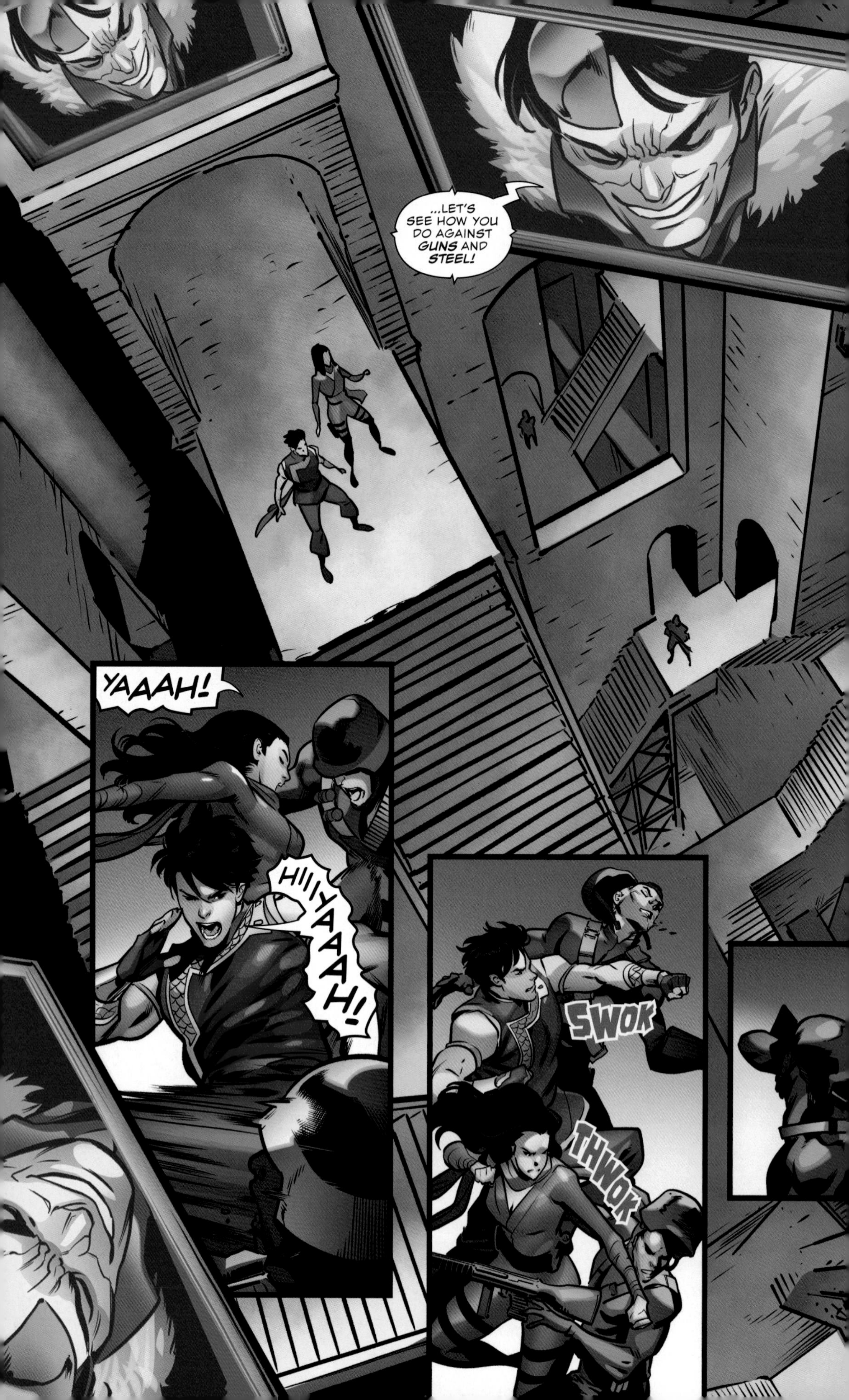
...LET'S SEE HOW YOU DO AGAINST GUNS AND STEEL!
YAAAH!
HIIIYAAAAH!
SWOK
THWOK

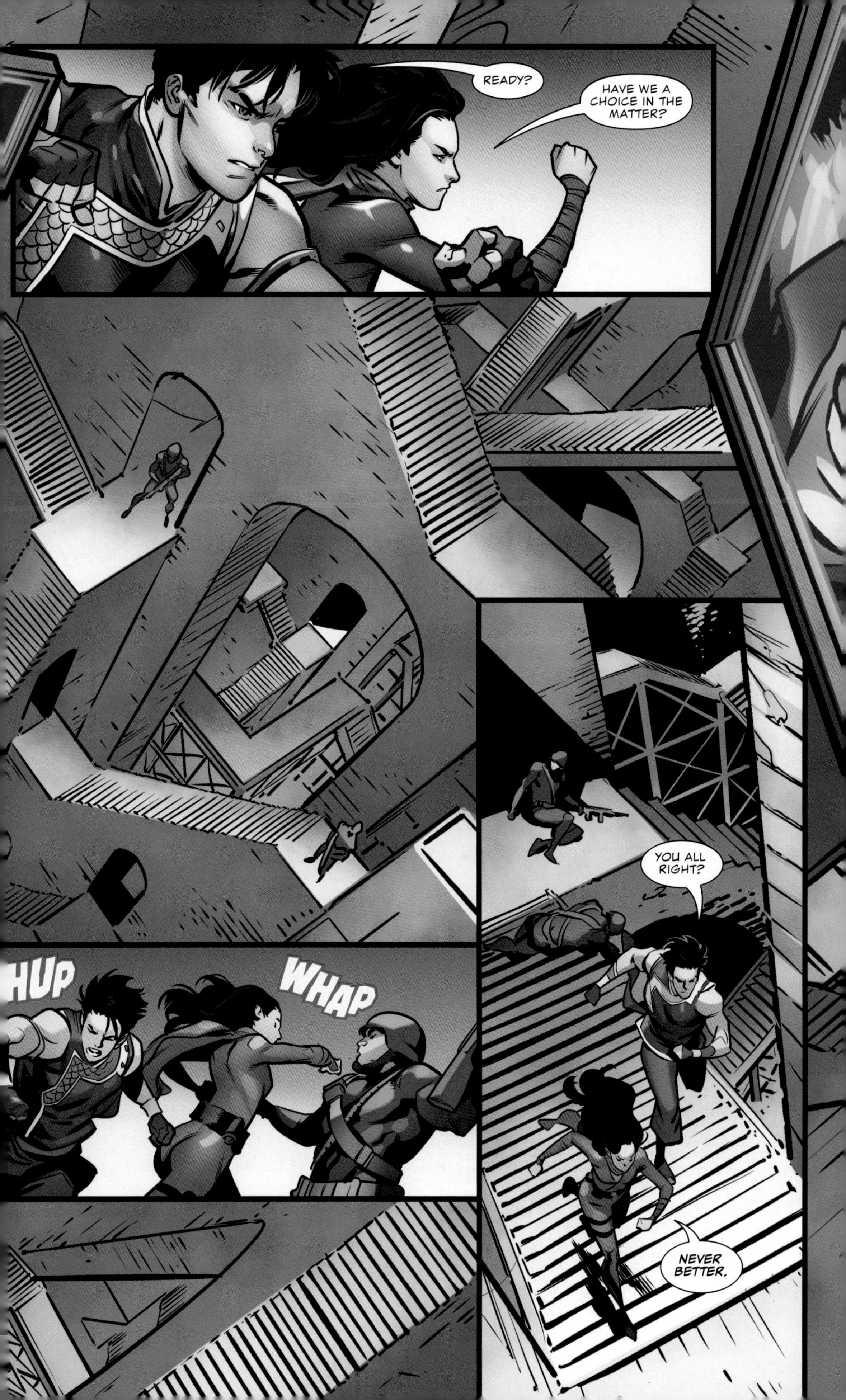
READY?
HAVE WE A CHOICE IN THE MATTER?
HUP
WHAP
YOU ALL RIGHT?
NEVER BETTER.

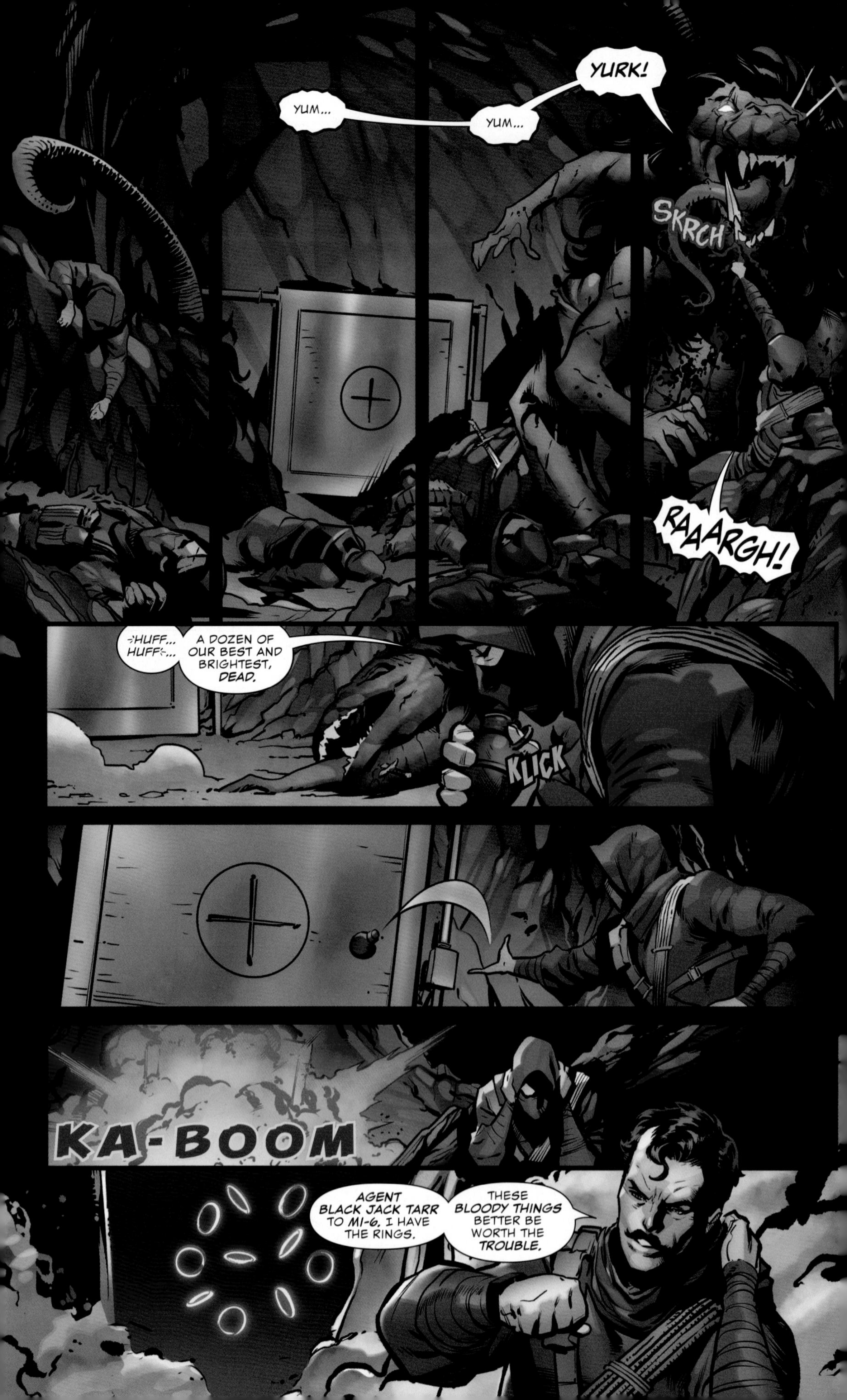
YUM...
YUM...
YURK!
SKRCH
RAAARGH!
HUFF... HUFF...
A DOZEN OF OUR BEST AND BRIGHTEST, DEAD.
KLICK
KA-BOOM
AGENT BLACK JACK TARR TO MI-6, I HAVE THE RINGS.
THESE BLOODY THINGS BETTER BE WORTH THE TROUBLE.

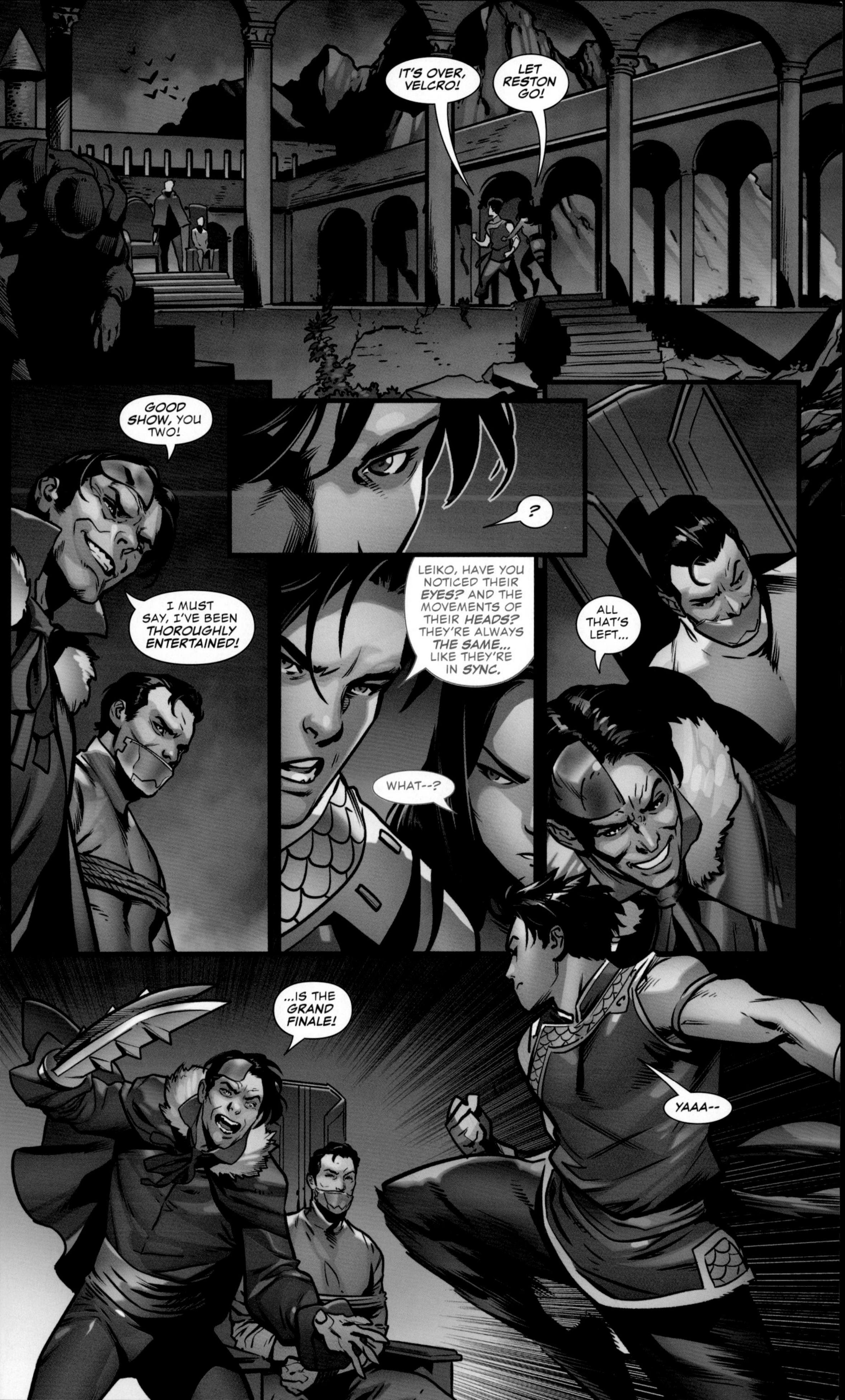
IT'S OVER, VELCRO!
LET RESTON GO!
GOOD SHOW, YOU TWO!
?
I MUST SAY, I'VE BEEN THOROUGHLY ENTERTAINED!
LEIKO, HAVE YOU NOTICED THEIR EYES? AND THE MOVEMENTS OF THEIR HEADS? THEY'RE ALWAYS THE SAME... LIKE THEY'RE IN SYNC.
WHAT--?
ALL THAT'S LEFT...
...IS THE GRAND FINALE!
YAAA--

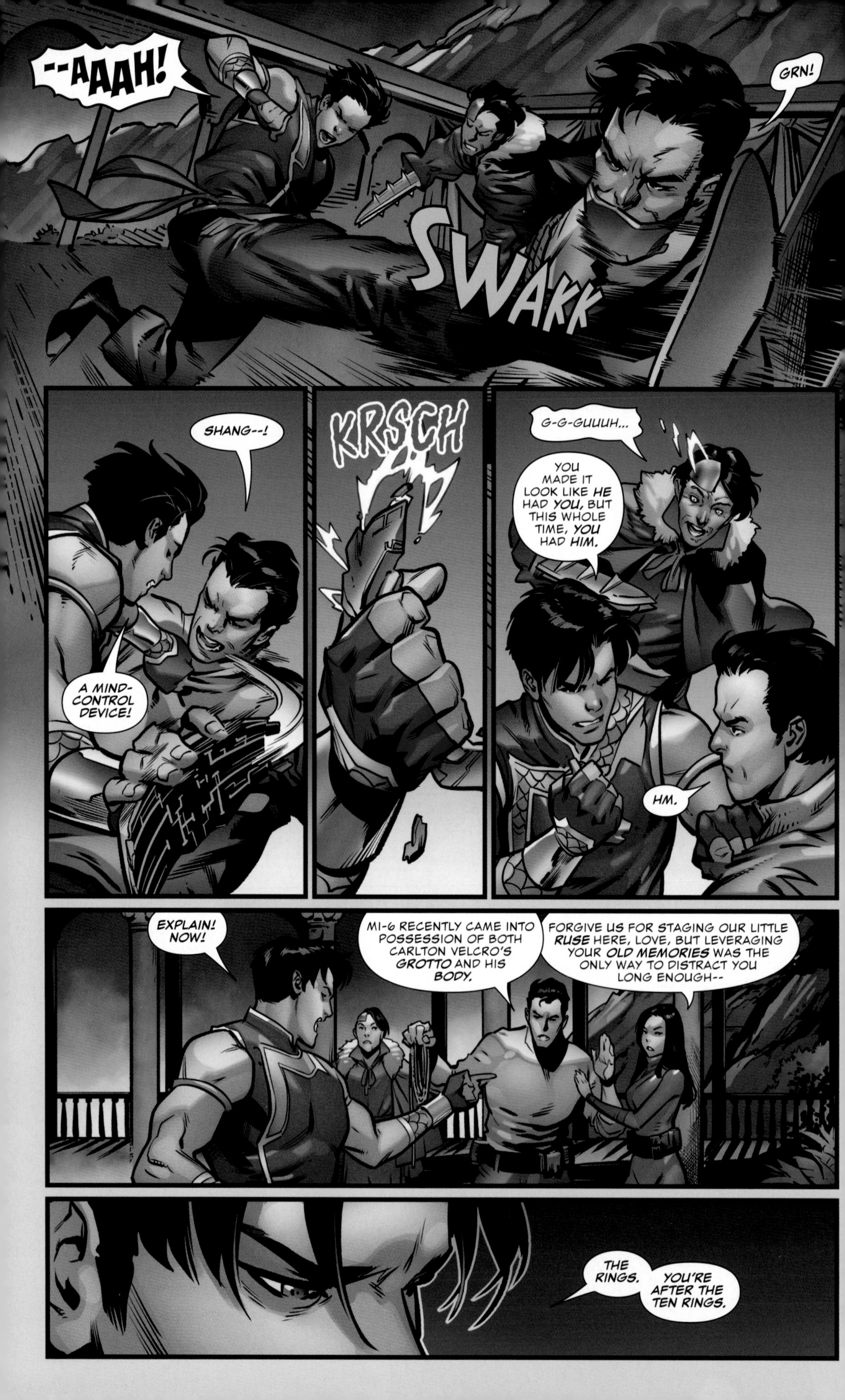
--AAAH!
GRN!
SWAKK
SHANG--!
A MIND-CONTROL DEVICE!
KRSCH
G-G-GUUUH...
YOU MADE IT LOOK LIKE HE HAD YOU, BUT THIS WHOLE TIME, YOU HAD HIM.
HM.
EXPLAIN! NOW!
MI-6 RECENTLY CAME INTO POSSESSION OF BOTH CARLTON VELCRO'S GROTTO AND HIS BODY.
FORGIVE US FOR STAGING OUR LITTLE RUSE HERE, LOVE, BUT LEVERAGING YOUR OLD MEMORIES WAS THE ONLY WAY TO DISTRACT YOU LONG ENOUGH--
THE RINGS.
YOU'RE AFTER THE TEN RINGS.

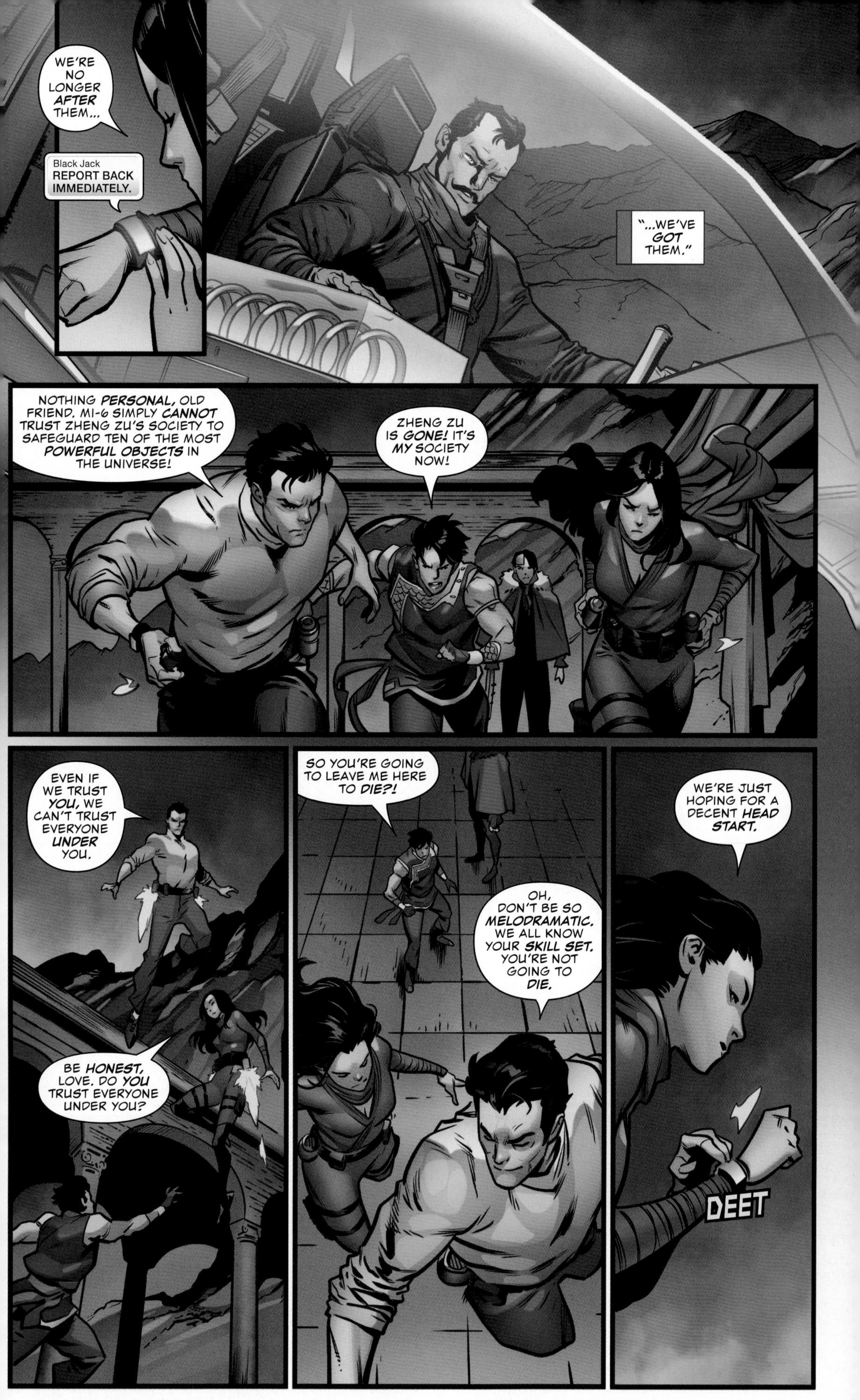
WE'RE NO LONGER AFTER THEM...
Black Jack
REPORT BACK IMMEDIATELY.
"...WE'VE GOT THEM."
NOTHING PERSONAL, OLD FRIEND. MI-6 SIMPLY CANNOT TRUST ZHENG ZU'S SOCIETY TO SAFEGUARD TEN OF THE MOST POWERFUL OBJECTS IN THE UNIVERSE!
ZHENG ZU IS GONE! IT'S MY SOCIETY NOW!
EVEN IF WE TRUST YOU, WE CAN'T TRUST EVERYONE UNDER YOU.
BE HONEST, LOVE. DO YOU TRUST EVERYONE UNDER YOU?
SO YOU'RE GOING TO LEAVE ME HERE TO DIE?!
OH, DON'T BE SO MELODRAMATIC. WE ALL KNOW YOUR SKILL SET. YOU'RE NOT GOING TO DIE.
WE'RE JUST HOPING FOR A DECENT HEAD START.
DEET

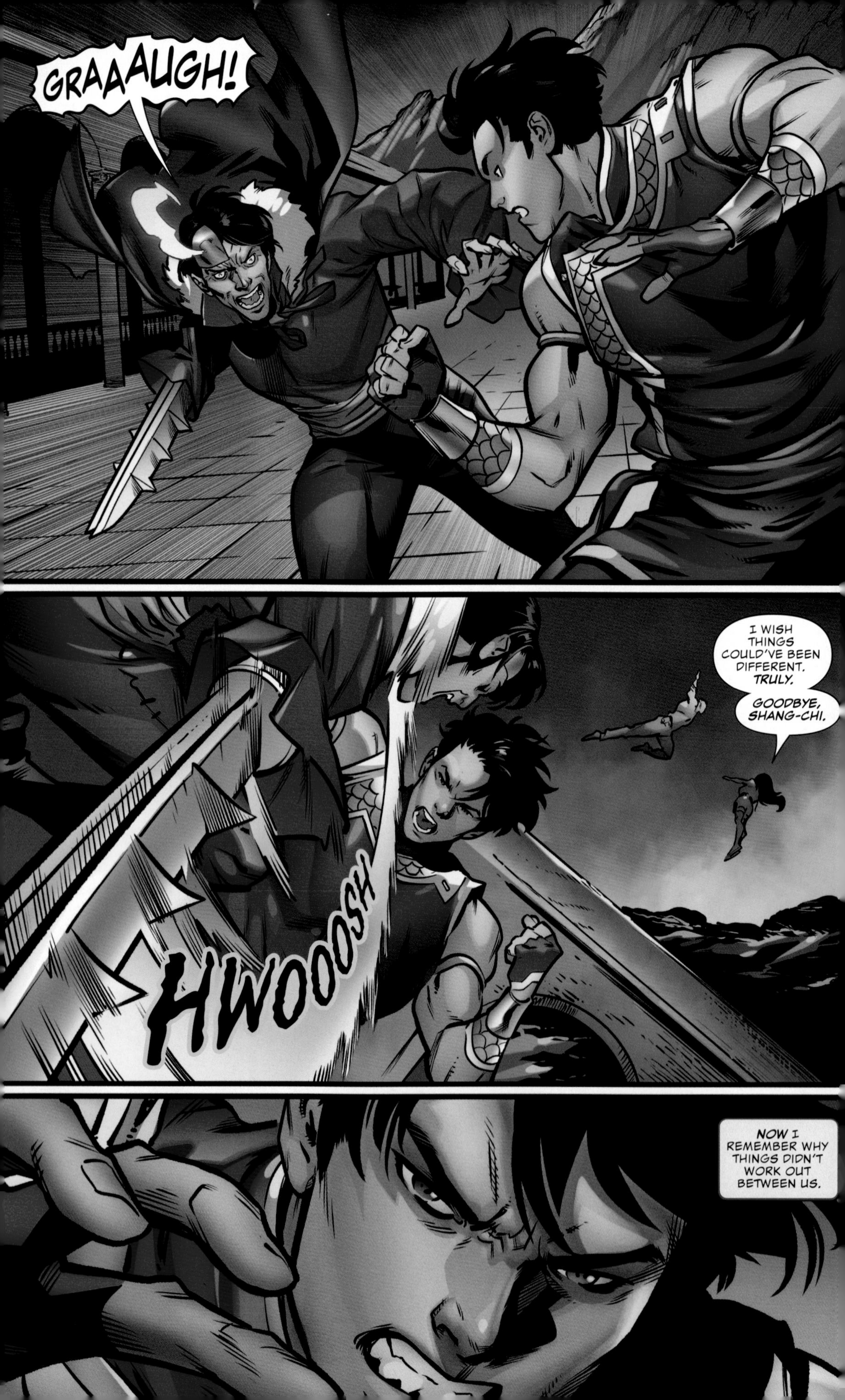
GRAAAUGH!
I WISH THINGS COULD'VE BEEN DIFFERENT. TRULY.
GOODBYE, SHANG-CHI.
HWOOOSH
NOW I REMEMBER WHY THINGS DIDN'T WORK OUT BETWEEN US.

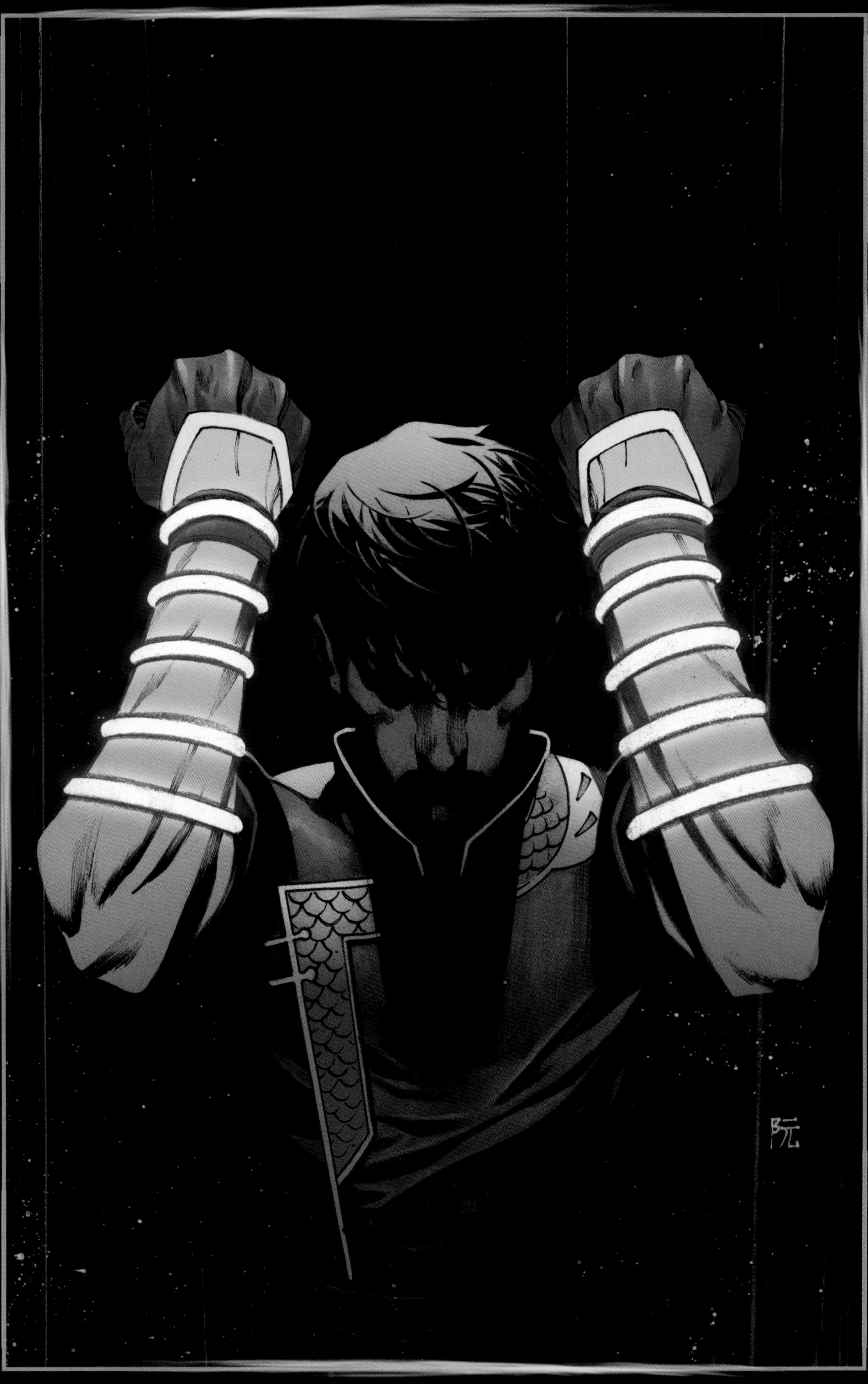

THREE

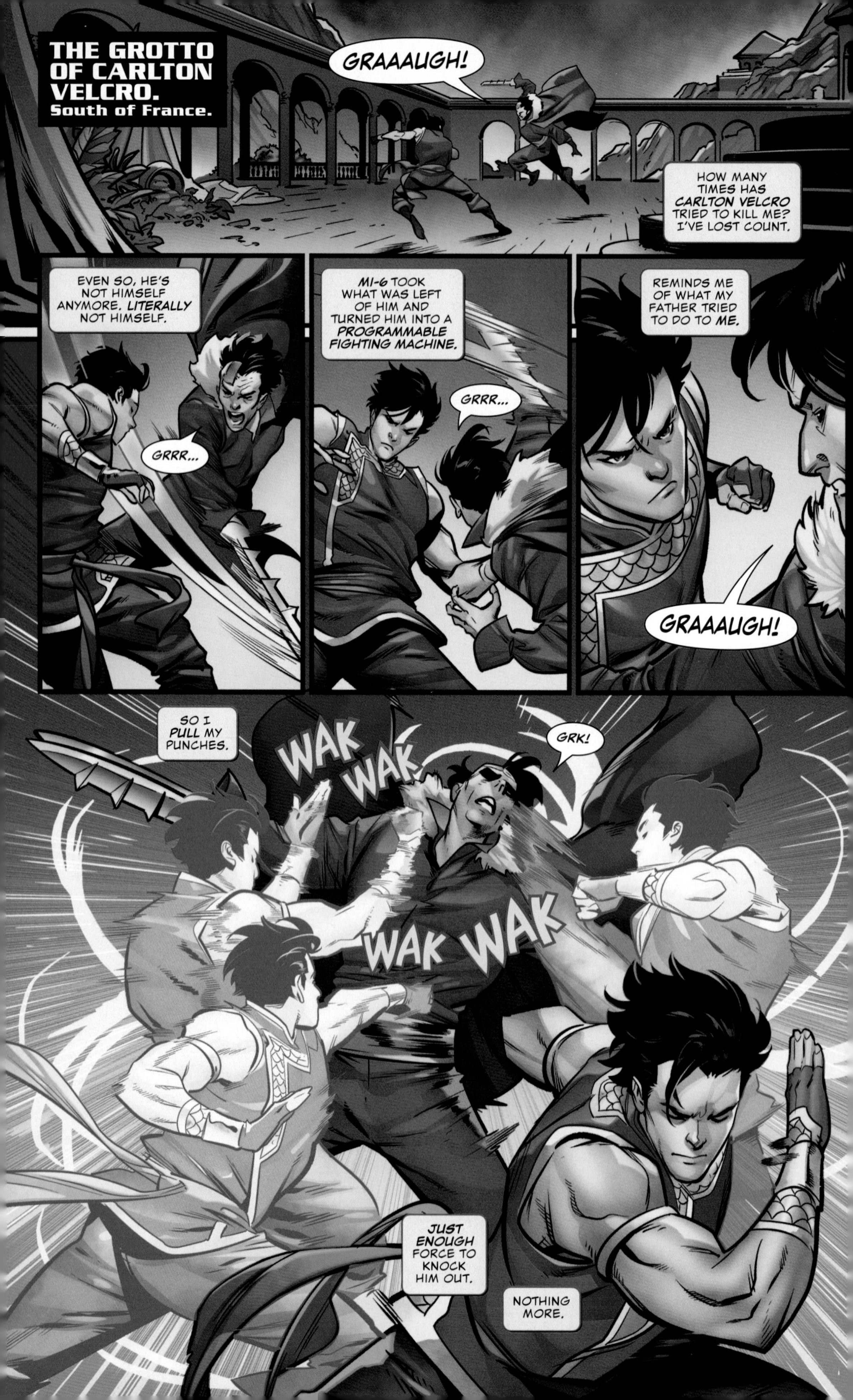
THE GROTTO OF CARLTON VELCRO. South of France.
GRAAAUGH!
HOW MANY TIMES HAS CARLTON VELCRO TRIED TO KILL ME? I'VE LOST COUNT.
EVEN SO, HE'S NOT HIMSELF ANYMORE. LITERALLY NOT HIMSELF.
GRRR...
MI-6 TOOK WHAT WAS LEFT OF HIM AND TURNED HIM INTO A PROGRAMMABLE FIGHTING MACHINE.
GRRR...
REMINDS ME OF WHAT MY FATHER TRIED TO DO TO ME.
GRAAAUGH!
SO I PULL MY PUNCHES.
WAK WAK
GRK!
WAK WAK
JUST ENOUGH FORCE TO KNOCK HIM OUT.
NOTHING MORE.

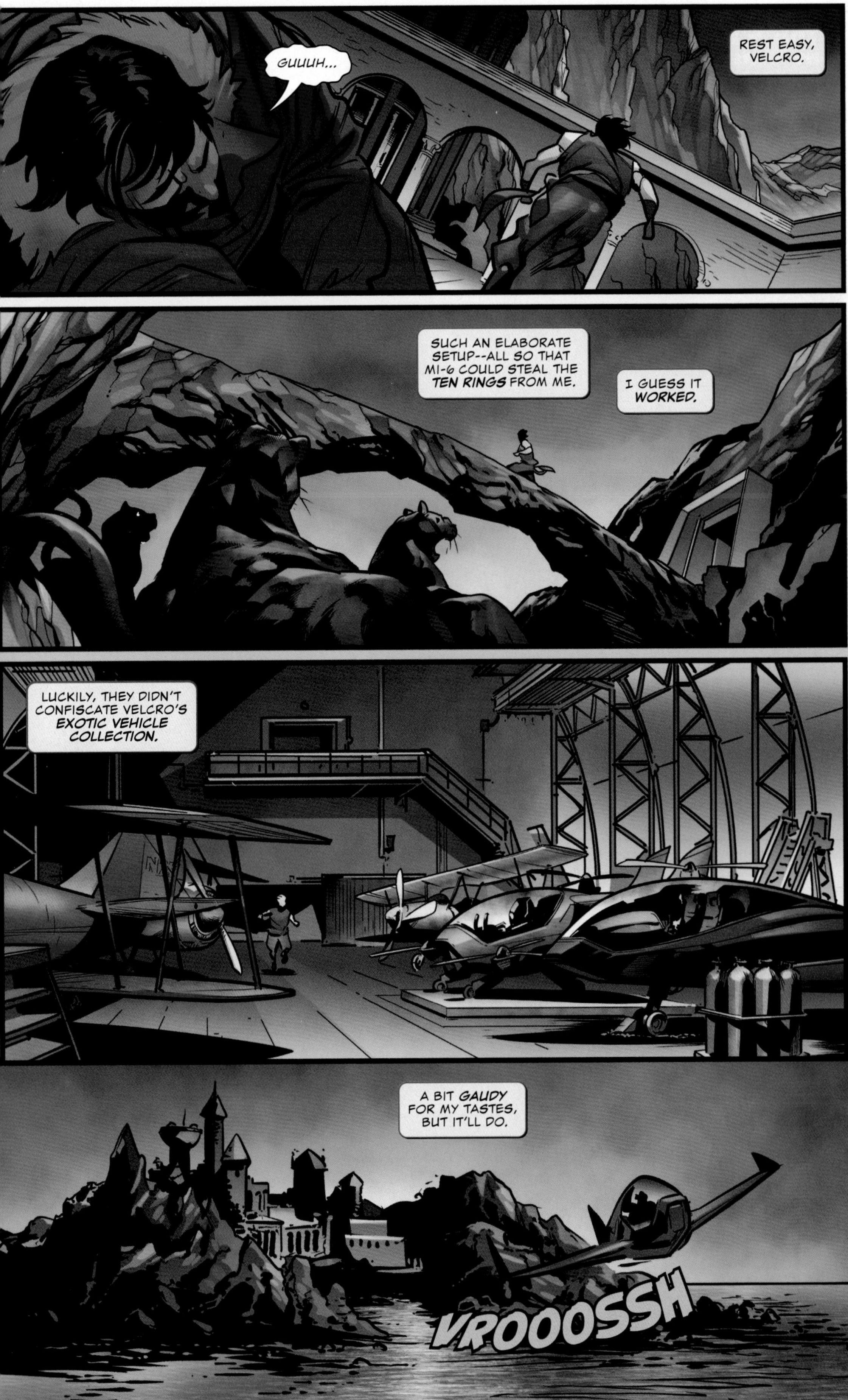
GUUUH...
REST EASY, VELCRO.
SUCH AN ELABORATE SETUP--ALL SO THAT MI-6 COULD STEAL THE TEN RINGS FROM ME.
I GUESS IT WORKED.
LUCKILY, THEY DIDN'T CONFISCATE VELCRO'S EXOTIC VEHICLE COLLECTION.
A BIT GAUDY FOR MY TASTES, BUT IT'LL DO.
VROOOSSH

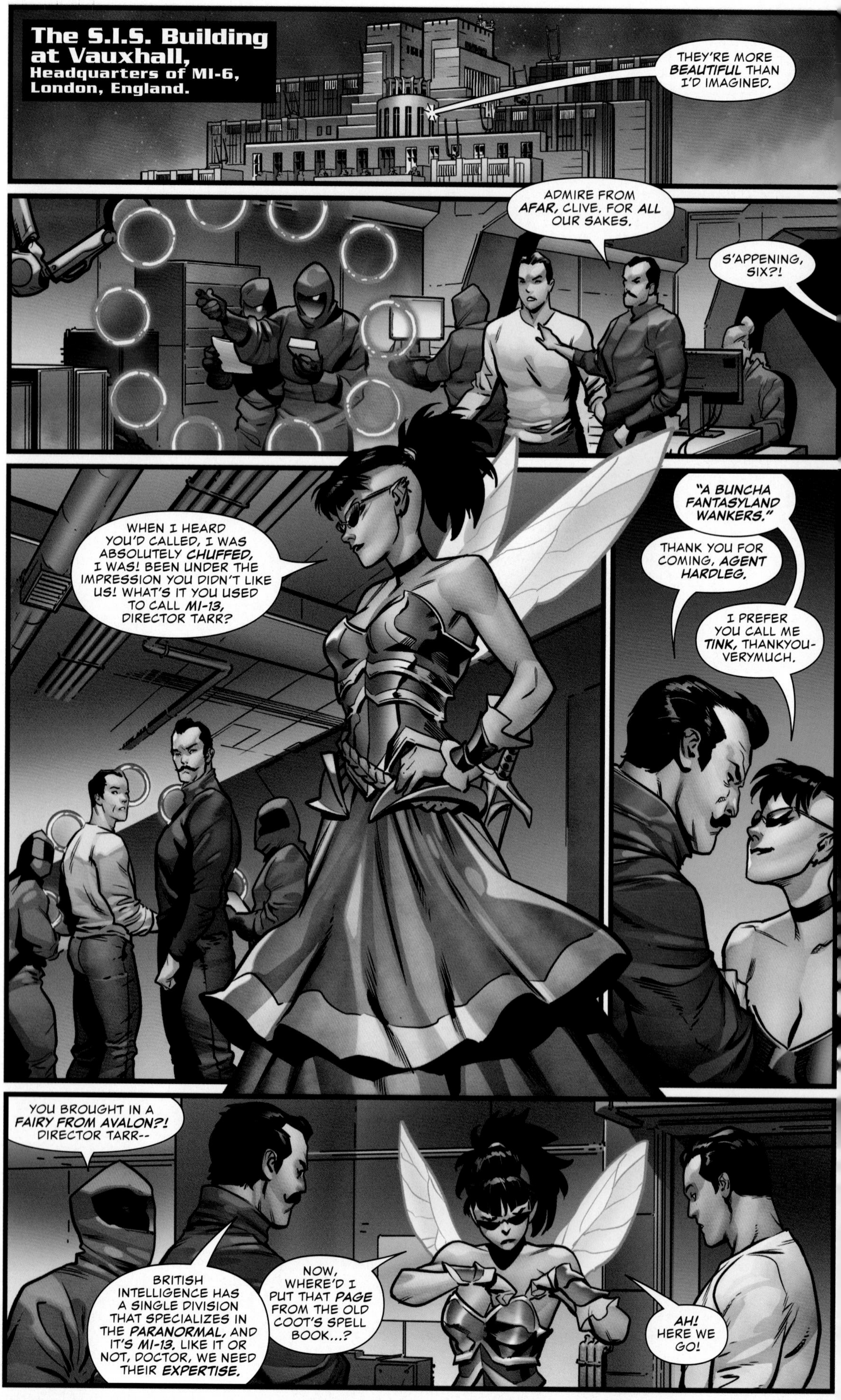

The S.I.S. Building at Vauxhall,
Headquarters of MI-6, London, England.
THEY'RE MORE BEAUTIFUL THAN I'D IMAGINED.
ADMIRE FROM AFAR, CLIVE. FOR ALL OUR SAKES.
S'APPENING, SIX?!
WHEN I HEARD YOU'D CALLED, I WAS ABSOLUTELY CHUFFED, I WAS! BEEN UNDER THE IMPRESSION YOU DIDN'T LIKE US! WHAT'S IT YOU USED TO CALL MI-13, DIRECTOR TARR?
"A BUNCHA FANTASYLAND WANKERS."
THANK YOU FOR COMING, AGENT HARDLEG.
I PREFER YOU CALL ME TINK, THANKYOU-VERYMUCH.
YOU BROUGHT IN A FAIRY FROM AVALON?! DIRECTOR TARR--
BRITISH INTELLIGENCE HAS A SINGLE DIVISION THAT SPECIALIZES IN THE PARANORMAL, AND IT'S MI-13. LIKE IT OR NOT, DOCTOR, WE NEED THEIR EXPERTISE.
NOW, WHERE'D I PUT THAT PAGE FROM THE OLD COOT'S SPELL BOOK...?
AH! HERE WE GO!

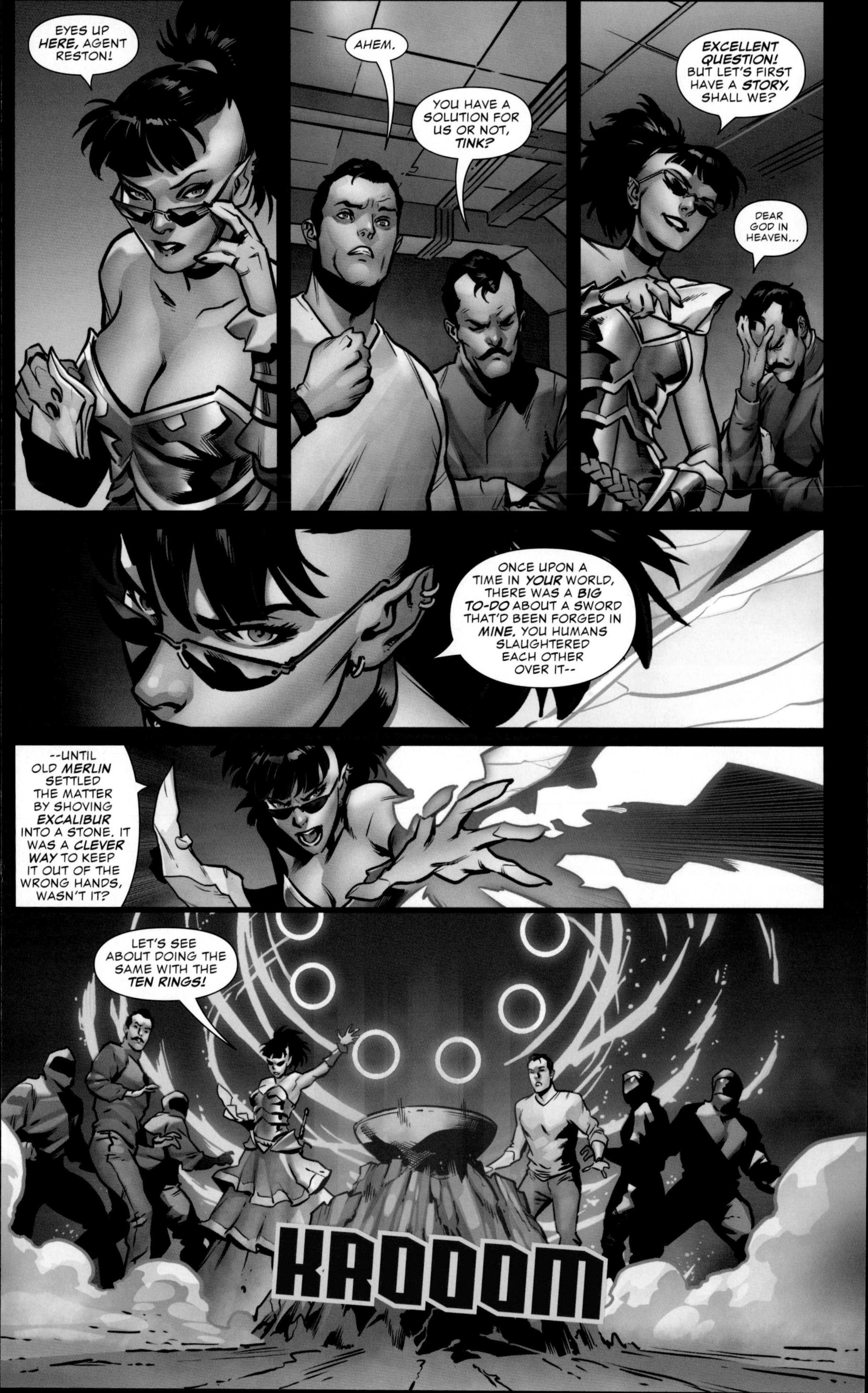
EYES UP HERE, AGENT RESTON!
AHEM.
YOU HAVE A SOLUTION FOR US OR NOT, TINK?
EXCELLENT QUESTION! BUT LET'S FIRST HAVE A STORY, SHALL WE?
DEAR GOD IN HEAVEN...
ONCE UPON A TIME IN YOUR WORLD, THERE WAS A BIG TO-DO ABOUT A SWORD THAT'D BEEN FORGED IN MINE. YOU HUMANS SLAUGHTERED EACH OTHER OVER IT--
--UNTIL OLD MERLIN SETTLED THE MATTER BY SHOVING EXCALIBUR INTO A STONE. IT WAS A CLEVER WAY TO KEEP IT OUT OF THE WRONG HANDS, WASN'T IT?
LET'S SEE ABOUT DOING THE SAME WITH THE TEN RINGS!
KROOOM

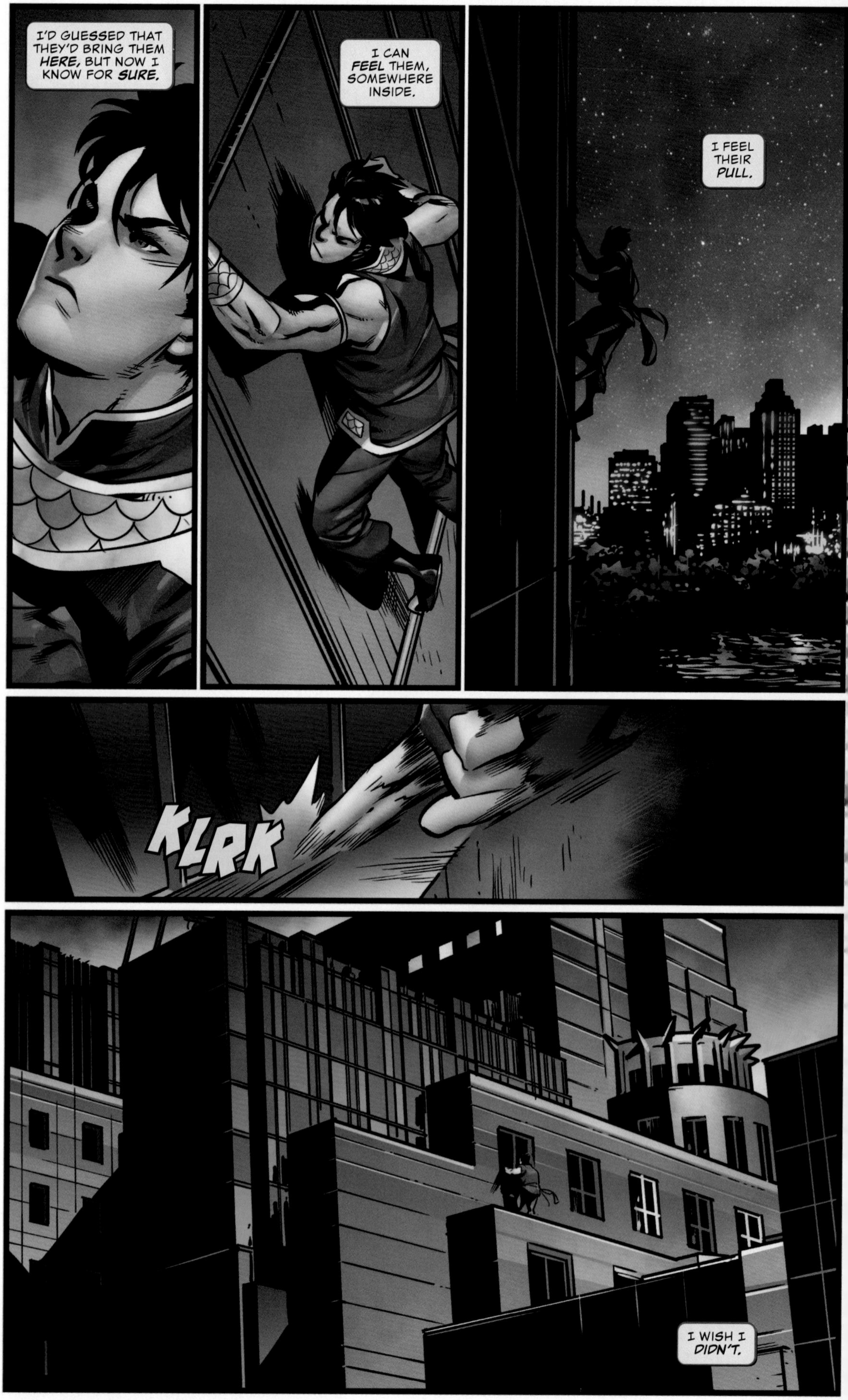
I'D GUESSED THAT THEY'D BRING THEM HERE, BUT NOW I KNOW FOR SURE.
I CAN FEEL THEM, SOMEWHERE INSIDE.
I FEEL THEIR PULL.
KLRK
I WISH I DIDN'T.

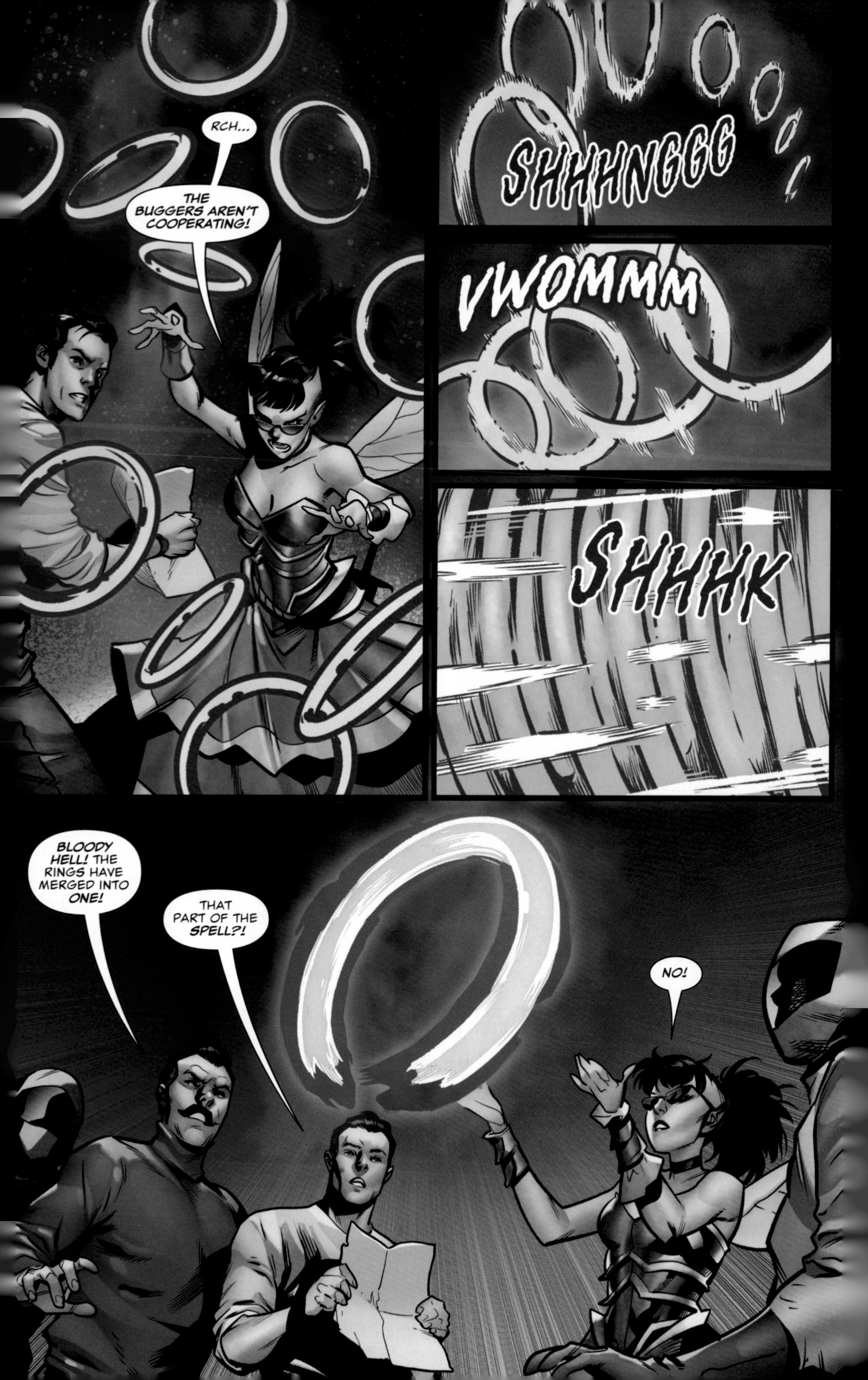
RCH...
THE BUGGERS AREN'T COOPERATING!
SHHHNGGG
VWOMMM
SHHHK
BLOODY HELL! THE RINGS HAVE MERGED INTO ONE!
THAT PART OF THE SPELL?!
NO!

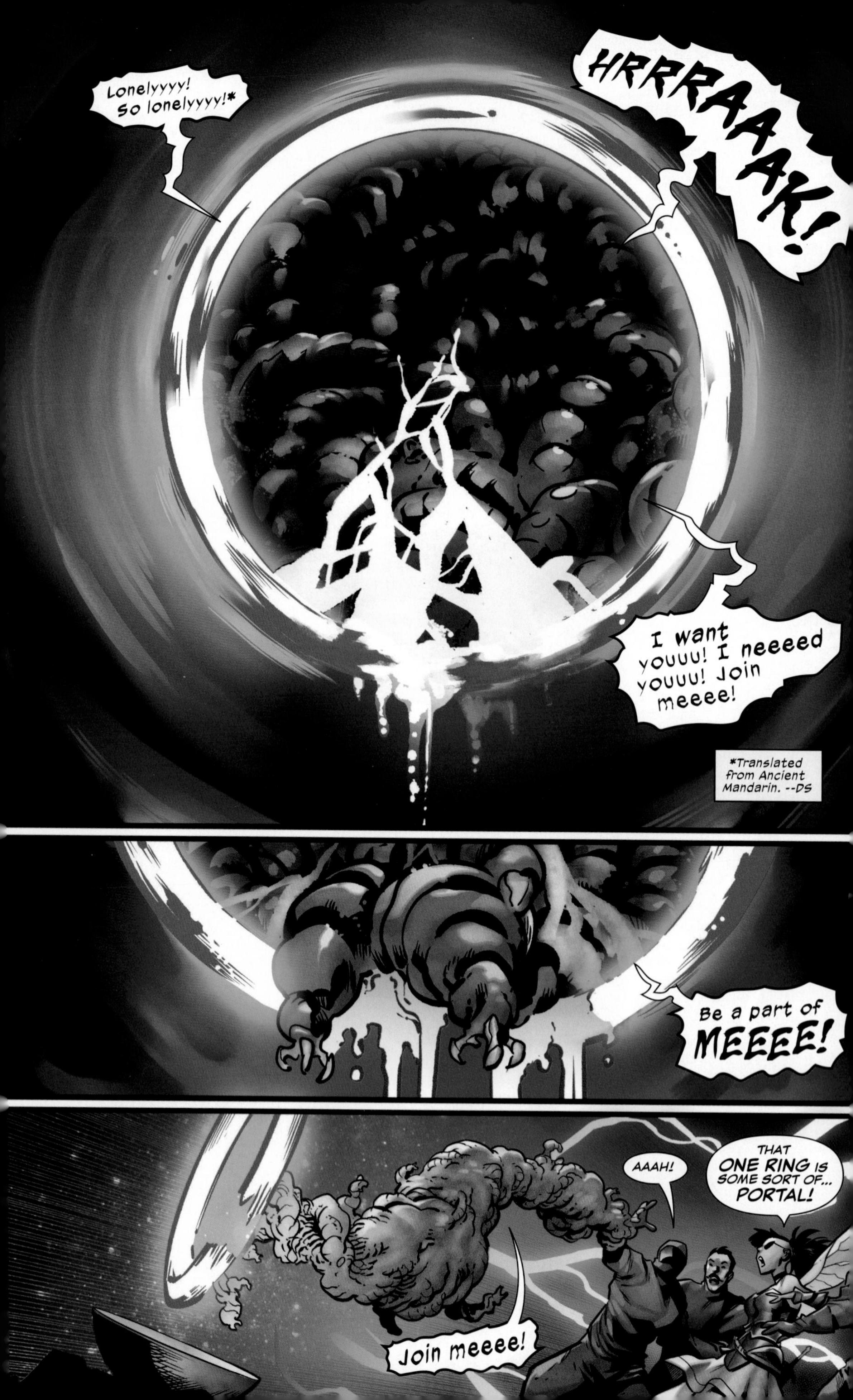
Lonelyyyy! So lonelyyyy!*
HRRRAAAK!
I want youuu! I neeeed youuu! Join meeee!
*Translated from Ancient Mandarin. --DS
Be a part of MEEEE!
AAAH!
THAT ONE RING IS SOME SORT OF... PORTAL!
Join meeee!

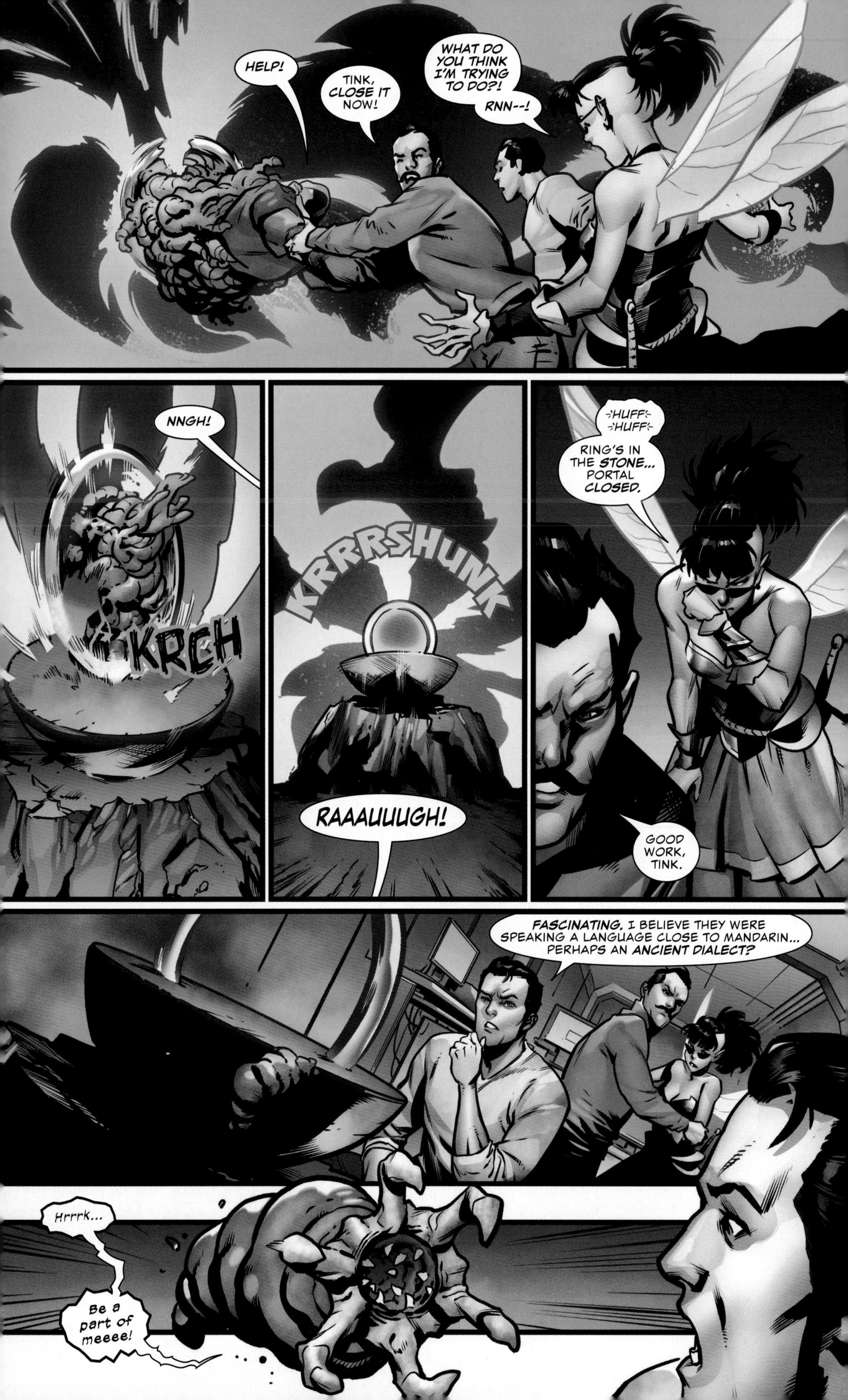
HELP!
TINK, CLOSE IT NOW!
WHAT DO YOU THINK I'M TRYING TO DO?!
RNN--!
NNGH!
KRCH
KRRRSHUNK
RAAAUUUGH!
HUFF HUFF
RING'S IN THE STONE... PORTAL CLOSED.
GOOD WORK, TINK.
FASCINATING. I BELIEVE THEY WERE SPEAKING A LANGUAGE CLOSE TO MANDARIN... PERHAPS AN ANCIENT DIALECT?
Hrrrk...
Be a part of meeee!

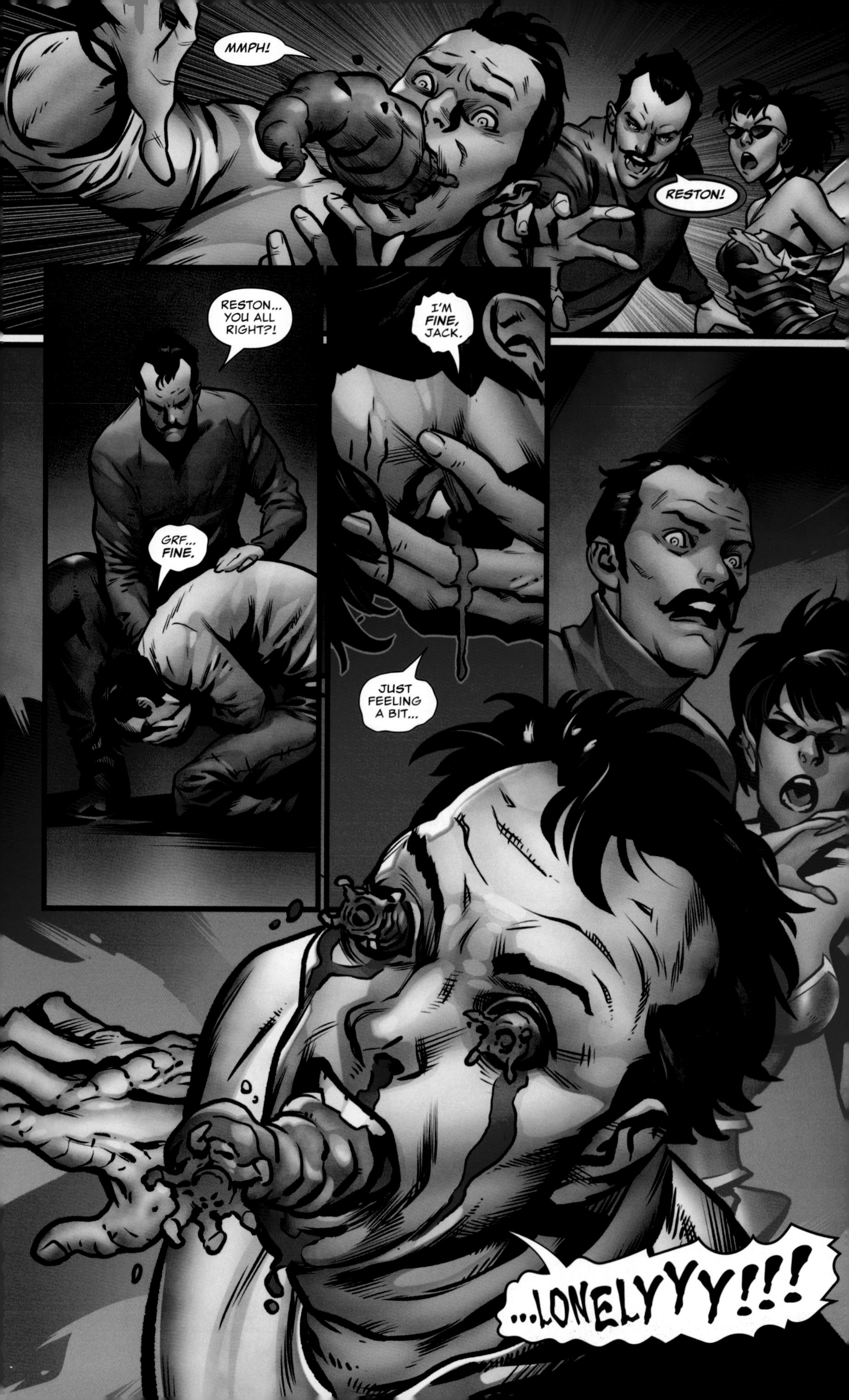
MMPH!
RESTON!
RESTON... YOU ALL RIGHT?!
GRF... FINE.
I'M FINE, JACK.
JUST FEELING A BIT...
...LONELYYY!!!

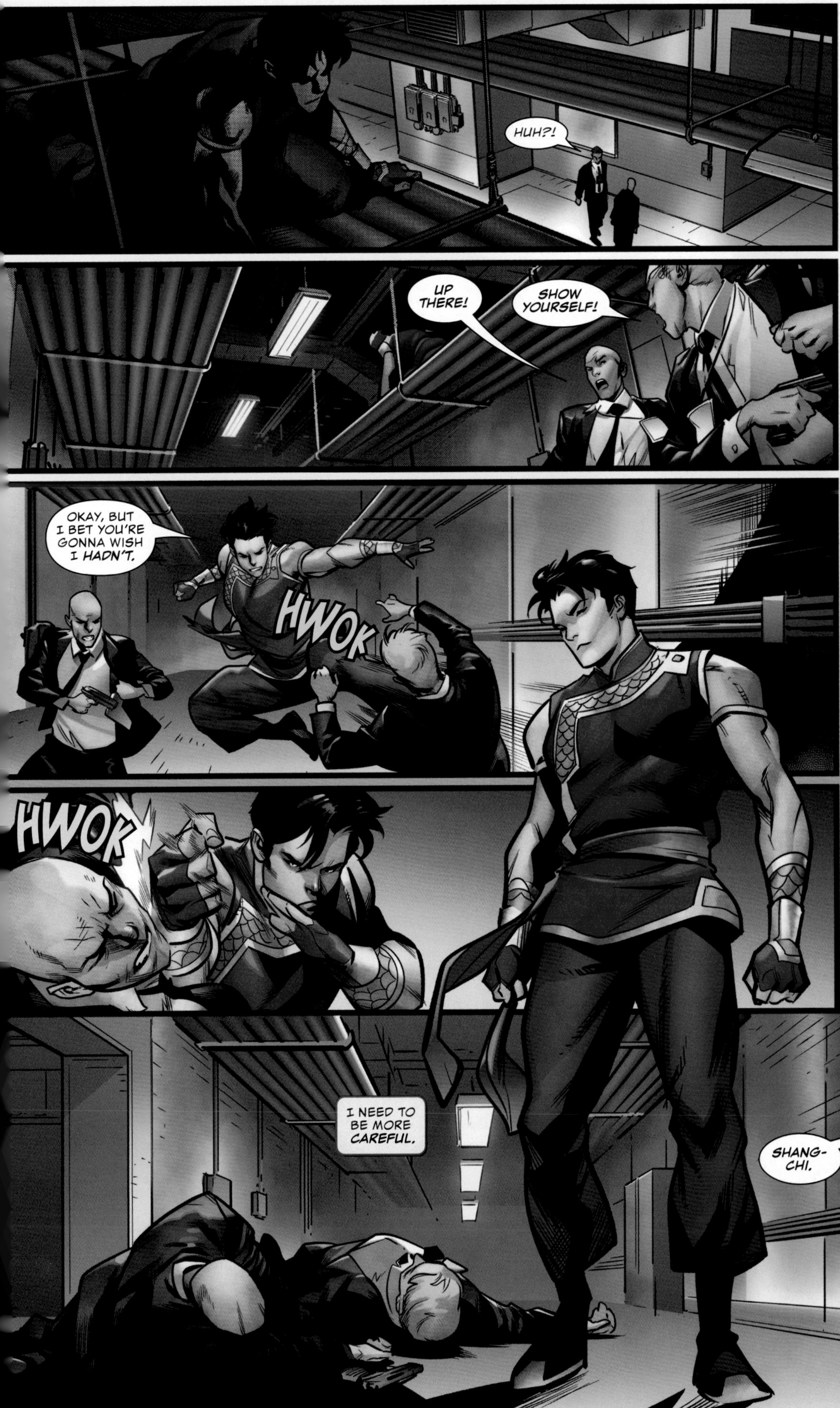
HUH?!
UP THERE!
SHOW YOURSELF!
OKAY, BUT I BET YOU'RE GONNA WISH I HADN'T.
HWOK
HWOK
I NEED TO BE MORE CAREFUL.
SHANG-CHI.

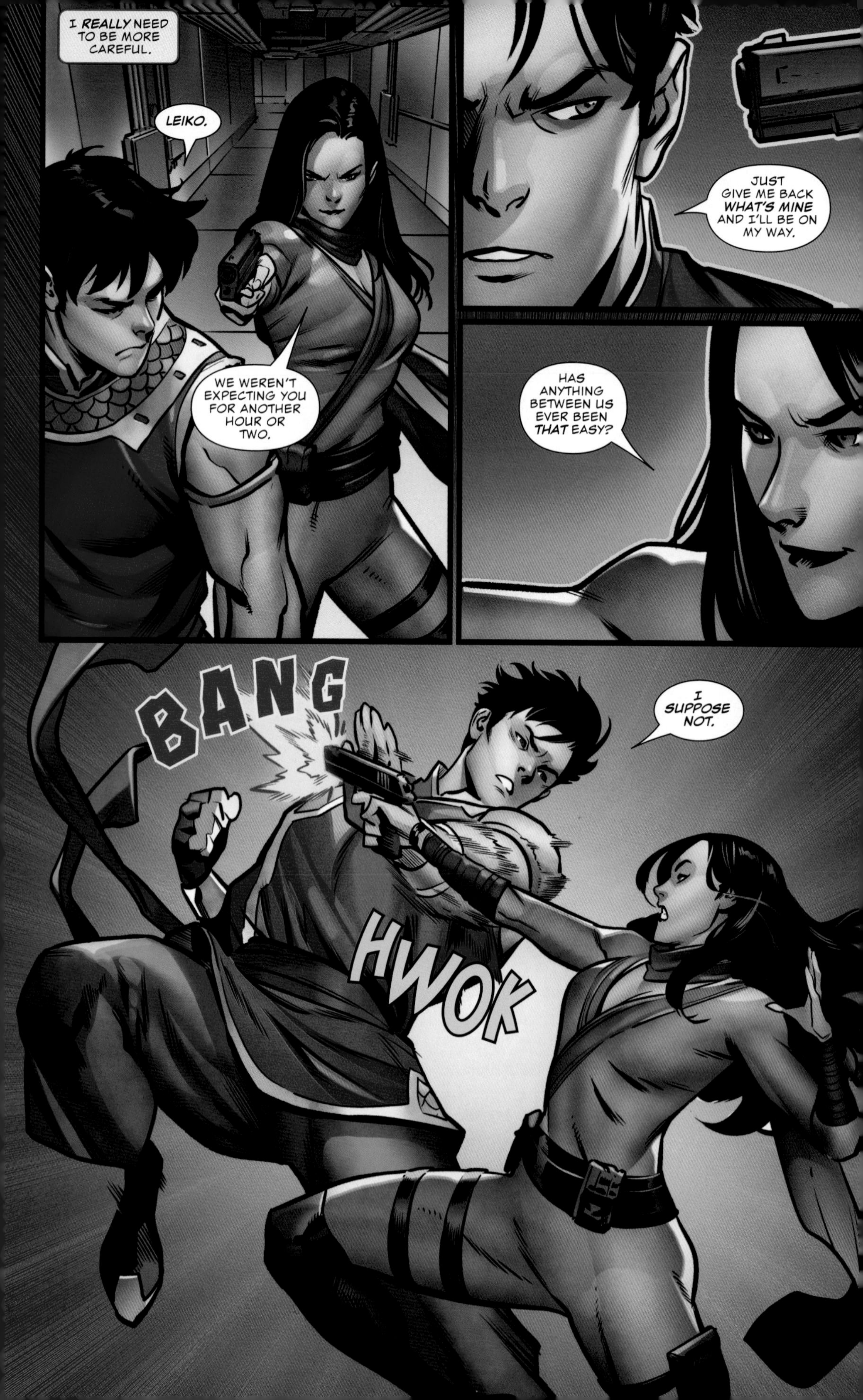
I REALLY NEED TO BE MORE CAREFUL.
LEIKO.
WE WEREN'T EXPECTING YOU FOR ANOTHER HOUR OR TWO.
JUST GIVE ME BACK WHAT'S MINE AND I'LL BE ON MY WAY.
HAS ANYTHING BETWEEN US EVER BEEN THAT EASY?
BANG
I SUPPOSE NOT.
HWOK

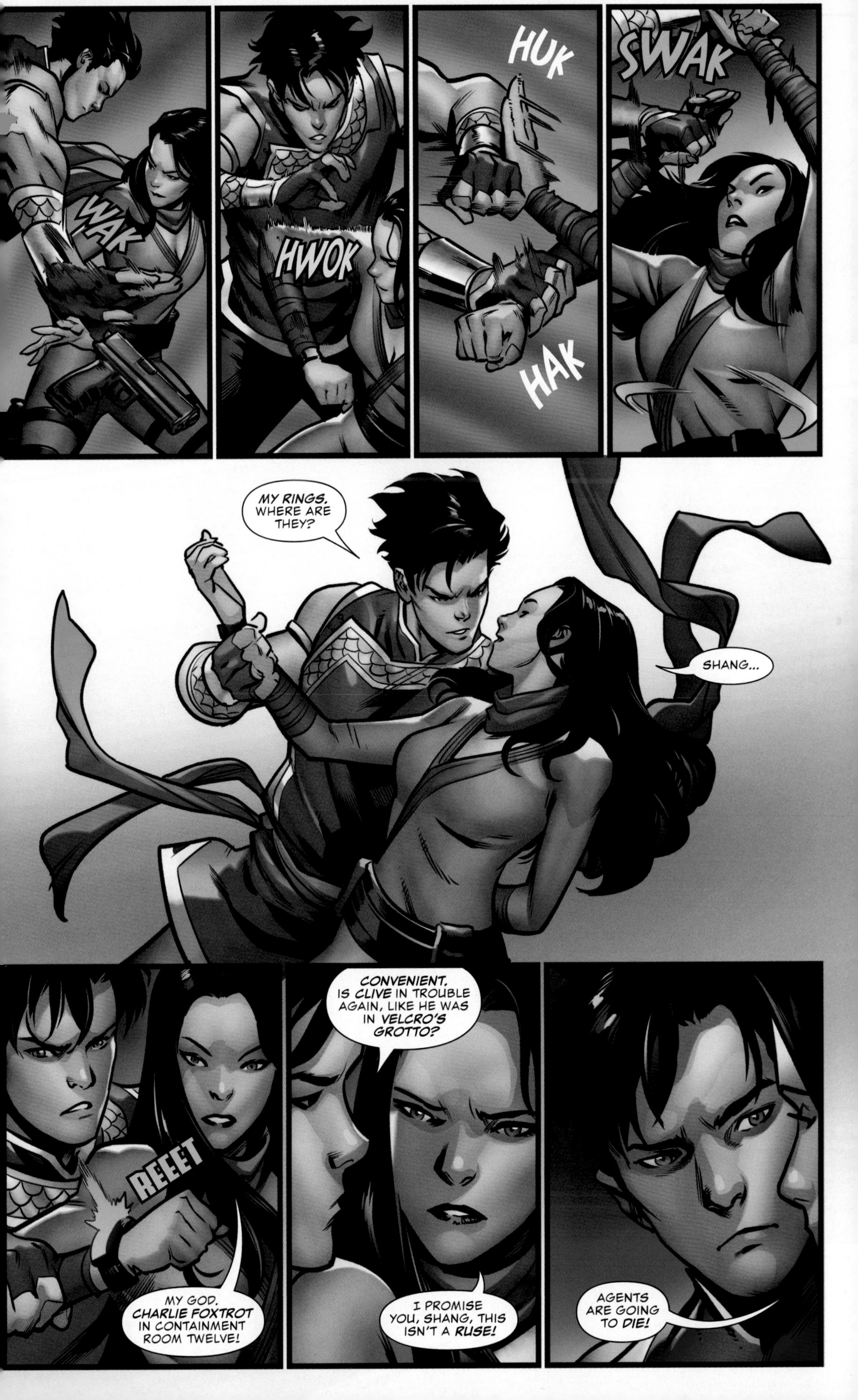
WAK
HWOK
HUK
HAK
SWAK
MY RINGS. WHERE ARE THEY?
SHANG...
REEET
MY GOD. CHARLIE FOXTROT IN CONTAINMENT ROOM TWELVE!
CONVENIENT. IS CLIVE IN TROUBLE AGAIN, LIKE HE WAS IN VELCRO'S GROTTO?
I PROMISE YOU, SHANG, THIS ISN'T A RUSE!
AGENTS ARE GOING TO DIE!

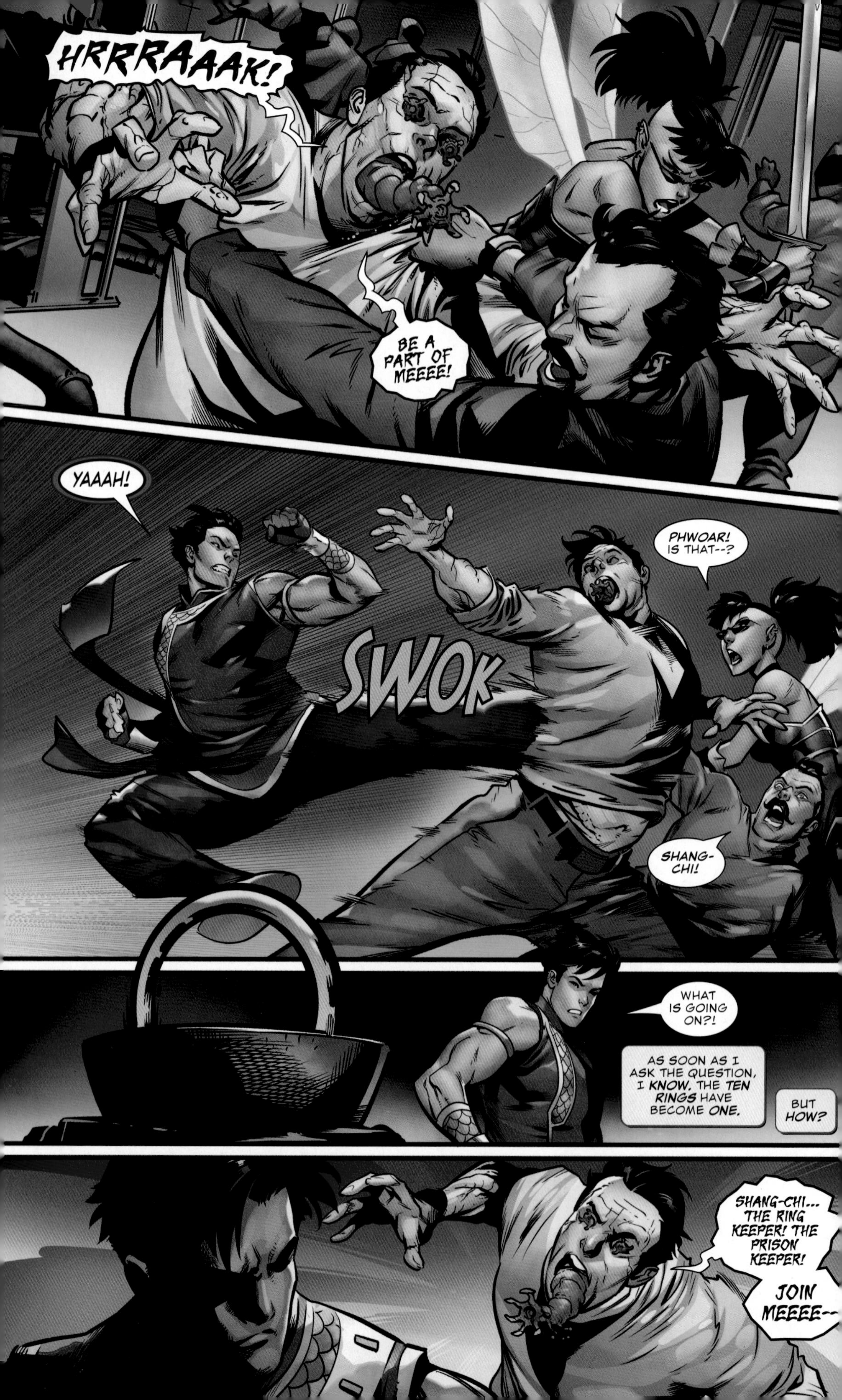
HRRRAAAK!
BE A PART OF MEEEE!
YAAAH!
PHWOAR! IS THAT--?
SWOK
SHANG-CHI!
WHAT IS GOING ON?!
AS SOON AS I ASK THE QUESTION, I KNOW. THE TEN RINGS HAVE BECOME ONE.
BUT HOW?
SHANG-CHI... THE RING KEEPER! THE PRISON KEEPER!
JOIN MEEEE--

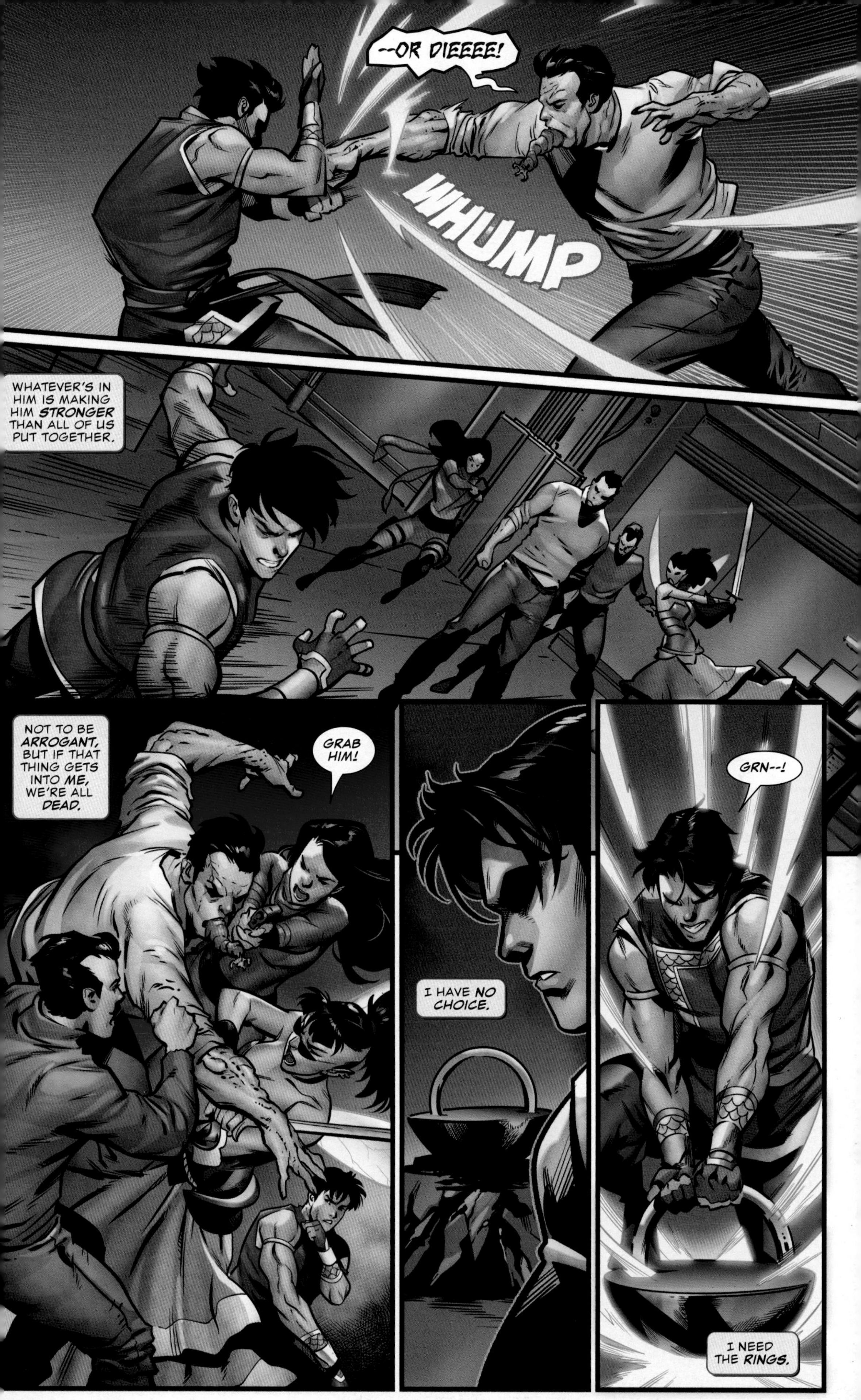
--OR DIEEEE!
WHUMP
WHATEVER'S IN HIM IS MAKING HIM STRONGER THAN ALL OF US PUT TOGETHER.
NOT TO BE ARROGANT, BUT IF THAT THING GETS INTO ME, WE'RE ALL DEAD.
GRAB HIM!
I HAVE NO CHOICE.
GRN--!
I NEED THE RINGS.

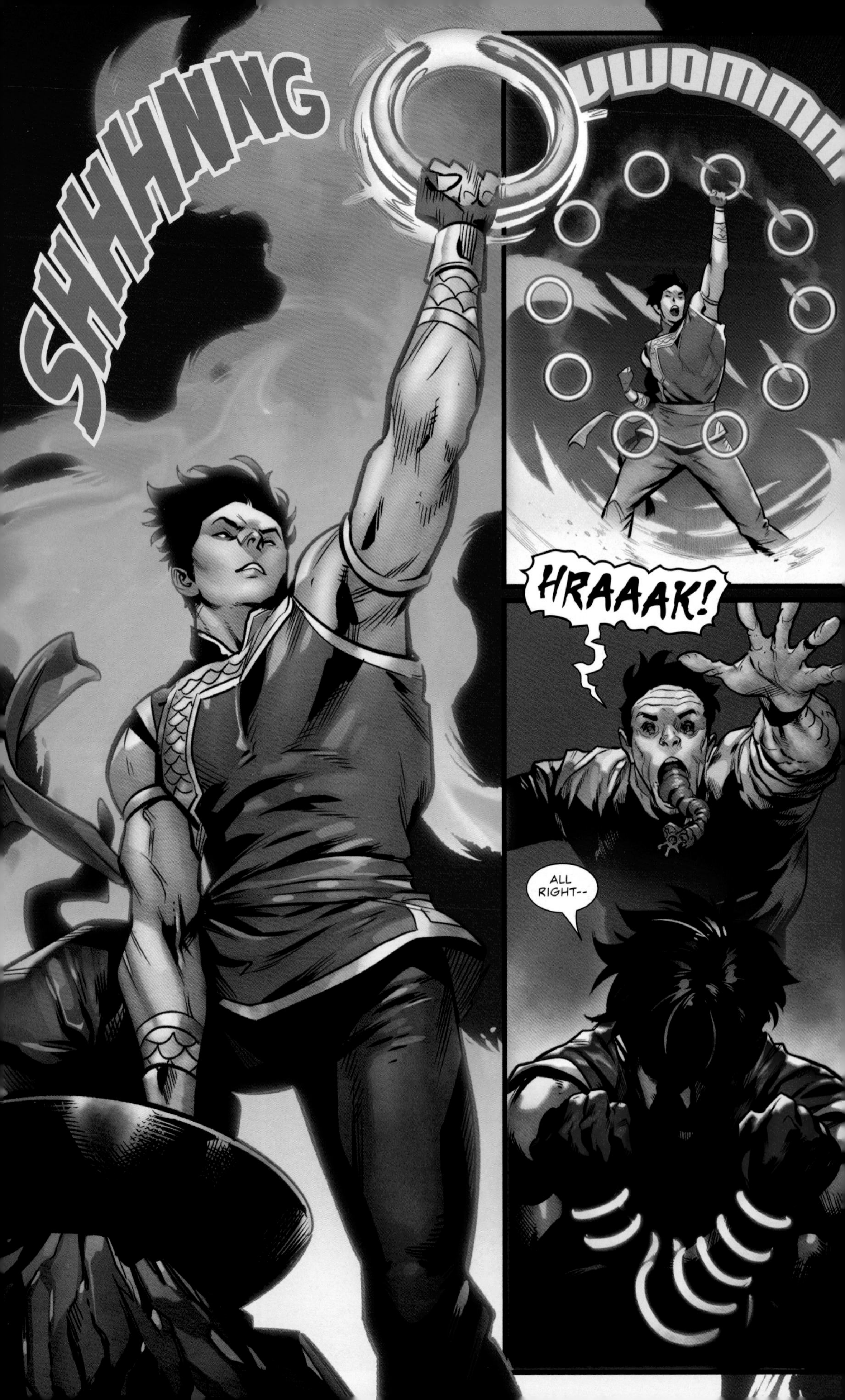
SHHHNNG
VWOMMMM
HRAAAK!
ALL RIGHT--

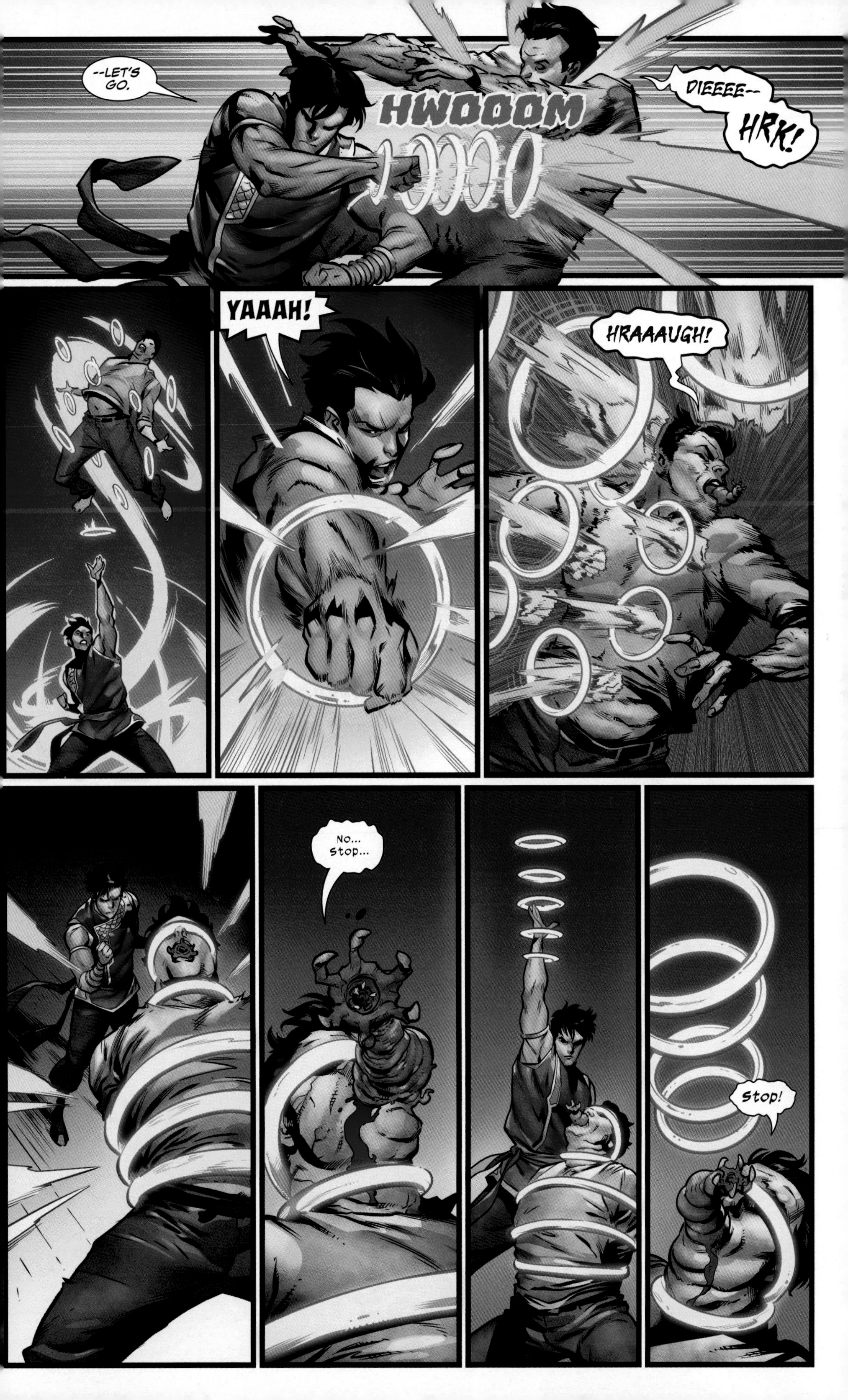
--LET'S GO.
HWOOOM
DIEEEE--
HRK!
YAAAH!
HRAAAUGH!
No... stop...
Stop!

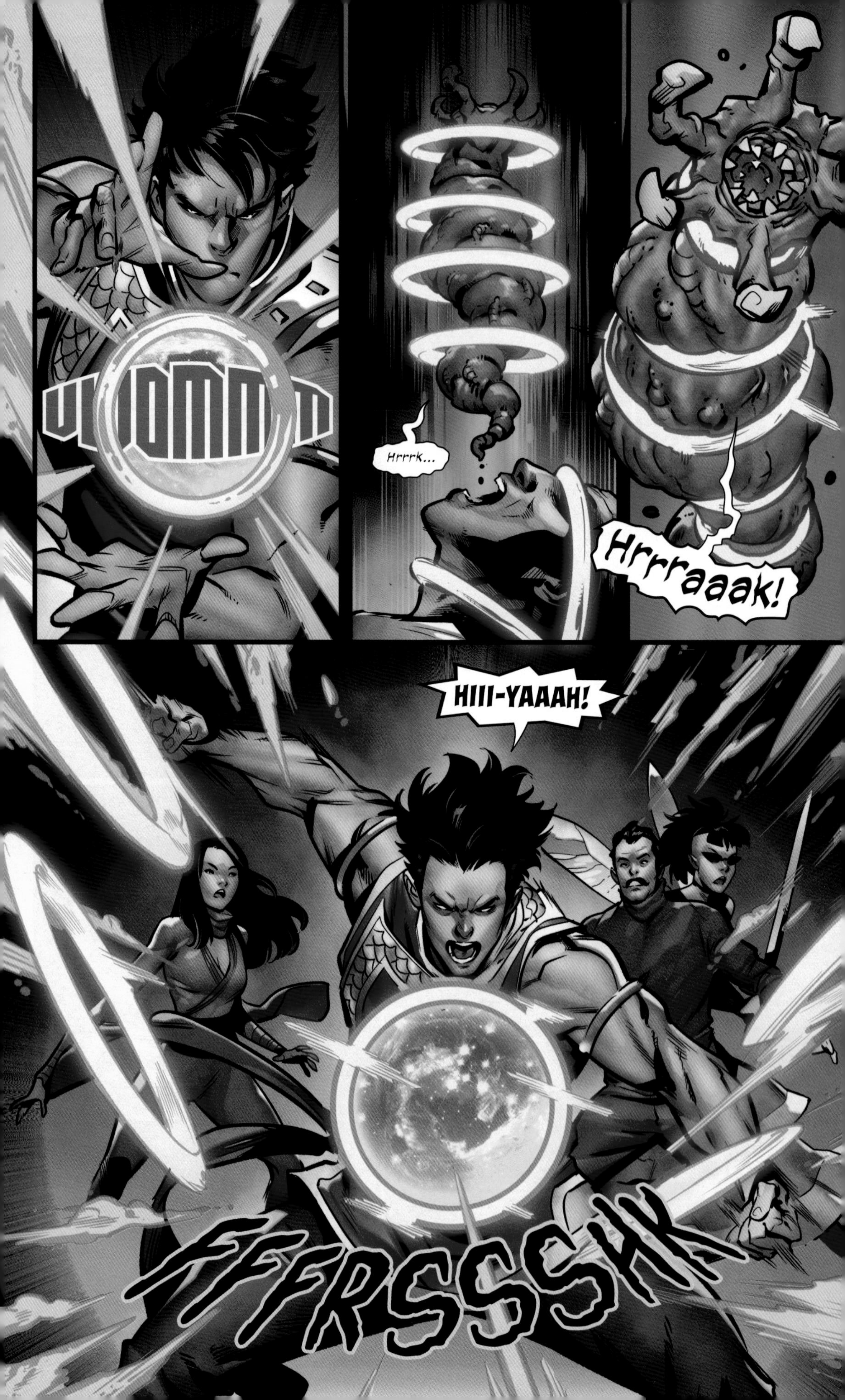
VVVOMMMM
Hrrrk...
Hrrraaak!
HIII-YAAAH!
FFFRSSSHK

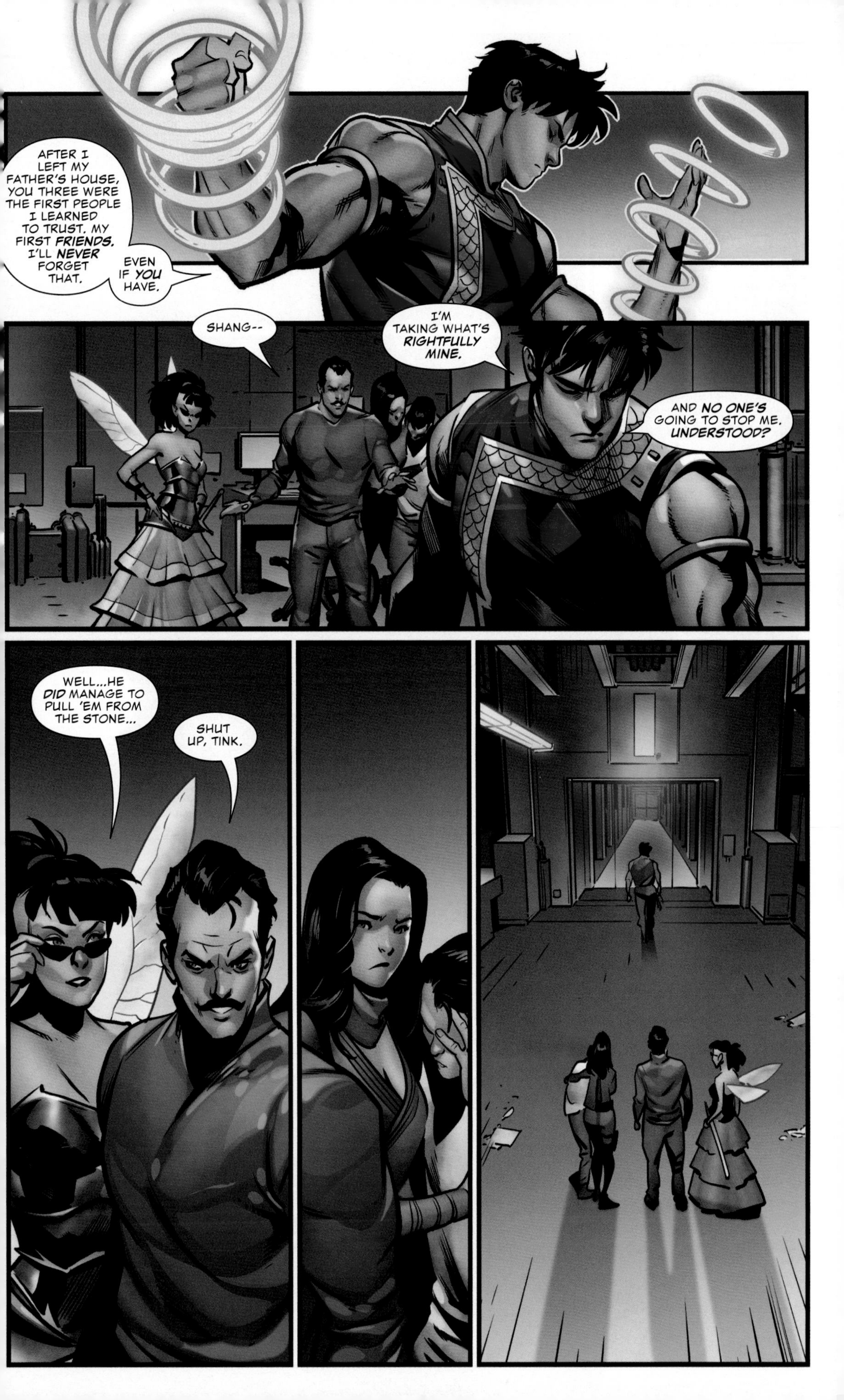
AFTER I LEFT MY FATHER'S HOUSE, YOU THREE WERE THE FIRST PEOPLE I LEARNED TO TRUST. MY FIRST FRIENDS. I'LL NEVER FORGET THAT.
EVEN IF YOU HAVE.
SHANG--
I'M TAKING WHAT'S RIGHTFULLY MINE.
AND NO ONE'S GOING TO STOP ME. UNDERSTOOD?
WELL...HE DID MANAGE TO PULL 'EM FROM THE STONE...
SHUT UP, TINK.

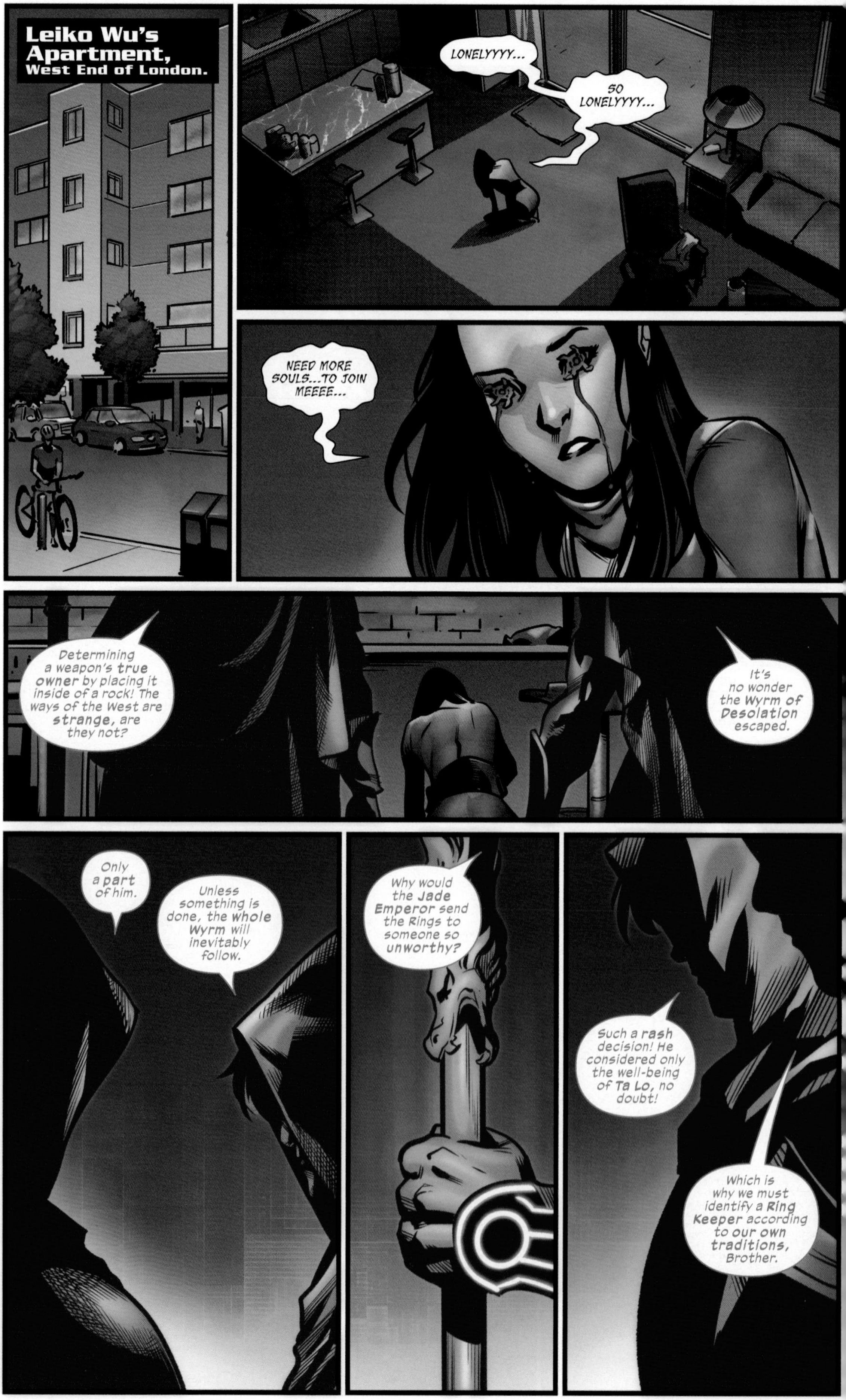

Leiko Wu's Apartment, West End of London.
LONELYYYY...
SO LONELYYYY...
NEED MORE SOULS...TO JOIN MEEEE...
Determining a weapon's true owner by placing it inside of a rock! The ways of the West are strange, are they not?
It's no wonder the Wyrm of Desolation escaped.
Only a part of him.
Unless something is done, the whole Wyrm will inevitably follow.
Why would the Jade Emperor send the Rings to someone so unworthy?
Such a rash decision! He considered only the well-being of Ta Lo, no doubt!
Which is why we must identify a Ring Keeper according to our own traditions, Brother.

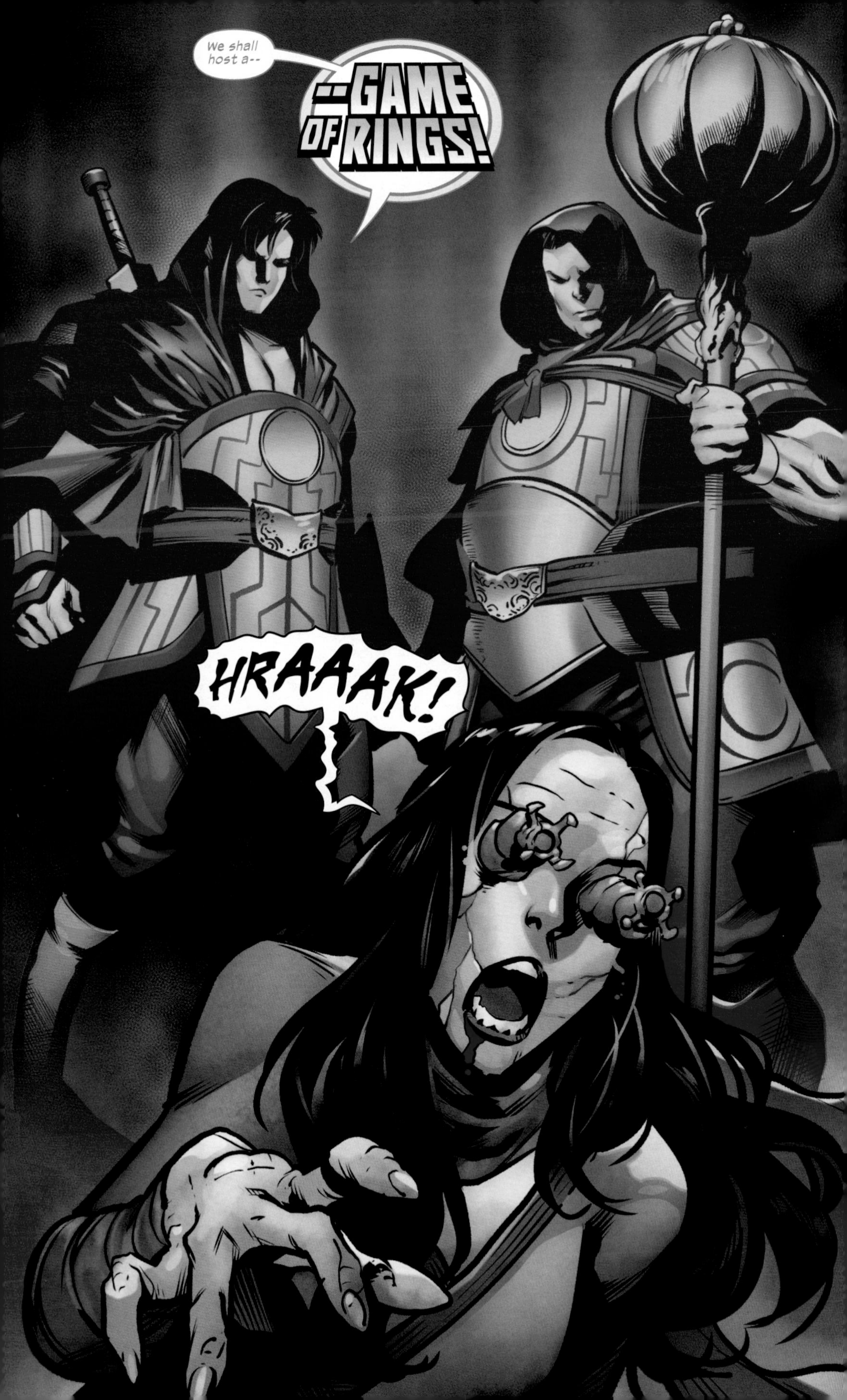
We shall host a--
--GAME OF RINGS!
HRAAAK!

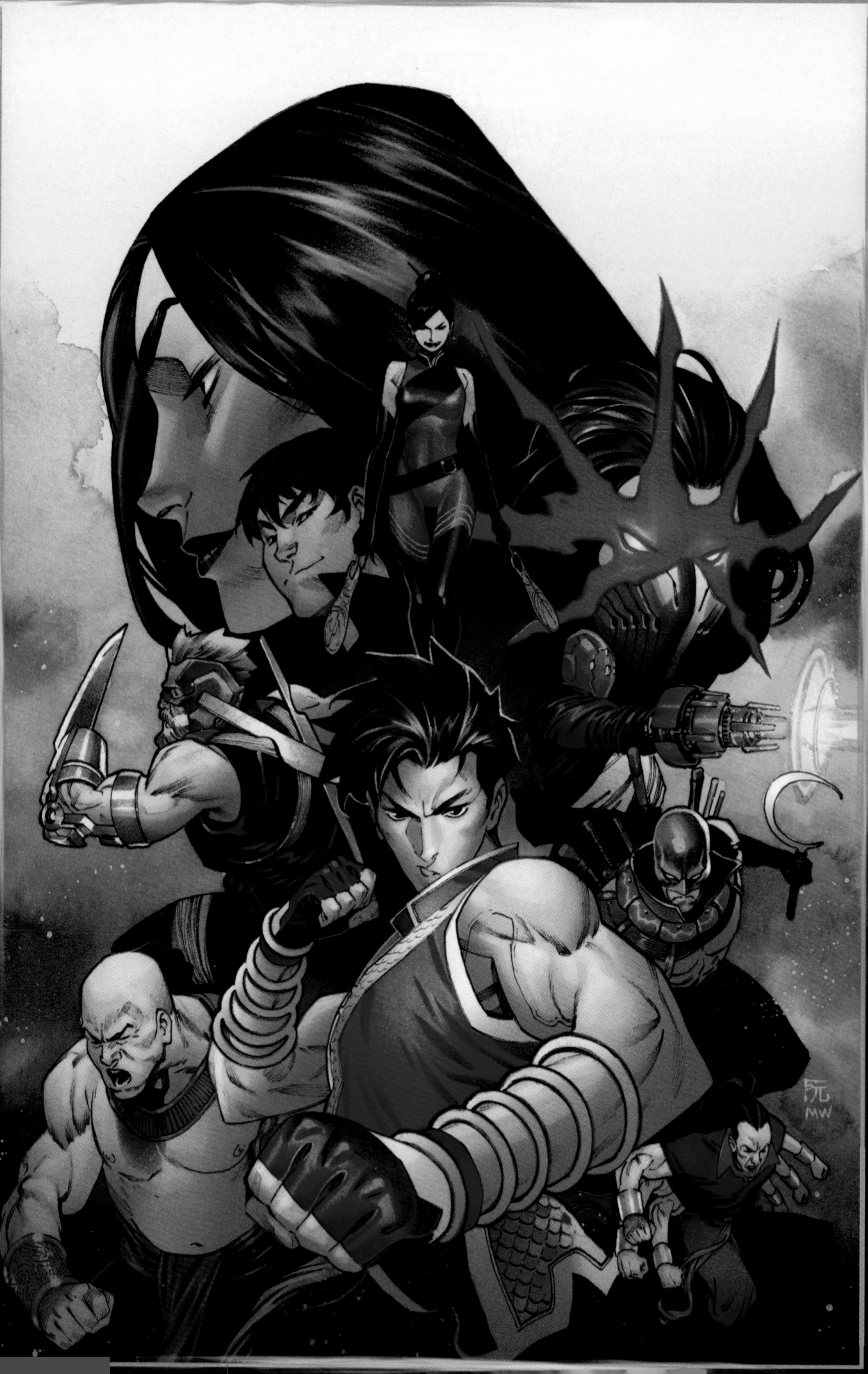

UR

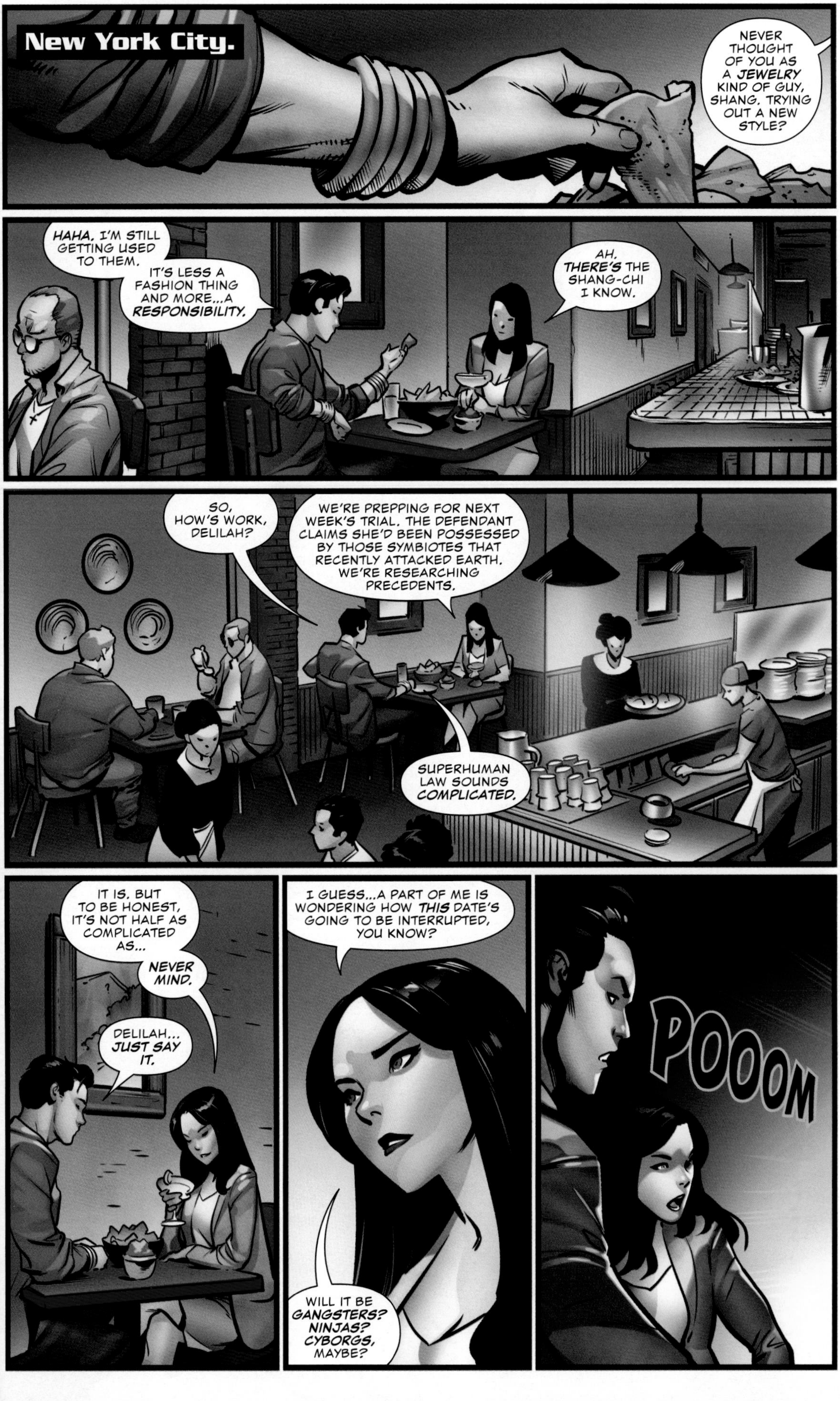
New York City.
NEVER THOUGHT OF YOU AS A JEWELRY KIND OF GUY, SHANG. TRYING OUT A NEW STYLE?
HAHA. I'M STILL GETTING USED TO THEM.
IT'S LESS A FASHION THING AND MORE...A RESPONSIBILITY.
AH. THERE'S THE SHANG-CHI I KNOW.
SO, HOW'S WORK, DELILAH?
WE'RE PREPPING FOR NEXT WEEK'S TRIAL. THE DEFENDANT CLAIMS SHE'D BEEN POSSESSED BY THOSE SYMBIOTES THAT RECENTLY ATTACKED EARTH. WE'RE RESEARCHING PRECEDENTS.
SUPERHUMAN LAW SOUNDS COMPLICATED.
IT IS. BUT TO BE HONEST, IT'S NOT HALF AS COMPLICATED AS...
NEVER MIND.
DELILAH... JUST SAY IT.
I GUESS...A PART OF ME IS WONDERING HOW THIS DATE'S GOING TO BE INTERRUPTED, YOU KNOW?
WILL IT BE GANGSTERS? NINJAS? CYBORGS, MAYBE?
POOOM

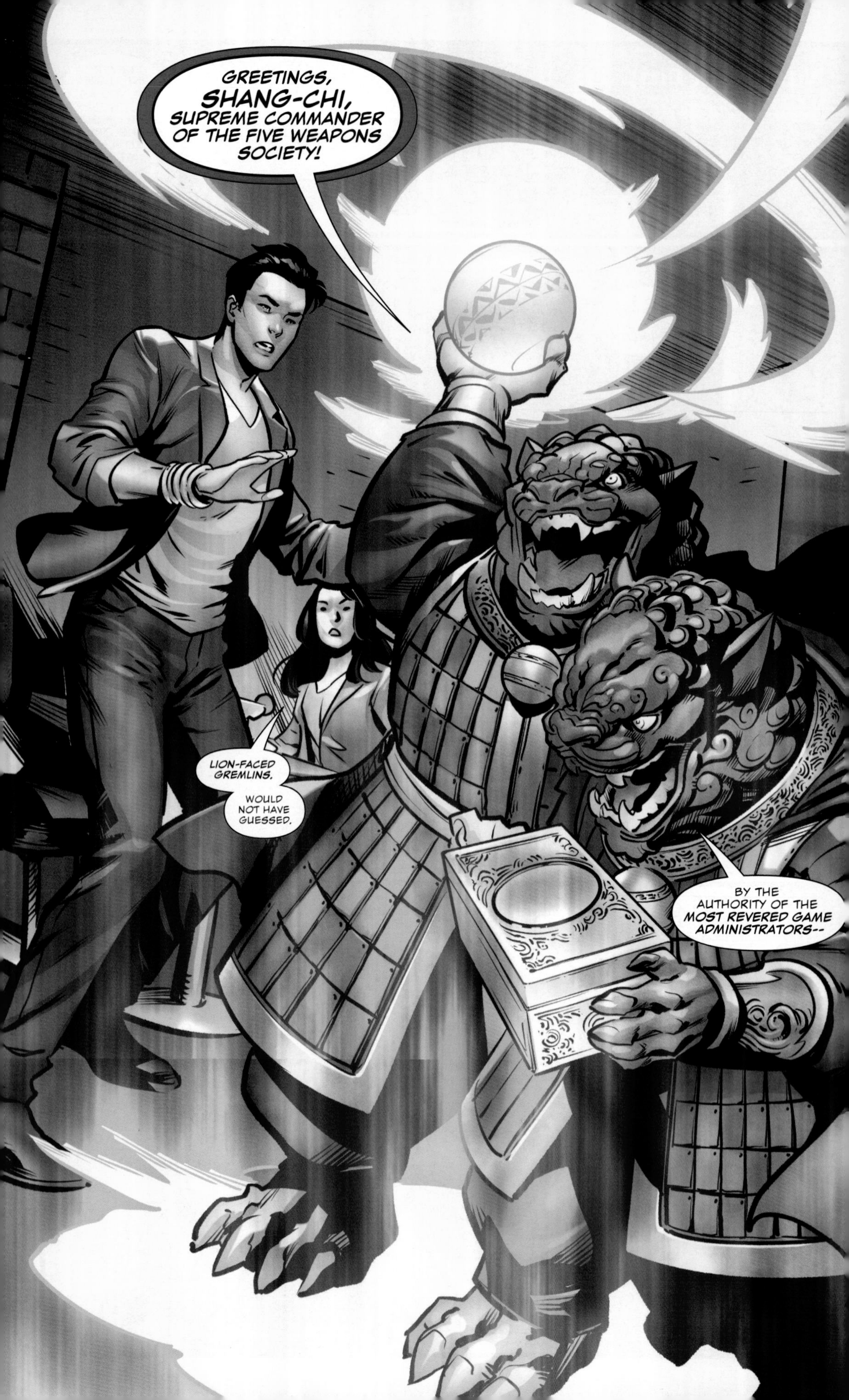
GREETINGS, SHANG-CHI, SUPREME COMMANDER OF THE FIVE WEAPONS SOCIETY!
LION-FACED GREMLINS.
WOULD NOT HAVE GUESSED.
BY THE AUTHORITY OF THE MOST REVERED GAME ADMINISTRATORS--

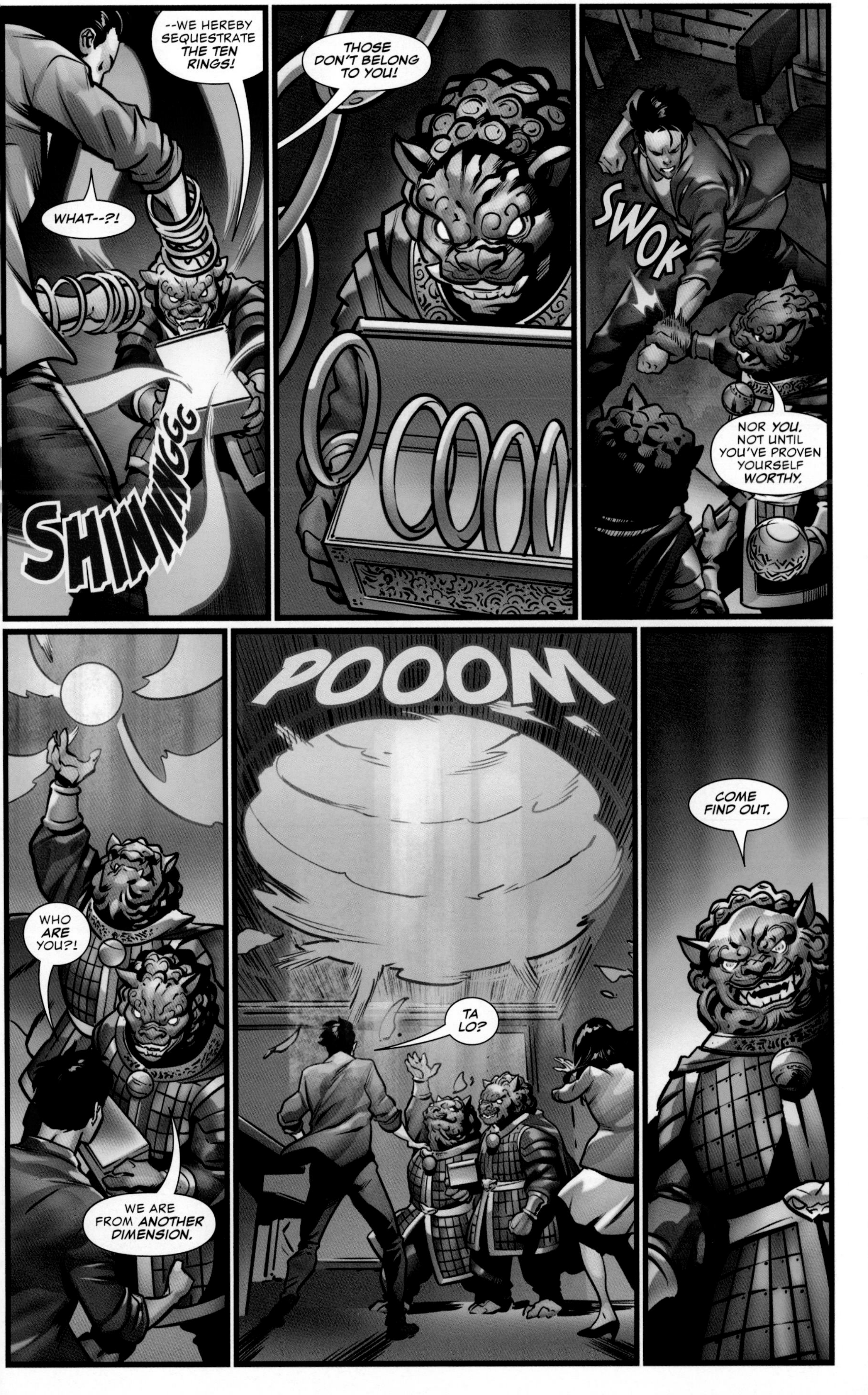

--WE HEREBY SEQUESTRATE THE TEN RINGS!
WHAT--?!
SHINNNGGG
THOSE DON'T BELONG TO YOU!
SWOK
NOR YOU. NOT UNTIL YOU'VE PROVEN YOURSELF WORTHY.
WHO ARE YOU?!
WE ARE FROM ANOTHER DIMENSION.
POOOM
TA LO?
COME FIND OUT.

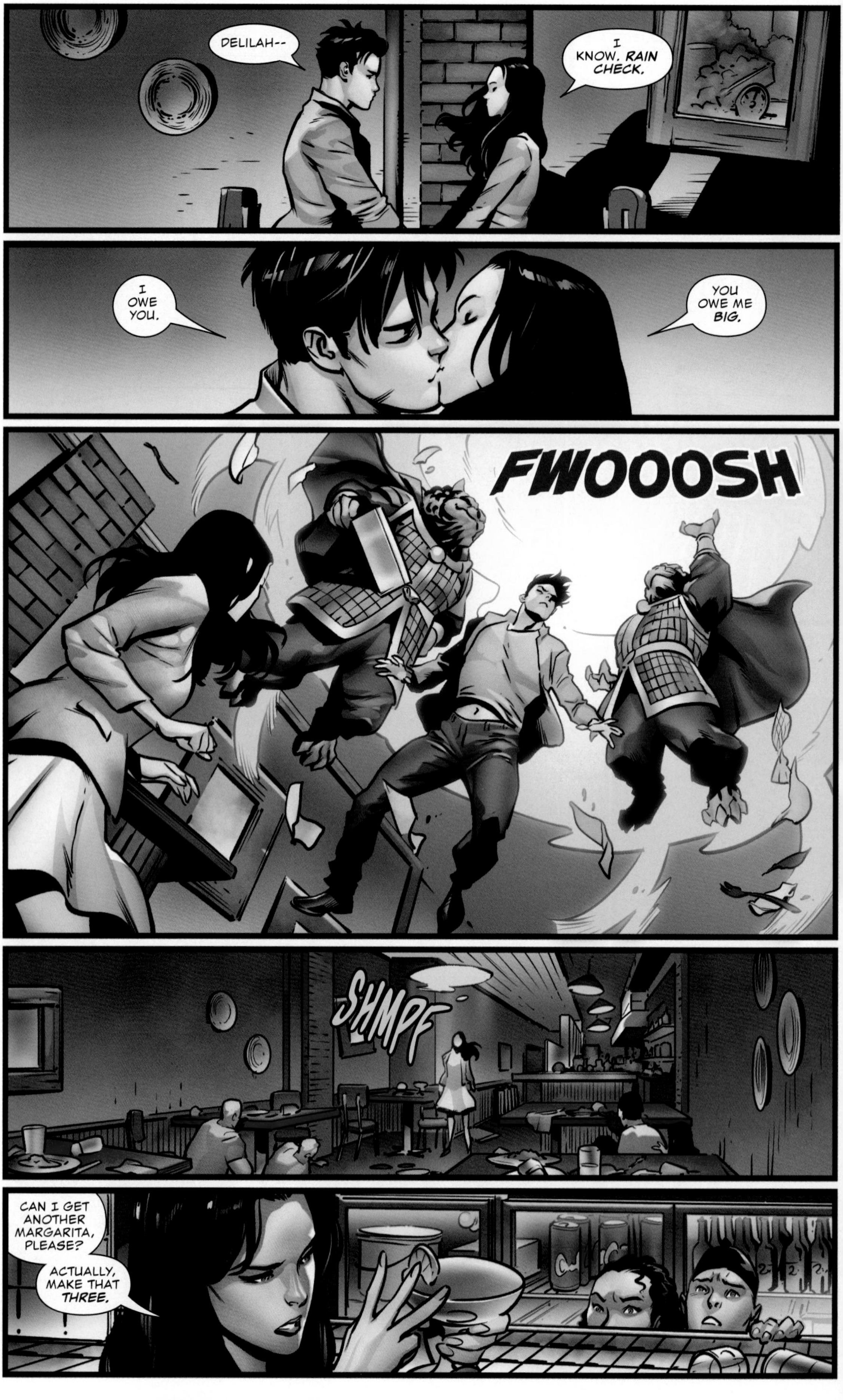
DELILAH--
I KNOW. RAIN CHECK.
I OWE YOU.
YOU OWE ME BIG.
FWOOOSH
SHMPF
CAN I GET ANOTHER MARGARITA, PLEASE?
ACTUALLY, MAKE THAT THREE.

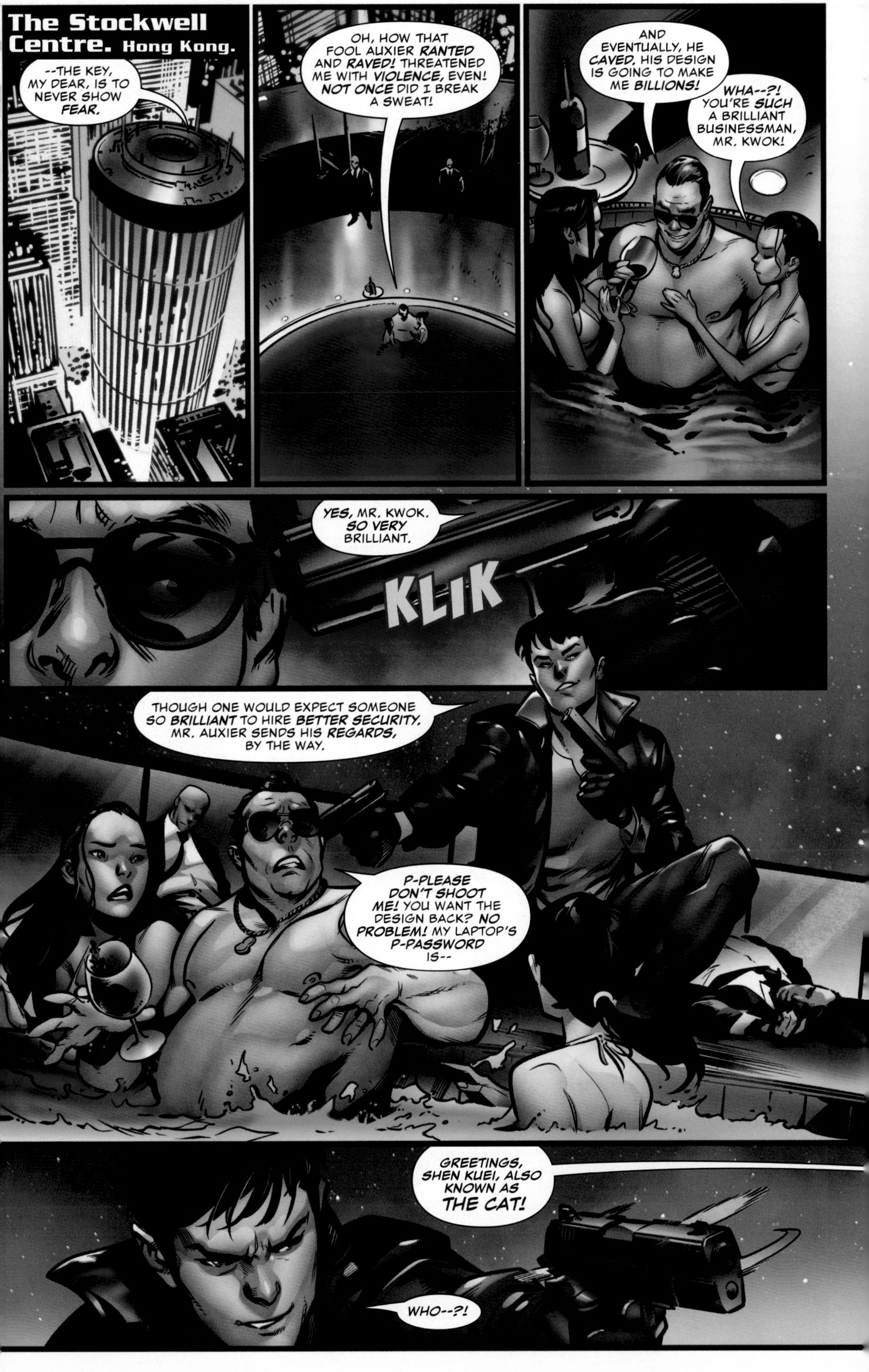
The Stockwell Centre. Hong Kong.
--THE KEY, MY DEAR, IS TO NEVER SHOW FEAR.
OH, HOW THAT FOOL AUXIER RANTED AND RAVED! THREATENED ME WITH VIOLENCE, EVEN! NOT ONCE DID I BREAK A SWEAT!
AND EVENTUALLY, HE CAVED. HIS DESIGN IS GOING TO MAKE ME BILLIONS!
WHA--?! YOU'RE SUCH A BRILLIANT BUSINESSMAN, MR. KWOK!
YES, MR. KWOK. SO VERY BRILLIANT.
KLIK
THOUGH ONE WOULD EXPECT SOMEONE SO BRILLIANT TO HIRE BETTER SECURITY. MR. AUXIER SENDS HIS REGARDS, BY THE WAY.
P-PLEASE DON'T SHOOT ME! YOU WANT THE DESIGN BACK? NO PROBLEM! MY LAPTOP'S P-PASSWORD IS--
GREETINGS, SHEN KUEI, ALSO KNOWN AS THE CAT!
WHO--?!

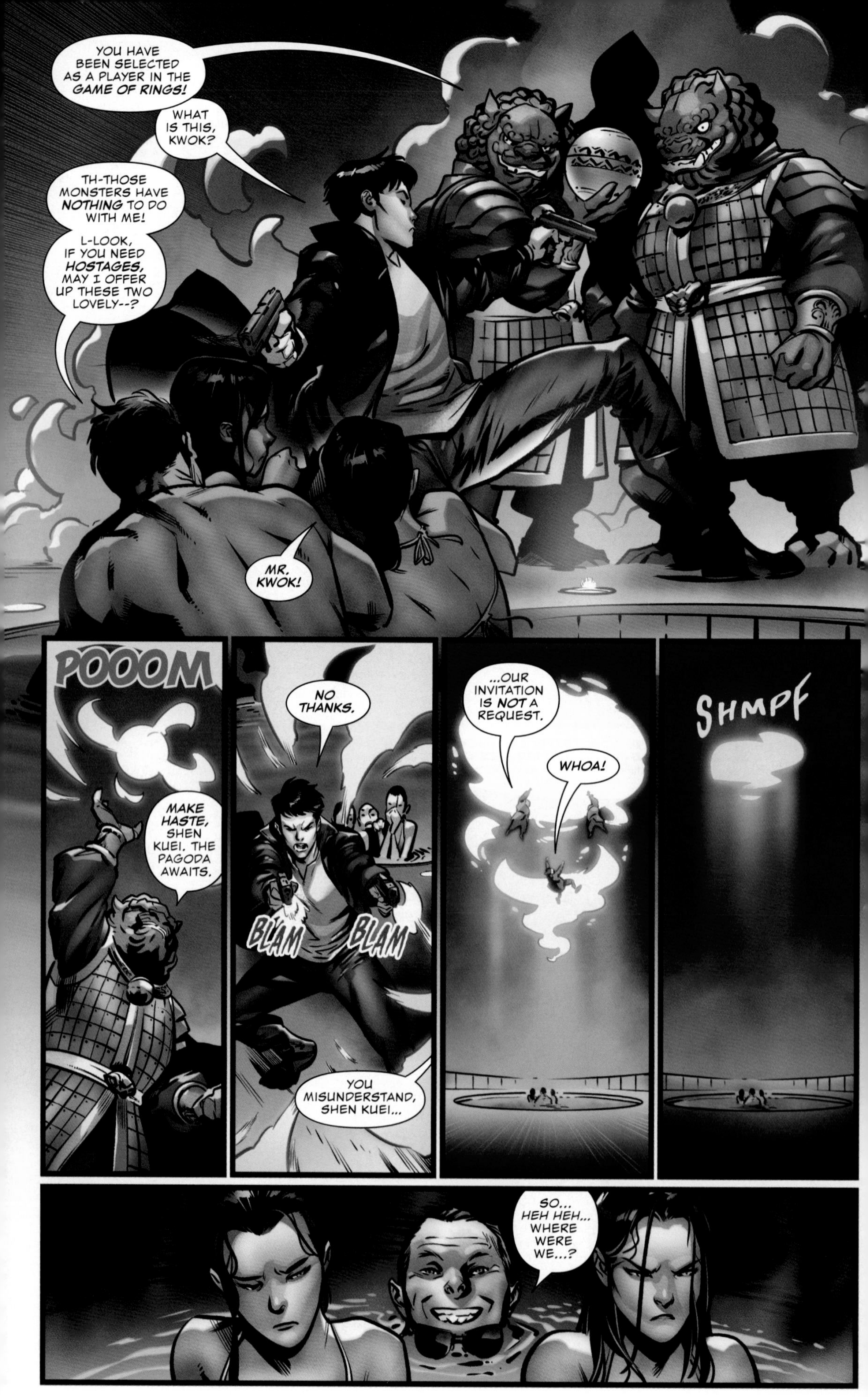

YOU HAVE BEEN SELECTED AS A PLAYER IN THE GAME OF RINGS!
WHAT IS THIS, KWOK?
TH-THOSE MONSTERS HAVE NOTHING TO DO WITH ME!
L-LOOK, IF YOU NEED HOSTAGES, MAY I OFFER UP THESE TWO LOVELY--?
MR. KWOK!
POOOM
MAKE HASTE, SHEN KUEI. THE PAGODA AWAITS.
NO THANKS.
BLAM
BLAM
YOU MISUNDERSTAND, SHEN KUEI...
...OUR INVITATION IS NOT A REQUEST.
WHOA!
SHMPF
SO... HEH HEH... WHERE WERE WE...?

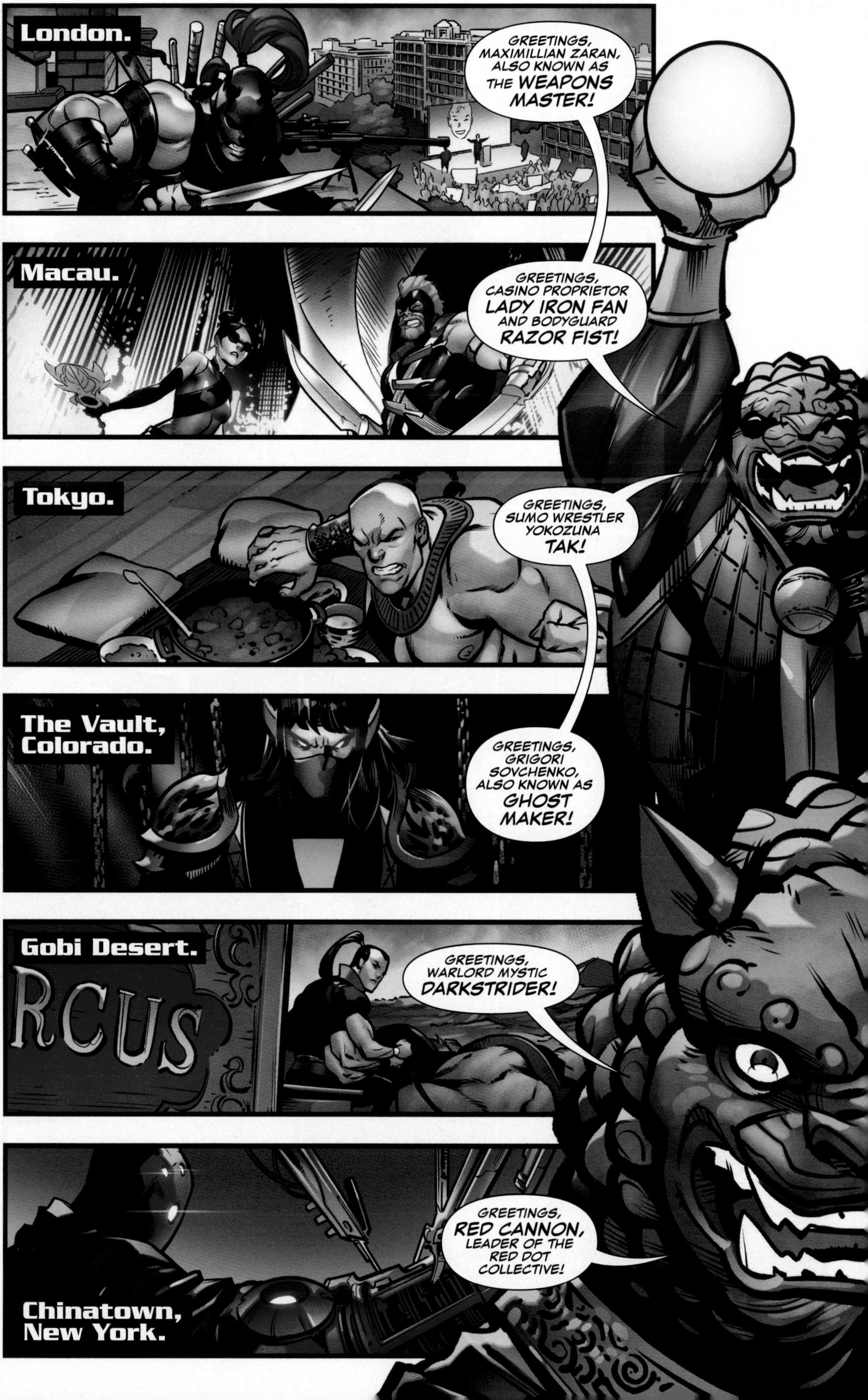
London.
GREETINGS, MAXIMILLIAN ZARAN, ALSO KNOWN AS THE WEAPONS MASTER!
Macau.
GREETINGS, CASINO PROPRIETOR LADY IRON FAN AND BODYGUARD RAZOR FIST!
Tokyo.
GREETINGS, SUMO WRESTLER YOKOZUNA TAK!
The Vault, Colorado.
GREETINGS, GRIGORI SOVCHENKO, ALSO KNOWN AS GHOST MAKER!
Gobi Desert.
RCUS
GREETINGS, WARLORD MYSTIC DARKSTRIDER!
GREETINGS, RED CANNON, LEADER OF THE RED DOT COLLECTIVE!
Chinatown, New York.

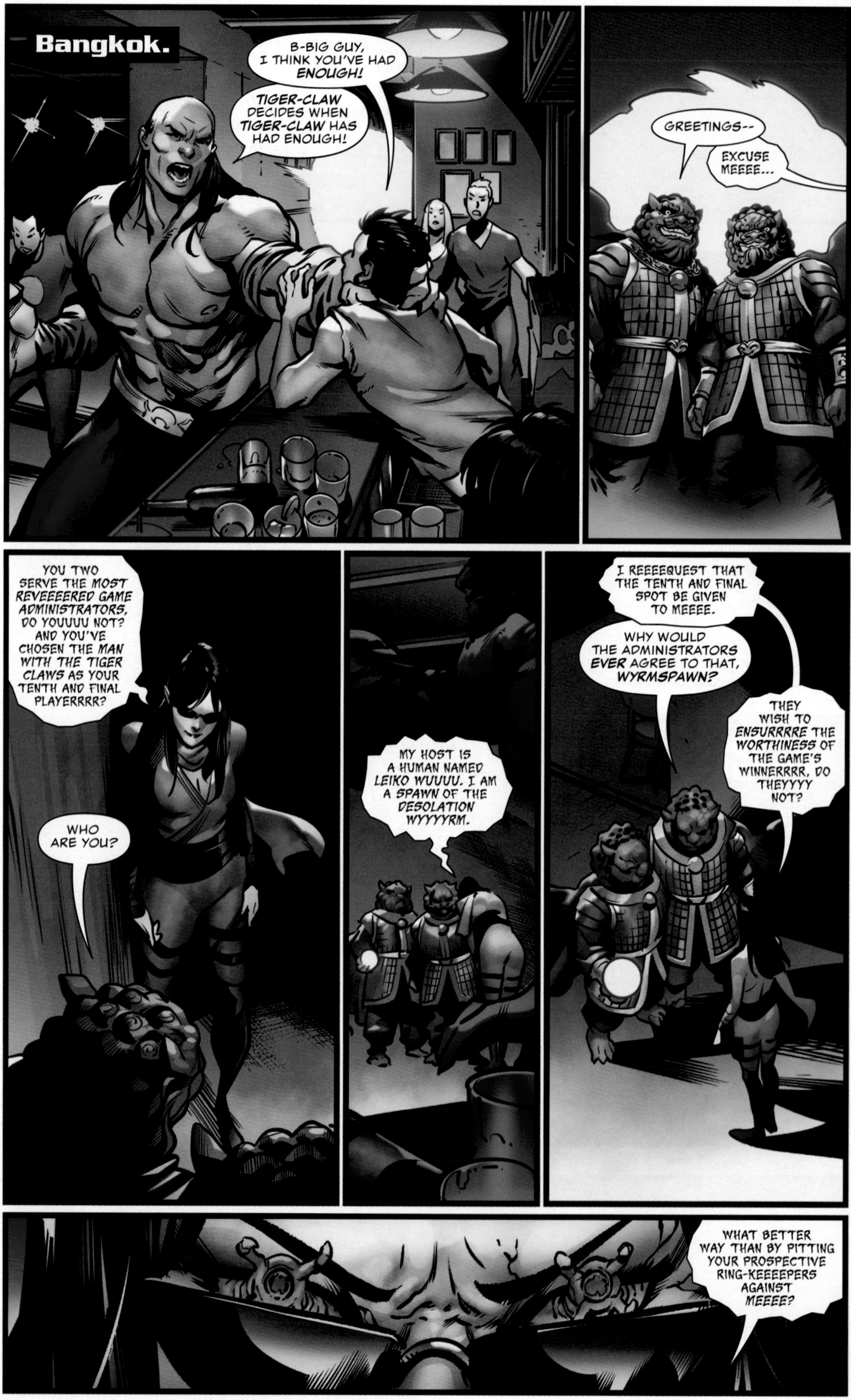
Bangkok.
B-BIG GUY, I THINK YOU'VE HAD ENOUGH!
TIGER-CLAW DECIDES WHEN TIGER-CLAW HAS HAD ENOUGH!
GREETINGS--
EXCUSE MEEEE...
YOU TWO SERVE THE MOST REVEEEERED GAME ADMINISTRATORS, DO YOUUUU NOT? AND YOU'VE CHOSEN THE MAN WITH THE TIGER CLAWS AS YOUR TENTH AND FINAL PLAYERRRR?
WHO ARE YOU?
MY HOST IS A HUMAN NAMED LEIKO WUUUU. I AM A SPAWN OF THE DESOLATION WYYYYRM.
I REEEEQUEST THAT THE TENTH AND FINAL SPOT BE GIVEN TO MEEEE.
WHY WOULD THE ADMINISTRATORS EVER AGREE TO THAT, WYRMSPAWN?
THEY WISH TO ENSURRRRE THE WORTHINESS OF THE GAME'S WINNERRRR, DO THEYYYY NOT?
WHAT BETTER WAY THAN BY PITTING YOUR PROSPECTIVE RING-KEEEEPERS AGAINST MEEEE?

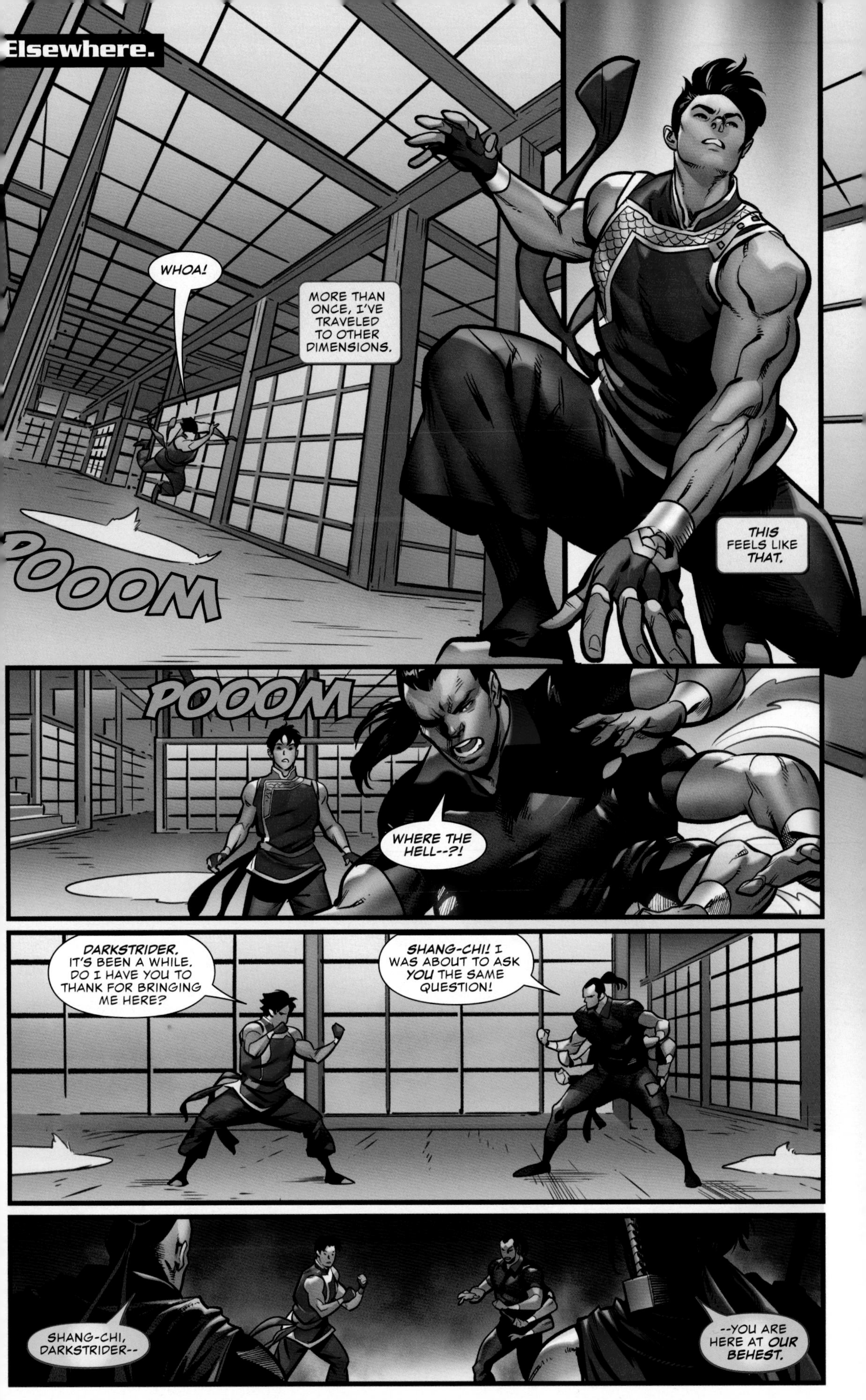
Elsewhere.
WHOA!
MORE THAN ONCE, I'VE TRAVELED TO OTHER DIMENSIONS.
POOOM
THIS FEELS LIKE THAT.
POOOM
WHERE THE HELL--?!
DARKSTRIDER. IT'S BEEN A WHILE. DO I HAVE YOU TO THANK FOR BRINGING ME HERE?
SHANG-CHI! I WAS ABOUT TO ASK YOU THE SAME QUESTION!
SHANG-CHI, DARKSTRIDER--
--YOU ARE HERE AT OUR BEHEST.

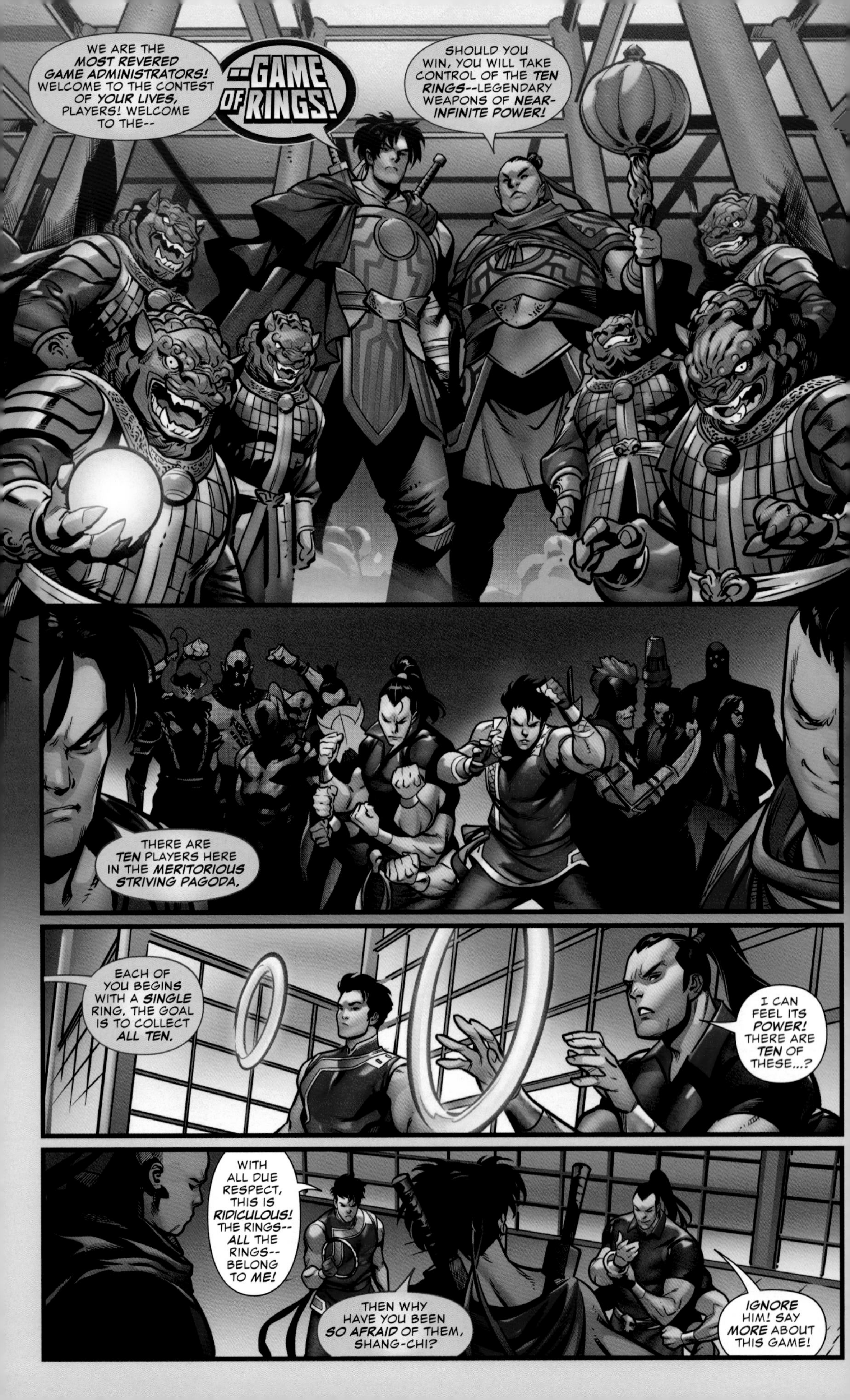
WE ARE THE MOST REVERED GAME ADMINISTRATORS! WELCOME TO THE CONTEST OF YOUR LIVES, PLAYERS! WELCOME TO THE--
--GAME OF RINGS!
SHOULD YOU WIN, YOU WILL TAKE CONTROL OF THE TEN RINGS--LEGENDARY WEAPONS OF NEAR-INFINITE POWER!
THERE ARE TEN PLAYERS HERE IN THE MERITORIOUS STRIVING PAGODA.
EACH OF YOU BEGINS WITH A SINGLE RING. THE GOAL IS TO COLLECT ALL TEN.
I CAN FEEL ITS POWER! THERE ARE TEN OF THESE...?
WITH ALL DUE RESPECT, THIS IS RIDICULOUS! THE RINGS--ALL THE RINGS--BELONG TO ME!
THEN WHY HAVE YOU BEEN SO AFRAID OF THEM, SHANG-CHI?
IGNORE HIM! SAY MORE ABOUT THIS GAME!

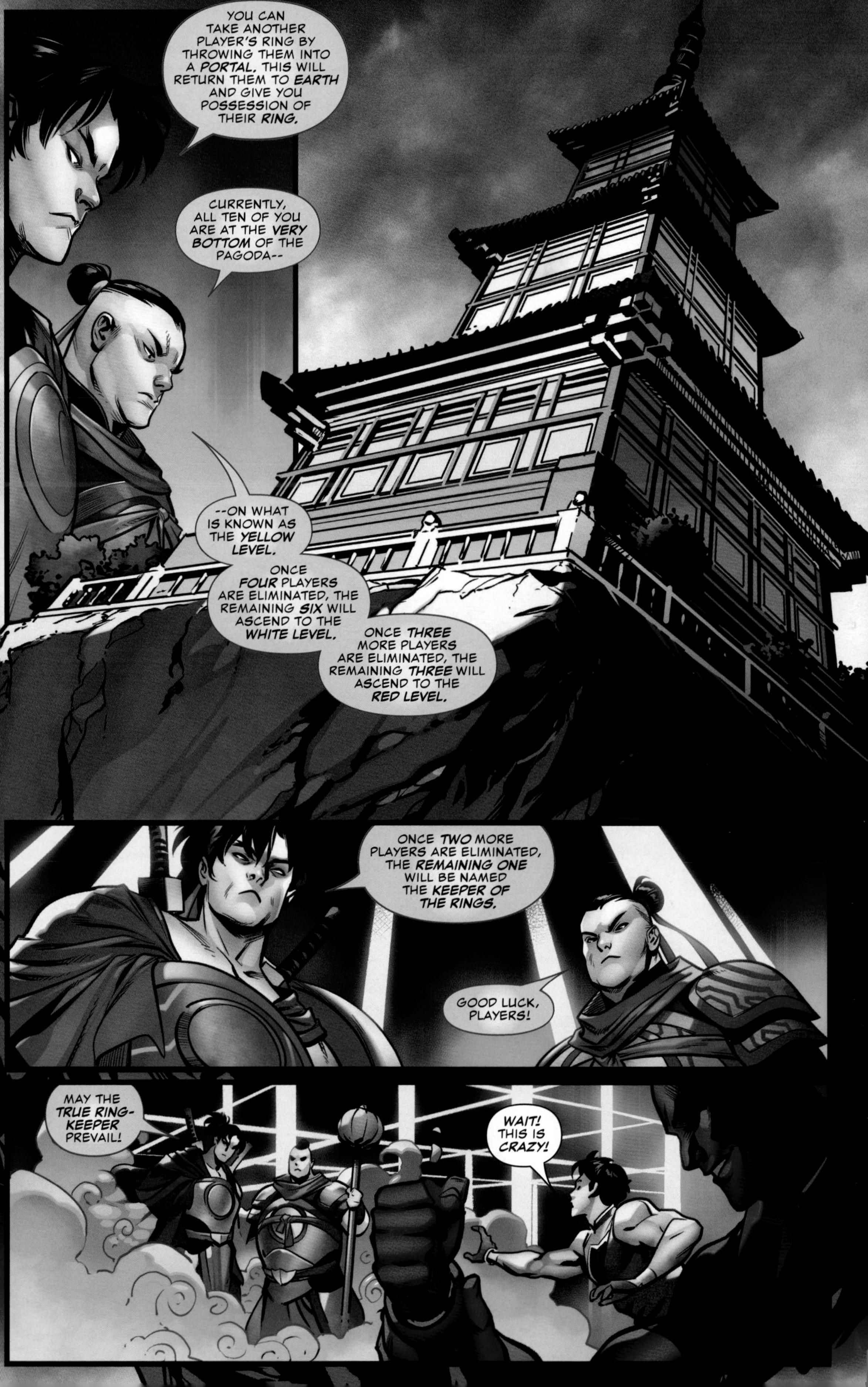
YOU CAN TAKE ANOTHER PLAYER'S RING BY THROWING THEM INTO A PORTAL. THIS WILL RETURN THEM TO EARTH AND GIVE YOU POSSESSION OF THEIR RING.
CURRENTLY, ALL TEN OF YOU ARE AT THE VERY BOTTOM OF THE PAGODA--
--ON WHAT IS KNOWN AS THE YELLOW LEVEL.
ONCE FOUR PLAYERS ARE ELIMINATED, THE REMAINING SIX WILL ASCEND TO THE WHITE LEVEL.
ONCE THREE MORE PLAYERS ARE ELIMINATED, THE REMAINING THREE WILL ASCEND TO THE RED LEVEL.
ONCE TWO MORE PLAYERS ARE ELIMINATED, THE REMAINING ONE WILL BE NAMED THE KEEPER OF THE RINGS.
GOOD LUCK, PLAYERS!
MAY THE TRUE RING-KEEPER PREVAIL!
WAIT! THIS IS CRAZY!

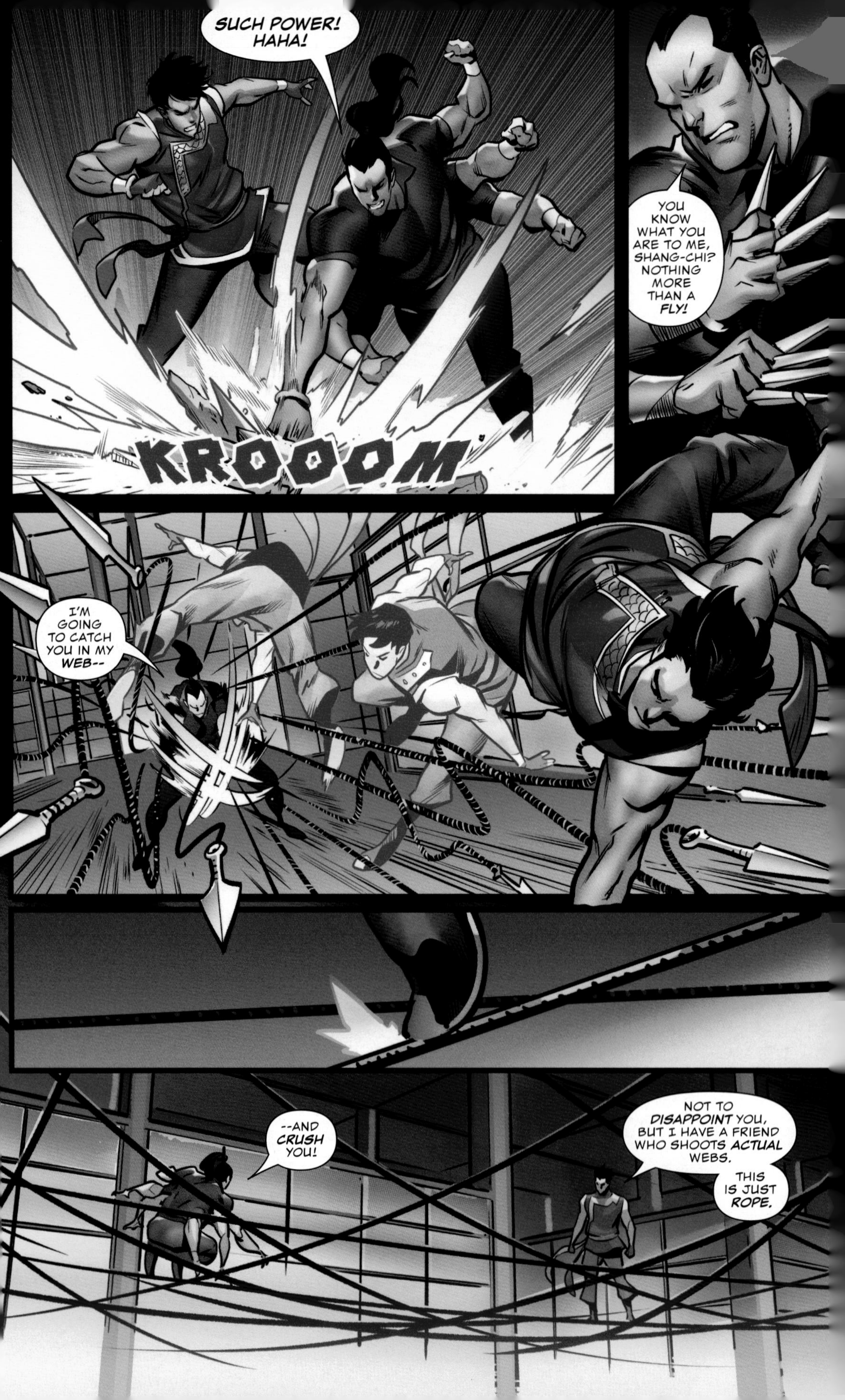
SUCH POWER! HAHA!
KROOOM
YOU KNOW WHAT YOU ARE TO ME, SHANG-CHI? NOTHING MORE THAN A FLY!
I'M GOING TO CATCH YOU IN MY WEB--
--AND CRUSH YOU!
NOT TO DISAPPOINT YOU, BUT I HAVE A FRIEND WHO SHOOTS ACTUAL WEBS.
THIS IS JUST ROPE.

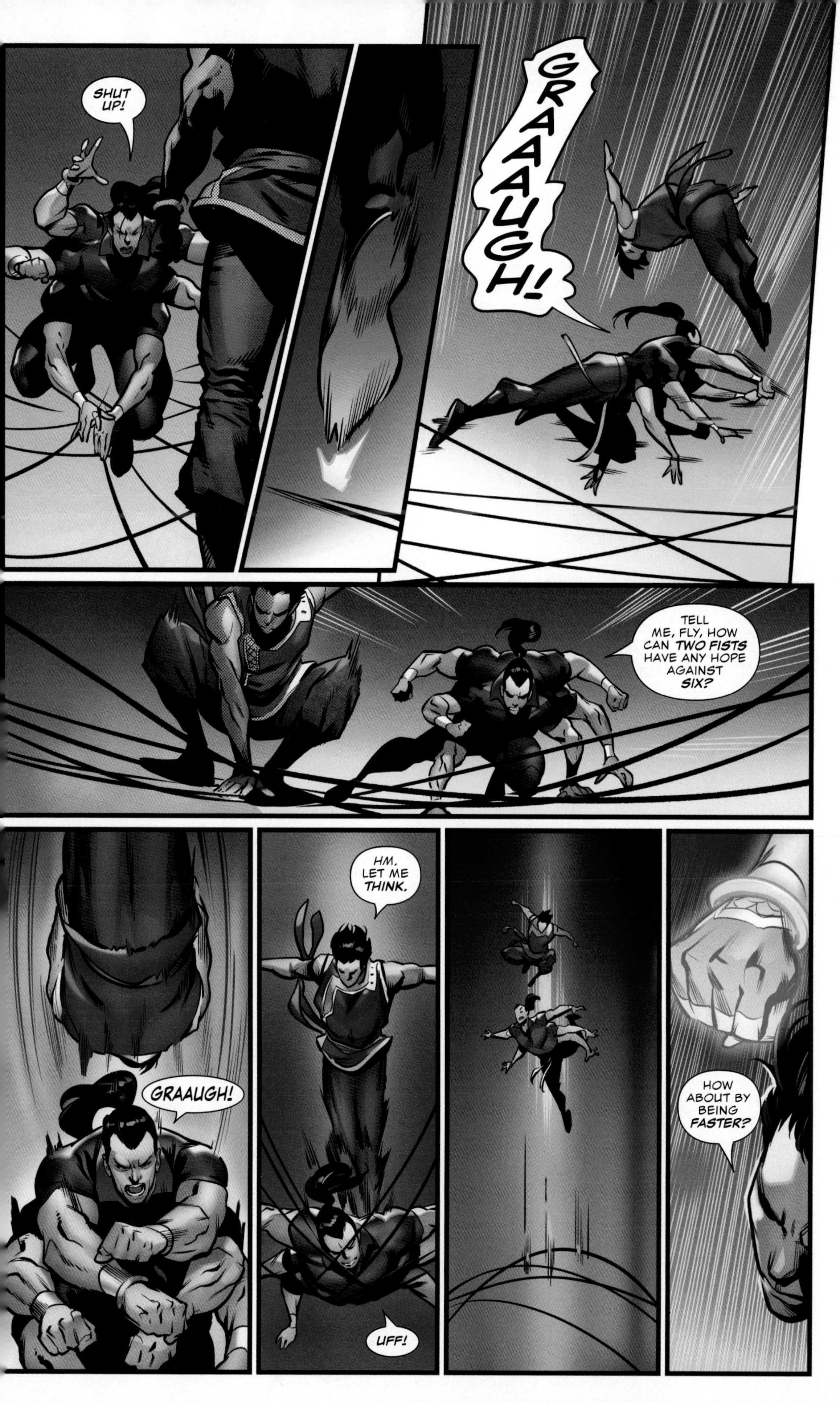
SHUT UP!
GRAAAUGH!
TELL ME, FLY, HOW CAN TWO FISTS HAVE ANY HOPE AGAINST SIX?
GRAAUGH!
HM. LET ME THINK.
UFF!
HOW ABOUT BY BEING FASTER?

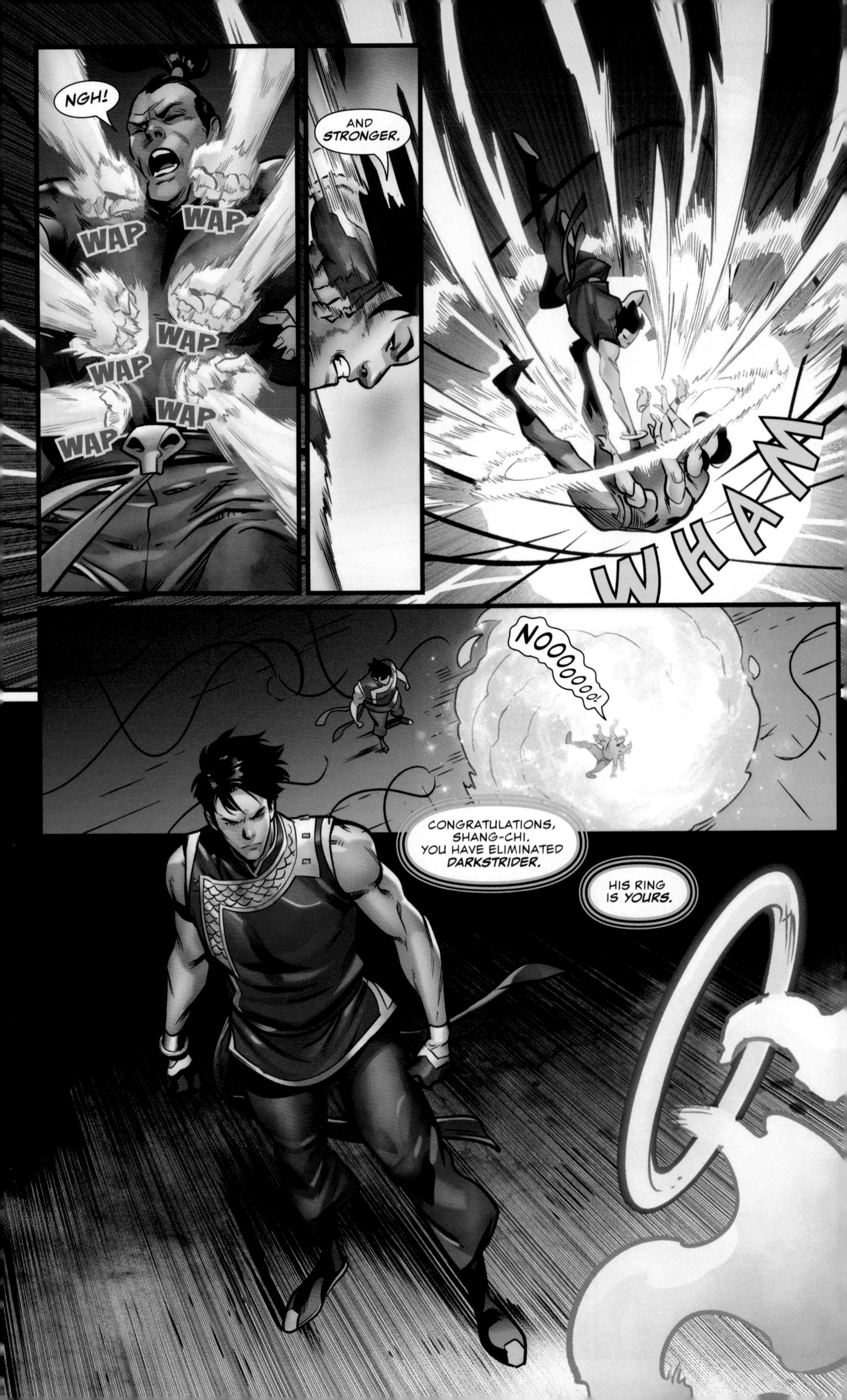
NGH!
WAP
WAP
WAP
WAP
WAP
WAP
AND STRONGER.
WHAM
NOOOOOOO!
CONGRATULATIONS, SHANG-CHI. YOU HAVE ELIMINATED DARKSTRIDER.
HIS RING IS YOURS.

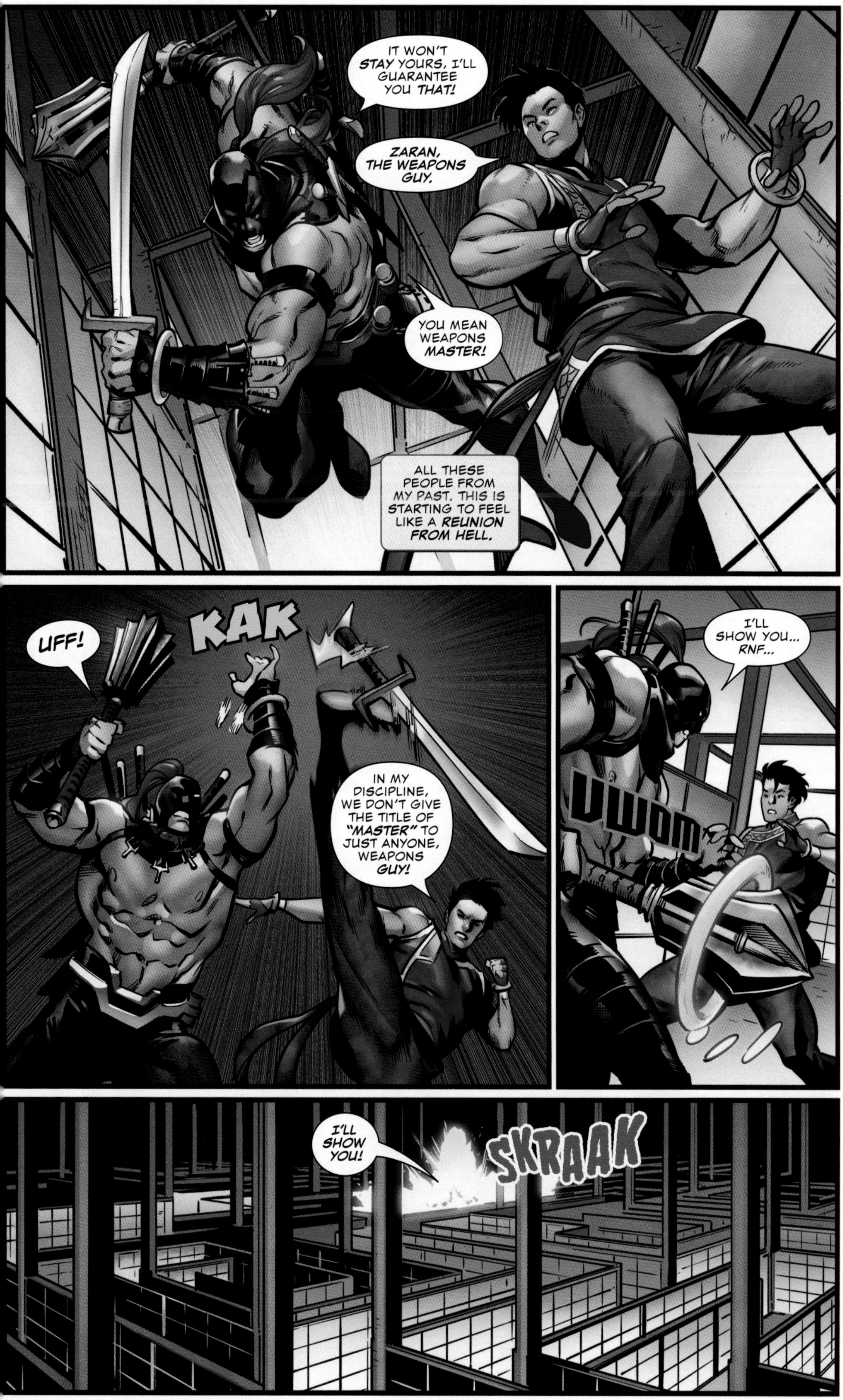
IT WON'T STAY YOURS, I'LL GUARANTEE YOU THAT!
ZARAN, THE WEAPONS GUY.
YOU MEAN WEAPONS MASTER!
ALL THESE PEOPLE FROM MY PAST. THIS IS STARTING TO FEEL LIKE A REUNION FROM HELL.
UFF!
KAK
IN MY DISCIPLINE, WE DON'T GIVE THE TITLE OF "MASTER" TO JUST ANYONE, WEAPONS GUY!
I'LL SHOW YOU... RNF...
VWOM
I'LL SHOW YOU!
SKRAAK

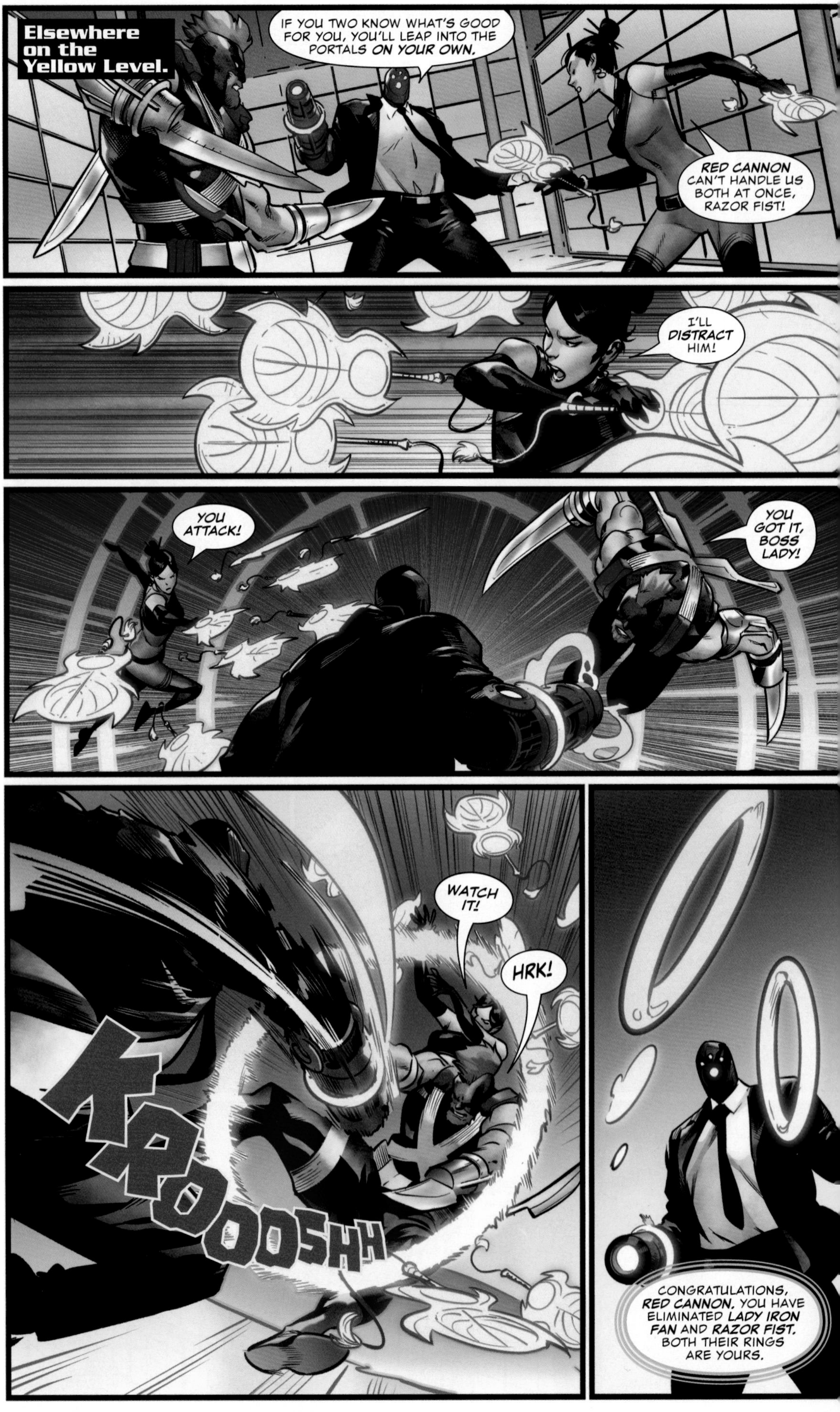
Elsewhere on the Yellow Level.
IF YOU TWO KNOW WHAT'S GOOD FOR YOU, YOU'LL LEAP INTO THE PORTALS ON YOUR OWN.
RED CANNON CAN'T HANDLE US BOTH AT ONCE, RAZOR FIST!
I'LL DISTRACT HIM!
YOU ATTACK!
YOU GOT IT, BOSS LADY!
WATCH IT!
HRK!
KROOOOSHH
CONGRATULATIONS, RED CANNON. YOU HAVE ELIMINATED LADY IRON FAN AND RAZOR FIST. BOTH THEIR RINGS ARE YOURS.

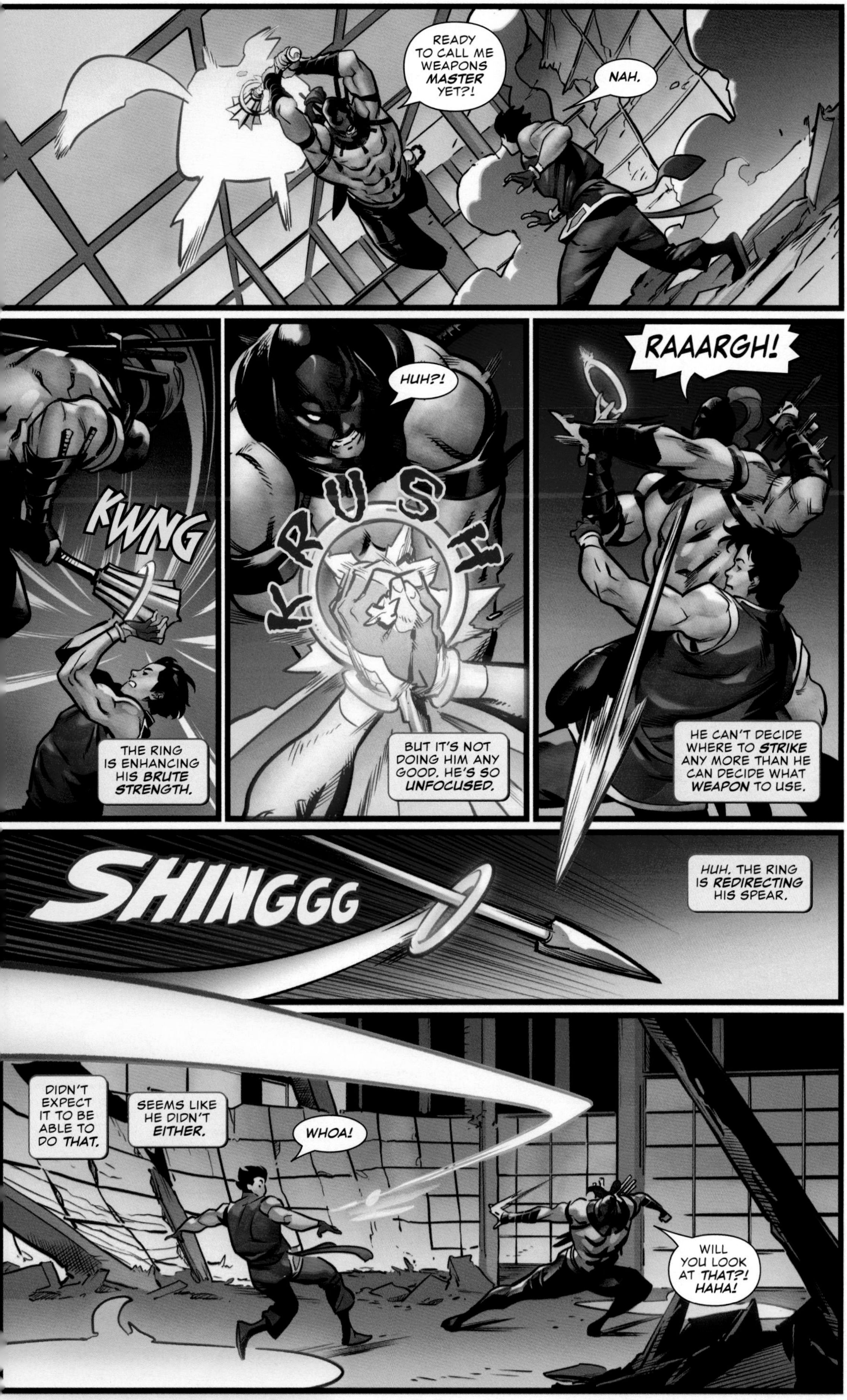
READY TO CALL ME WEAPONS MASTER YET?!
NAH.
KWNG
THE RING IS ENHANCING HIS BRUTE STRENGTH.
HUH?!
KRUSH
BUT IT'S NOT DOING HIM ANY GOOD. HE'S SO UNFOCUSED.
RAAARGH!
HE CAN'T DECIDE WHERE TO STRIKE ANY MORE THAN HE CAN DECIDE WHAT WEAPON TO USE.
SHINGGG
HUH. THE RING IS REDIRECTING HIS SPEAR.
DIDN'T EXPECT IT TO BE ABLE TO DO THAT.
SEEMS LIKE HE DIDN'T EITHER.
WHOA!
WILL YOU LOOK AT THAT?! HAHA!

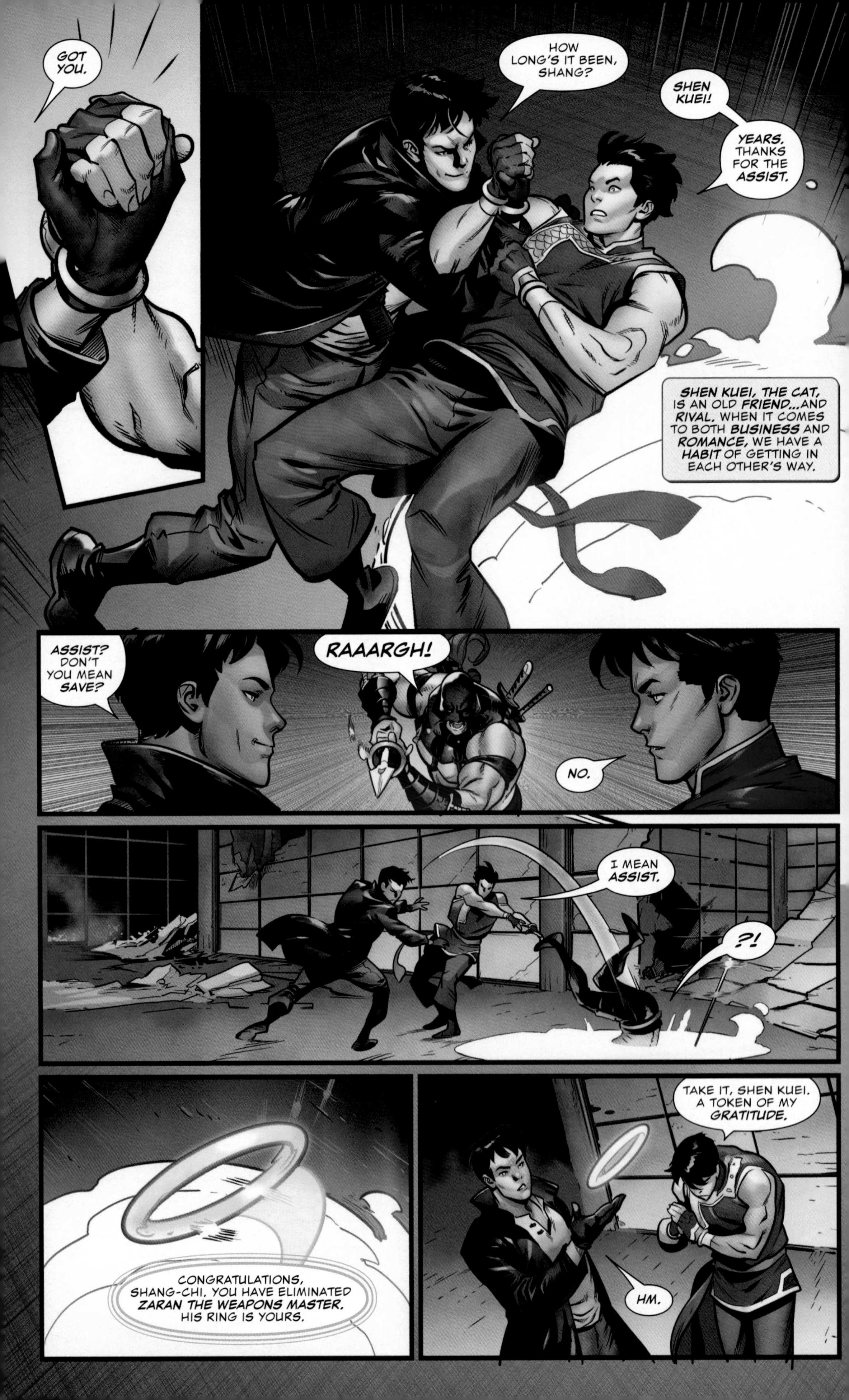
GOT YOU.
HOW LONG'S IT BEEN, SHANG?
SHEN KUEI!
YEARS. THANKS FOR THE ASSIST.
SHEN KUEI, THE CAT, IS AN OLD FRIEND...AND RIVAL. WHEN IT COMES TO BOTH BUSINESS AND ROMANCE, WE HAVE A HABIT OF GETTING IN EACH OTHER'S WAY.
ASSIST? DON'T YOU MEAN SAVE?
RAAARGH!
NO.
I MEAN ASSIST.
?!
CONGRATULATIONS, SHANG-CHI. YOU HAVE ELIMINATED ZARAN THE WEAPONS MASTER. HIS RING IS YOURS.
TAKE IT, SHEN KUEI. A TOKEN OF MY GRATITUDE.
HM.

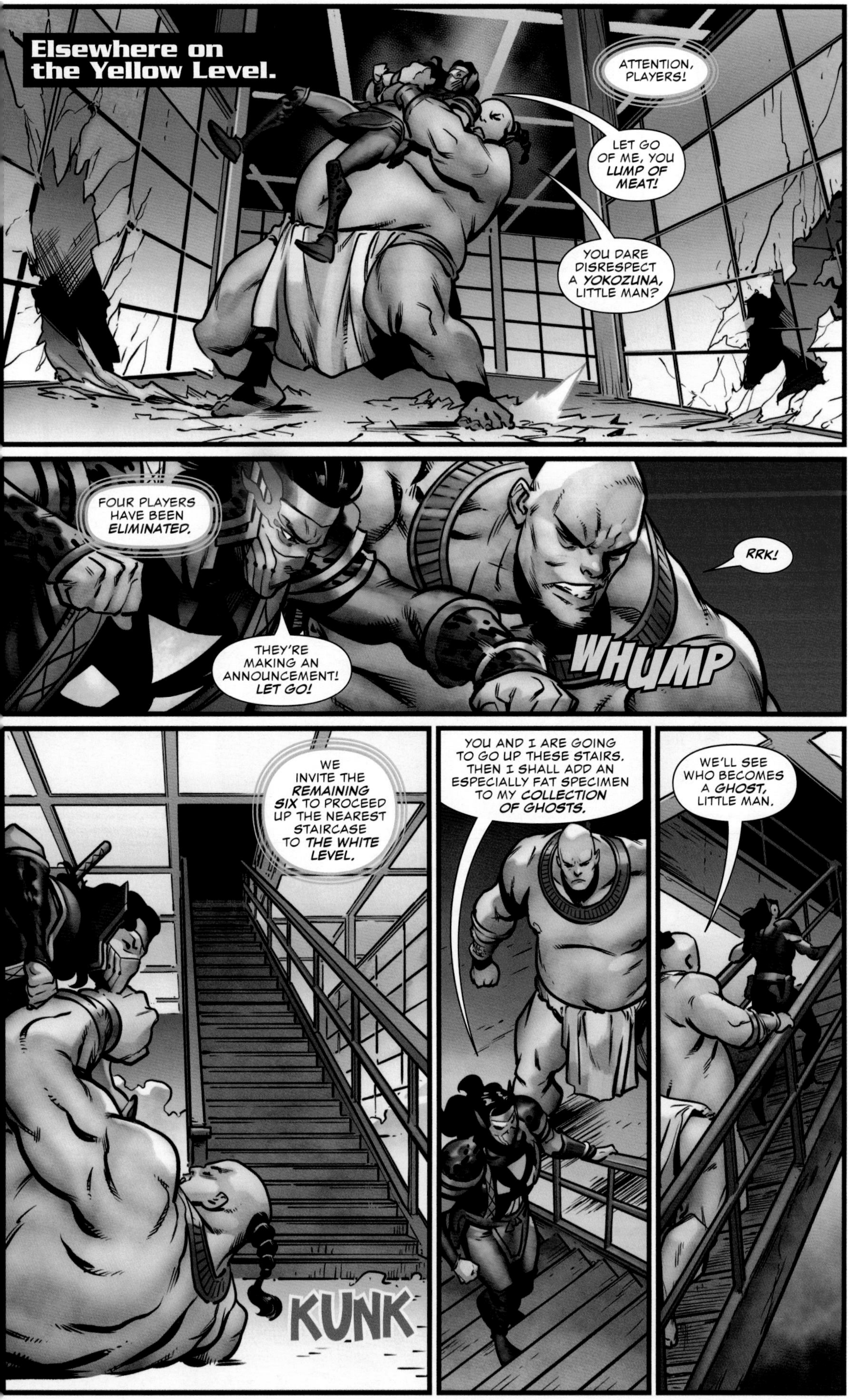
Elsewhere on the Yellow Level.
ATTENTION, PLAYERS!
LET GO OF ME, YOU LUMP OF MEAT!
YOU DARE DISRESPECT A YOKOZUNA, LITTLE MAN?
FOUR PLAYERS HAVE BEEN ELIMINATED.
THEY'RE MAKING AN ANNOUNCEMENT! LET GO!
RRK!
WHUMP
WE INVITE THE REMAINING SIX TO PROCEED UP THE NEAREST STAIRCASE TO THE WHITE LEVEL.
KUNK
YOU AND I ARE GOING TO GO UP THESE STAIRS. THEN I SHALL ADD AN ESPECIALLY FAT SPECIMEN TO MY COLLECTION OF GHOSTS.
WE'LL SEE WHO BECOMES A GHOST, LITTLE MAN.

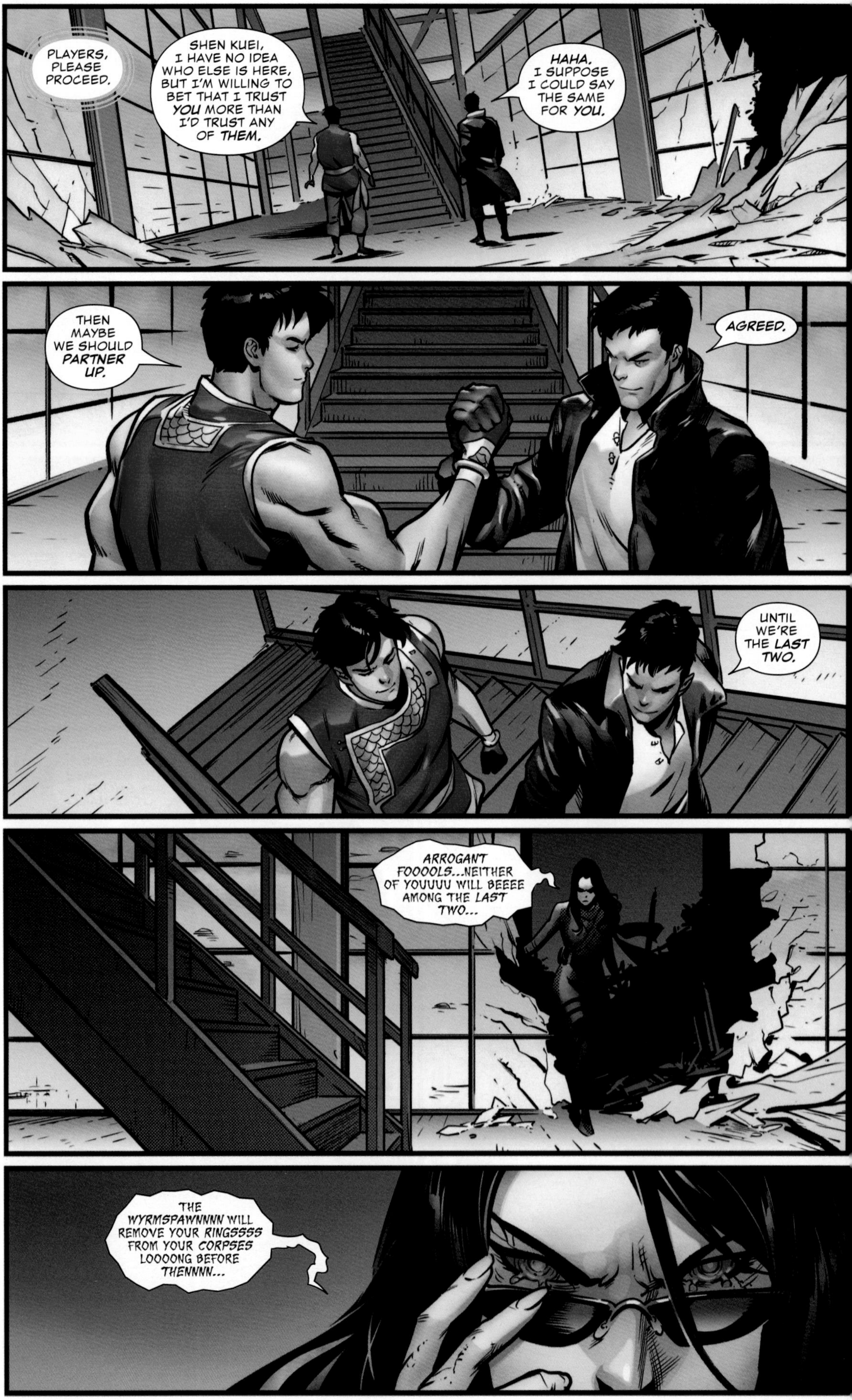
PLAYERS, PLEASE PROCEED.
SHEN KUEI, I HAVE NO IDEA WHO ELSE IS HERE, BUT I'M WILLING TO BET THAT I TRUST YOU MORE THAN I'D TRUST ANY OF THEM.
HAHA. I SUPPOSE I COULD SAY THE SAME FOR YOU.
THEN MAYBE WE SHOULD PARTNER UP.
AGREED.
UNTIL WE'RE THE LAST TWO.
ARROGANT FOOOOLS...NEITHER OF YOUUUU WILL BEEEE AMONG THE LAST TWO...
THE WYRMSPAWNNNN WILL REMOVE YOUR RINGSSSS FROM YOUR CORPSES LOOOONG BEFORE THENNNN...

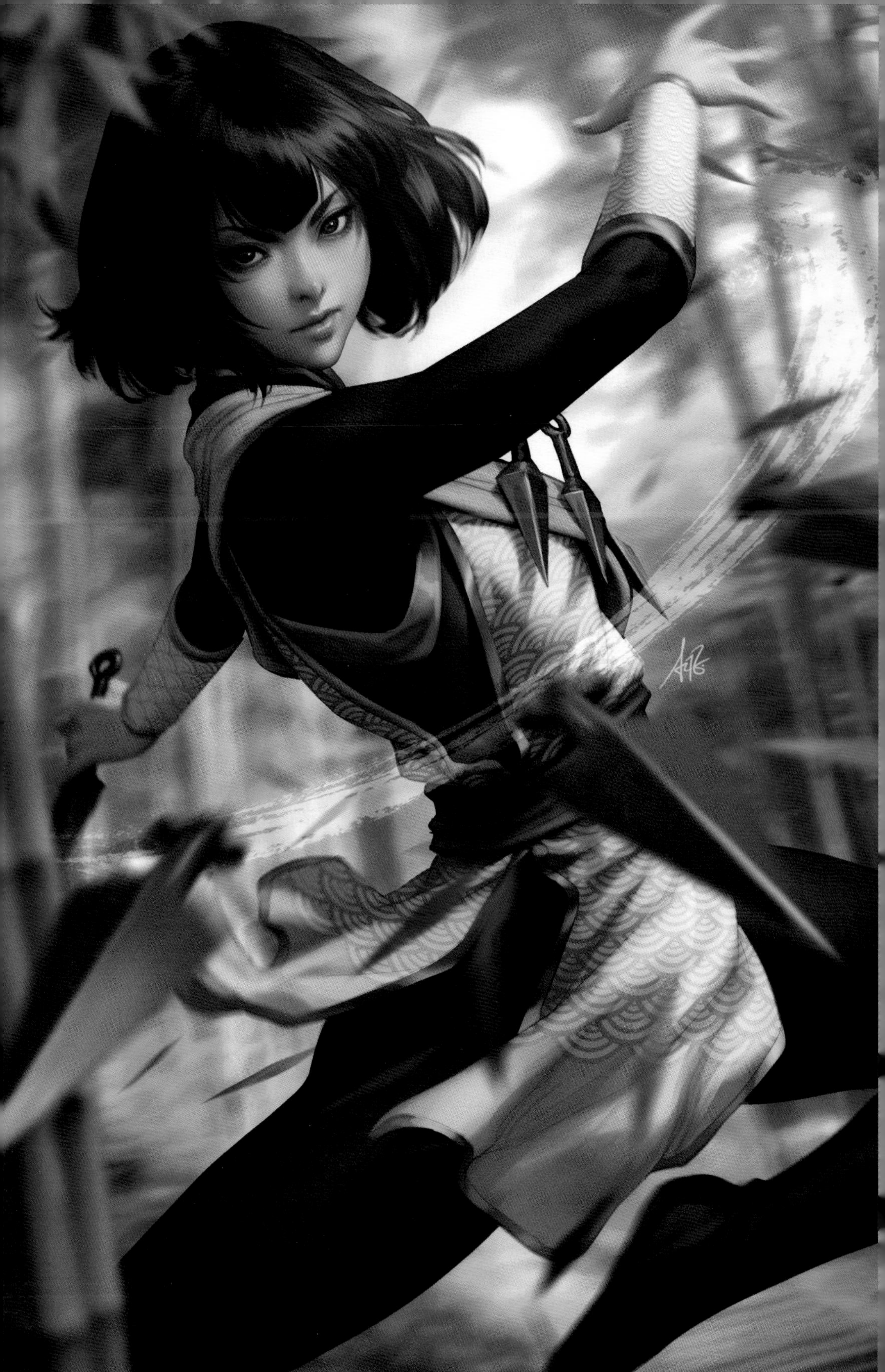

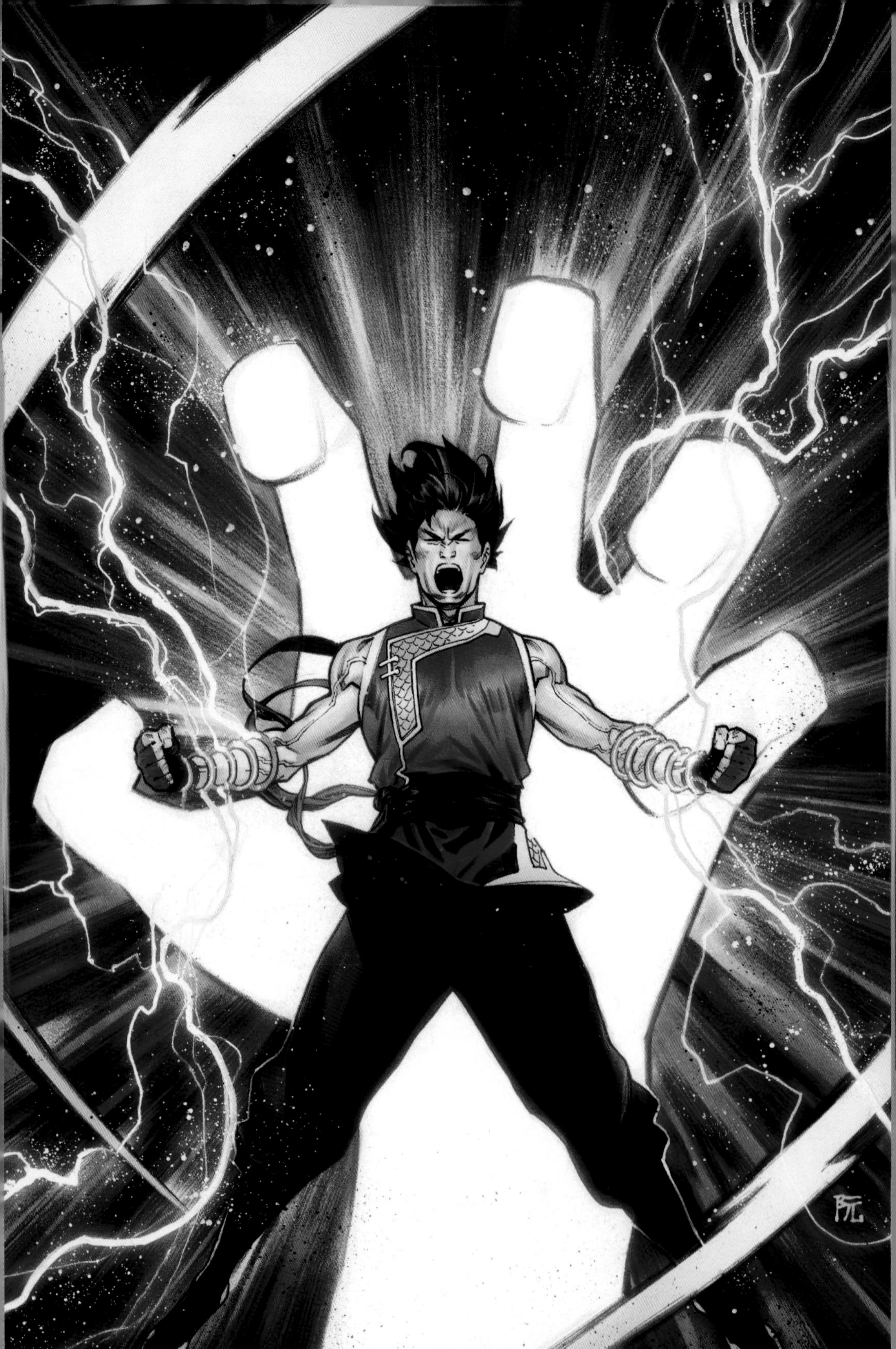

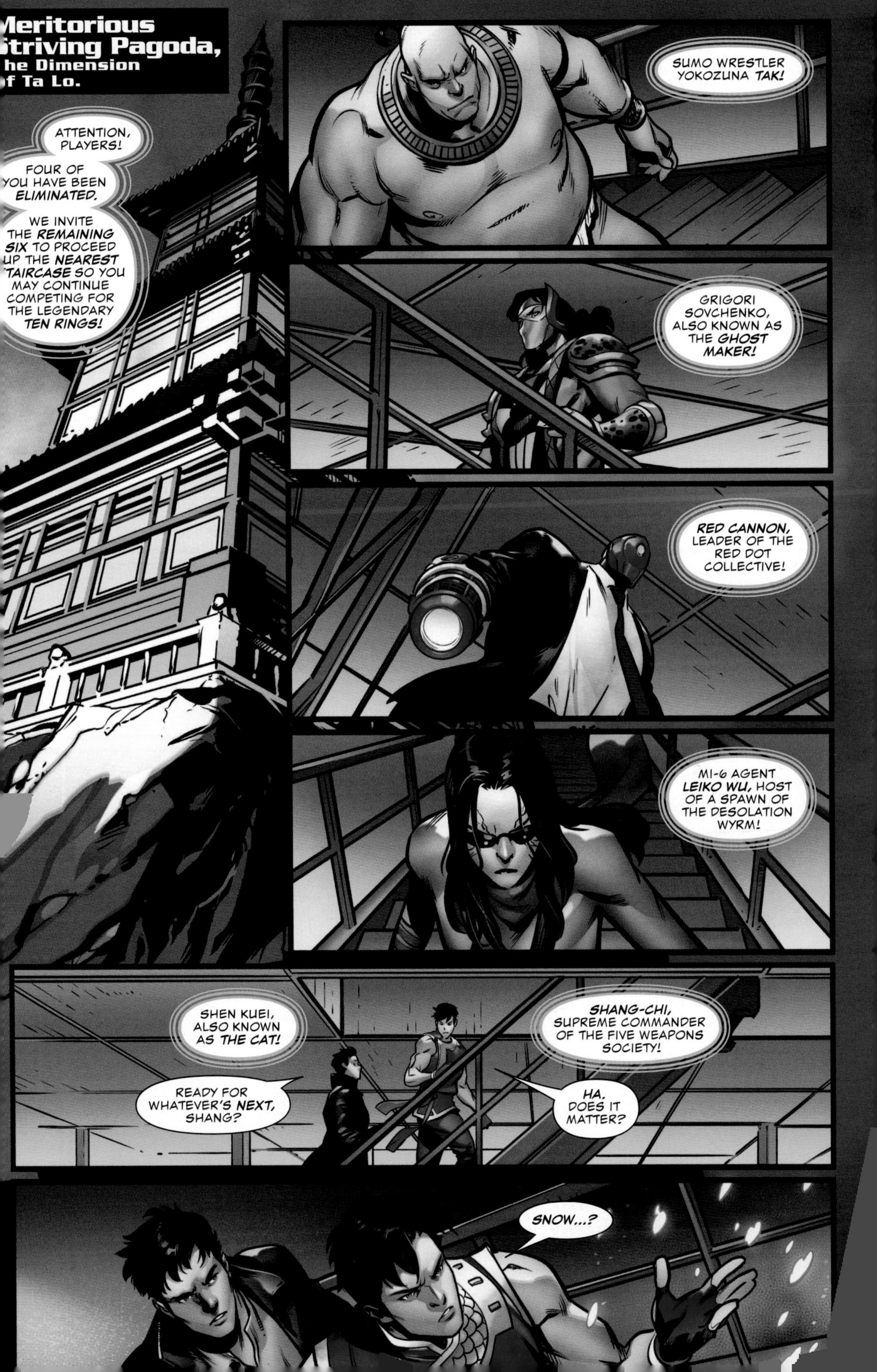

Meritorious Striving Pagoda, the Dimension of Ta Lo.
ATTENTION, PLAYERS!
FOUR OF YOU HAVE BEEN ELIMINATED.
WE INVITE THE REMAINING SIX TO PROCEED UP THE NEAREST STAIRCASE SO YOU MAY CONTINUE COMPETING FOR THE LEGENDARY TEN RINGS!
SUMO WRESTLER YOKOZUNA TAK!
GRIGORI SOVCHENKO, ALSO KNOWN AS THE GHOST MAKER!
RED CANNON, LEADER OF THE RED DOT COLLECTIVE!
MI-6 AGENT LEIKO WU, HOST OF A SPAWN OF THE DESOLATION WYRM!
SHEN KUEI, ALSO KNOWN AS THE CAT!
SHANG-CHI, SUPREME COMMANDER OF THE FIVE WEAPONS SOCIETY!
READY FOR WHATEVER'S NEXT, SHANG?
HA. DOES IT MATTER?
SNOW...?

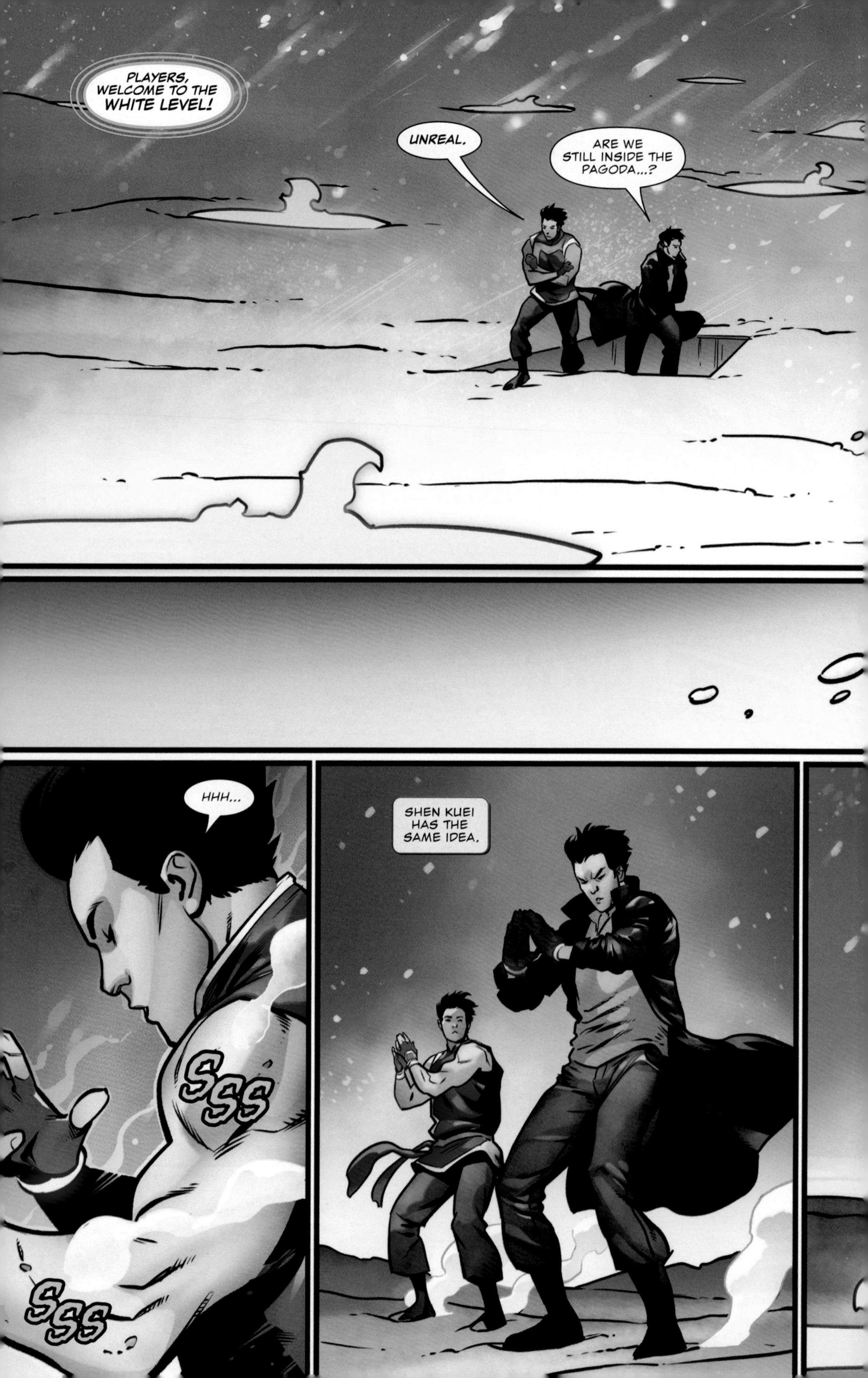
PLAYERS, WELCOME TO THE WHITE LEVEL!
UNREAL.
ARE WE STILL INSIDE THE PAGODA...?
HHH...
SSS
SSS
SHEN KUEI HAS THE SAME IDEA.

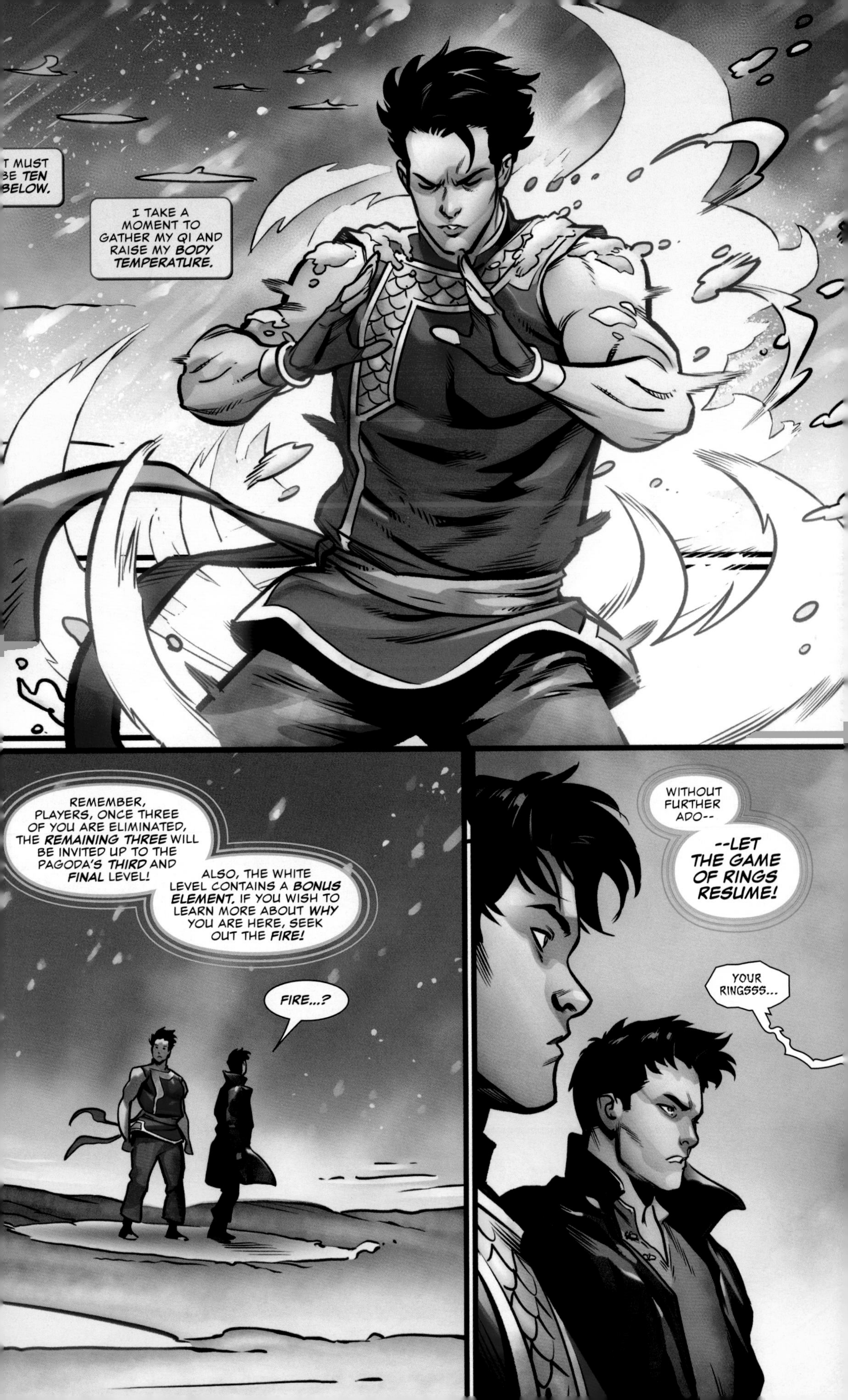
T MUST
BE TEN
BELOW.
I TAKE A MOMENT TO GATHER MY QI AND RAISE MY BODY TEMPERATURE.
REMEMBER, PLAYERS, ONCE THREE OF YOU ARE ELIMINATED, THE REMAINING THREE WILL BE INVITED UP TO THE PAGODA'S THIRD AND FINAL LEVEL!
ALSO, THE WHITE LEVEL CONTAINS A BONUS ELEMENT. IF YOU WISH TO LEARN MORE ABOUT WHY YOU ARE HERE, SEEK OUT THE FIRE!
FIRE...?
WITHOUT FURTHER ADO--
--LET THE GAME OF RINGS RESUME!
YOUR RINGSSS...

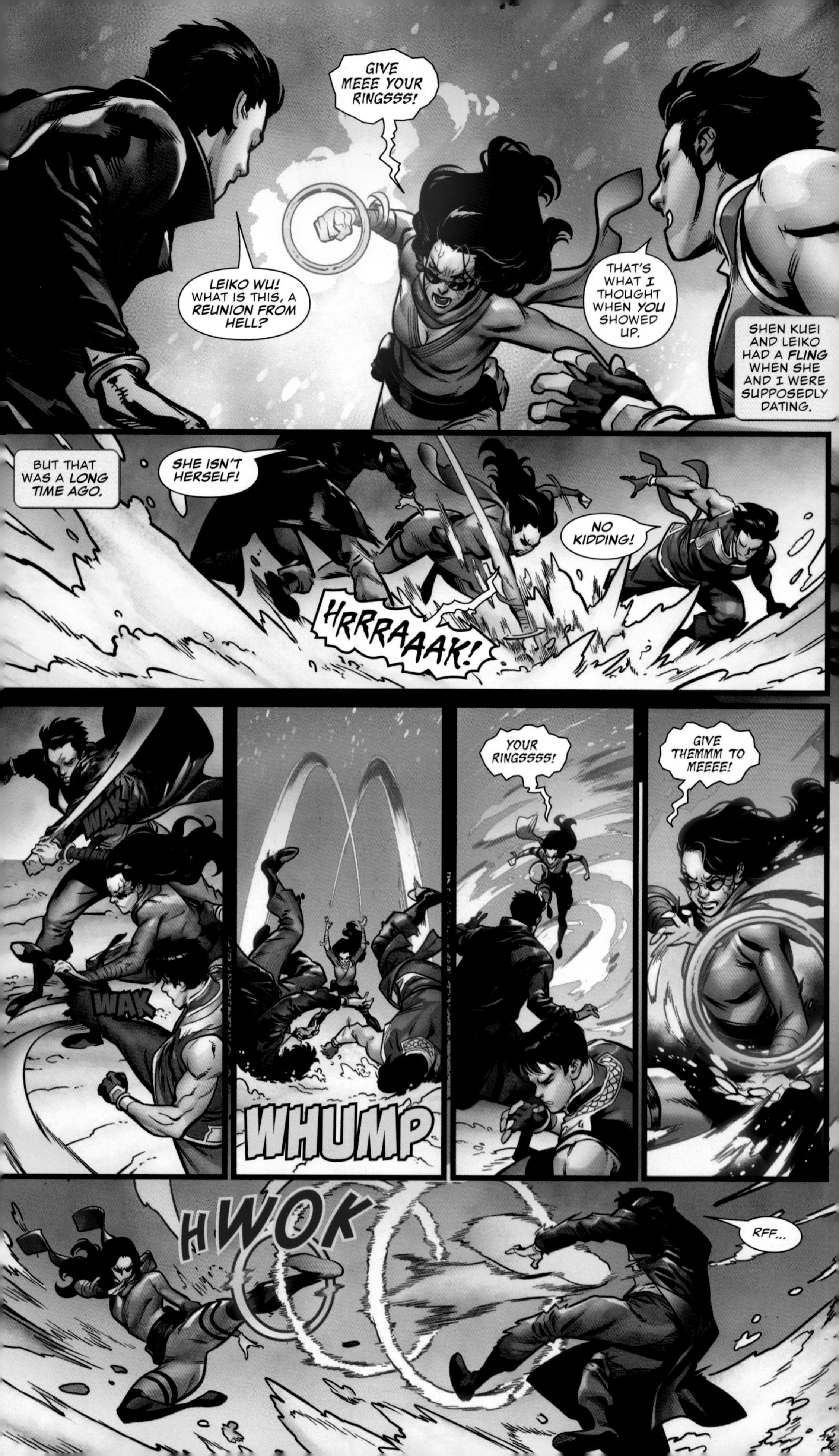
GIVE MEEE YOUR RINGSSS!
LEIKO WU! WHAT IS THIS, A REUNION FROM HELL?
THAT'S WHAT I THOUGHT WHEN YOU SHOWED UP.
SHEN KUEI AND LEIKO HAD A FLING WHEN SHE AND I WERE SUPPOSEDLY DATING.
BUT THAT WAS A LONG TIME AGO.
SHE ISN'T HERSELF!
NO KIDDING!
HRRRAAAK!
WAK
WAK
WHUMP
YOUR RINGSSSS!
GIVE THEMMM TO MEEEE!
HWOK
RFF...

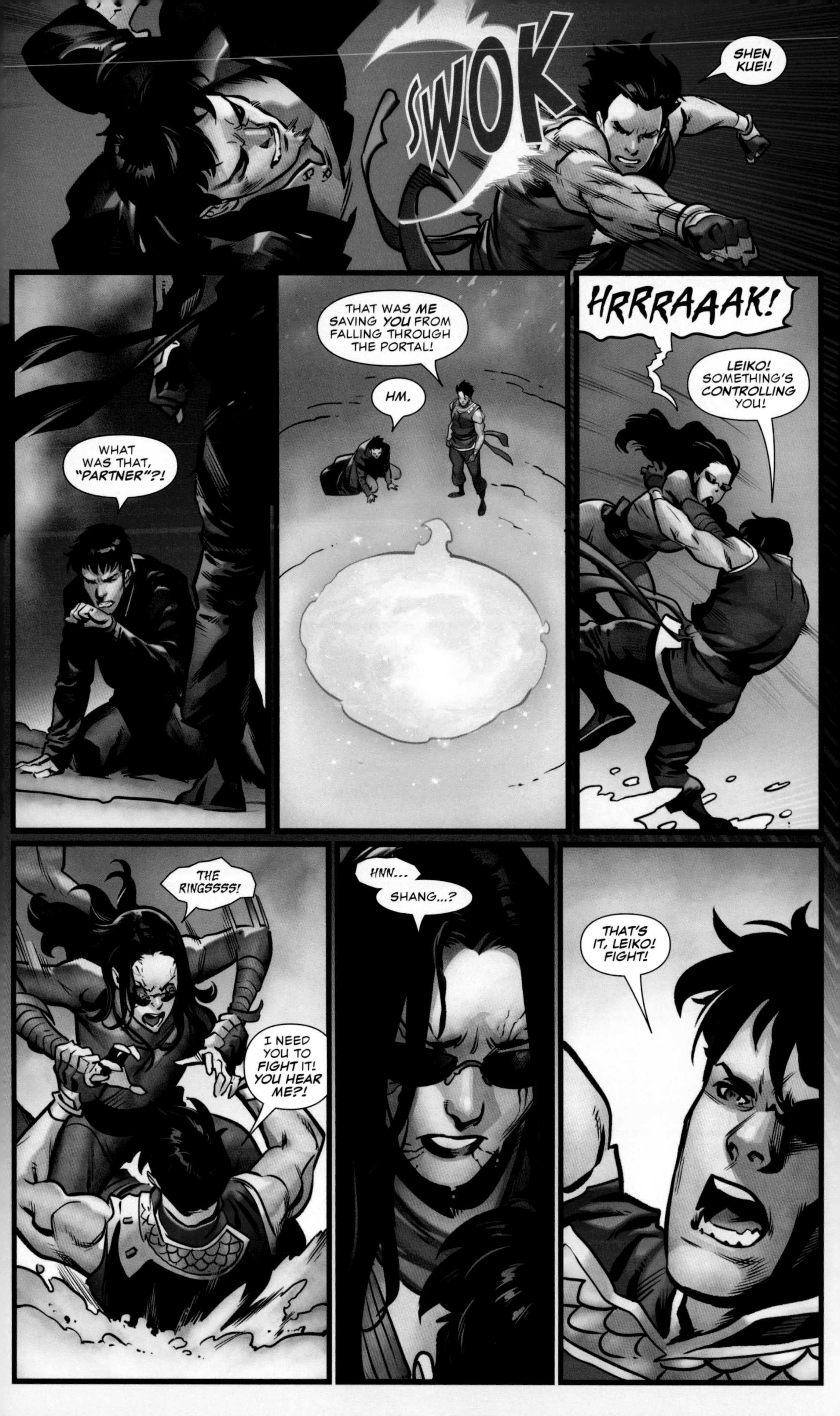
SWOK
SHEN KUEI!
WHAT WAS THAT, "PARTNER"?!
THAT WAS ME SAVING YOU FROM FALLING THROUGH THE PORTAL!
HM.
HRRRAAAK!
LEIKO! SOMETHING'S CONTROLLING YOU!
THE RINGSSSS!
I NEED YOU TO FIGHT IT! YOU HEAR ME?!
HNN...
SHANG...?
THAT'S IT, LEIKO! FIGHT!

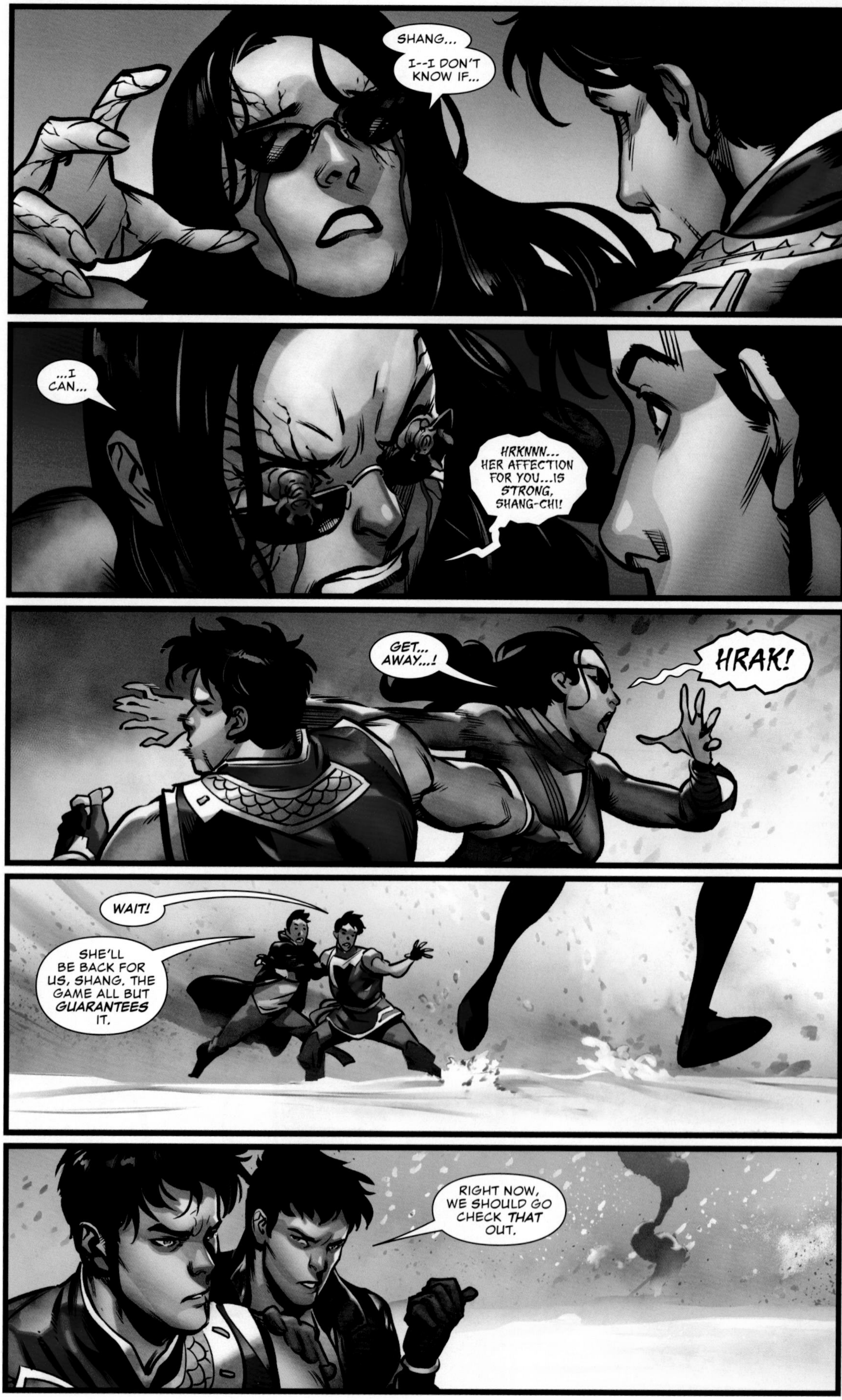

SHANG...
I--I DON'T KNOW IF...
...I CAN...
HRKNNN... HER AFFECTION FOR YOU...IS STRONG, SHANG-CHI!
GET... AWAY...!
HRAK!
WAIT!
SHE'LL BE BACK FOR US, SHANG. THE GAME ALL BUT GUARANTEES IT.
RIGHT NOW, WE SHOULD GO CHECK THAT OUT.

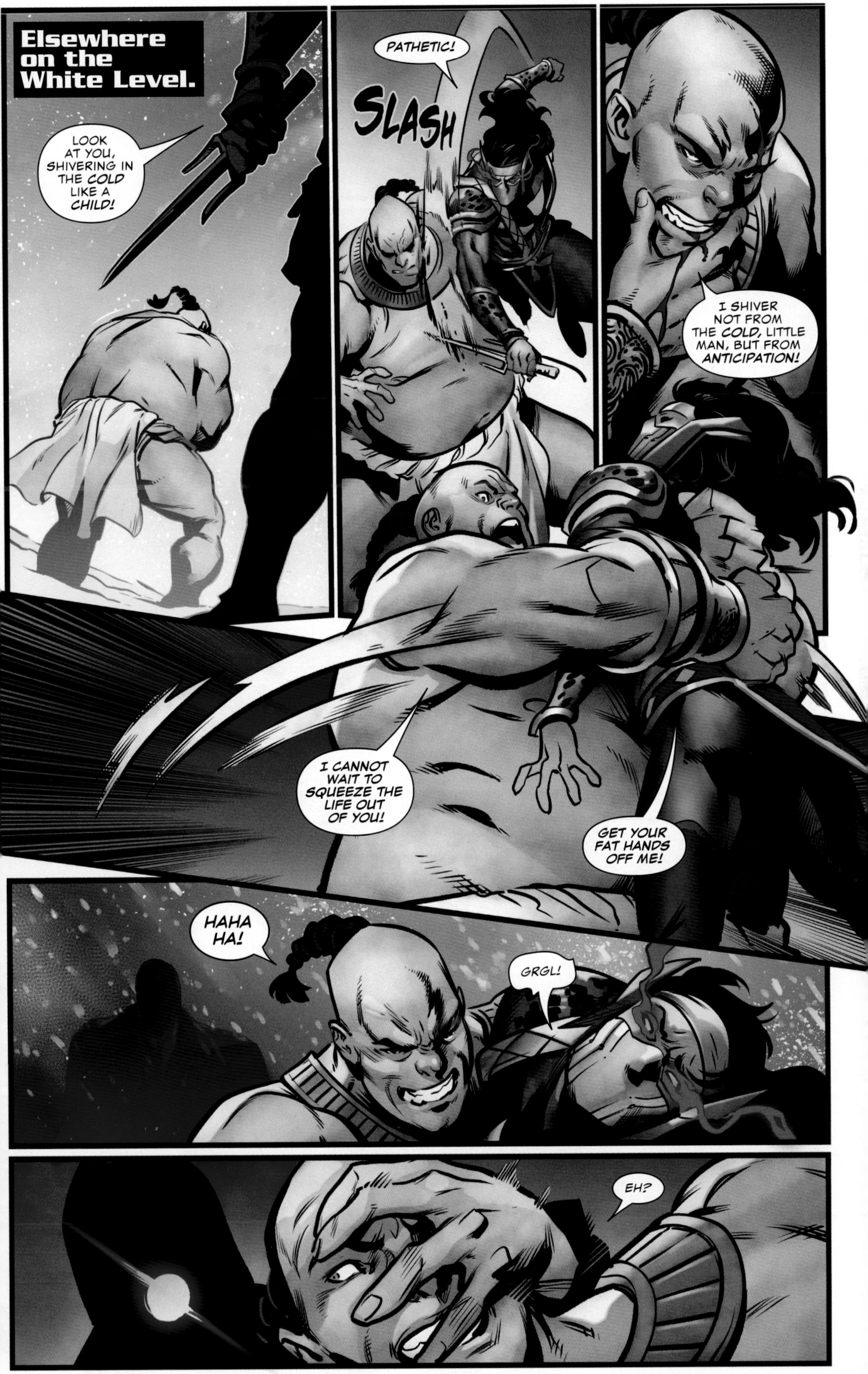
Elsewhere on the White Level.
LOOK AT YOU, SHIVERING IN THE COLD LIKE A CHILD!
PATHETIC!
SLASH
I SHIVER NOT FROM THE COLD, LITTLE MAN, BUT FROM ANTICIPATION!
I CANNOT WAIT TO SQUEEZE THE LIFE OUT OF YOU!
GET YOUR FAT HANDS OFF ME!
HAHA HA!
GRGL!
EH?

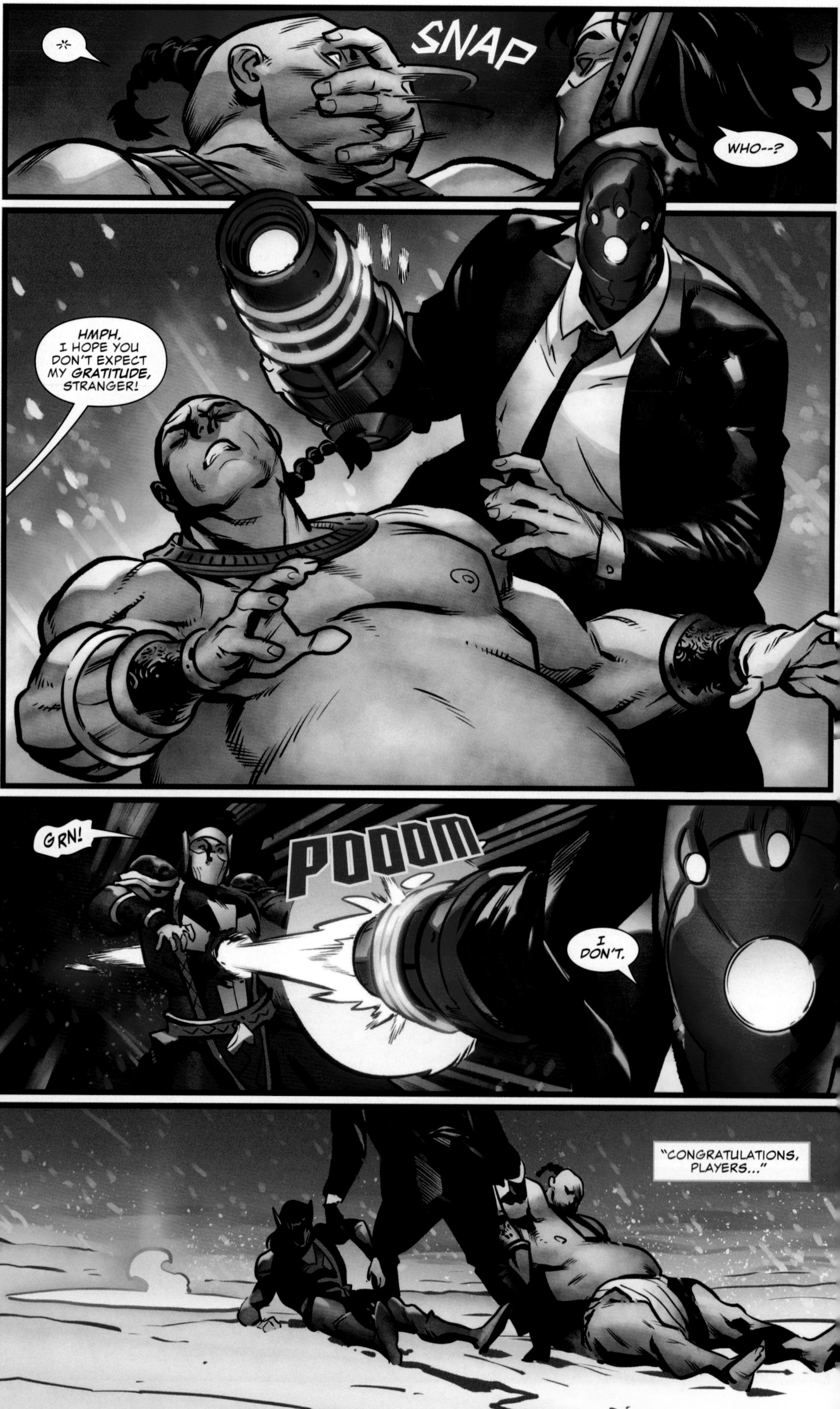

!
SNAP
WHO--?
HMPH. I HOPE YOU DON'T EXPECT MY GRATITUDE, STRANGER!
GRN!
POOOM
I DON'T.
"CONGRATULATIONS, PLAYERS..."

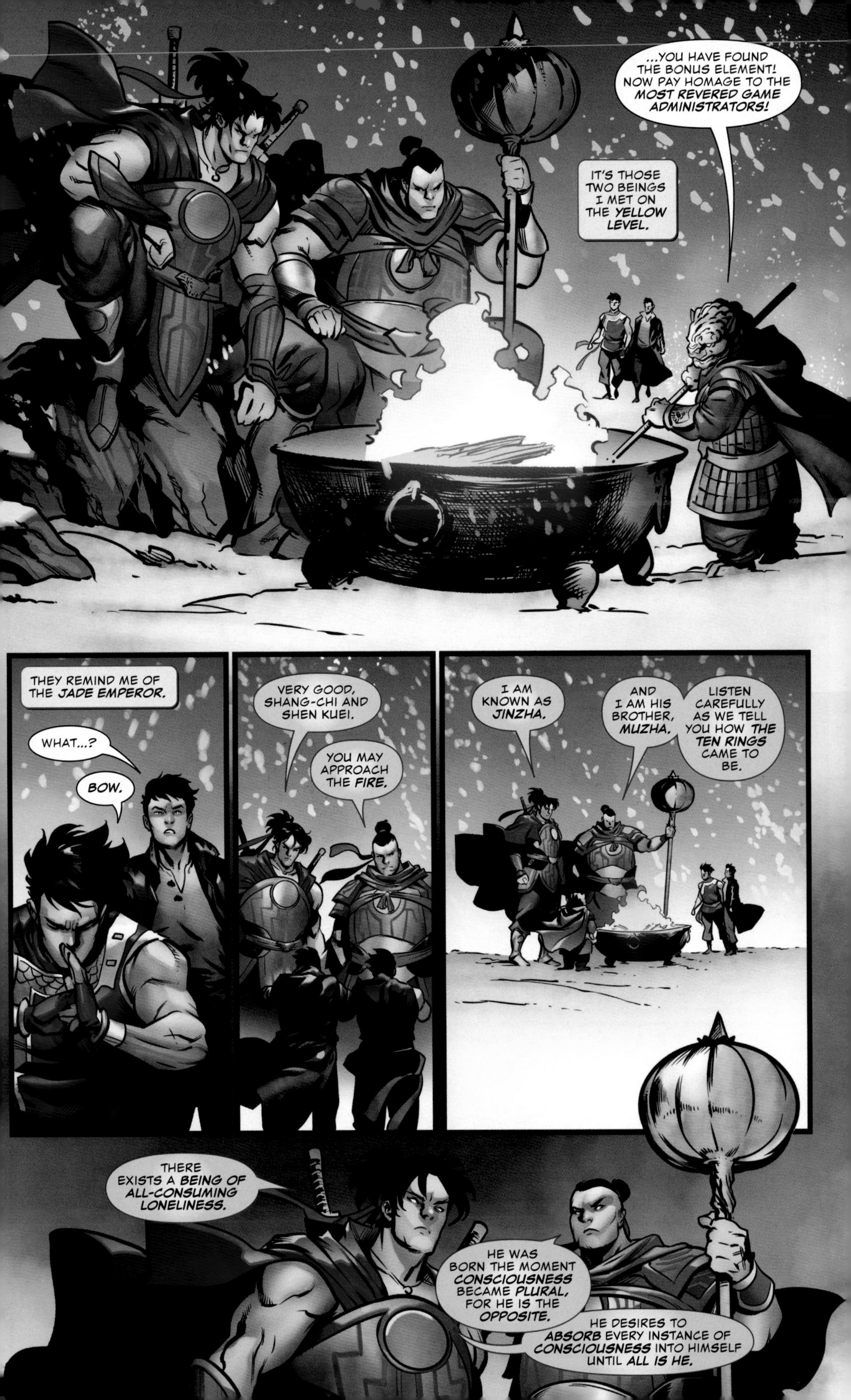

...YOU HAVE FOUND THE BONUS ELEMENT! NOW PAY HOMAGE TO THE MOST REVERED GAME ADMINISTRATORS!
IT'S THOSE TWO BEINGS I MET ON THE YELLOW LEVEL.
THEY REMIND ME OF THE JADE EMPEROR.
WHAT...?
BOW.
VERY GOOD, SHANG-CHI AND SHEN KUEI.
YOU MAY APPROACH THE FIRE.
I AM KNOWN AS JINZHA.
AND I AM HIS BROTHER, MUZHA.
LISTEN CAREFULLY AS WE TELL YOU HOW THE TEN RINGS CAME TO BE.
THERE EXISTS A BEING OF ALL-CONSUMING LONELINESS.
HE WAS BORN THE MOMENT CONSCIOUSNESS BECAME PLURAL, FOR HE IS THE OPPOSITE.
HE DESIRES TO ABSORB EVERY INSTANCE OF CONSCIOUSNESS INTO HIMSELF UNTIL ALL IS HE.

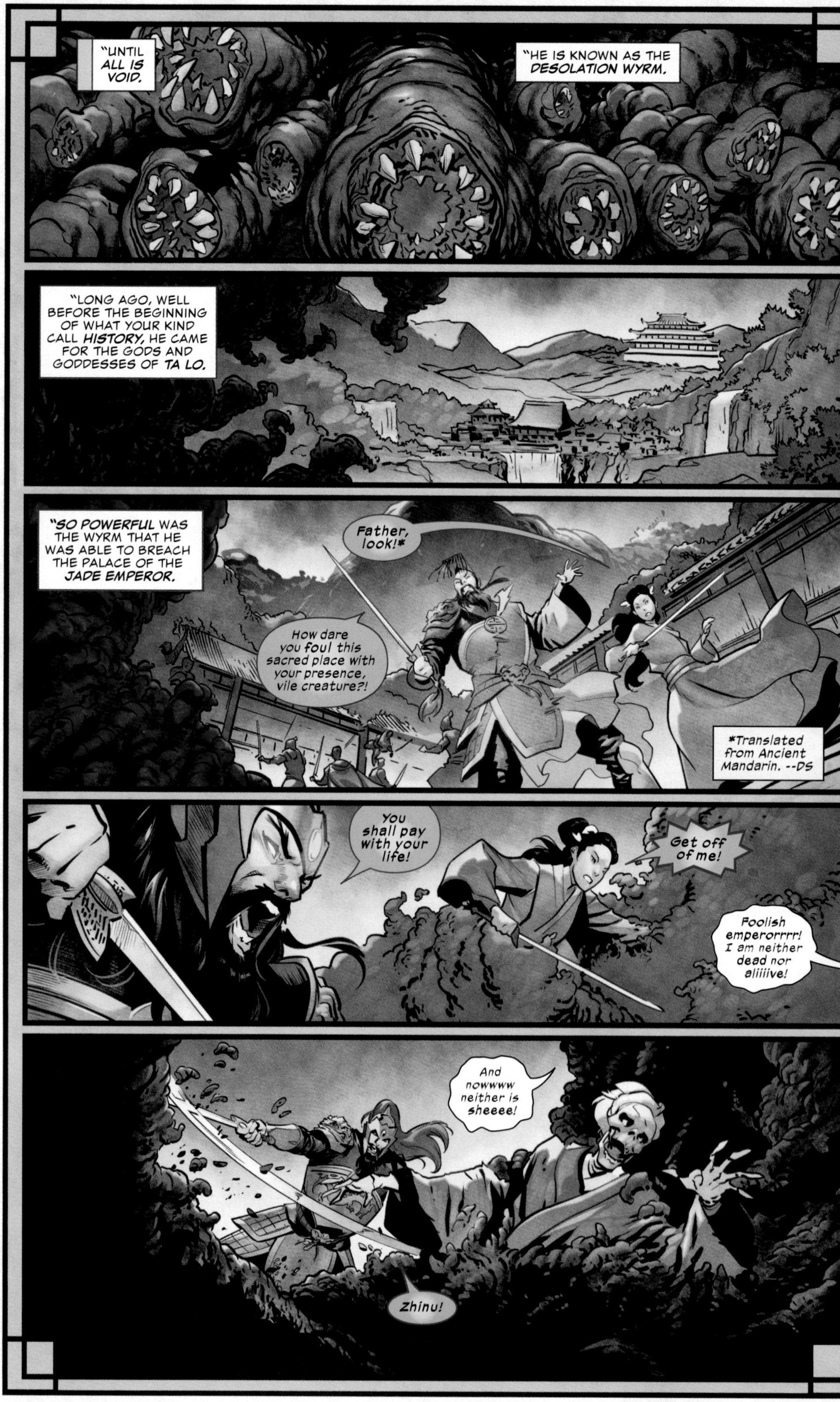
"UNTIL ALL IS VOID.
"HE IS KNOWN AS THE DESOLATION WYRM.
"LONG AGO, WELL BEFORE THE BEGINNING OF WHAT YOUR KIND CALL HISTORY, HE CAME FOR THE GODS AND GODDESSES OF TA LO.
"SO POWERFUL WAS THE WYRM THAT HE WAS ABLE TO BREACH THE PALACE OF THE JADE EMPEROR.
Father, look!*
How dare you foul this sacred place with your presence, vile creature?!
*Translated from Ancient Mandarin. --DS
You shall pay with your life!
Get off of me!
Foolish emperorrrr! I am neither dead nor aliiiive!
And nowwww neither is sheeee!
Zhinu!

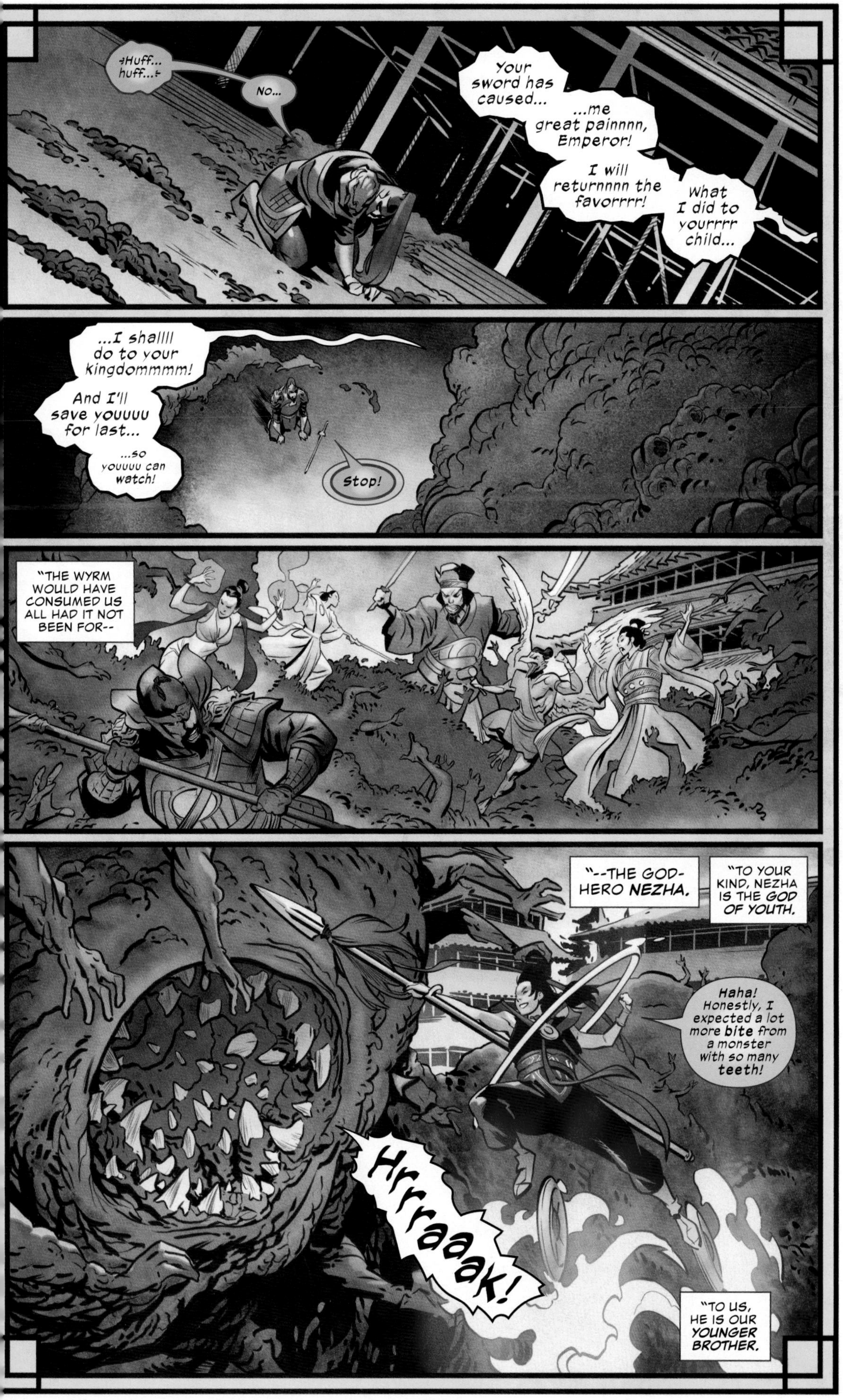
Huff... huff...
No...
Your sword has caused...
...me great painnnn, Emperor!
I will returnnnn the favorrrr!
What I did to yourrrr child...
...I shallll do to your kingdommmm!
And I'll save youuuu for last...
...so youuuu can watch!
Stop!
"THE WYRM WOULD HAVE CONSUMED US ALL HAD IT NOT BEEN FOR--
"--THE GOD-HERO NEZHA.
"TO YOUR KIND, NEZHA IS THE GOD OF YOUTH.
Haha! Honestly, I expected a lot more bite from a monster with so many teeth!
Hrrraaak!
"TO US, HE IS OUR YOUNGER BROTHER.

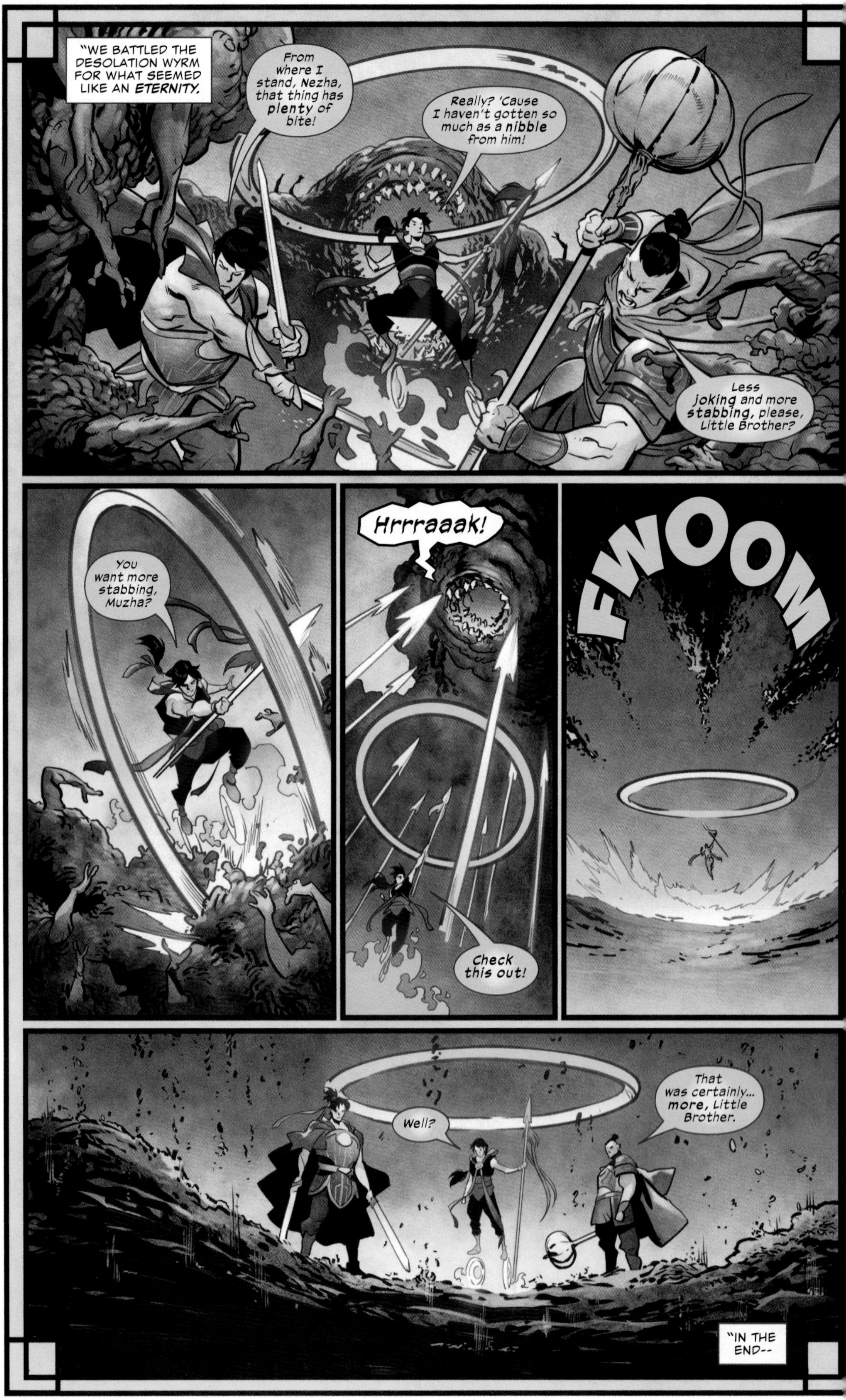

"WE BATTLED THE DESOLATION WYRM FOR WHAT SEEMED LIKE AN *ETERNITY.*
From where I stand, Nezha, that thing has **plenty** of bite!
Really? 'Cause I haven't gotten so much as a **nibble** from him!
Less **joking** and more **stabbing,** please, Little Brother?
You want more stabbing, Muzha?
Hrrraaak!
Check this out!
FWOOM
Well?
That was certainly... **more,** Little Brother.
"IN THE END--

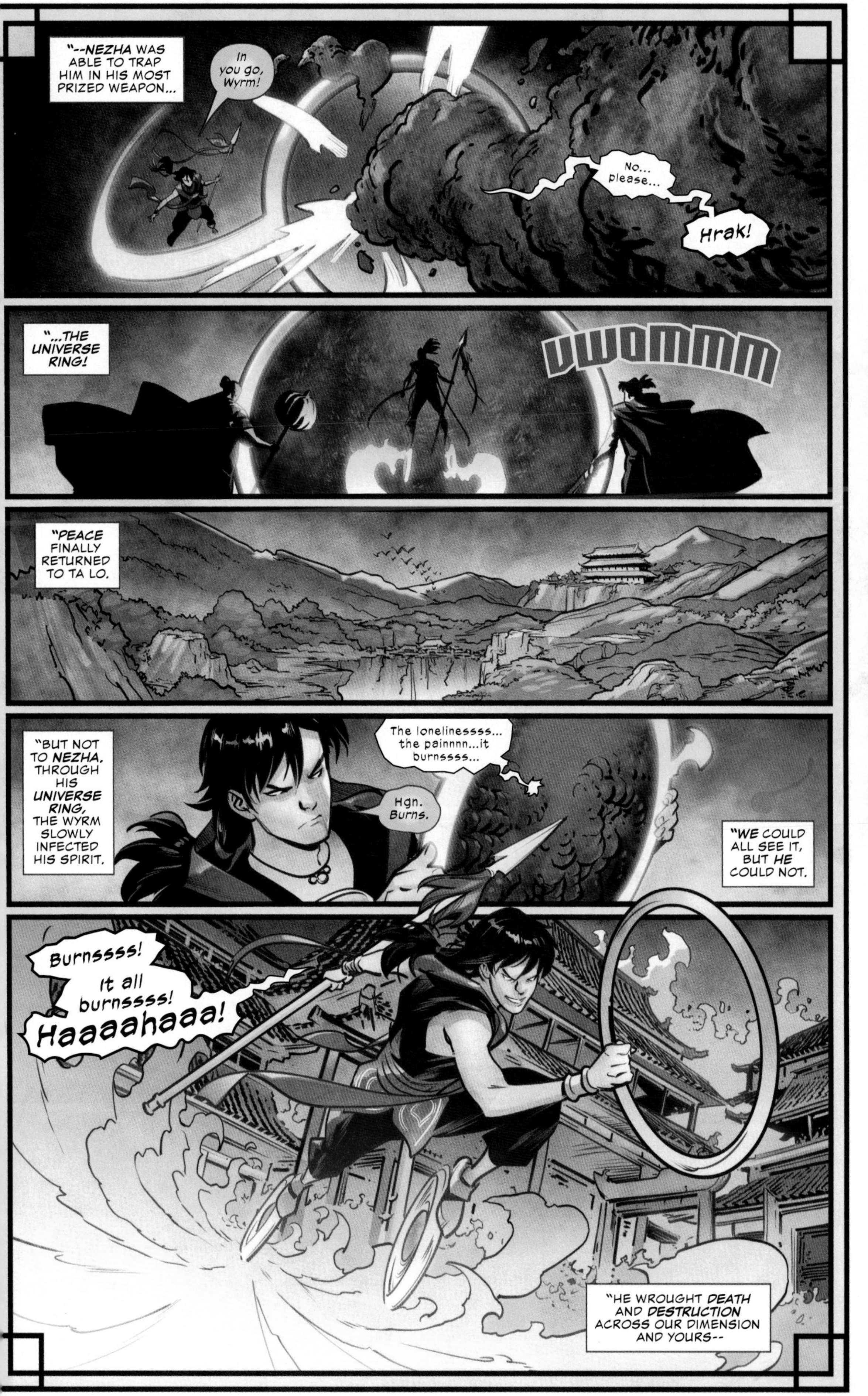
"--NEZHA WAS ABLE TO TRAP HIM IN HIS MOST PRIZED WEAPON...
In you go, Wyrm!
No... please...
Hrak!
"...THE UNIVERSE RING!
VWOMMM
"PEACE FINALLY RETURNED TO TA LO.
"BUT NOT TO NEZHA. THROUGH HIS UNIVERSE RING, THE WYRM SLOWLY INFECTED HIS SPIRIT.
The lonelinessss... the painnnn...it burnssss...
Hgn. Burns.
"WE COULD ALL SEE IT, BUT HE COULD NOT.
Burnssss!
It all burnssss!
Haaaahaaa!
"HE WROUGHT DEATH AND DESTRUCTION ACROSS OUR DIMENSION AND YOURS--

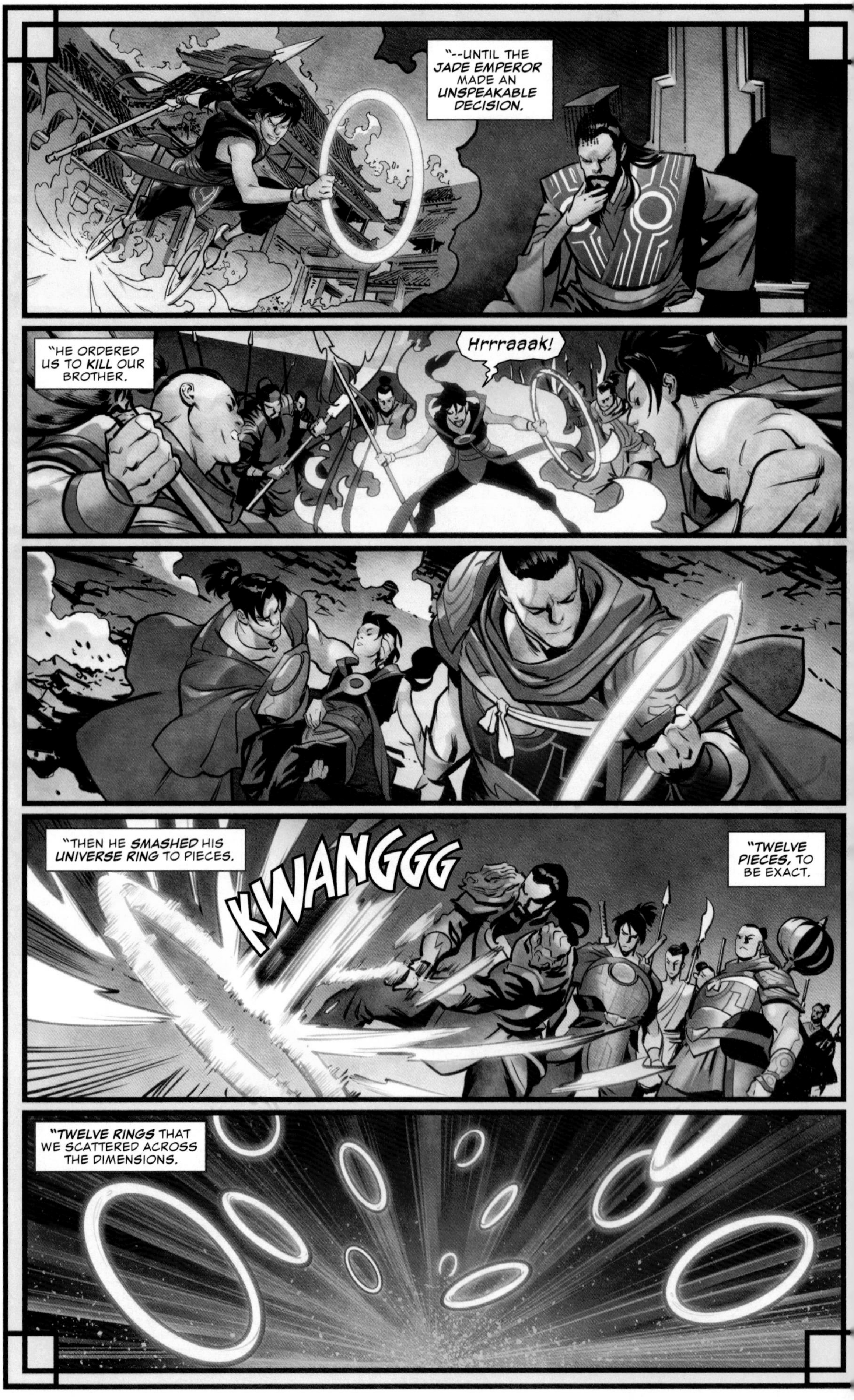
"--UNTIL THE JADE EMPEROR MADE AN UNSPEAKABLE DECISION.
"HE ORDERED US TO KILL OUR BROTHER.
Hrrraaak!
"THEN HE SMASHED HIS UNIVERSE RING TO PIECES.
KWANGGG
"TWELVE PIECES, TO BE EXACT.
"TWELVE RINGS THAT WE SCATTERED ACROSS THE DIMENSIONS.

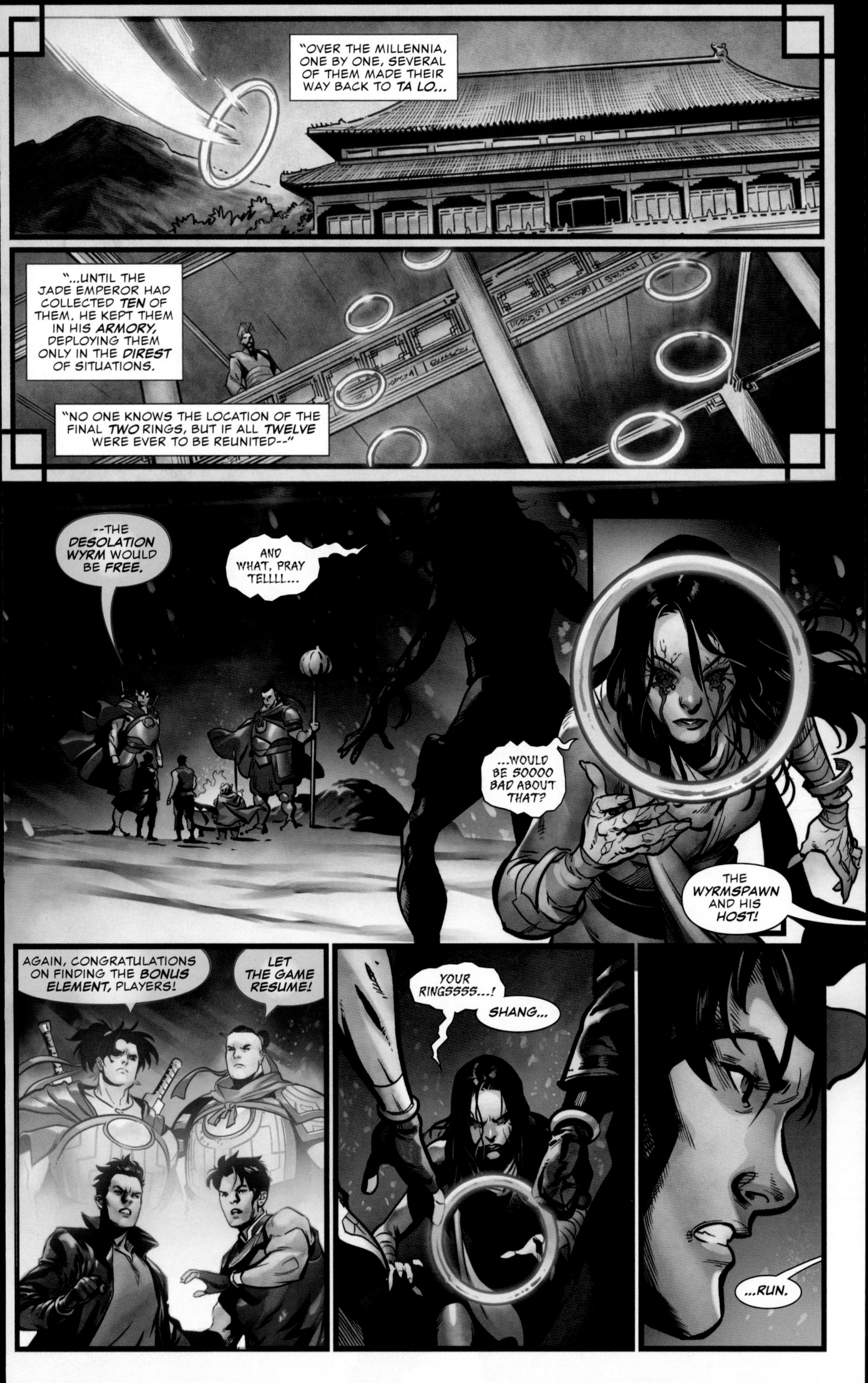
"OVER THE MILLENNIA, ONE BY ONE, SEVERAL OF THEM MADE THEIR WAY BACK TO TA LO...
"...UNTIL THE JADE EMPEROR HAD COLLECTED TEN OF THEM. HE KEPT THEM IN HIS ARMORY, DEPLOYING THEM ONLY IN THE DIREST OF SITUATIONS.
"NO ONE KNOWS THE LOCATION OF THE FINAL TWO RINGS, BUT IF ALL TWELVE WERE EVER TO BE REUNITED--"
--THE DESOLATION WYRM WOULD BE FREE.
AND WHAT, PRAY TELLLL...
...WOULD BE SOOOO BAD ABOUT THAT?
THE WYRMSPAWN AND HIS HOST!
AGAIN, CONGRATULATIONS ON FINDING THE BONUS ELEMENT, PLAYERS!
LET THE GAME RESUME!
YOUR RINGSSSS...!
SHANG...
...RUN.

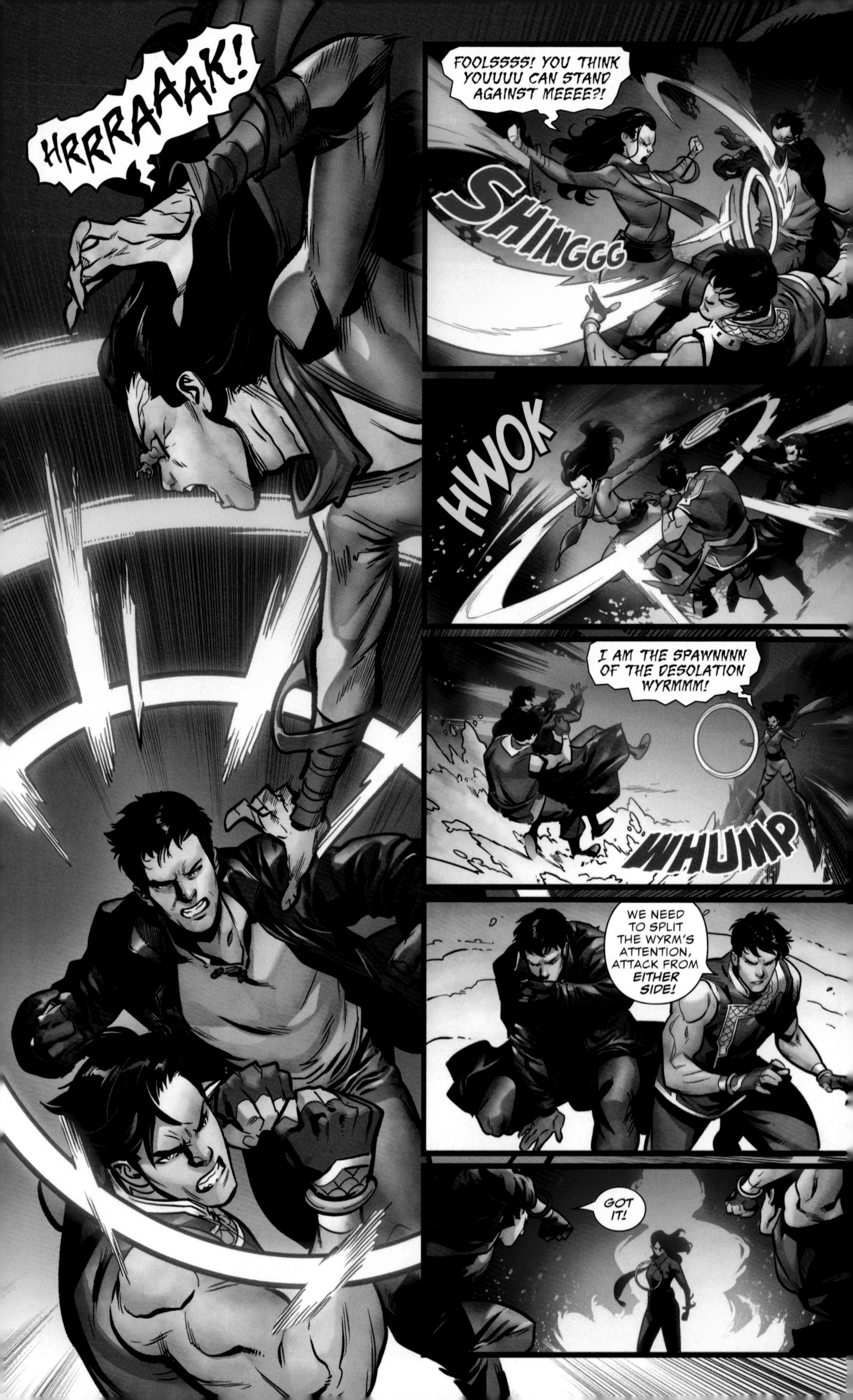
HRRRAAAK!
FOOLSSSS! YOU THINK YOUUUU CAN STAND AGAINST MEEEE?!
SHINGGG
HWOK
I AM THE SPAWNNNN OF THE DESOLATION WYRMMM!
WHUMP
WE NEED TO SPLIT THE WYRM'S ATTENTION, ATTACK FROM EITHER SIDE!
GOT IT!

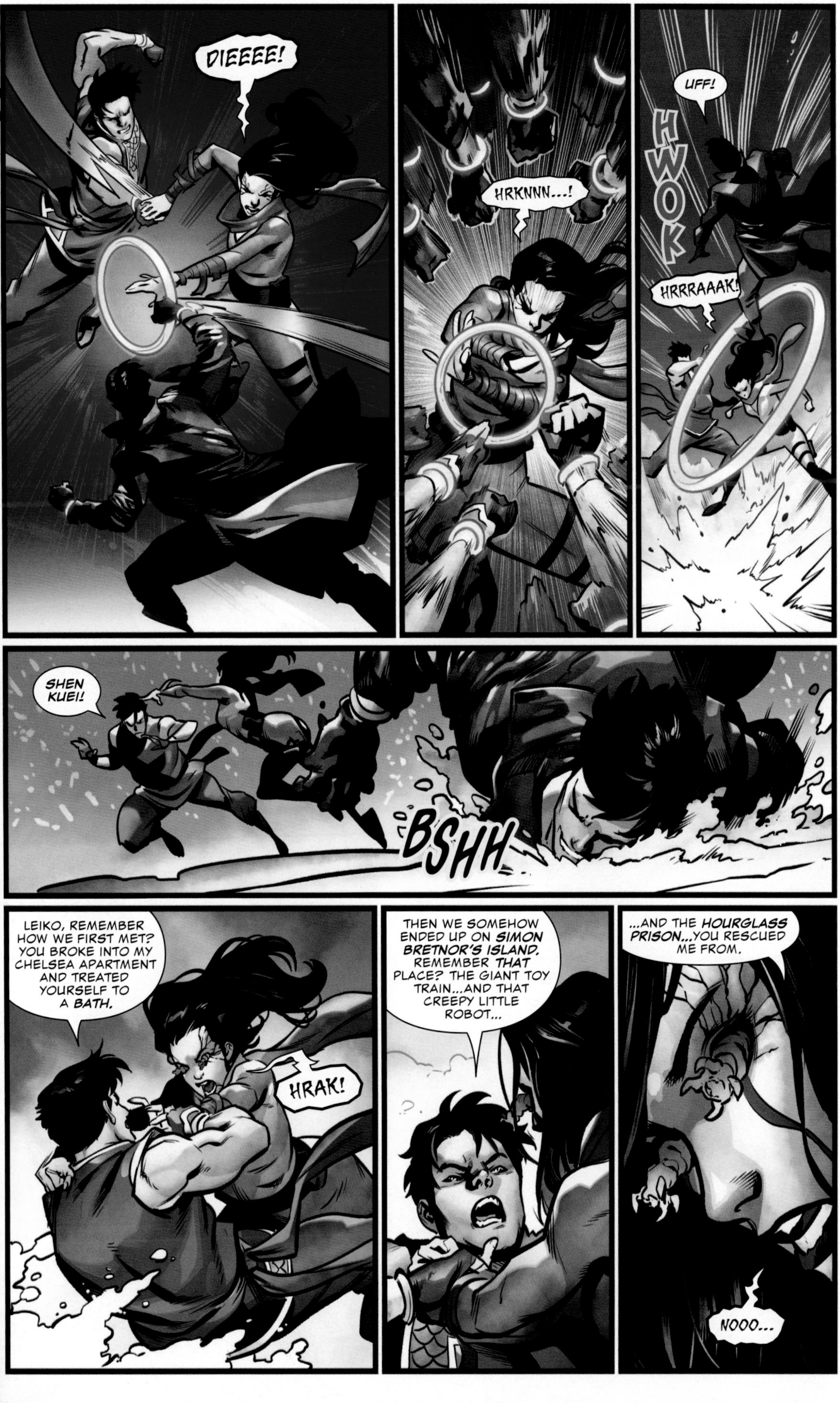
DIEEEE!
HRKNNN...!
UFF!
HWOK
HRRRAAAK!
SHEN KUEI!
BSHH
LEIKO, REMEMBER HOW WE FIRST MET? YOU BROKE INTO MY CHELSEA APARTMENT AND TREATED YOURSELF TO A BATH.
HRAK!
THEN WE SOMEHOW ENDED UP ON SIMON BRETNOR'S ISLAND. REMEMBER THAT PLACE? THE GIANT TOY TRAIN...AND THAT CREEPY LITTLE ROBOT...
...AND THE HOURGLASS PRISON...YOU RESCUED ME FROM.
NOOO...

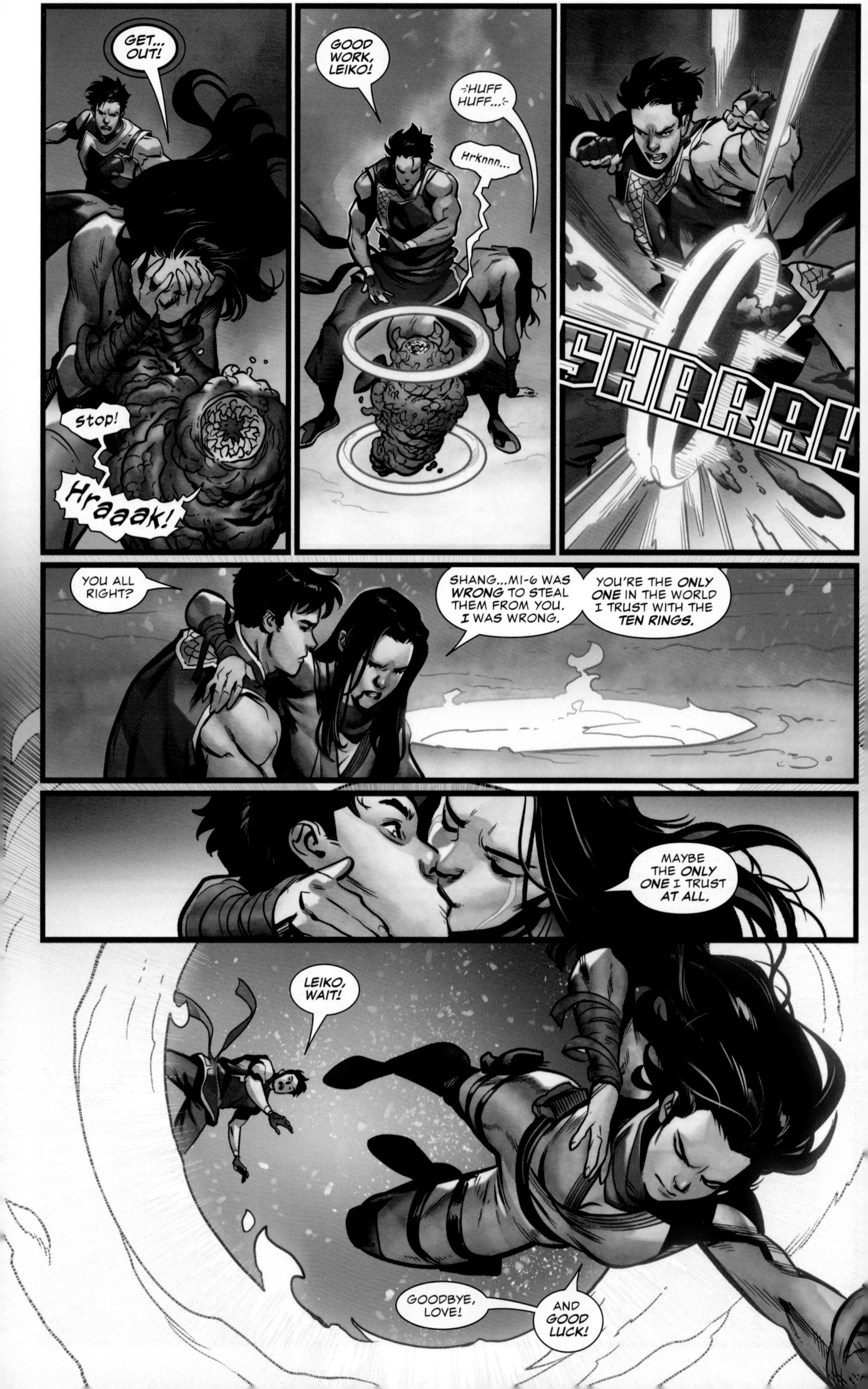
GET... OUT!
stop!
Hraaak!
GOOD WORK, LEIKO!
HUFF HUFF...
Hrknnn...
SHARRAK
YOU ALL RIGHT?
SHANG...MI-6 WAS WRONG TO STEAL THEM FROM YOU. I WAS WRONG.
YOU'RE THE ONLY ONE IN THE WORLD I TRUST WITH THE TEN RINGS.
MAYBE THE ONLY ONE I TRUST AT ALL.
LEIKO, WAIT!
GOODBYE, LOVE!
AND GOOD LUCK!

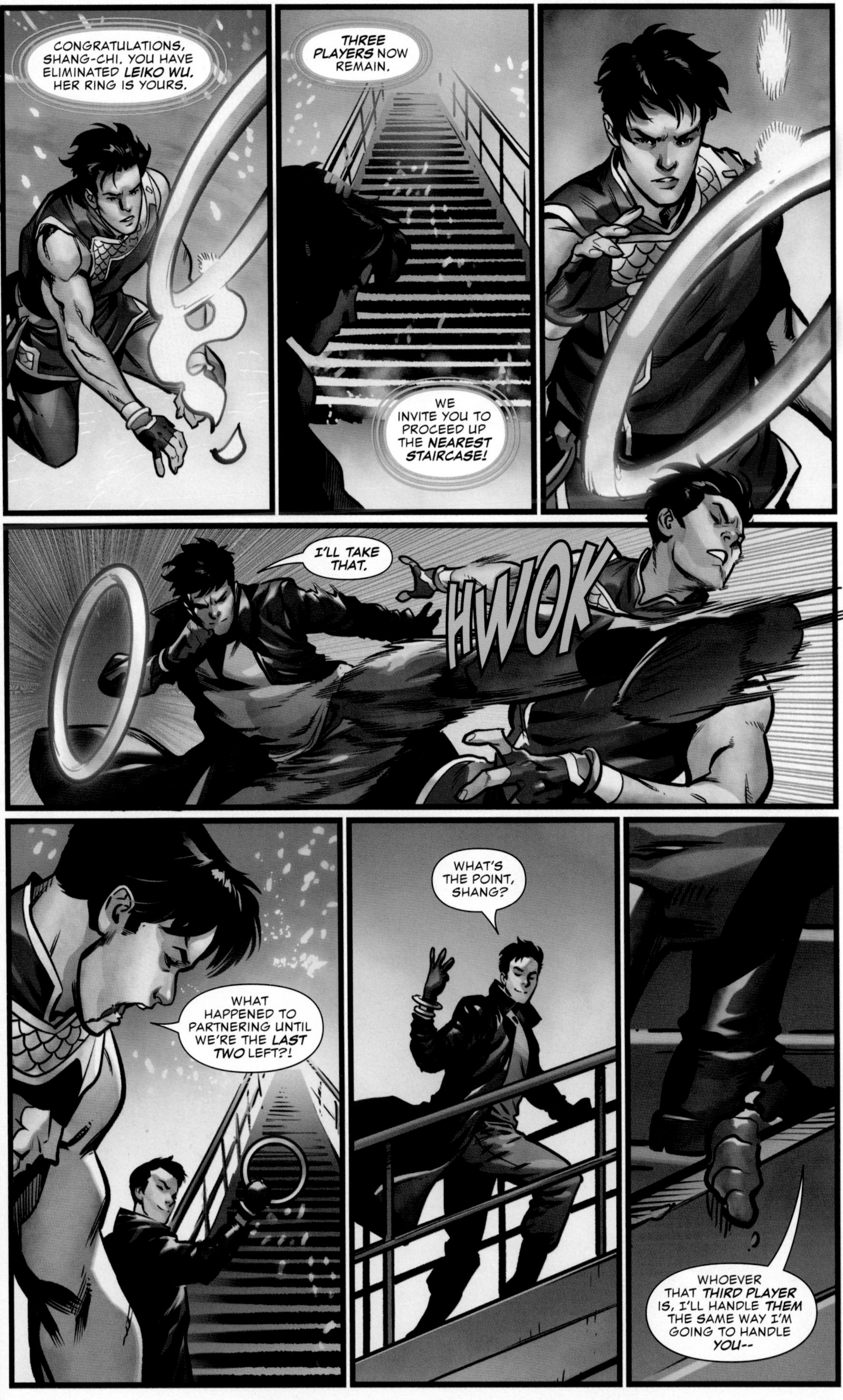
CONGRATULATIONS, SHANG-CHI. YOU HAVE ELIMINATED LEIKO WU. HER RING IS YOURS.
THREE PLAYERS NOW REMAIN.
WE INVITE YOU TO PROCEED UP THE NEAREST STAIRCASE!
I'LL TAKE THAT.
HWOK
WHAT HAPPENED TO PARTNERING UNTIL WE'RE THE LAST TWO LEFT?!
WHAT'S THE POINT, SHANG?
WHOEVER THAT THIRD PLAYER IS, I'LL HANDLE THEM THE SAME WAY I'M GOING TO HANDLE YOU--

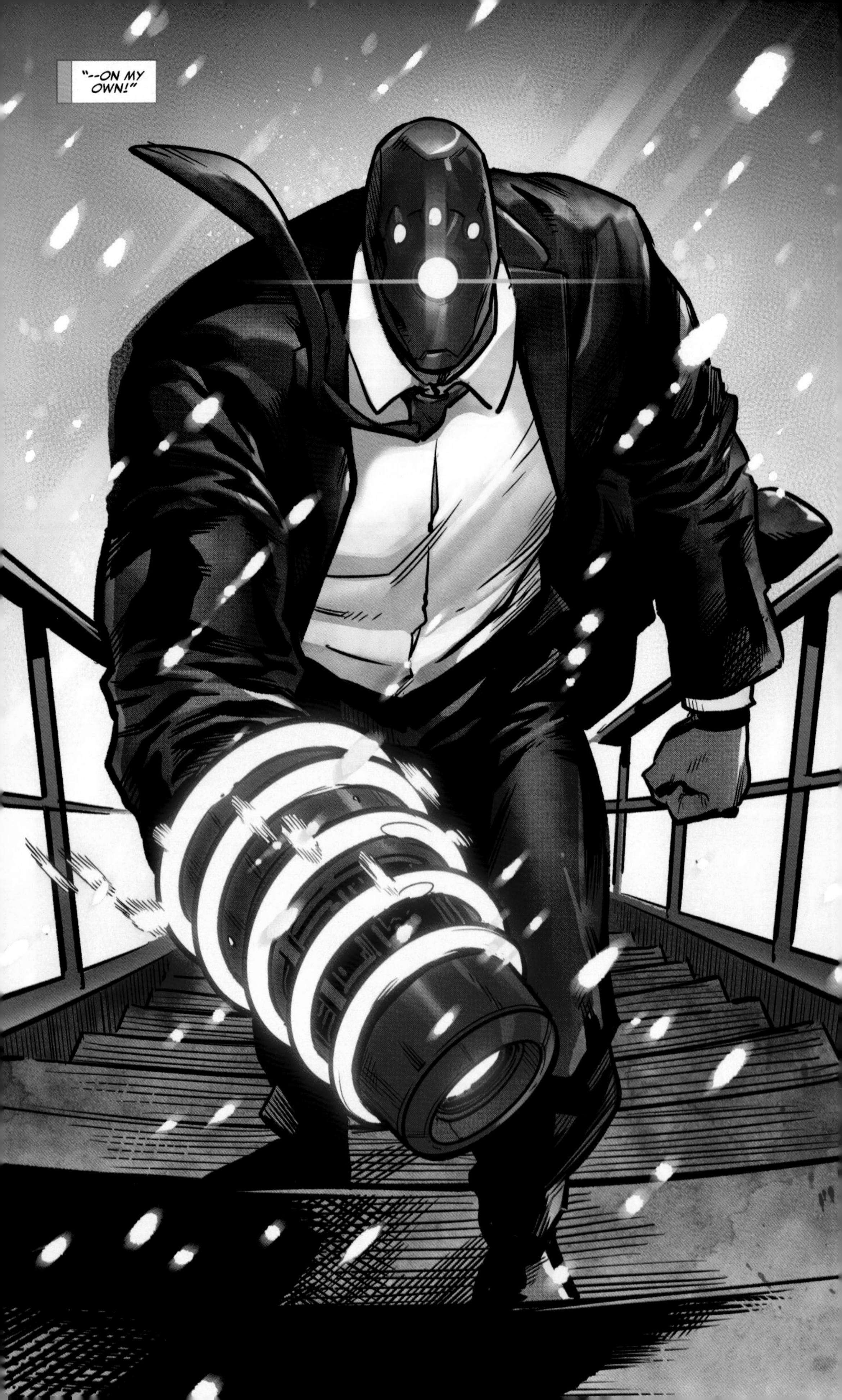
"--ON MY OWN!"

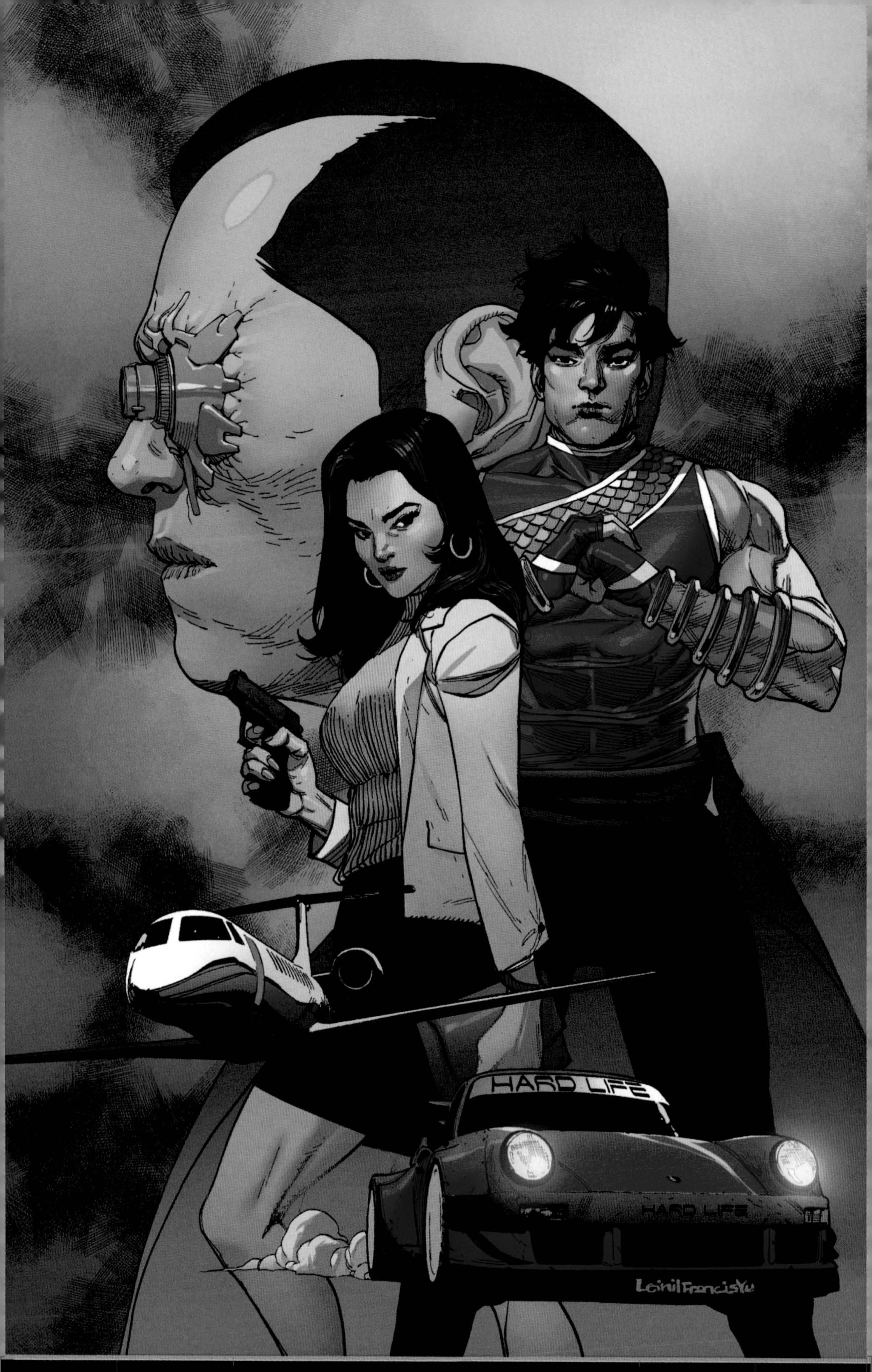
HARD LIFE
HARD LIFE
LeinilFrancisYu

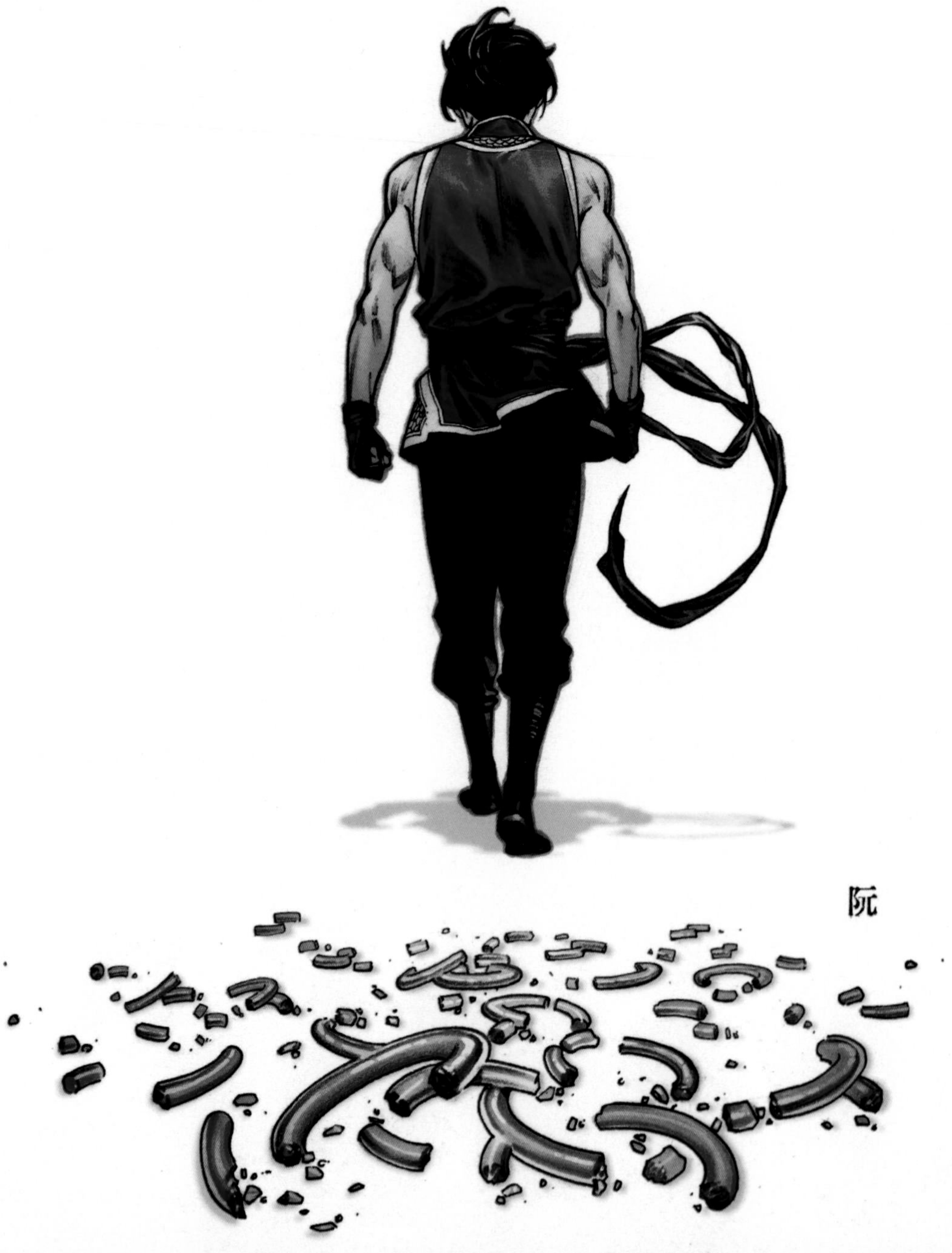
阮

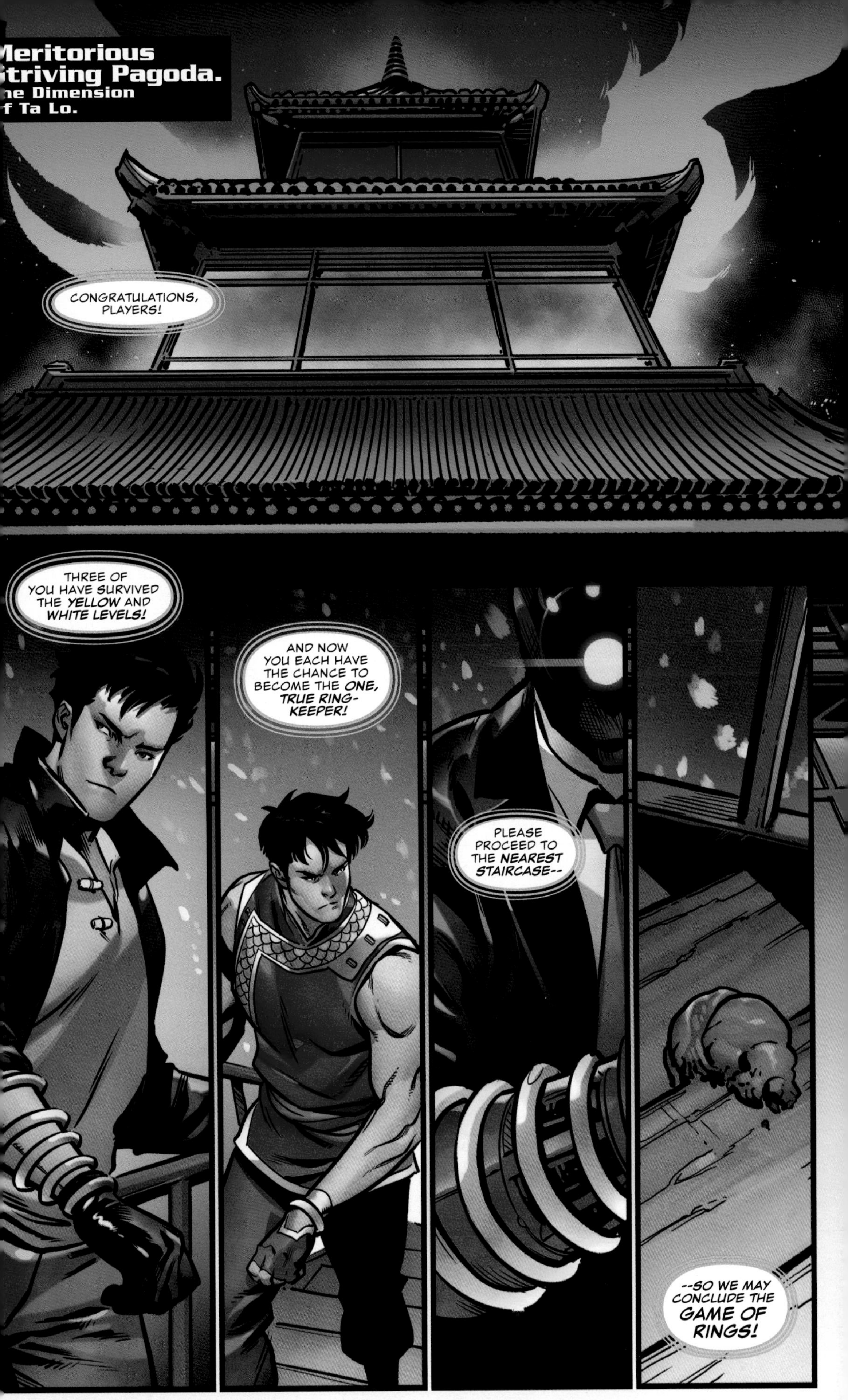

Meritorious Striving Pagoda. The Dimension of Ta Lo.
CONGRATULATIONS, PLAYERS!
THREE OF YOU HAVE SURVIVED THE YELLOW AND WHITE LEVELS!
AND NOW YOU EACH HAVE THE CHANCE TO BECOME THE ONE, TRUE RING-KEEPER!
PLEASE PROCEED TO THE NEAREST STAIRCASE--
--SO WE MAY CONCLUDE THE GAME OF RINGS!

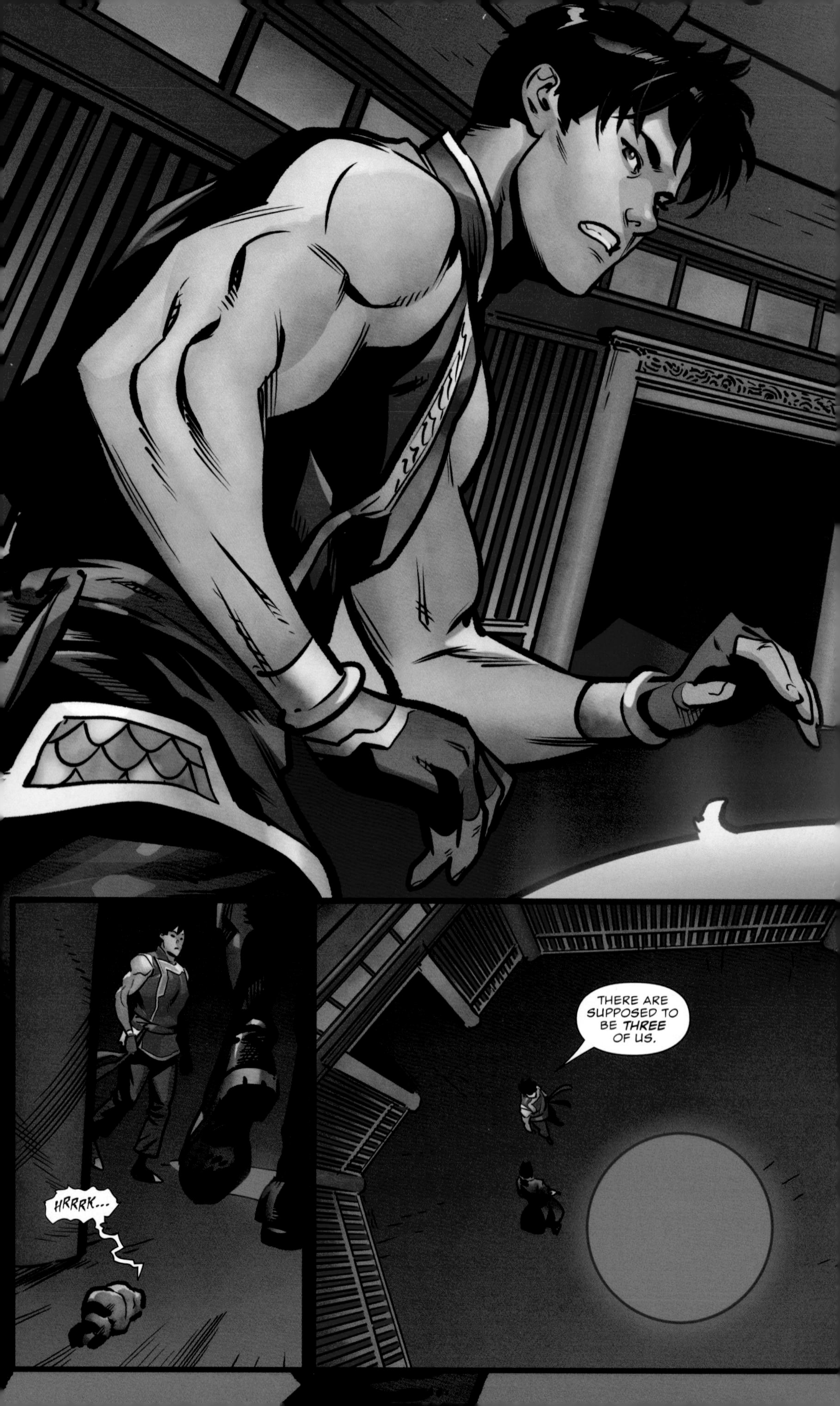
HRRRK...
THERE ARE SUPPOSED TO BE THREE OF US.

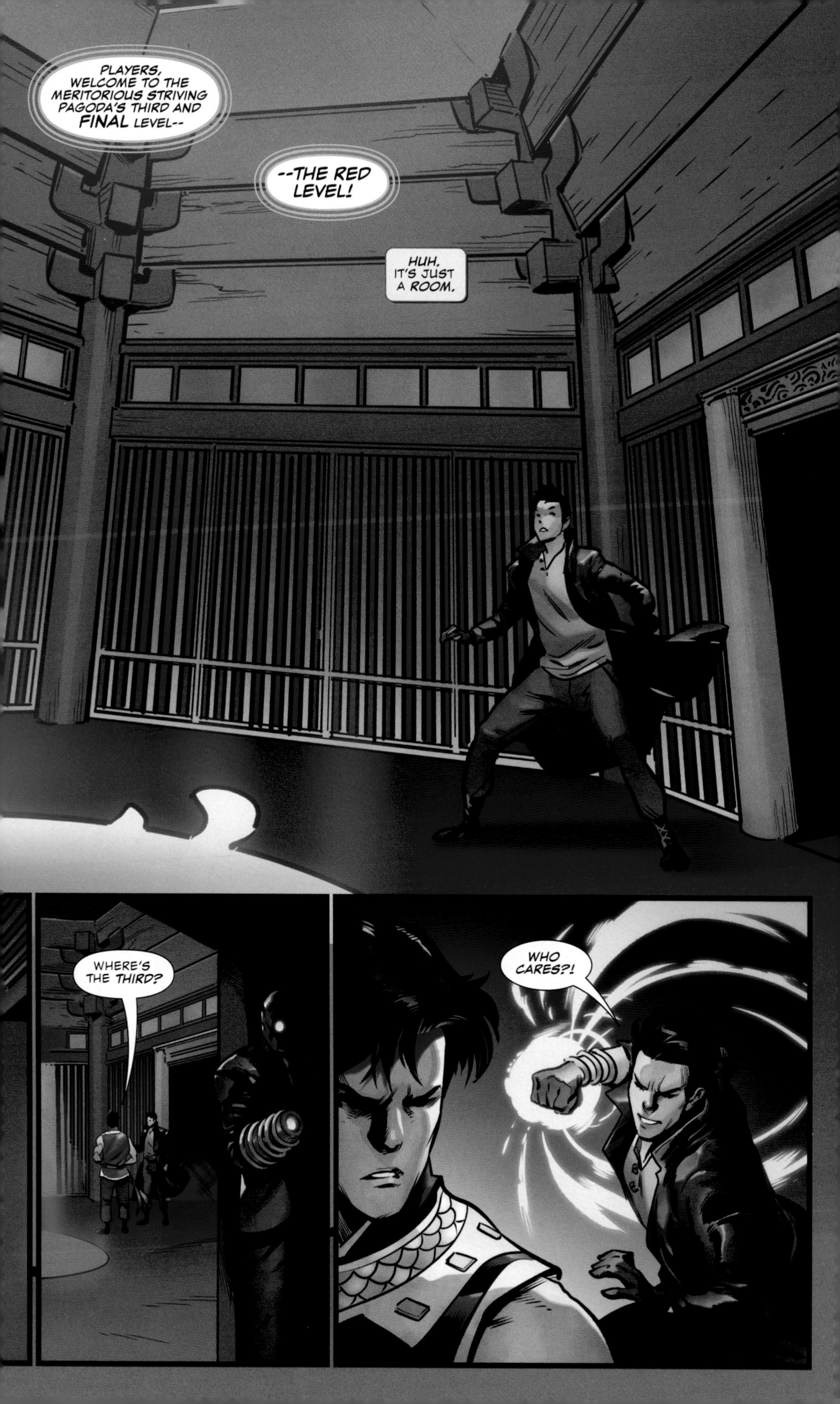
PLAYERS, WELCOME TO THE MERITORIOUS STRIVING PAGODA'S THIRD AND FINAL LEVEL--
--THE RED LEVEL!
HUH. IT'S JUST A ROOM.
WHERE'S THE THIRD?
WHO CARES?!

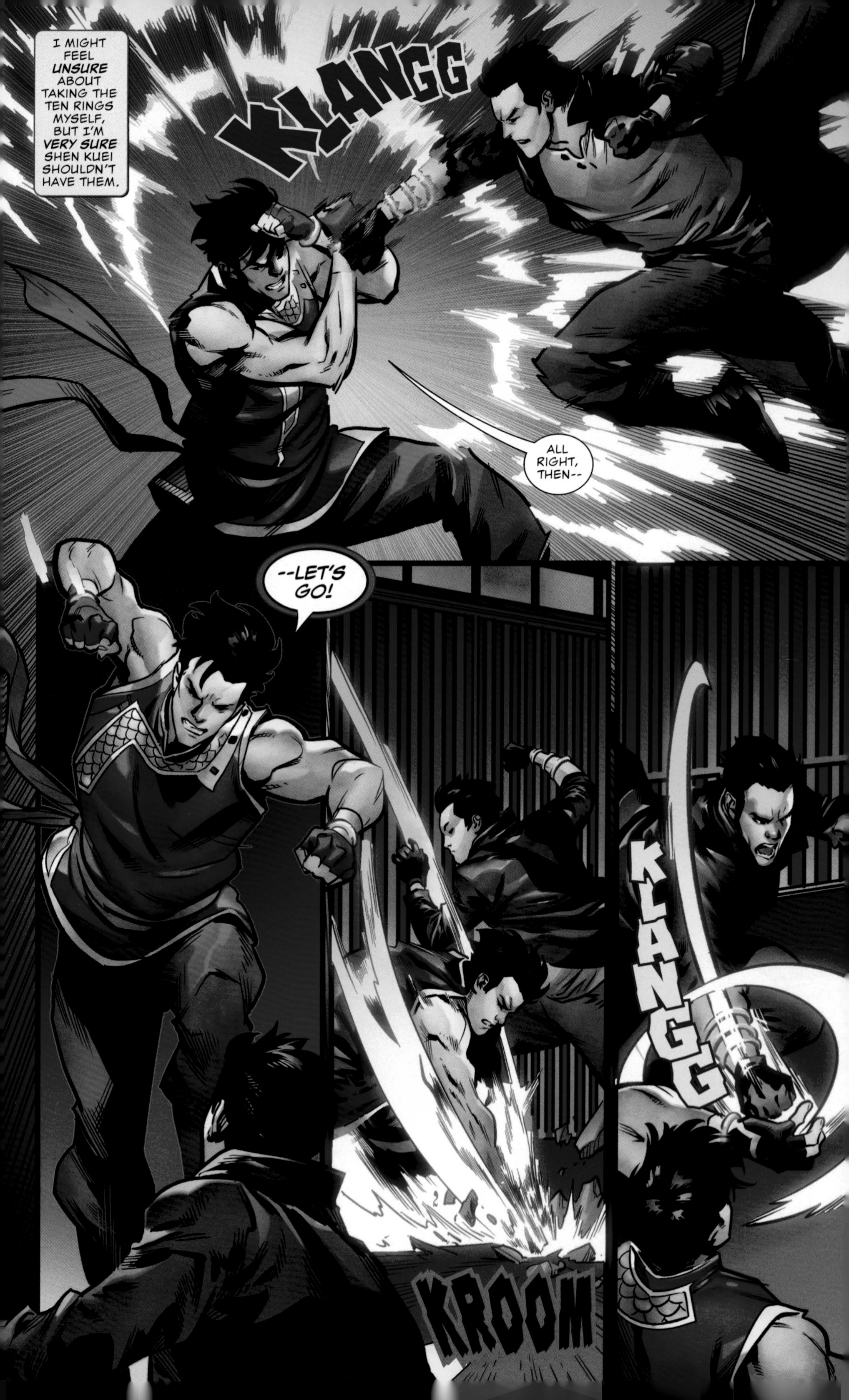
I MIGHT FEEL **UNSURE** ABOUT TAKING THE TEN RINGS MYSELF, BUT I'M **VERY SURE** SHEN KUEI SHOULDN'T HAVE THEM.
KLANGG
ALL RIGHT, THEN--
--LET'S GO!
KROOM
KLANGG

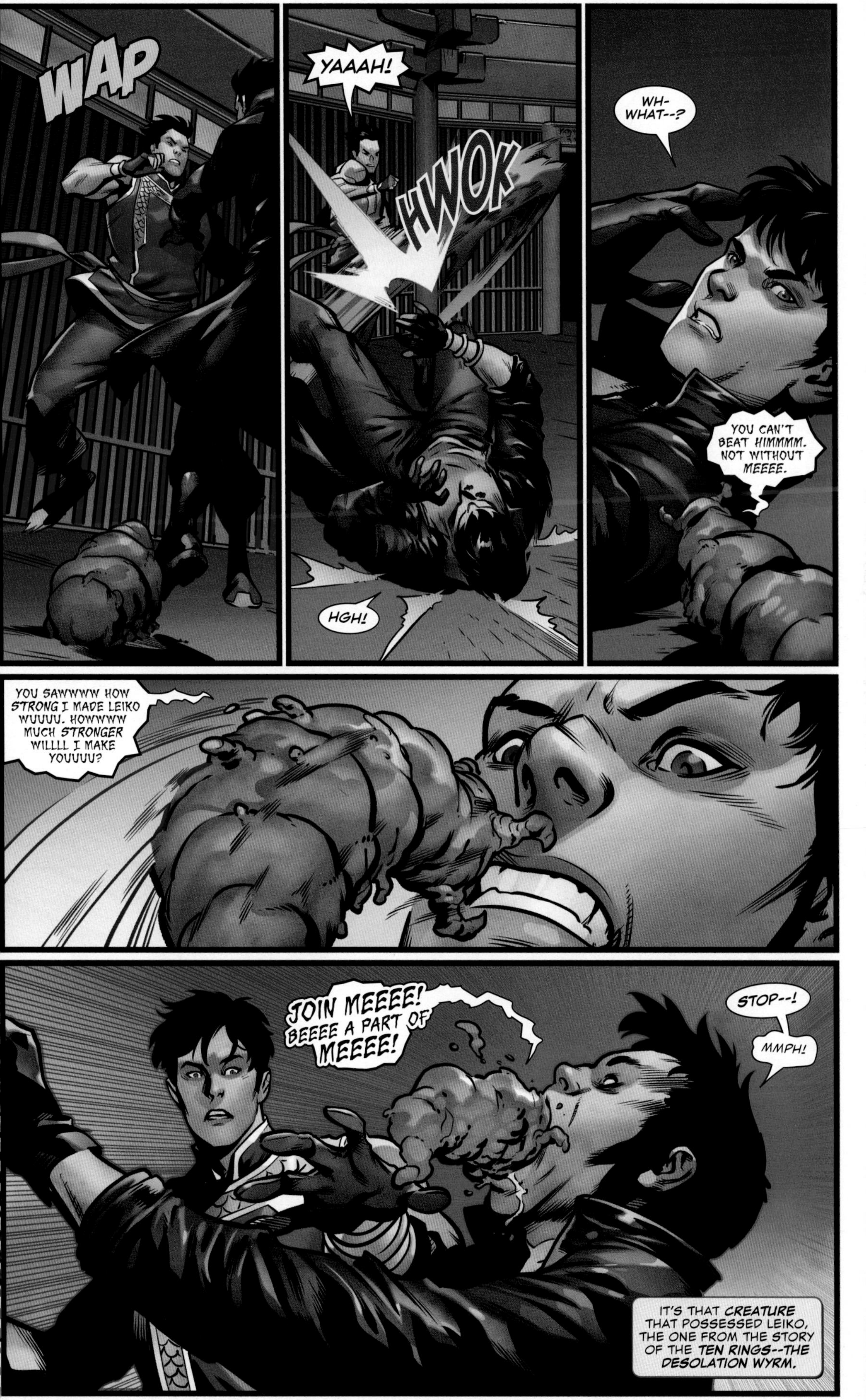

WAP
YAAAH!
HWOK
HGH!
WH- WHAT--?
YOU CAN'T BEAT HIMMMM. NOT WITHOUT MEEEE.
YOU SAWWWW HOW STRONG I MADE LEIKO WUUUU. HOWWWW MUCH STRONGER WILLLL I MAKE YOUUUU?
JOIN MEEEE! BEEEE A PART OF MEEEE!
STOP--!
MMPH!
IT'S THAT CREATURE THAT POSSESSED LEIKO, THE ONE FROM THE STORY OF THE TEN RINGS--THE DESOLATION WYRM.

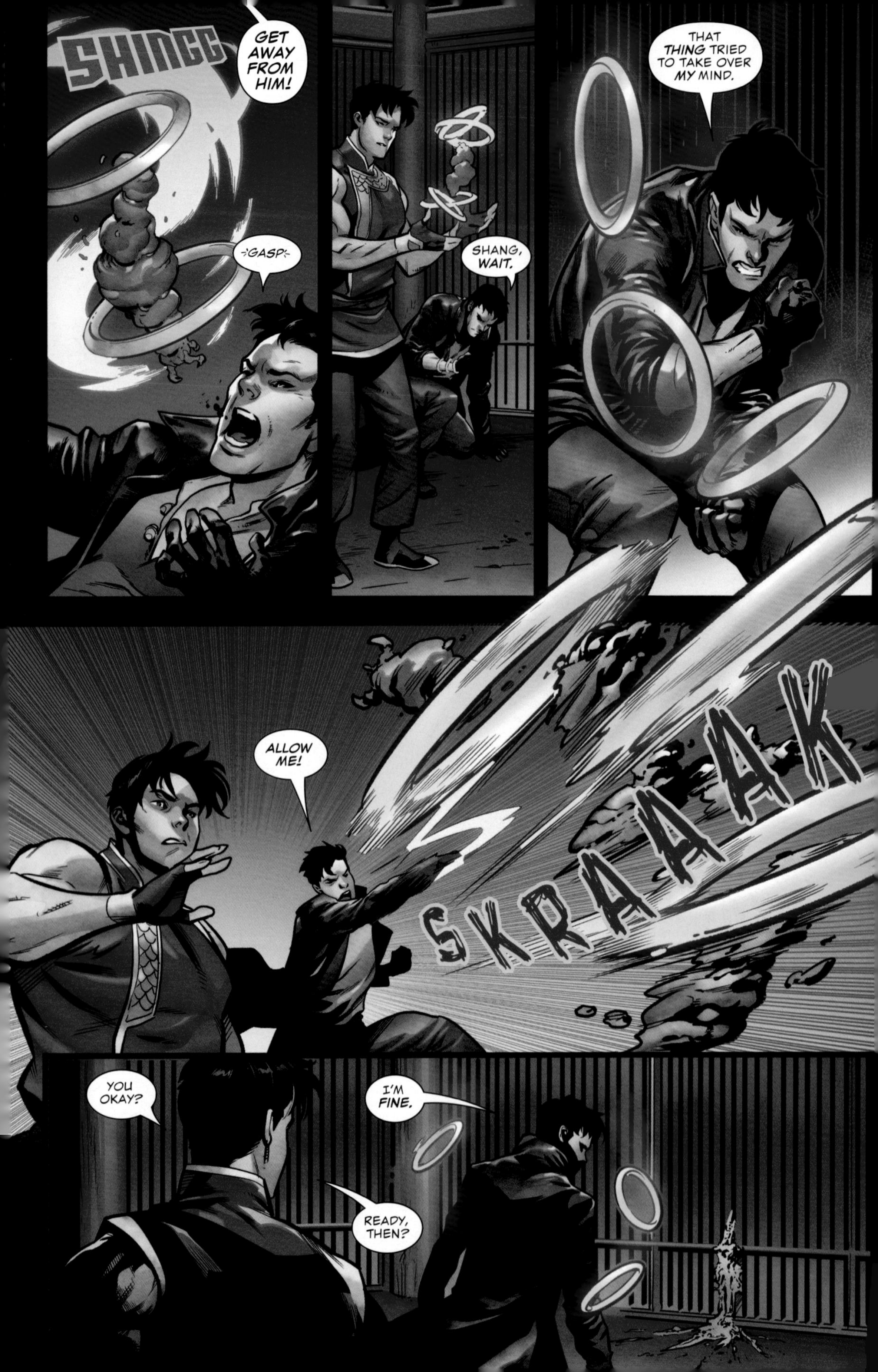
SHINGG
GET AWAY FROM HIM!
GASP
SHANG, WAIT.
THAT THING TRIED TO TAKE OVER MY MIND.
ALLOW ME!
SKRAAAAK
YOU OKAY?
I'M FINE.
READY, THEN?

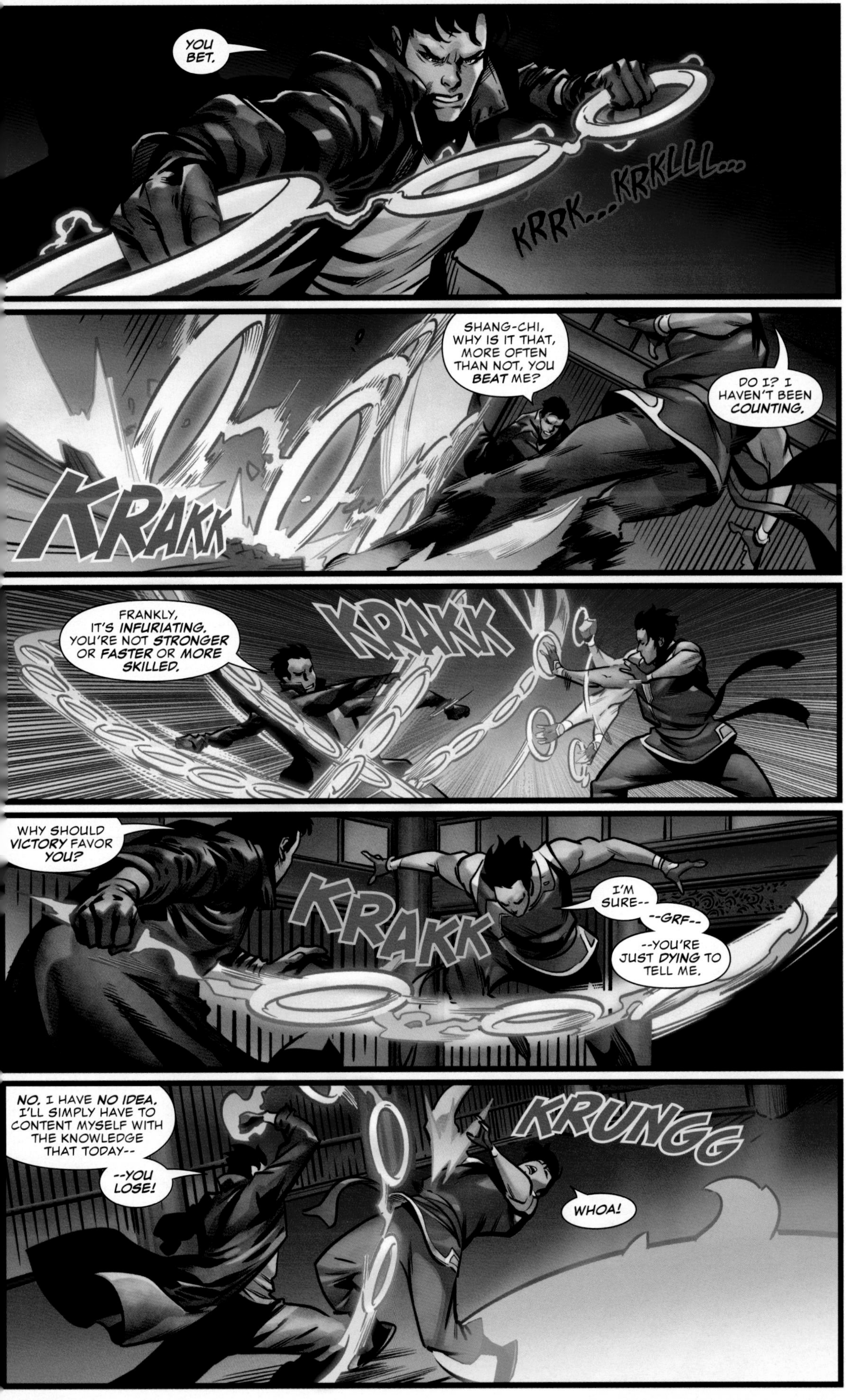
YOU BET.
KRRK...KRKLLL...
SHANG-CHI, WHY IS IT THAT, MORE OFTEN THAN NOT, YOU BEAT ME?
DO I? I HAVEN'T BEEN COUNTING.
KRAKK
FRANKLY, IT'S INFURIATING. YOU'RE NOT STRONGER OR FASTER OR MORE SKILLED.
KRAKK
WHY SHOULD VICTORY FAVOR YOU?
KRAKK
I'M SURE--
--GRF--
--YOU'RE JUST DYING TO TELL ME.
NO. I HAVE NO IDEA. I'LL SIMPLY HAVE TO CONTENT MYSELF WITH THE KNOWLEDGE THAT TODAY--
--YOU LOSE!
KRUNGG
WHOA!

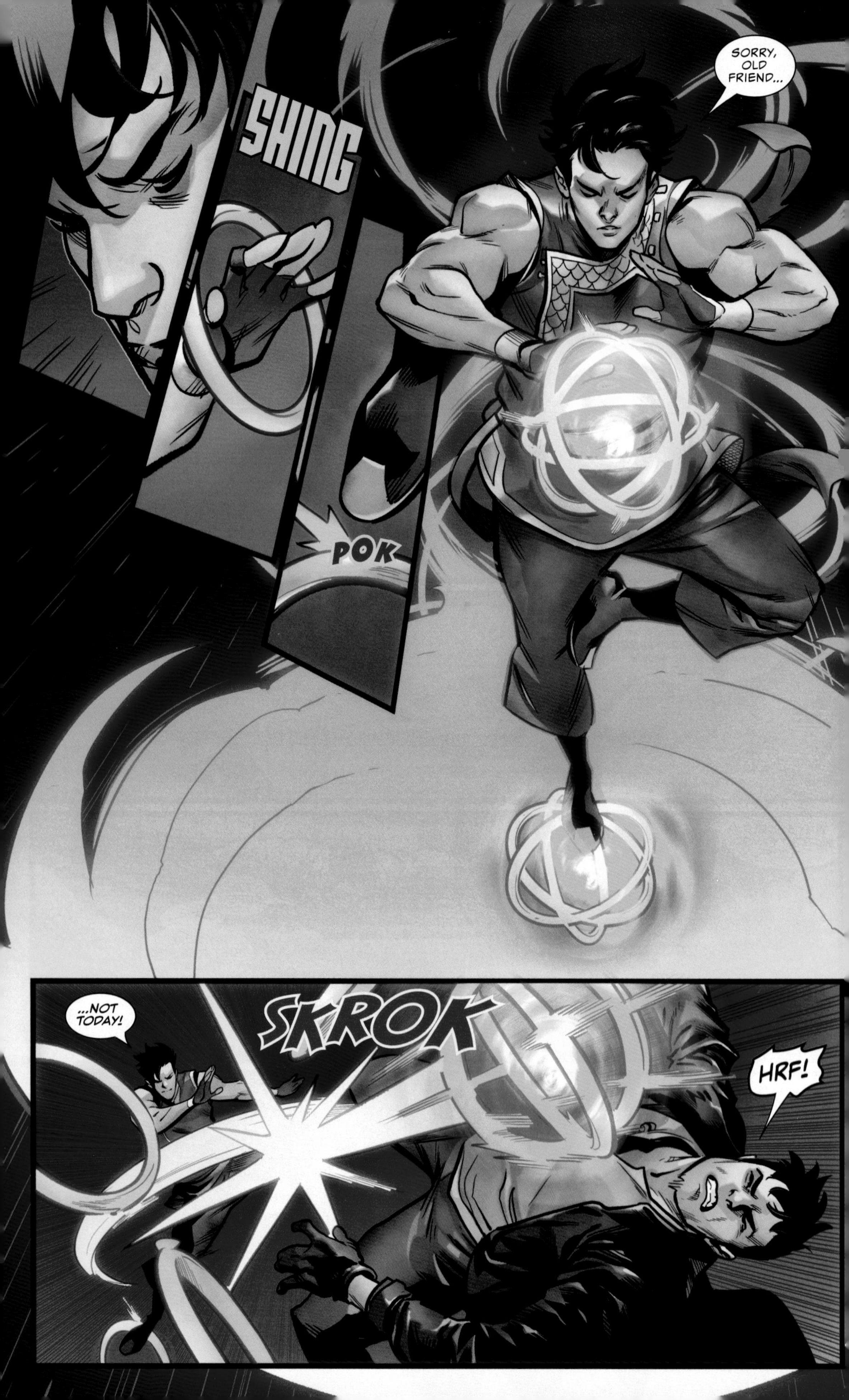
SHING
SORRY, OLD FRIEND...
POK
...NOT TODAY!
SKROK
HRF!

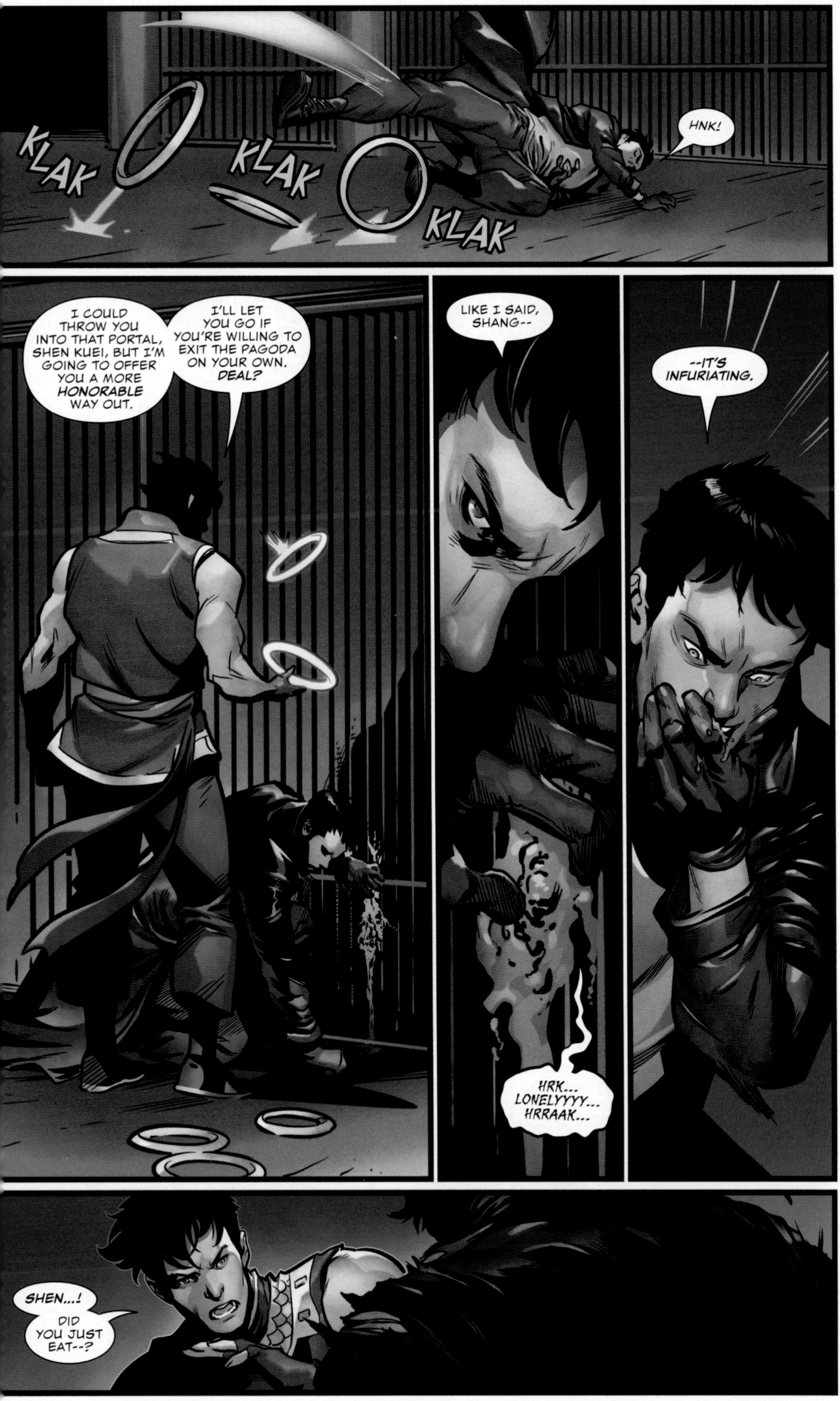

KLAK
KLAK
KLAK
HNK!
I COULD THROW YOU INTO THAT PORTAL, SHEN KUEI, BUT I'M GOING TO OFFER YOU A MORE HONORABLE WAY OUT.
I'LL LET YOU GO IF YOU'RE WILLING TO EXIT THE PAGODA ON YOUR OWN. DEAL?
LIKE I SAID, SHANG--
HRK... LONELYYYY... HRRAAK...
--IT'S INFURIATING.
SHEN...! DID YOU JUST EAT--?

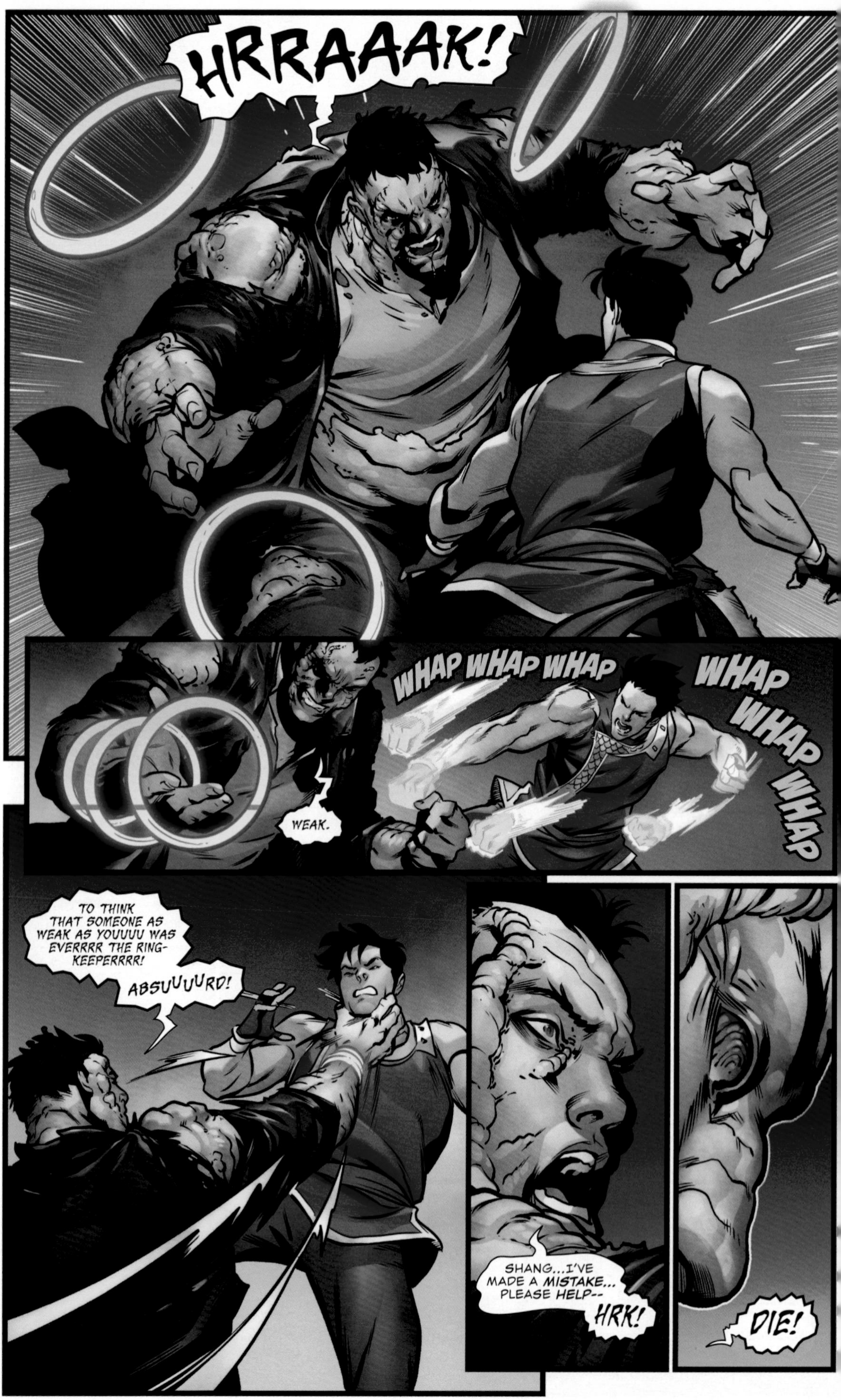
HRRAAAK!
WHAP WHAP WHAP
WHAP WHAP WHAP WHAP
WEAK.
TO THINK THAT SOMEONE AS WEAK AS YOUUUU WAS EVERRRR THE RING-KEEPERRRR!
ABSUUUURD!
SHANG...I'VE MADE A MISTAKE... PLEASE HELP--
HRK!
DIE!

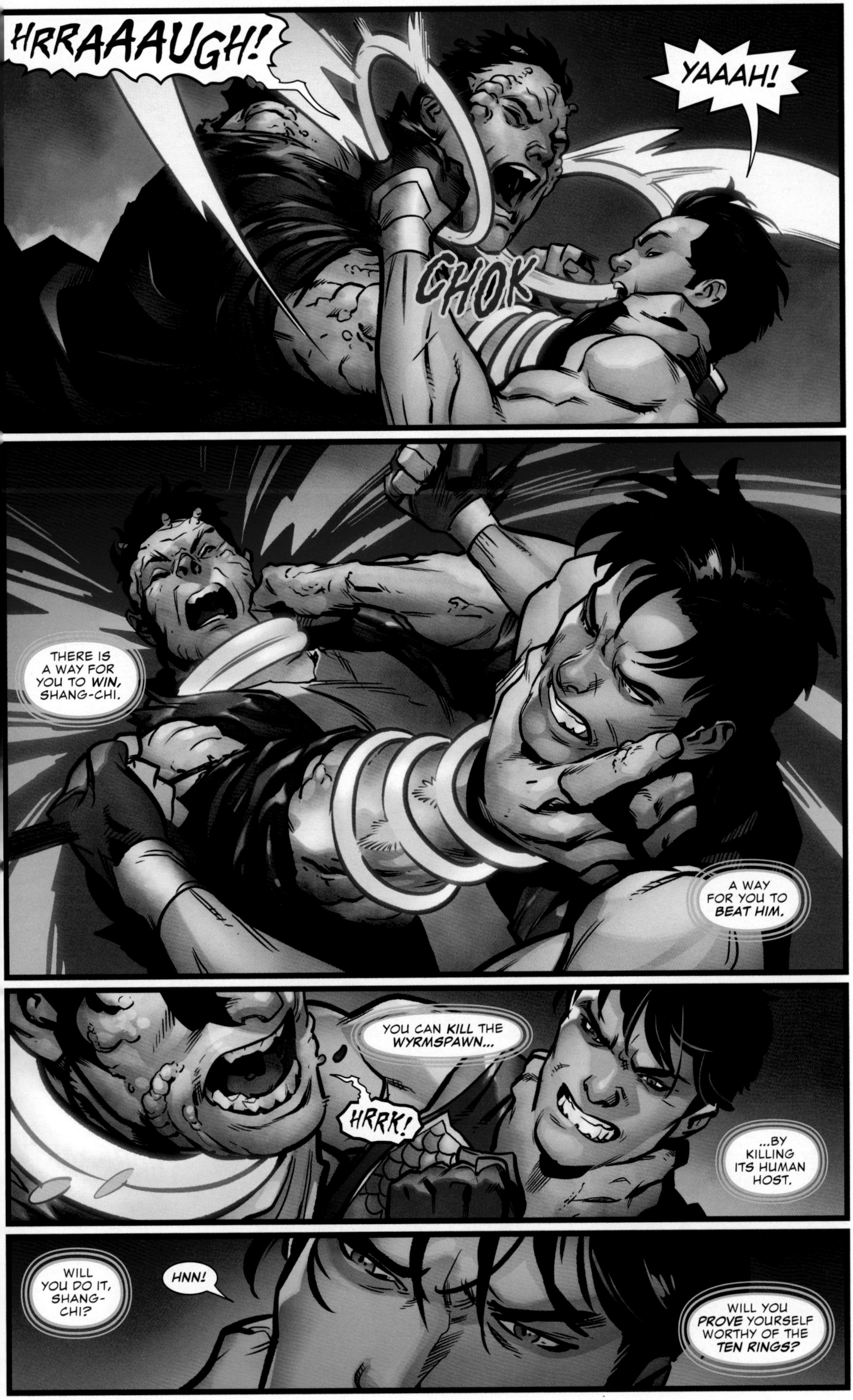
HRRAAAUGH!
YAAAH!
CHOK
THERE IS A WAY FOR YOU TO WIN, SHANG-CHI.
A WAY FOR YOU TO BEAT HIM.
YOU CAN KILL THE WYRMSPAWN...
HRRK!
...BY KILLING ITS HUMAN HOST.
WILL YOU DO IT, SHANG-CHI?
HNN!
WILL YOU PROVE YOURSELF WORTHY OF THE TEN RINGS?

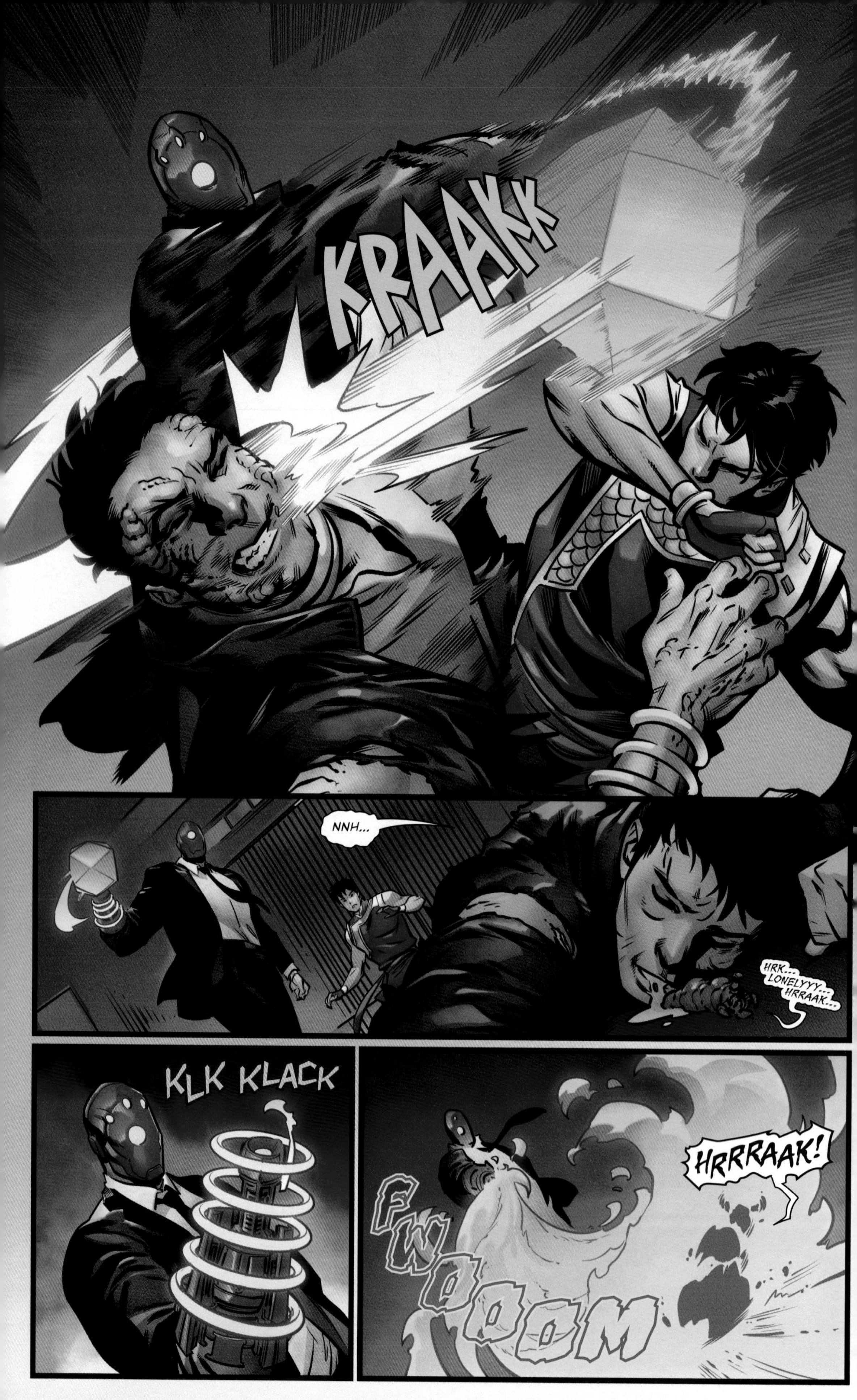
KRAAKK
NNH...
HRK... LONELYYY... HRRAAK...
KLK KLACK
HRRRAAK!
FWOOOOM

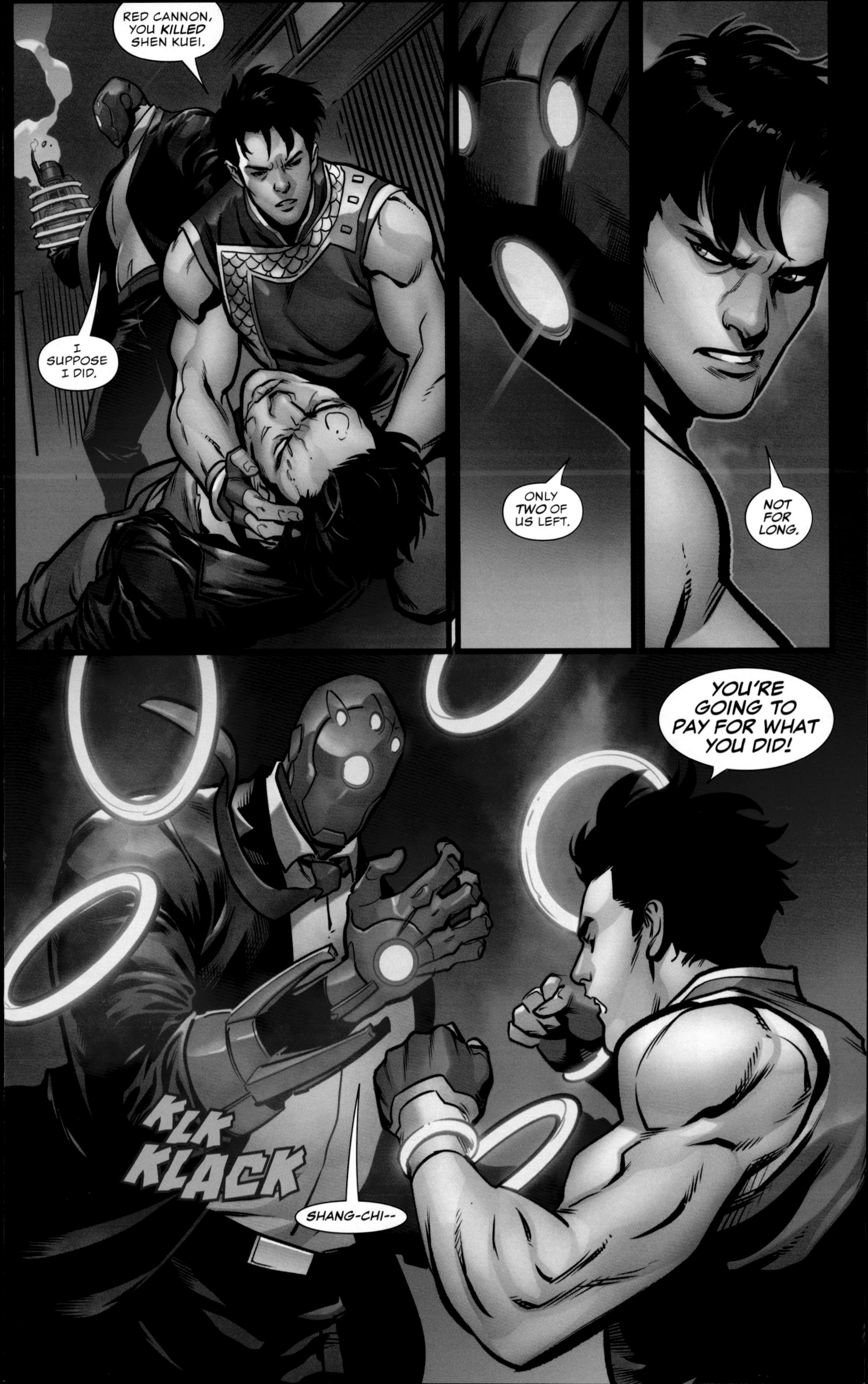
RED CANNON, YOU KILLED SHEN KUEI.
I SUPPOSE I DID.
ONLY TWO OF US LEFT.
NOT FOR LONG.
YOU'RE GOING TO PAY FOR WHAT YOU DID!
KLK KLACK
SHANG-CHI--

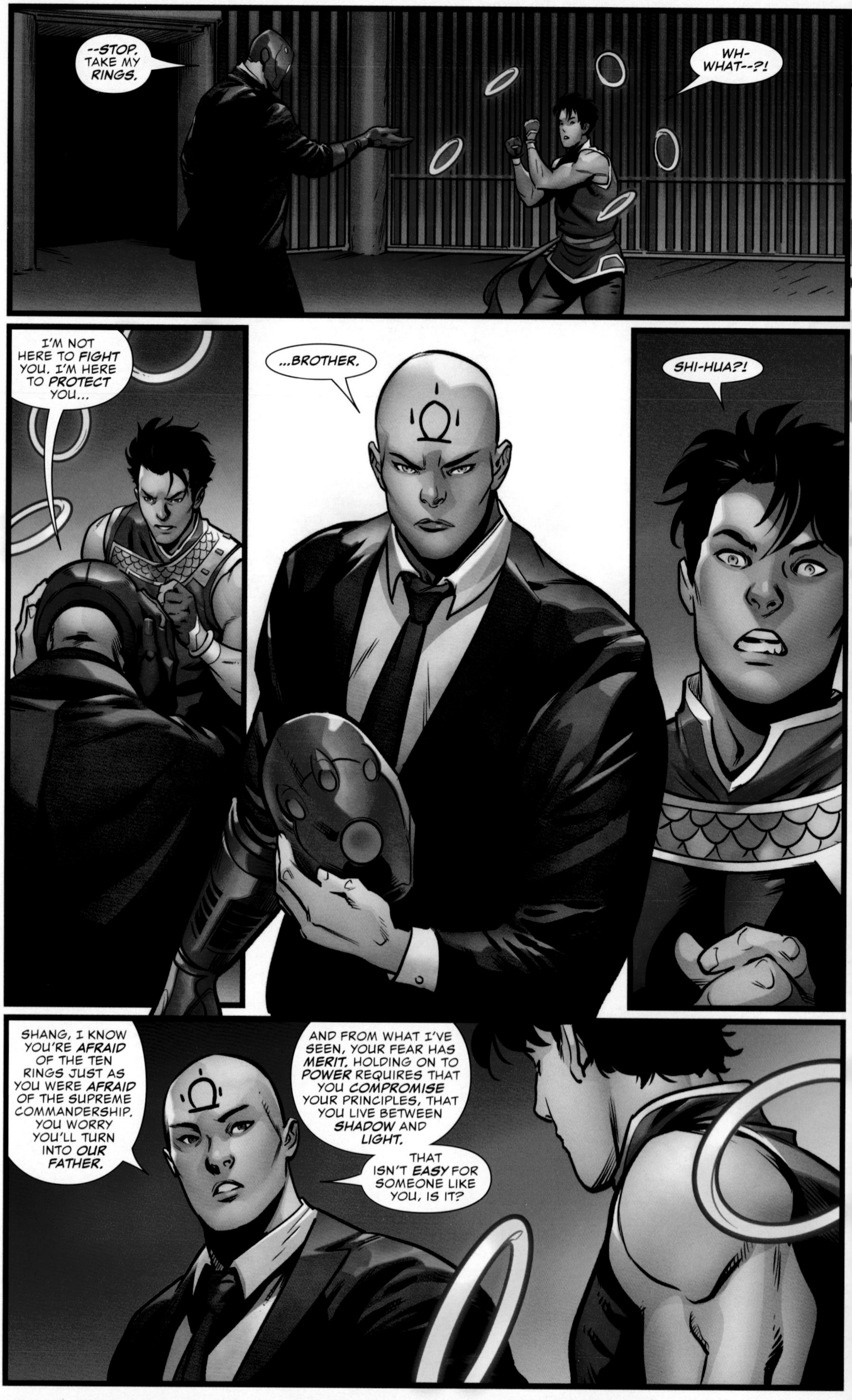
--STOP. TAKE MY RINGS.
WH- WHAT--?!
I'M NOT HERE TO FIGHT YOU. I'M HERE TO PROTECT YOU...
...BROTHER.
SHI-HUA?!
SHANG, I KNOW YOU'RE AFRAID OF THE TEN RINGS JUST AS YOU WERE AFRAID OF THE SUPREME COMMANDERSHIP. YOU WORRY YOU'LL TURN INTO OUR FATHER.
AND FROM WHAT I'VE SEEN, YOUR FEAR HAS MERIT. HOLDING ON TO POWER REQUIRES THAT YOU COMPROMISE YOUR PRINCIPLES, THAT YOU LIVE BETWEEN SHADOW AND LIGHT.
THAT ISN'T EASY FOR SOMEONE LIKE YOU, IS IT?

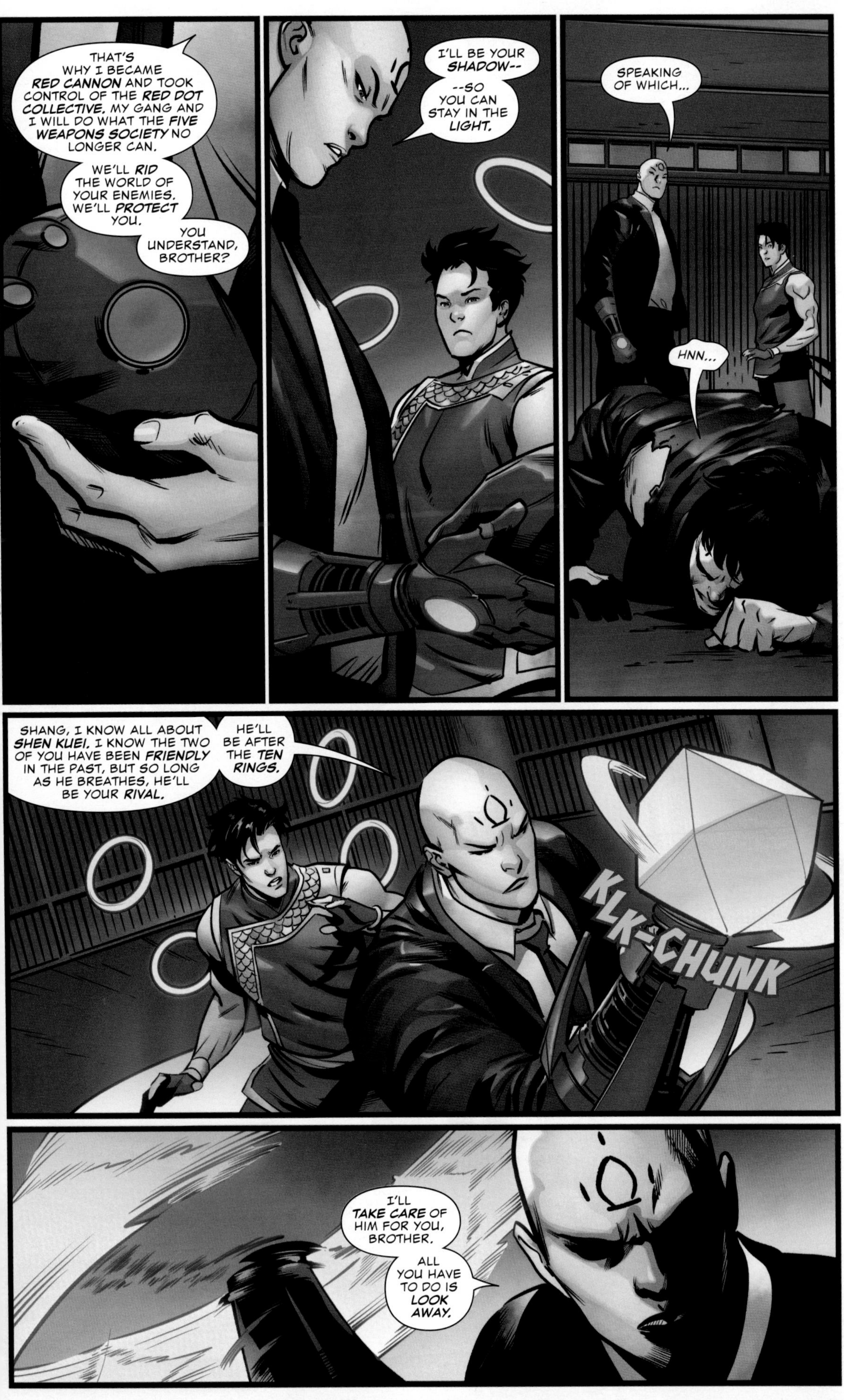
THAT'S WHY I BECAME RED CANNON AND TOOK CONTROL OF THE RED DOT COLLECTIVE. MY GANG AND I WILL DO WHAT THE FIVE WEAPONS SOCIETY NO LONGER CAN.
WE'LL RID THE WORLD OF YOUR ENEMIES. WE'LL PROTECT YOU.
YOU UNDERSTAND, BROTHER?
I'LL BE YOUR SHADOW--
--SO YOU CAN STAY IN THE LIGHT.
SPEAKING OF WHICH...
HNN...
SHANG, I KNOW ALL ABOUT SHEN KUEI. I KNOW THE TWO OF YOU HAVE BEEN FRIENDLY IN THE PAST, BUT SO LONG AS HE BREATHES, HE'LL BE YOUR RIVAL.
HE'LL BE AFTER THE TEN RINGS.
KLK-CHUNK
I'LL TAKE CARE OF HIM FOR YOU, BROTHER.
ALL YOU HAVE TO DO IS LOOK AWAY.

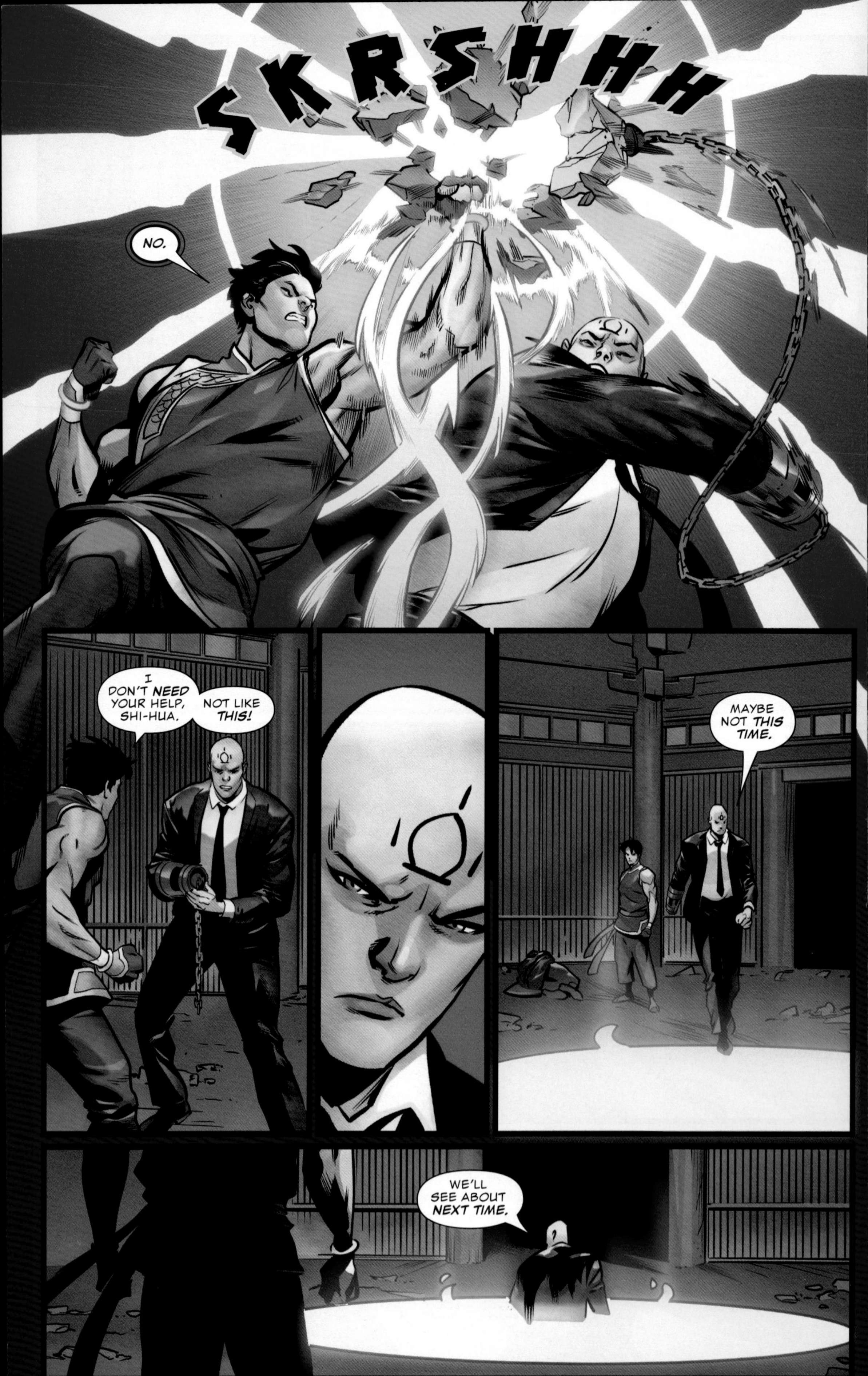
SKRSHHH
NO.
I DON'T NEED YOUR HELP, SHI-HUA.
NOT LIKE THIS!
MAYBE NOT THIS TIME.
WE'LL SEE ABOUT NEXT TIME.

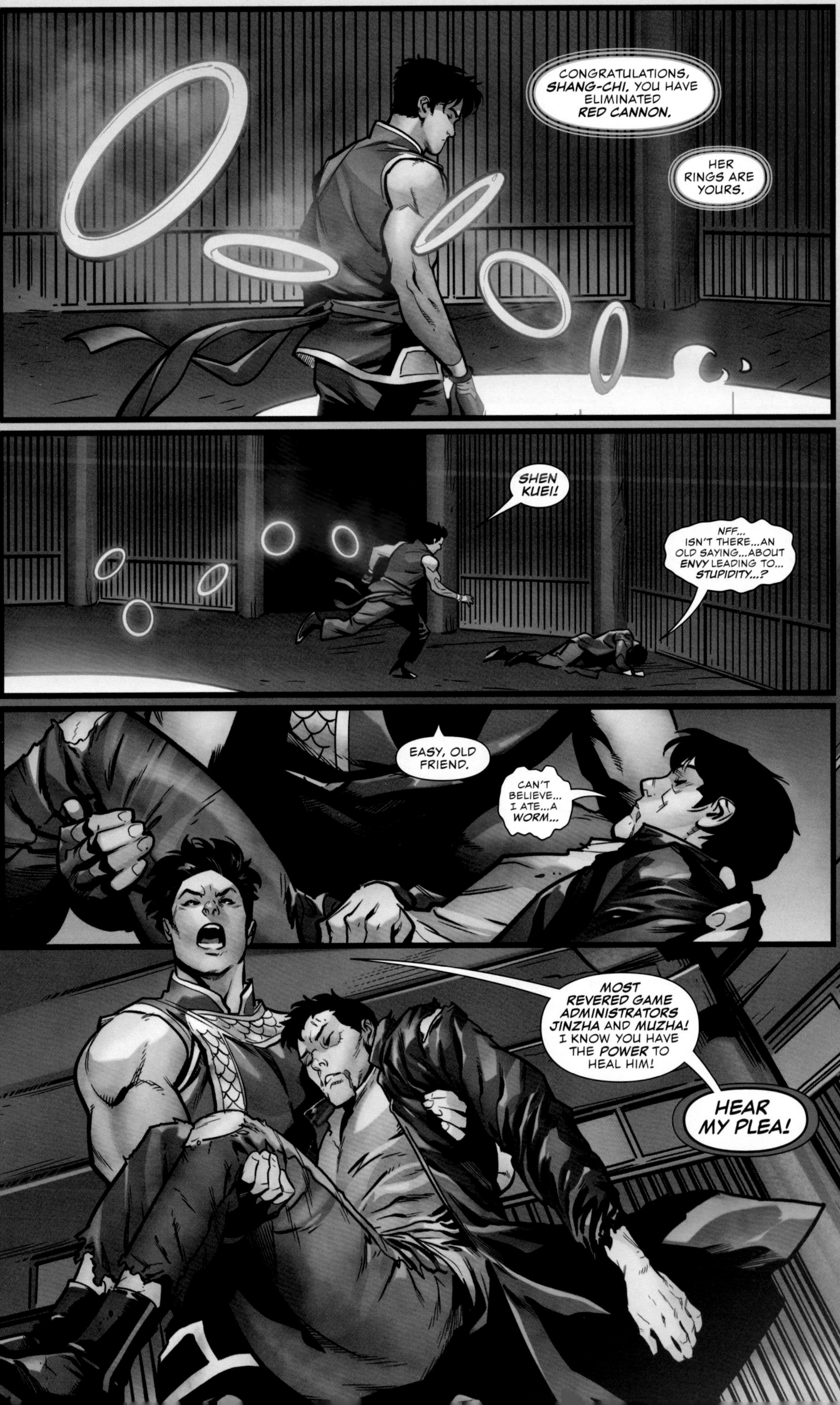
CONGRATULATIONS, SHANG-CHI. YOU HAVE ELIMINATED RED CANNON.
HER RINGS ARE YOURS.
SHEN KUEI!
NFF... ISN'T THERE...AN OLD SAYING...ABOUT ENVY LEADING TO... STUPIDITY...?
EASY, OLD FRIEND.
CAN'T BELIEVE... I ATE...A WORM...
MOST REVERED GAME ADMINISTRATORS JINZHA AND MUZHA! I KNOW YOU HAVE THE POWER TO HEAL HIM!
HEAR MY PLEA!

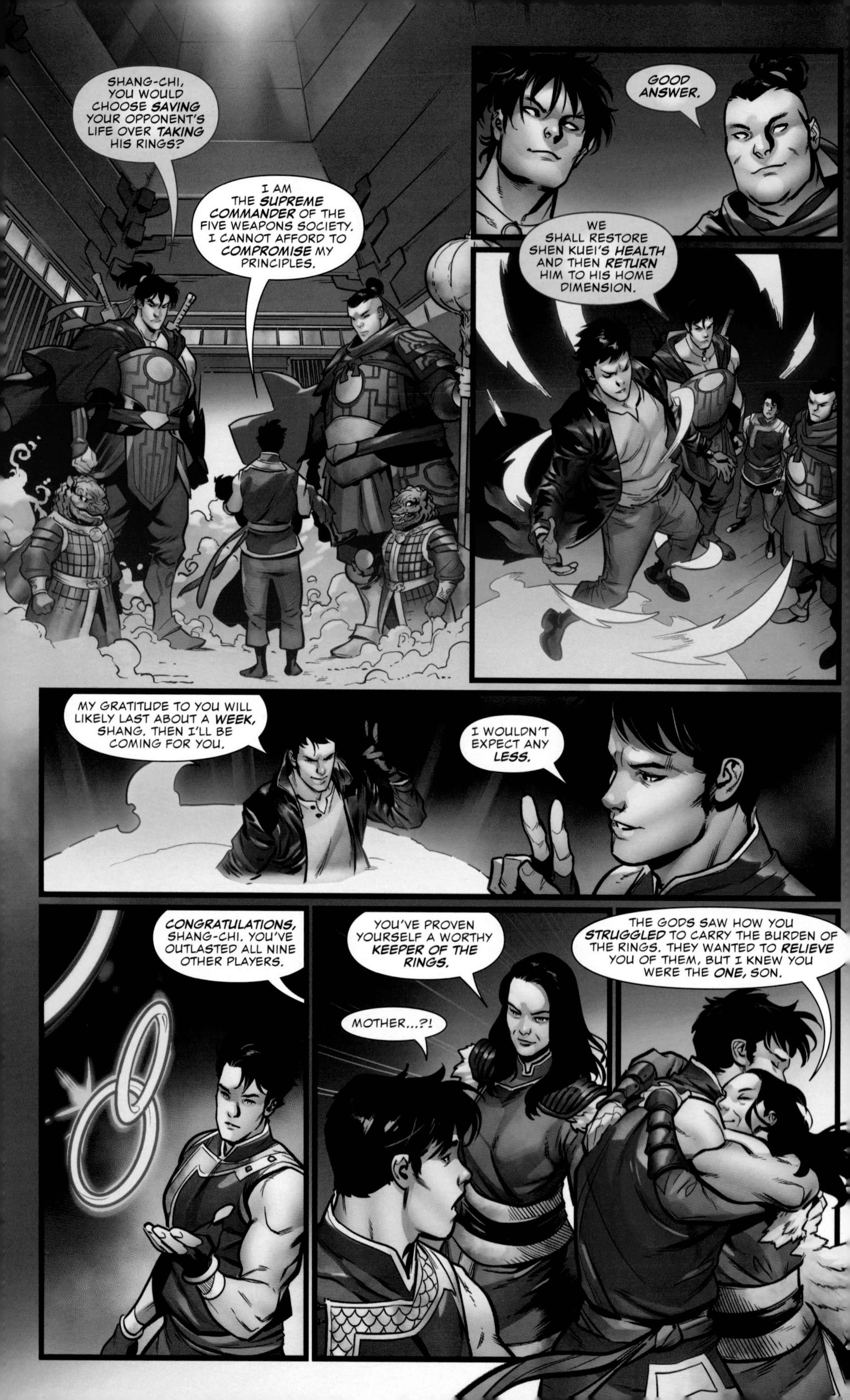
SHANG-CHI, YOU WOULD CHOOSE SAVING YOUR OPPONENT'S LIFE OVER TAKING HIS RINGS?
I AM THE SUPREME COMMANDER OF THE FIVE WEAPONS SOCIETY. I CANNOT AFFORD TO COMPROMISE MY PRINCIPLES.
GOOD ANSWER.
WE SHALL RESTORE SHEN KUEI'S HEALTH AND THEN RETURN HIM TO HIS HOME DIMENSION.
MY GRATITUDE TO YOU WILL LIKELY LAST ABOUT A WEEK, SHANG. THEN I'LL BE COMING FOR YOU.
I WOULDN'T EXPECT ANY LESS.
CONGRATULATIONS, SHANG-CHI. YOU'VE OUTLASTED ALL NINE OTHER PLAYERS.
YOU'VE PROVEN YOURSELF A WORTHY KEEPER OF THE RINGS.
MOTHER...?!
THE GODS SAW HOW YOU STRUGGLED TO CARRY THE BURDEN OF THE RINGS. THEY WANTED TO RELIEVE YOU OF THEM, BUT I KNEW YOU WERE THE ONE, SON.

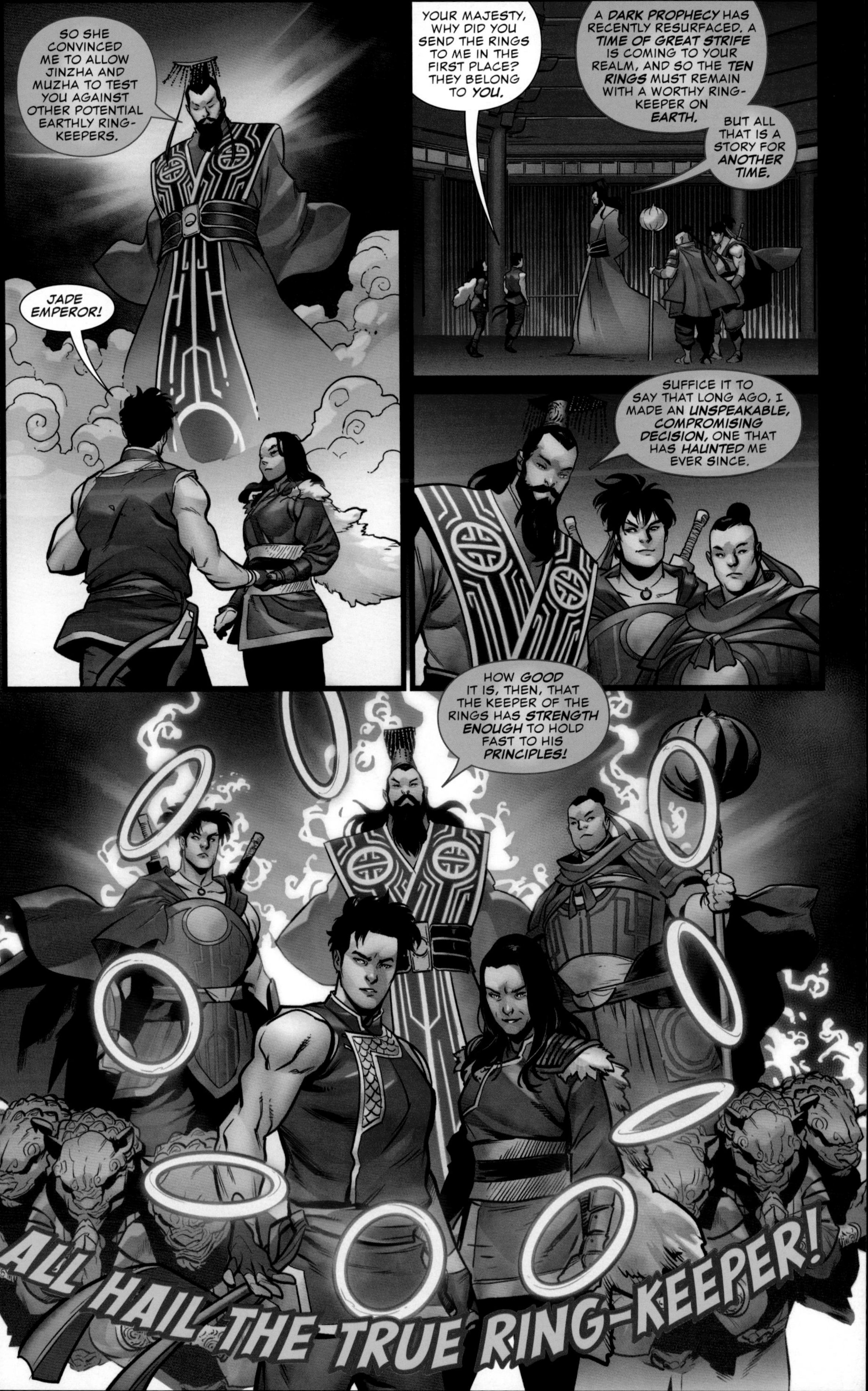
SO SHE CONVINCED ME TO ALLOW JINZHA AND MUZHA TO TEST YOU AGAINST OTHER POTENTIAL EARTHLY RING-KEEPERS.
JADE EMPEROR!
YOUR MAJESTY, WHY DID YOU SEND THE RINGS TO ME IN THE FIRST PLACE? THEY BELONG TO YOU.
A DARK PROPHECY HAS RECENTLY RESURFACED. A TIME OF GREAT STRIFE IS COMING TO YOUR REALM, AND SO THE TEN RINGS MUST REMAIN WITH A WORTHY RING-KEEPER ON EARTH.
BUT ALL THAT IS A STORY FOR ANOTHER TIME.
SUFFICE IT TO SAY THAT LONG AGO, I MADE AN UNSPEAKABLE, COMPROMISING DECISION, ONE THAT HAS HAUNTED ME EVER SINCE.
HOW GOOD IT IS, THEN, THAT THE KEEPER OF THE RINGS HAS STRENGTH ENOUGH TO HOLD FAST TO HIS PRINCIPLES!
ALL HAIL THE TRUE RING-KEEPER!

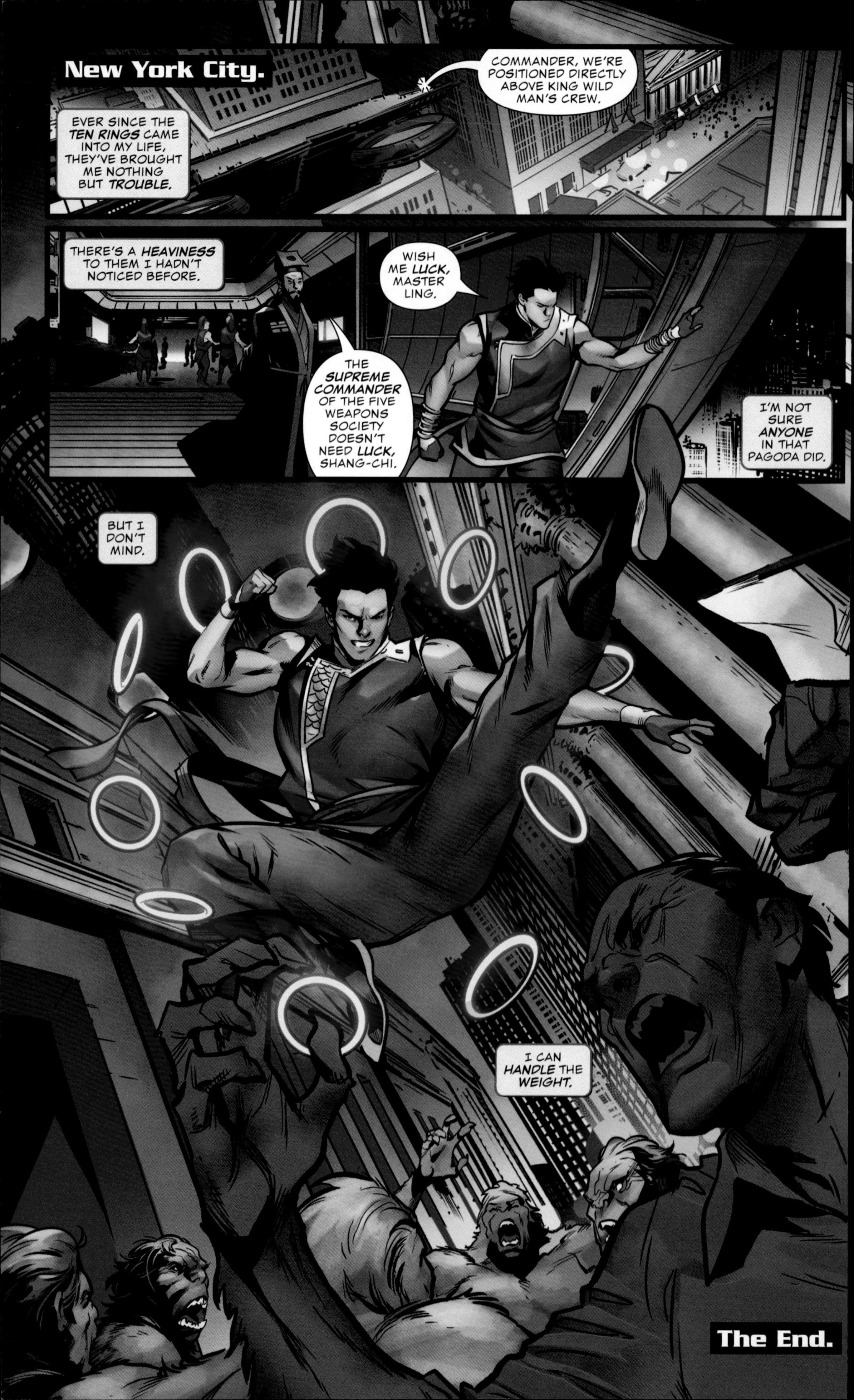
New York City.
EVER SINCE THE TEN RINGS CAME INTO MY LIFE, THEY'VE BROUGHT ME NOTHING BUT TROUBLE.
COMMANDER, WE'RE POSITIONED DIRECTLY ABOVE KING WILD MAN'S CREW.
THERE'S A HEAVINESS TO THEM I HADN'T NOTICED BEFORE.
WISH ME LUCK, MASTER LING.
THE SUPREME COMMANDER OF THE FIVE WEAPONS SOCIETY DOESN'T NEED LUCK, SHANG-CHI.
I'M NOT SURE ANYONE IN THAT PAGODA DID.
BUT I DON'T MIND.
I CAN HANDLE THE WEIGHT.
The End.

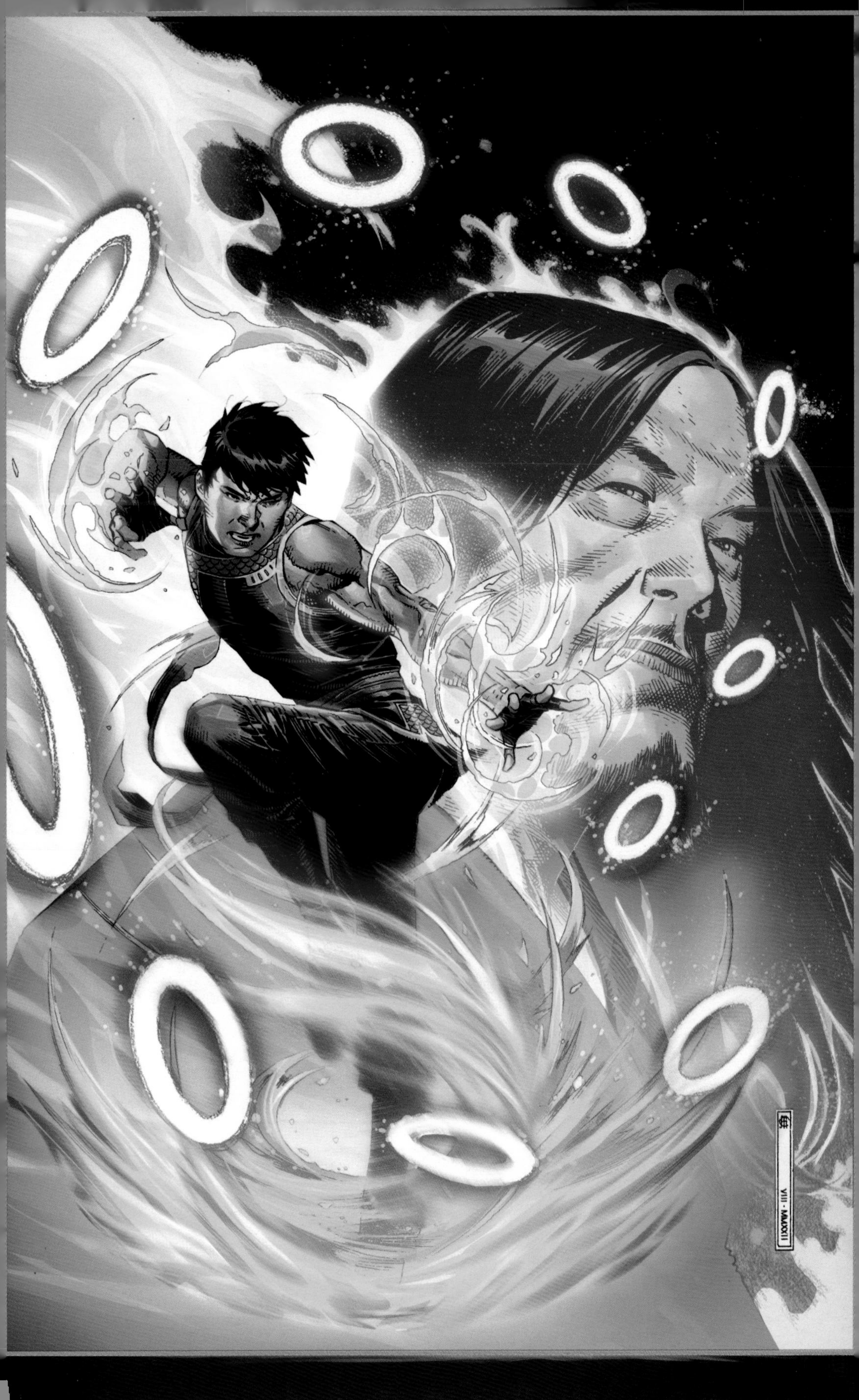
VIII - MMXXII

SHANG-CHI: MASTER OF THE TEN RINGS

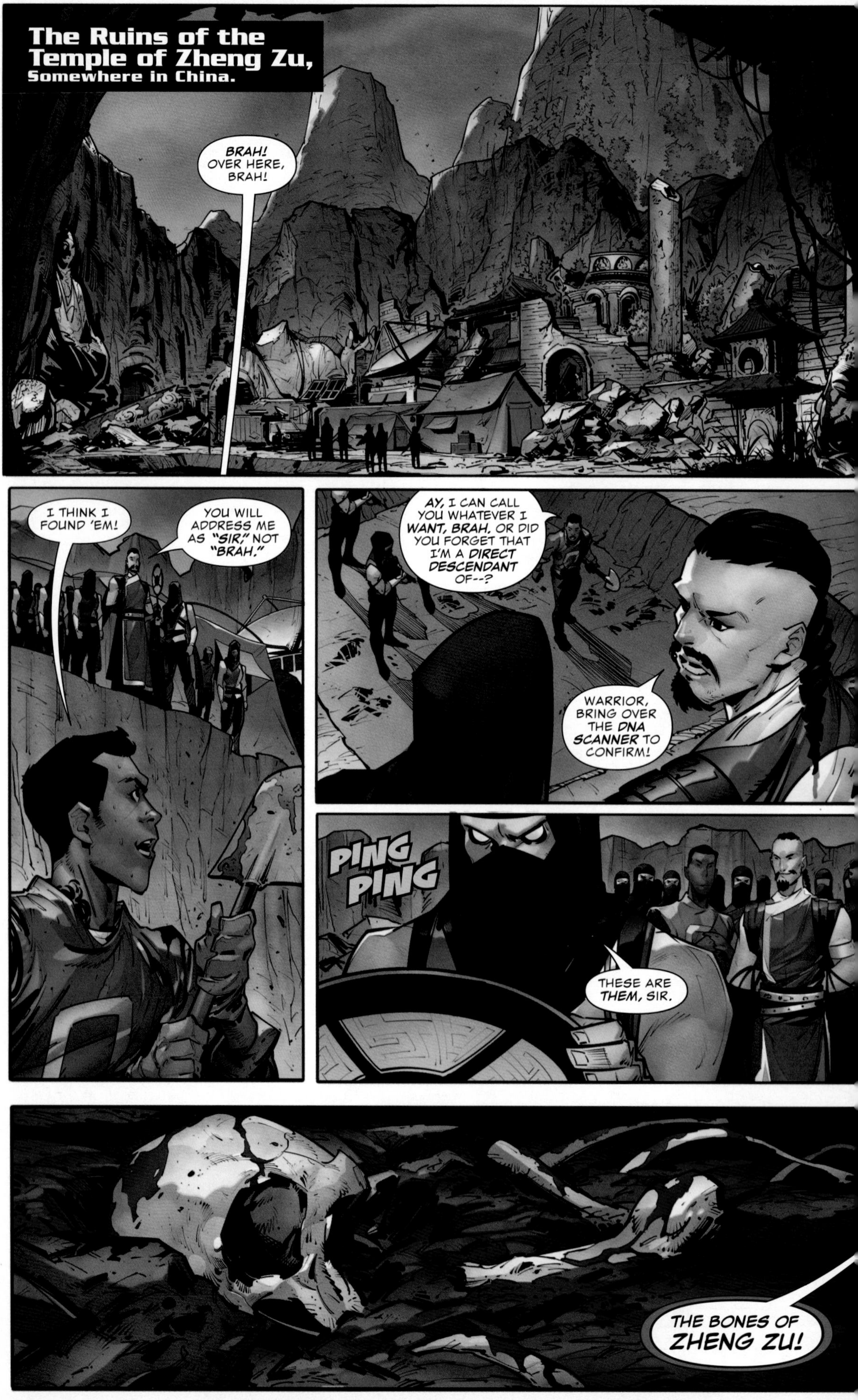
The Ruins of the Temple of Zheng Zu,
Somewhere in China.
BRAH! OVER HERE, BRAH!
I THINK I FOUND 'EM!
YOU WILL ADDRESS ME AS "SIR," NOT "BRAH."
AY, I CAN CALL YOU WHATEVER I WANT, BRAH, OR DID YOU FORGET THAT I'M A DIRECT DESCENDANT OF--?
WARRIOR, BRING OVER THE DNA SCANNER TO CONFIRM!
PING PING
THESE ARE THEM, SIR.
THE BONES OF ZHENG ZU!

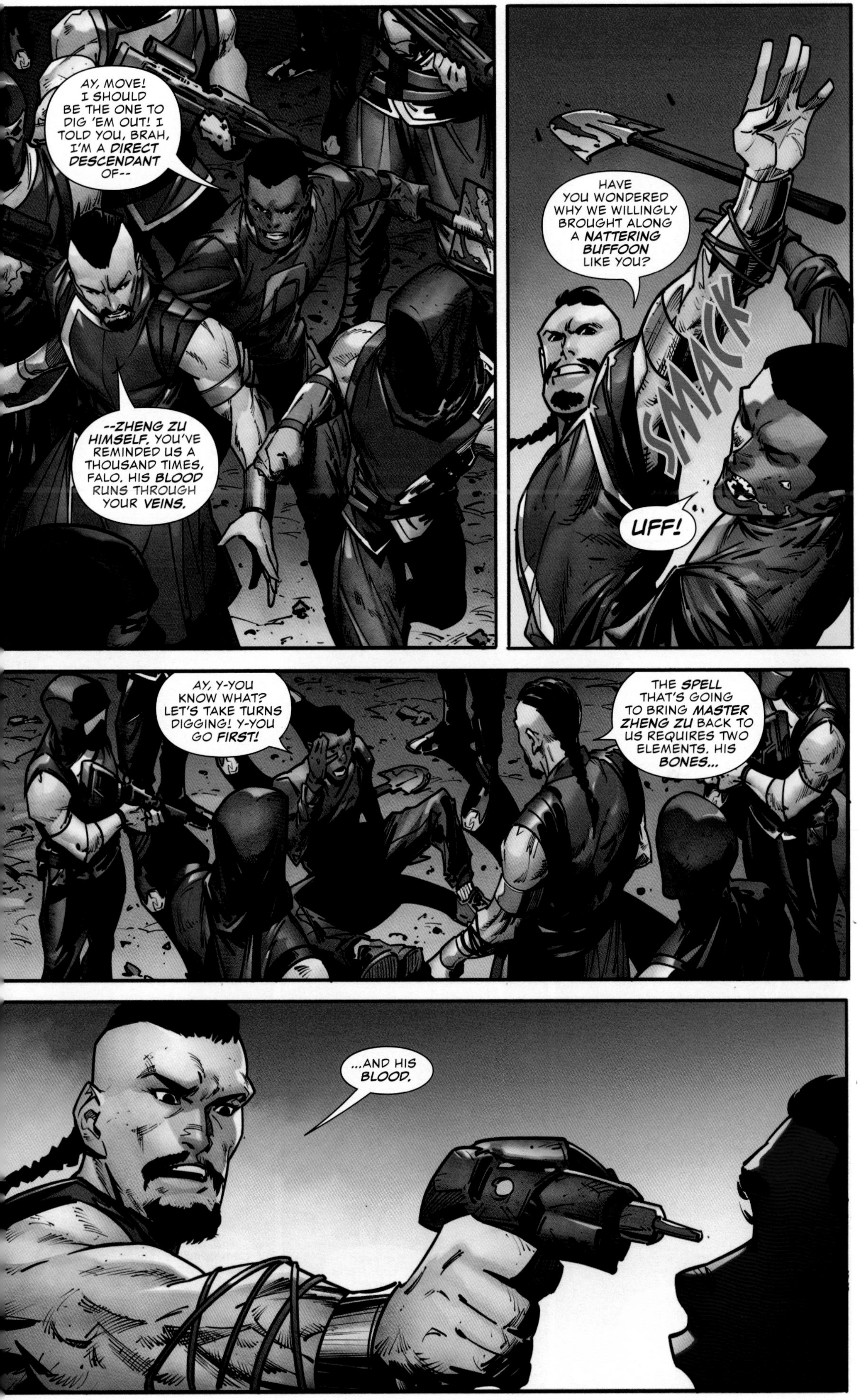
AY, MOVE! I SHOULD BE THE ONE TO DIG 'EM OUT! I TOLD YOU, BRAH, I'M A DIRECT DESCENDANT OF--
--ZHENG ZU HIMSELF. YOU'VE REMINDED US A THOUSAND TIMES, FALO. HIS BLOOD RUNS THROUGH YOUR VEINS.
HAVE YOU WONDERED WHY WE WILLINGLY BROUGHT ALONG A NATTERING BUFFOON LIKE YOU?
SMACK
UFF!
AY, Y-YOU KNOW WHAT? LET'S TAKE TURNS DIGGING! Y-YOU GO FIRST!
THE SPELL THAT'S GOING TO BRING MASTER ZHENG ZU BACK TO US REQUIRES TWO ELEMENTS. HIS BONES...
...AND HIS BLOOD.

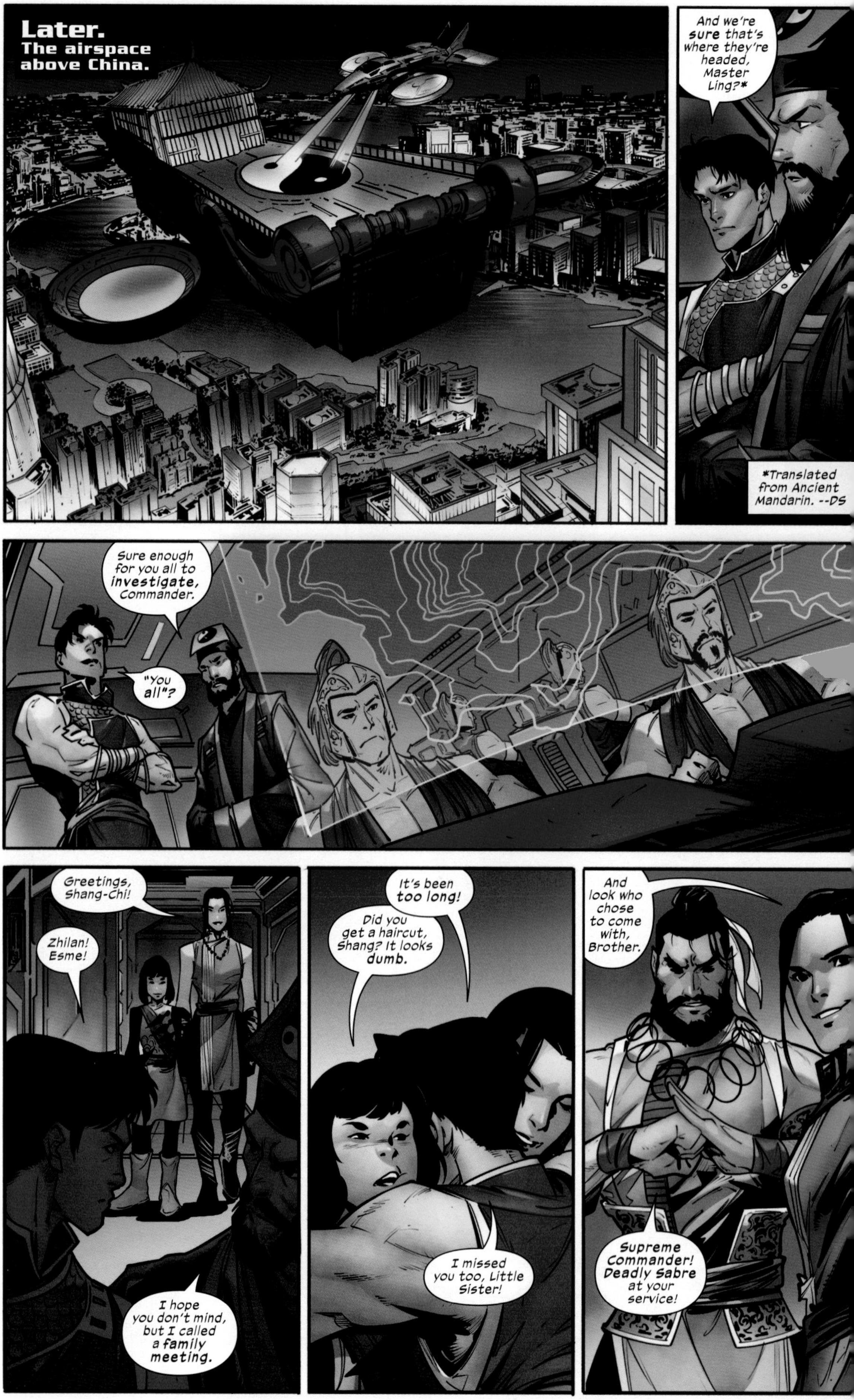
Later.
The airspace above China.
And we're sure that's where they're headed, Master Ling?*
*Translated from Ancient Mandarin. --DS
Sure enough for you all to investigate, Commander.
"You all"?
Greetings, Shang-Chi!
Zhilan! Esme!
I hope you don't mind, but I called a family meeting.
It's been too long!
Did you get a haircut, Shang? It looks dumb.
I missed you too, Little Sister!
And look who chose to come with, Brother.
Supreme Commander! Deadly Sabre at your service!

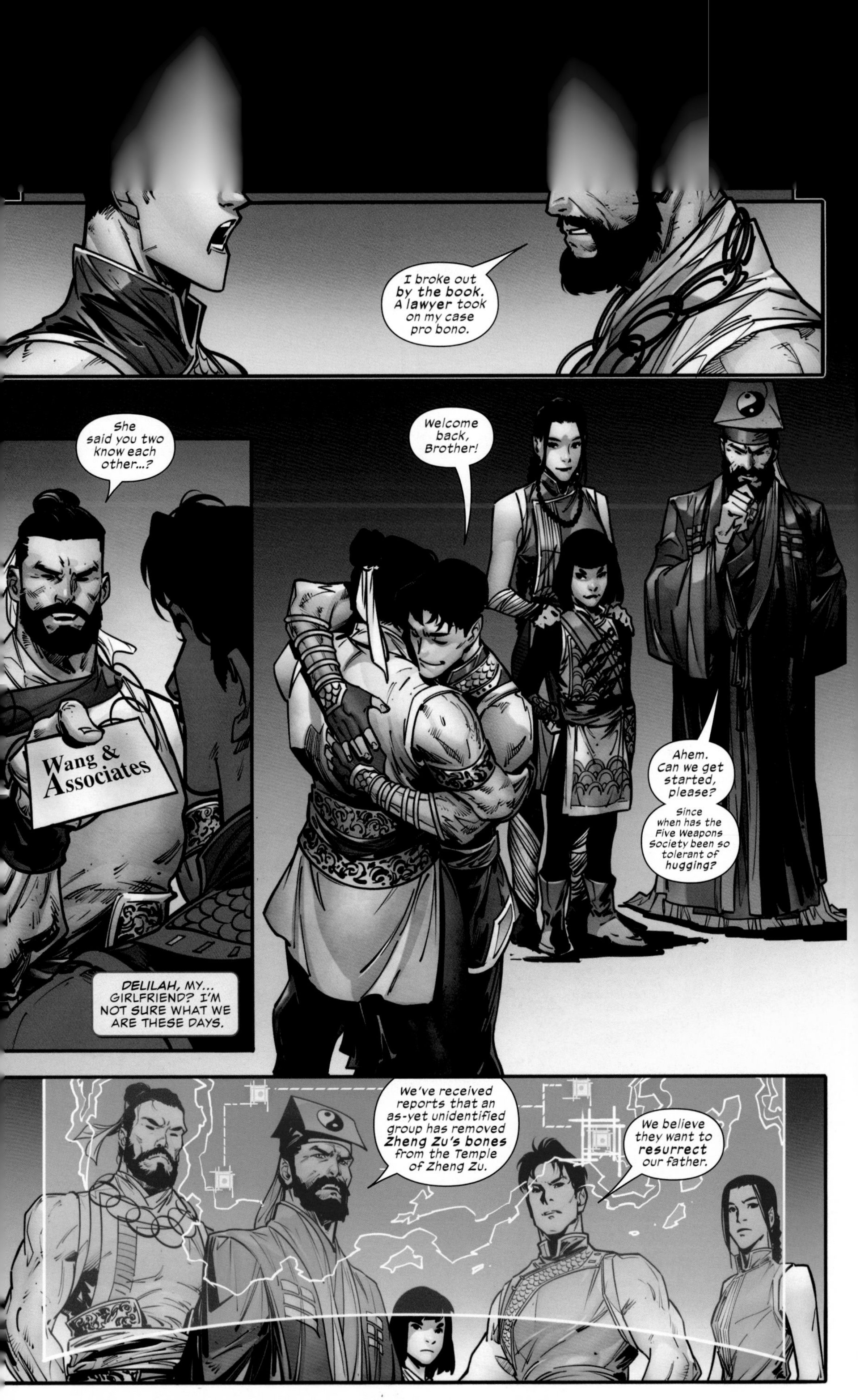
I broke out by the book. A lawyer took on my case pro bono.
She said you two know each other...?
Wang & Associates
DELILAH, MY... GIRLFRIEND? I'M NOT SURE WHAT WE ARE THESE DAYS.
Welcome back, Brother!
Ahem. Can we get started, please?
Since when has the Five Weapons Society been so tolerant of hugging?
We've received reports that an as-yet unidentified group has removed Zheng Zu's bones from the Temple of Zheng Zu.
We believe they want to resurrect our father.

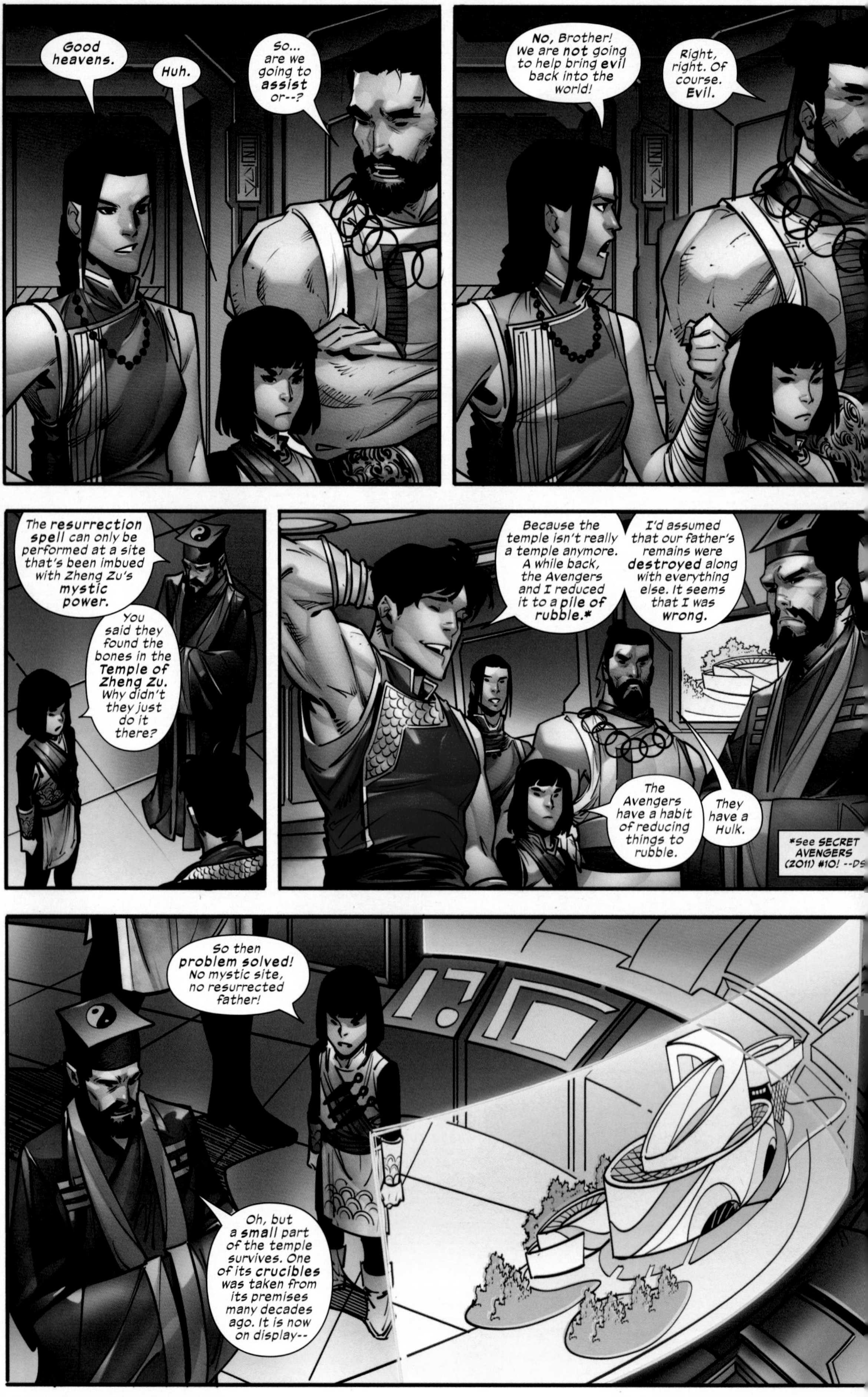
Good heavens.
Huh.
So... are we going to assist or--?
No, Brother! We are not going to help bring evil back into the world!
Right, right. Of course. Evil.
The resurrection spell can only be performed at a site that's been imbued with Zheng Zu's mystic power.
You said they found the bones in the Temple of Zheng Zu. Why didn't they just do it there?
Because the temple isn't really a temple anymore. A while back, the Avengers and I reduced it to a pile of rubble.*
I'd assumed that our father's remains were destroyed along with everything else. It seems that I was wrong.
The Avengers have a habit of reducing things to rubble.
They have a Hulk.
*See SECRET AVENGERS (2011) #10! --DS
So then problem solved! No mystic site, no resurrected father!
Oh, but a small part of the temple survives. One of its crucibles was taken from its premises many decades ago. It is now on display--

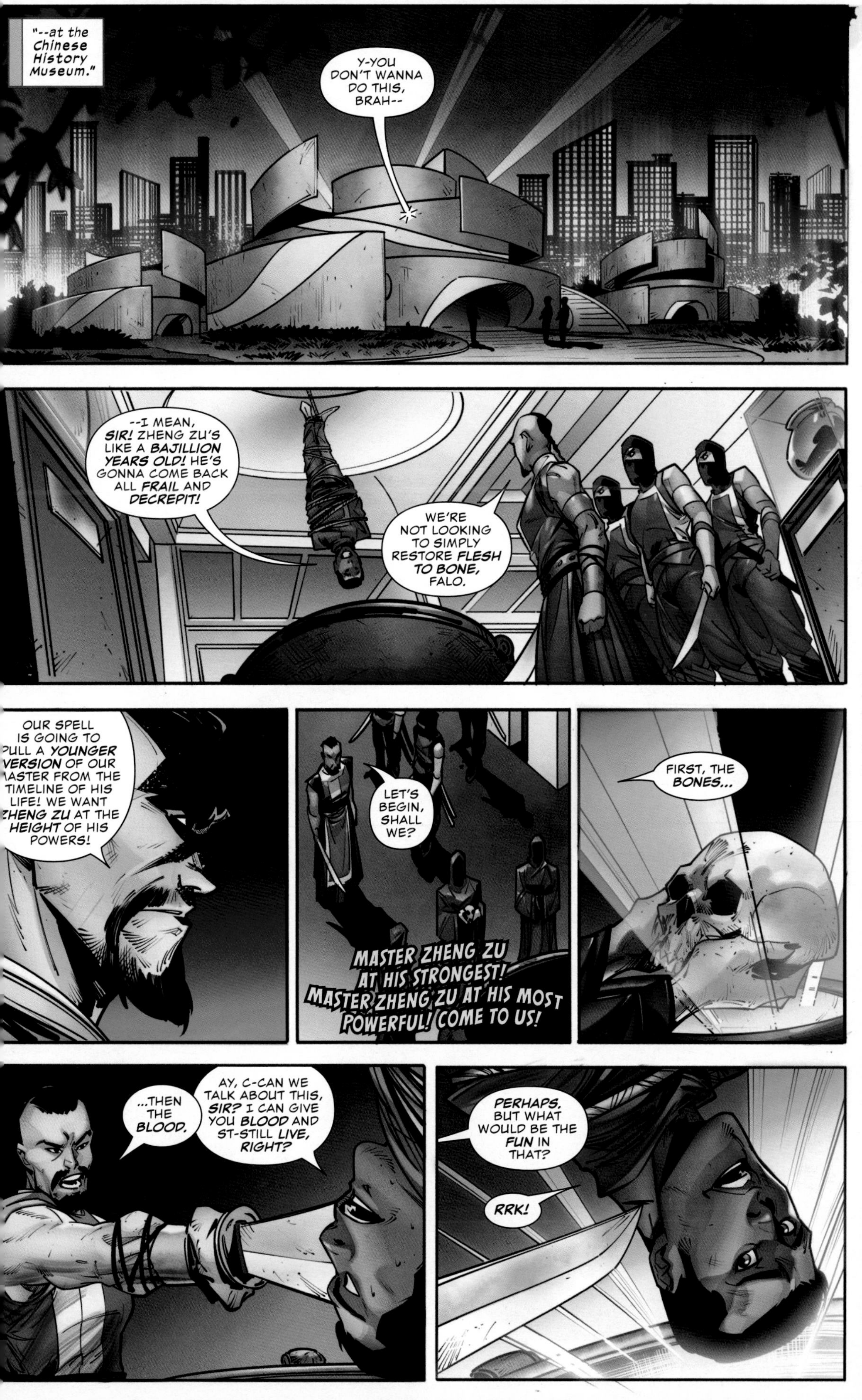
"--at the Chinese History Museum."
Y-YOU DON'T WANNA DO THIS, BRAH--
--I MEAN, SIR! ZHENG ZU'S LIKE A BAJILLION YEARS OLD! HE'S GONNA COME BACK ALL FRAIL AND DECREPIT!
WE'RE NOT LOOKING TO SIMPLY RESTORE FLESH TO BONE, FALO.
OUR SPELL IS GOING TO PULL A YOUNGER VERSION OF OUR MASTER FROM THE TIMELINE OF HIS LIFE! WE WANT ZHENG ZU AT THE HEIGHT OF HIS POWERS!
LET'S BEGIN, SHALL WE?
MASTER ZHENG ZU AT HIS STRONGEST! MASTER ZHENG ZU AT HIS MOST POWERFUL! COME TO US!
FIRST, THE BONES...
...THEN THE BLOOD.
AY, C-CAN WE TALK ABOUT THIS, SIR? I CAN GIVE YOU BLOOD AND ST-STILL LIVE, RIGHT?
PERHAPS. BUT WHAT WOULD BE THE FUN IN THAT?
RRK!

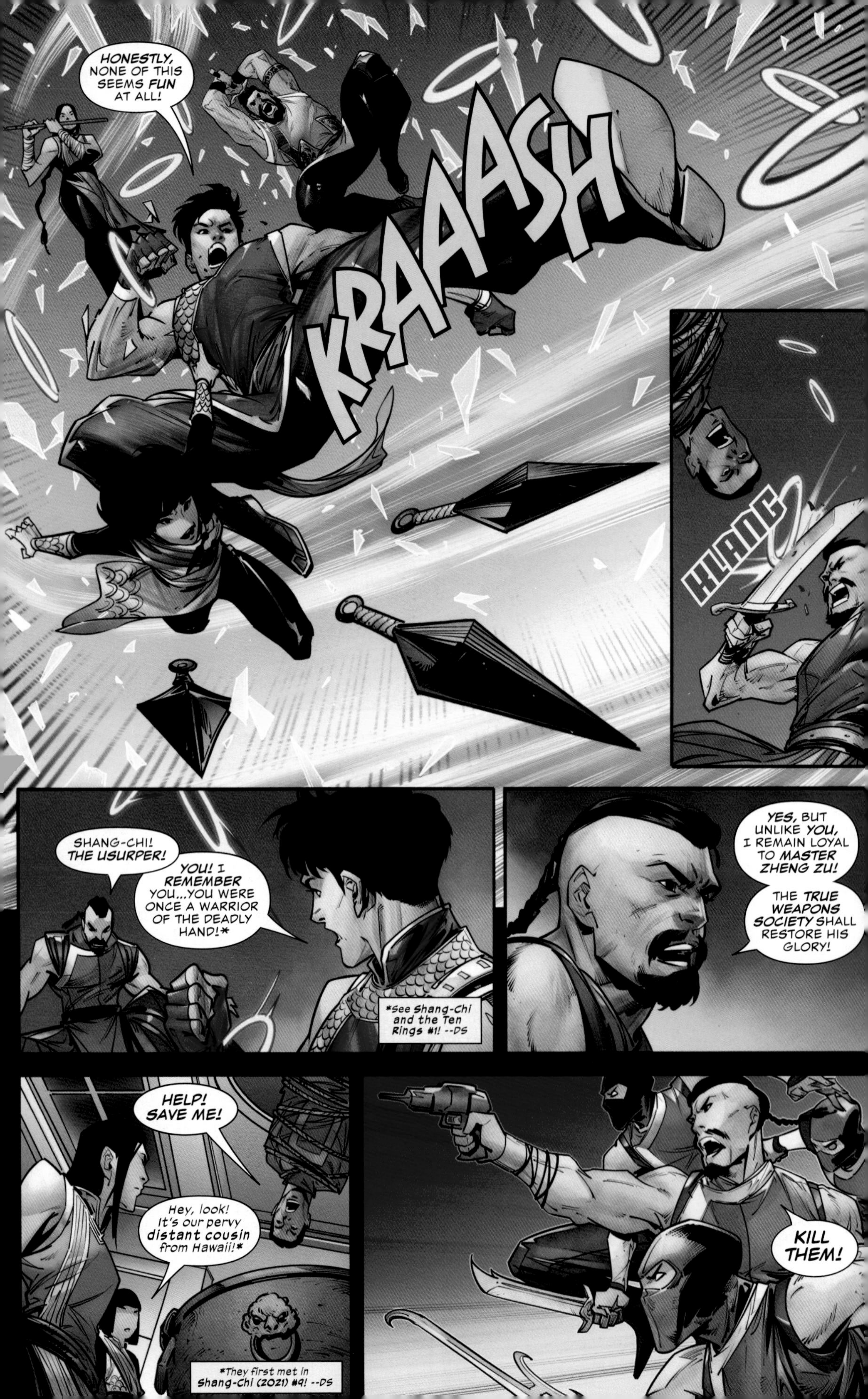
HONESTLY, NONE OF THIS SEEMS FUN AT ALL!
KRAAASH
KLANG
SHANG-CHI! THE USURPER!
YOU! I REMEMBER YOU...YOU WERE ONCE A WARRIOR OF THE DEADLY HAND!*
*See Shang-Chi and the Ten Rings #1! --DS
YES, BUT UNLIKE YOU, I REMAIN LOYAL TO MASTER ZHENG ZU!
THE TRUE WEAPONS SOCIETY SHALL RESTORE HIS GLORY!
HELP! SAVE ME!
Hey, look! It's our pervy distant cousin from Hawaii!*
*They first met in Shang-Chi (2021) #9! --DS
KILL THEM!

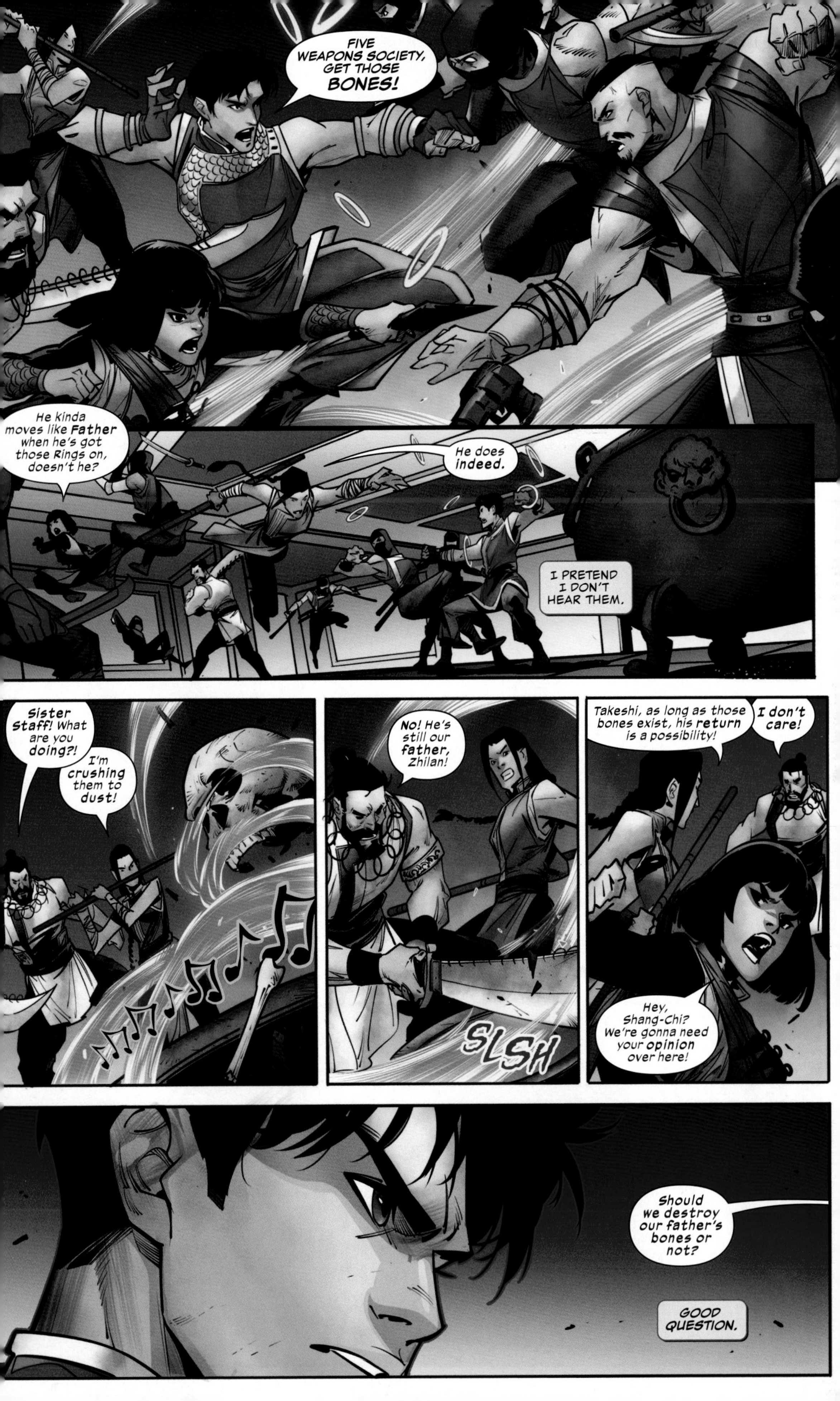
FIVE WEAPONS SOCIETY, GET THOSE BONES!
He kinda moves like Father when he's got those Rings on, doesn't he?
He does indeed.
I PRETEND I DON'T HEAR THEM.
Sister Staff! What are you doing?!
I'm crushing them to dust!
No! He's still our father, Zhilan!
SLSH
Takeshi, as long as those bones exist, his return is a possibility!
I don't care!
Hey, Shang-Chi? We're gonna need your opinion over here!
Should we destroy our father's bones or not?
GOOD QUESTION.

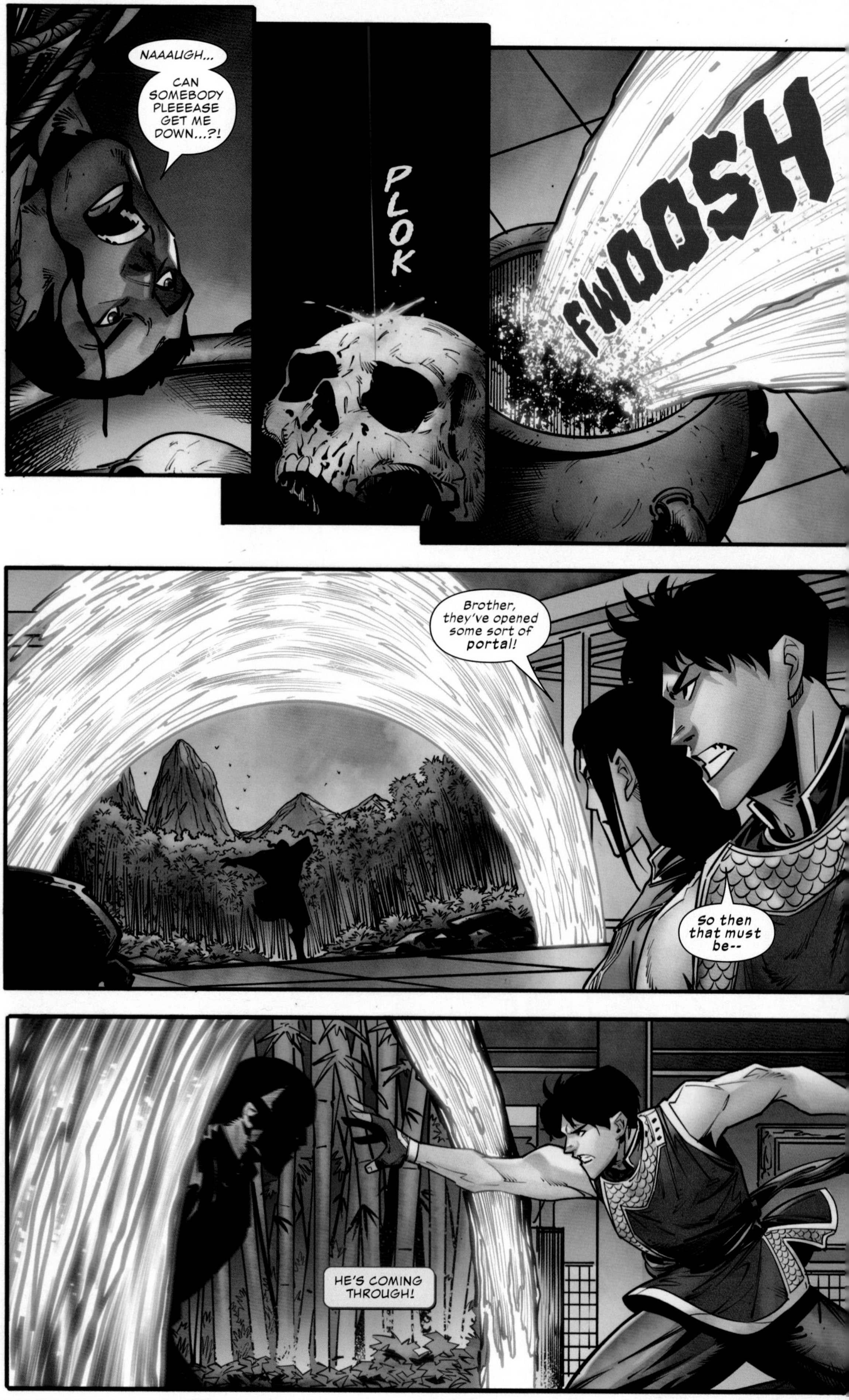
NAAAUGH...
CAN SOMEBODY PLEEEASE GET ME DOWN...?!
PLOK
FWOOSH
Brother, they've opened some sort of portal!
So then that must be--
HE'S COMING THROUGH!

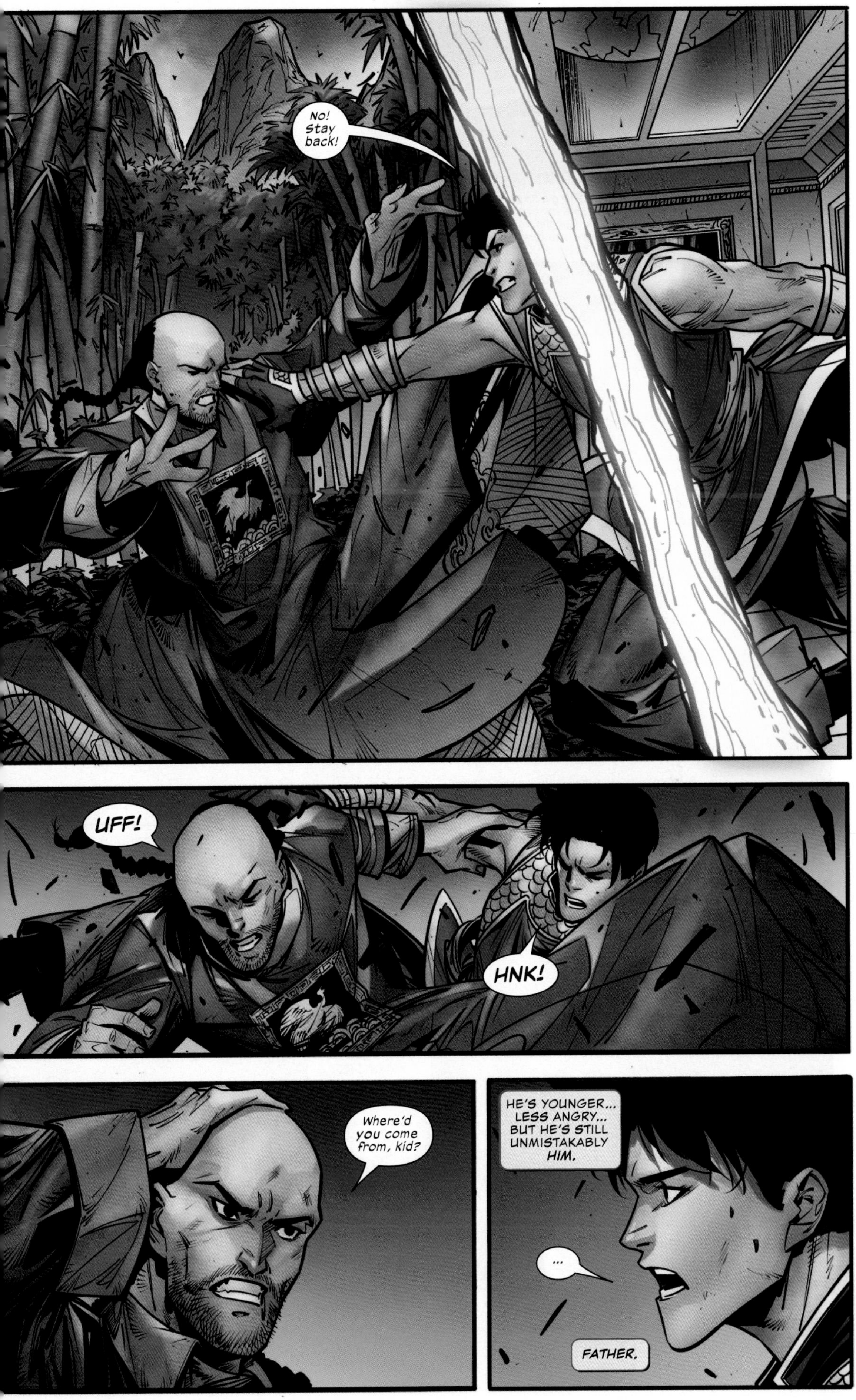

No! Stay back!
UFF!
HNK!
Where'd you come from, kid?
HE'S YOUNGER... LESS ANGRY... BUT HE'S STILL UNMISTAKABLY HIM.
...
FATHER.

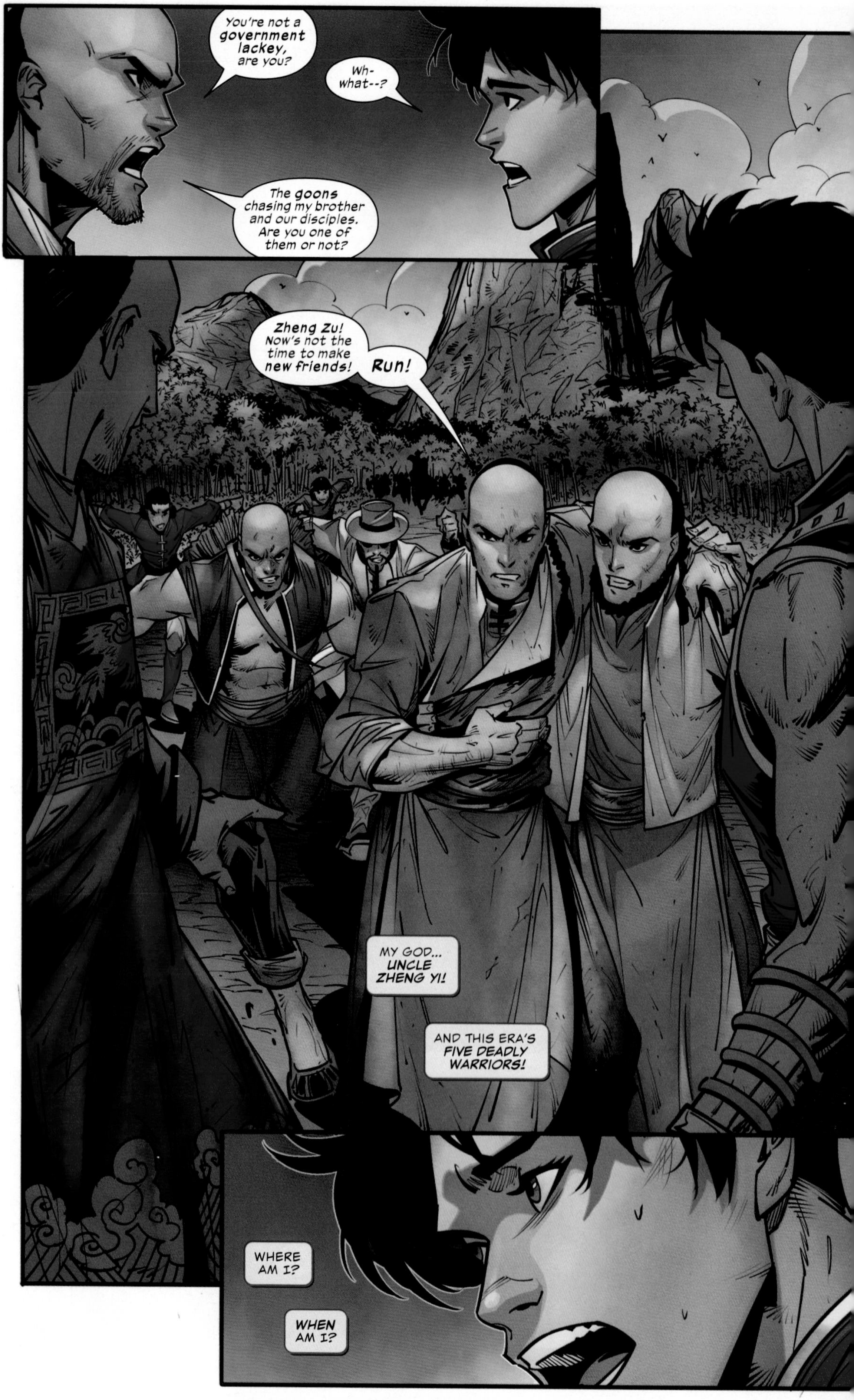
You're not a government lackey, are you?
Wh- what--?
The goons chasing my brother and our disciples. Are you one of them or not?
Zheng Zu! Now's not the time to make new friends!
Run!
MY GOD... UNCLE ZHENG YI!
AND THIS ERA'S FIVE DEADLY WARRIORS!
WHERE AM I?
WHEN AM I?

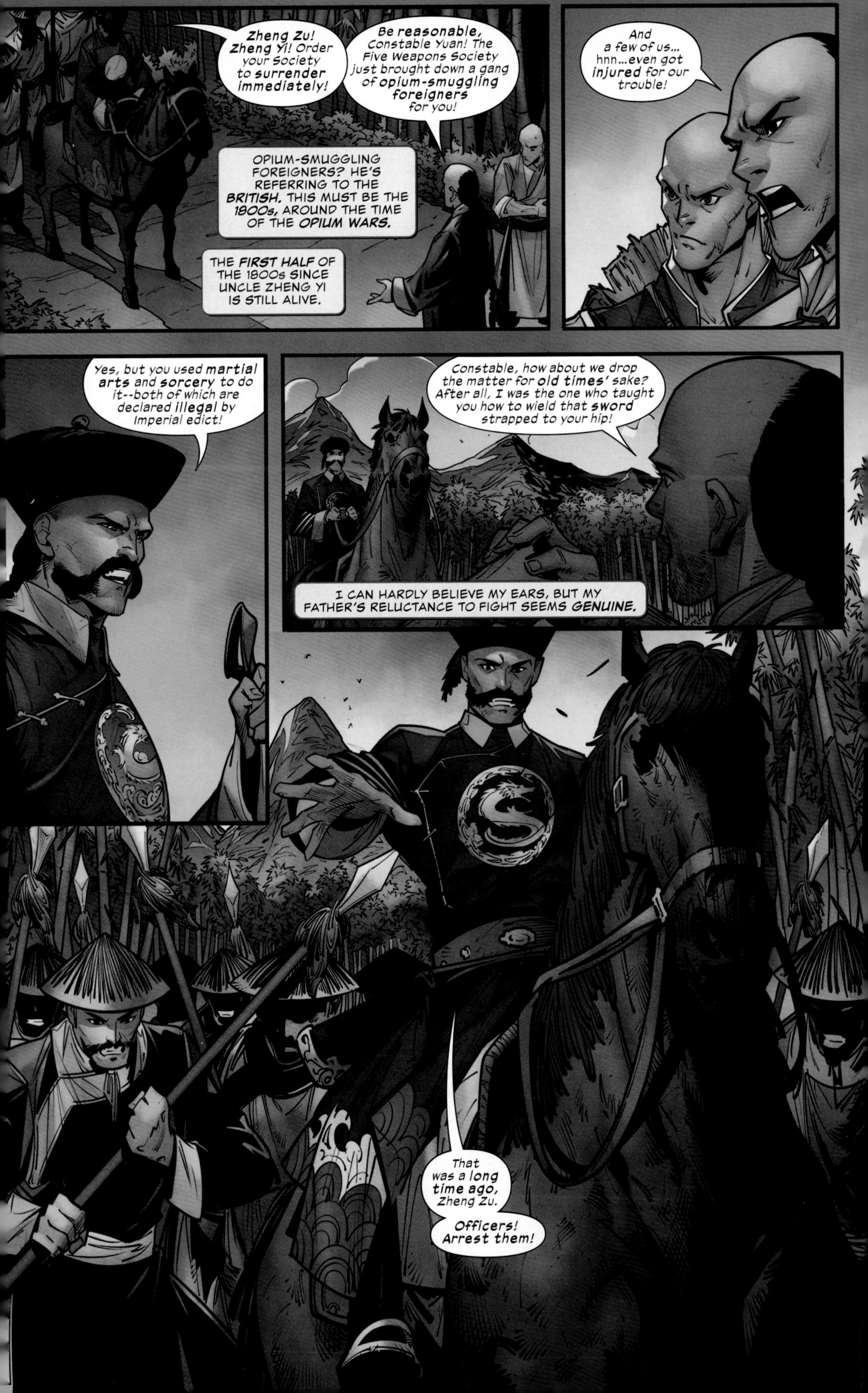
Zheng Zu! Zheng Yi! Order your Society to surrender immediately!
Be reasonable, Constable Yuan! The Five Weapons Society just brought down a gang of opium-smuggling foreigners for you!
OPIUM-SMUGGLING FOREIGNERS? HE'S REFERRING TO THE BRITISH. THIS MUST BE THE 1800s, AROUND THE TIME OF THE OPIUM WARS.
THE FIRST HALF OF THE 1800s SINCE UNCLE ZHENG YI IS STILL ALIVE.
And a few of us... hnn...even got injured for our trouble!
Yes, but you used martial arts and sorcery to do it--both of which are declared illegal by Imperial edict!
Constable, how about we drop the matter for old times' sake? After all, I was the one who taught you how to wield that sword strapped to your hip!
I CAN HARDLY BELIEVE MY EARS, BUT MY FATHER'S RELUCTANCE TO FIGHT SEEMS GENUINE.
That was a long time ago, Zheng Zu.
Officers! Arrest them!

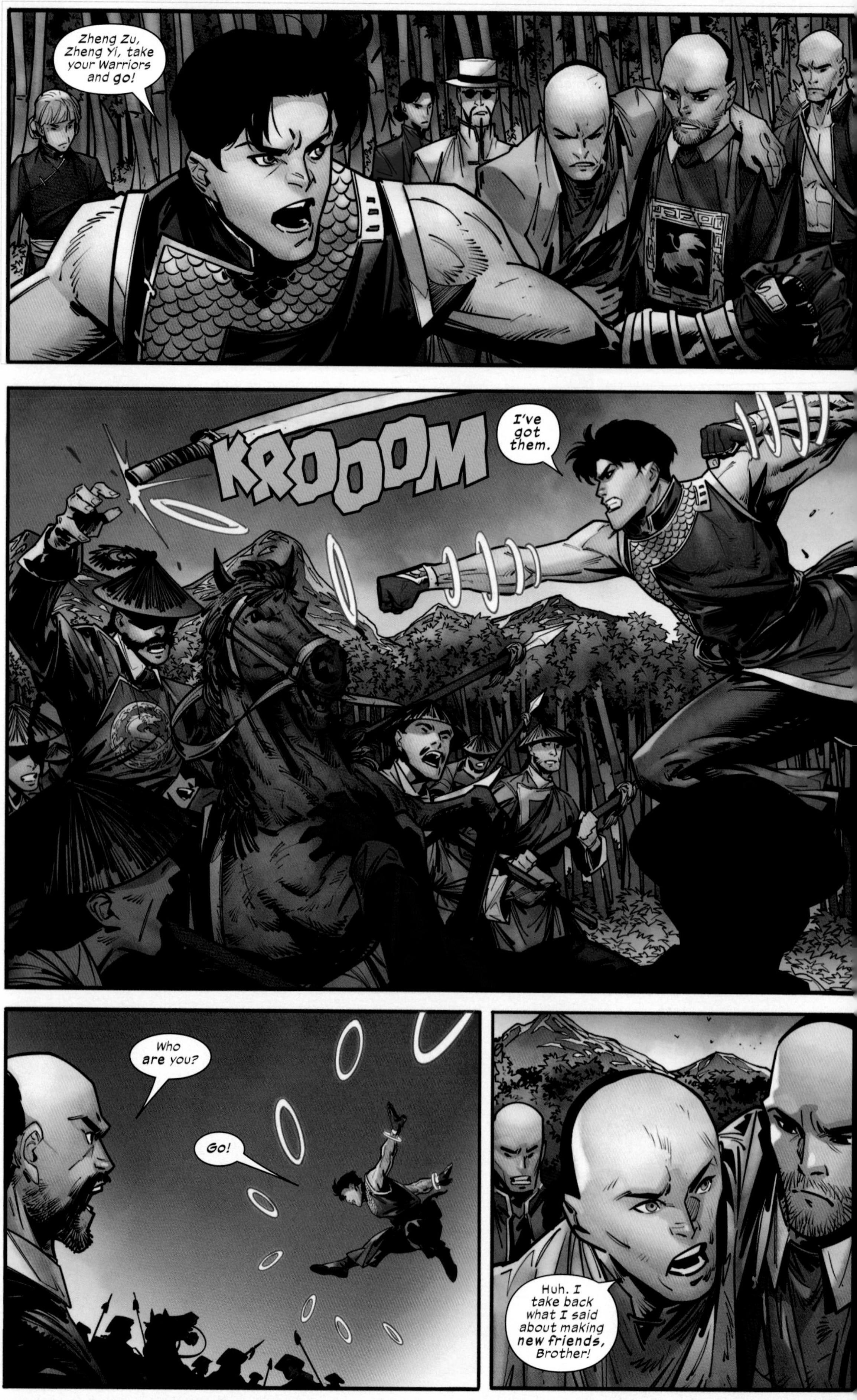

Zheng Zu, Zheng Yi, take your Warriors and go!
KROOOM
I've got them.
Who are you?
Go!
Huh. I take back what I said about making new friends, Brother!

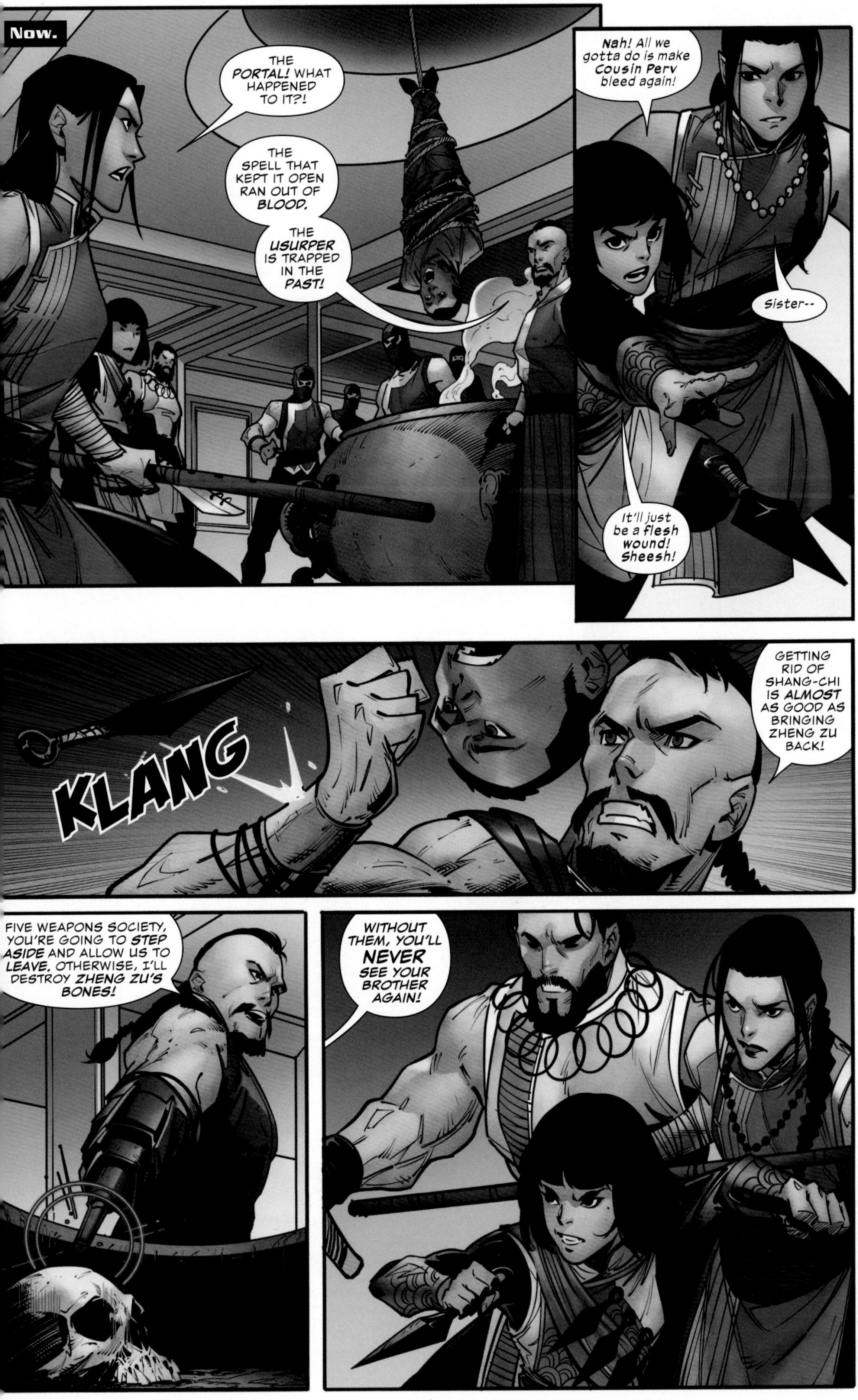
Now.
THE PORTAL! WHAT HAPPENED TO IT?!
THE SPELL THAT KEPT IT OPEN RAN OUT OF BLOOD.
THE USURPER IS TRAPPED IN THE PAST!
Nah! All we gotta do is make Cousin Perv bleed again!
Sister--
It'll just be a flesh wound! Sheesh!
KLANG
GETTING RID OF SHANG-CHI IS ALMOST AS GOOD AS BRINGING ZHENG ZU BACK!
FIVE WEAPONS SOCIETY, YOU'RE GOING TO STEP ASIDE AND ALLOW US TO LEAVE. OTHERWISE, I'LL DESTROY ZHENG ZU'S BONES!
WITHOUT THEM, YOU'LL NEVER SEE YOUR BROTHER AGAIN!

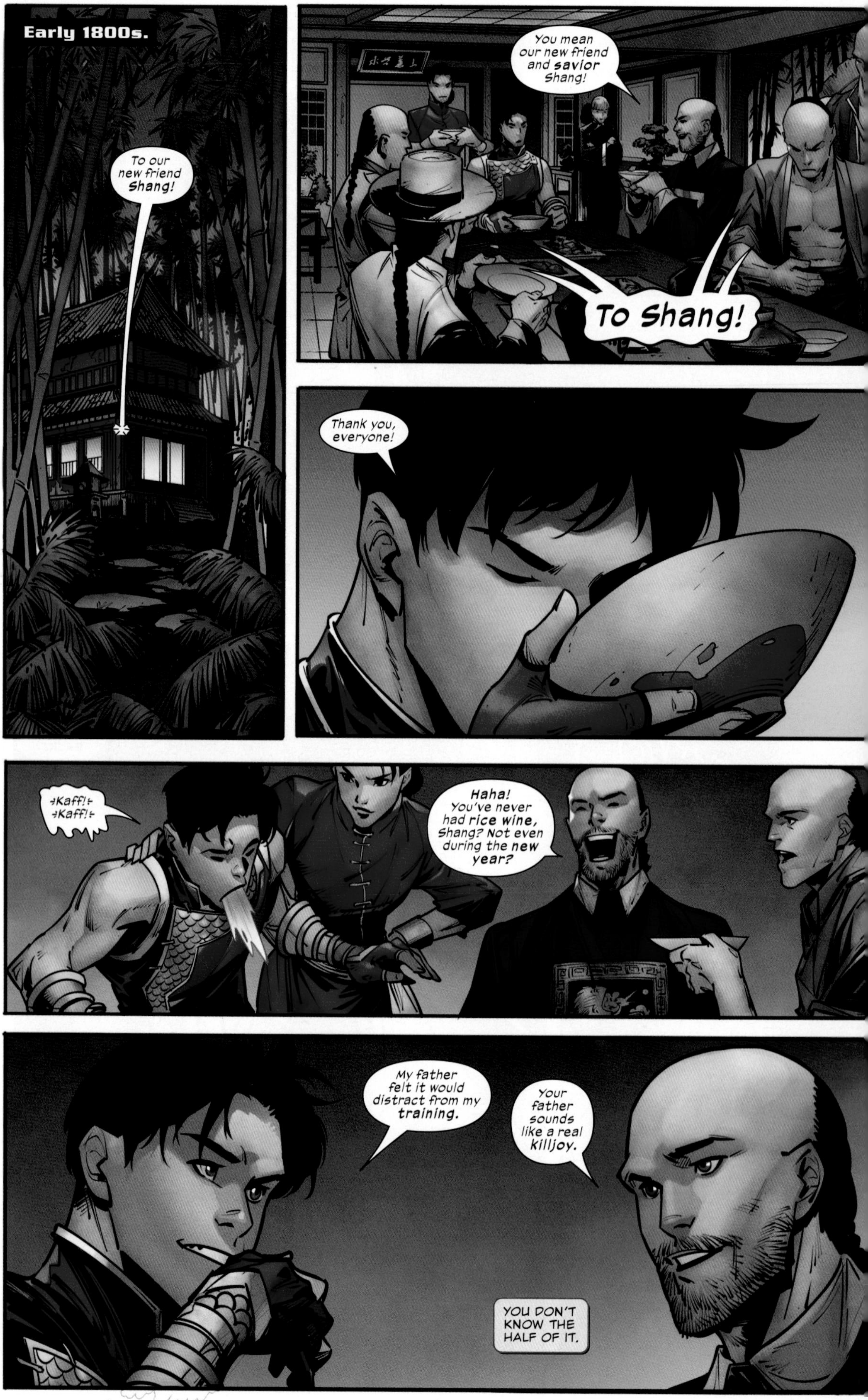
Early 1800s.
To our new friend Shang!
You mean our new friend and savior Shang!
To Shang!
Thank you, everyone!
Kaff! Kaff!
Haha! You've never had rice wine, Shang? Not even during the new year?
My father felt it would distract from my training.
Your father sounds like a real killjoy.
YOU DON'T KNOW THE HALF OF IT.

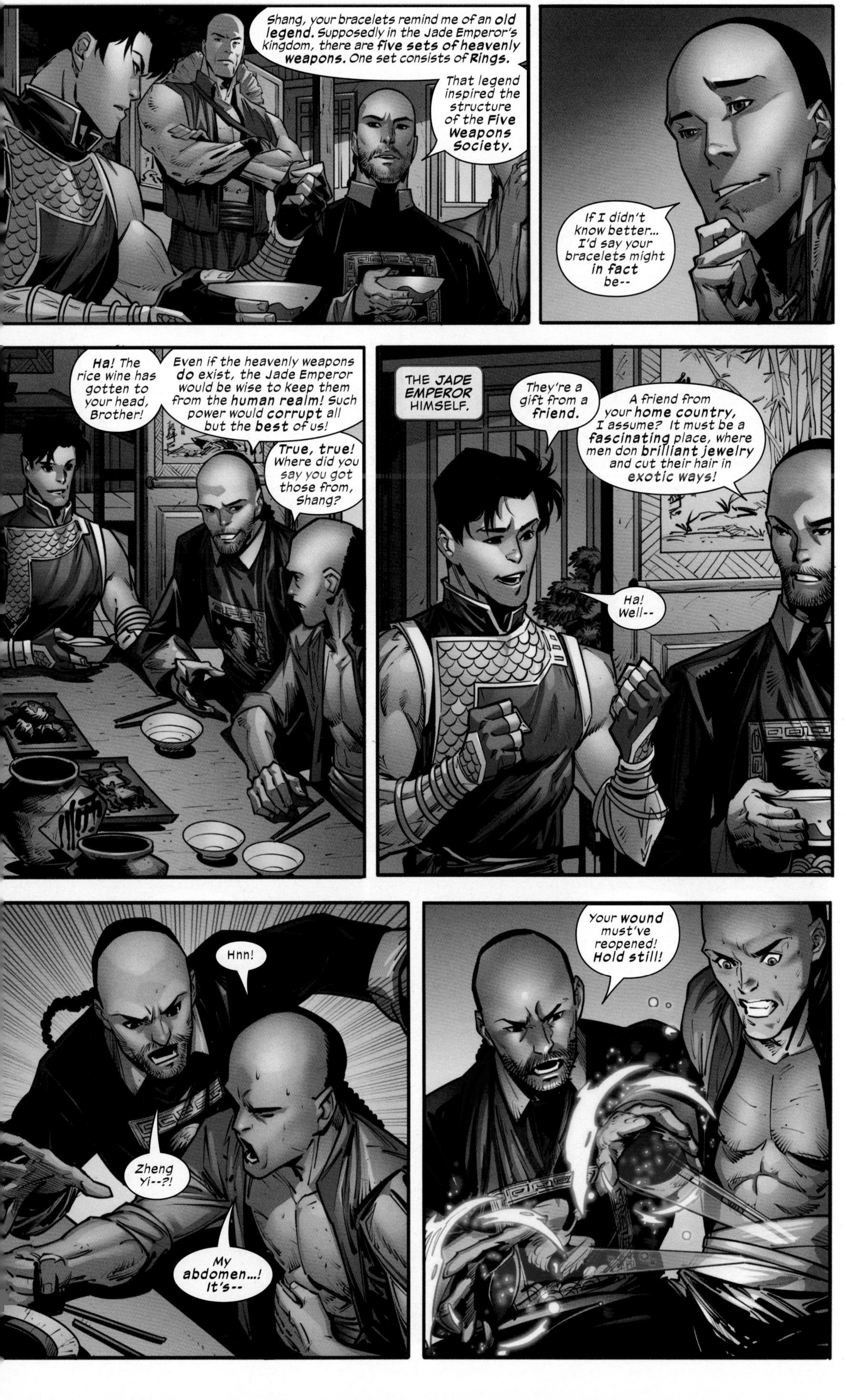
Shang, your bracelets remind me of an old legend. Supposedly in the Jade Emperor's kingdom, there are five sets of heavenly weapons. One set consists of Rings.
That legend inspired the structure of the Five Weapons Society.
If I didn't know better... I'd say your bracelets might in fact be--
Ha! The rice wine has gotten to your head, Brother!
Even if the heavenly weapons do exist, the Jade Emperor would be wise to keep them from the human realm! Such power would corrupt all but the best of us!
True, true! Where did you say you got those from, Shang?
They're a gift from a friend.
THE JADE EMPEROR HIMSELF.
A friend from your home country, I assume? It must be a fascinating place, where men don brilliant jewelry and cut their hair in exotic ways!
Ha! Well--
Hnn!
Zheng Yi--?!
My abdomen...! It's--
Your wound must've reopened! Hold still!

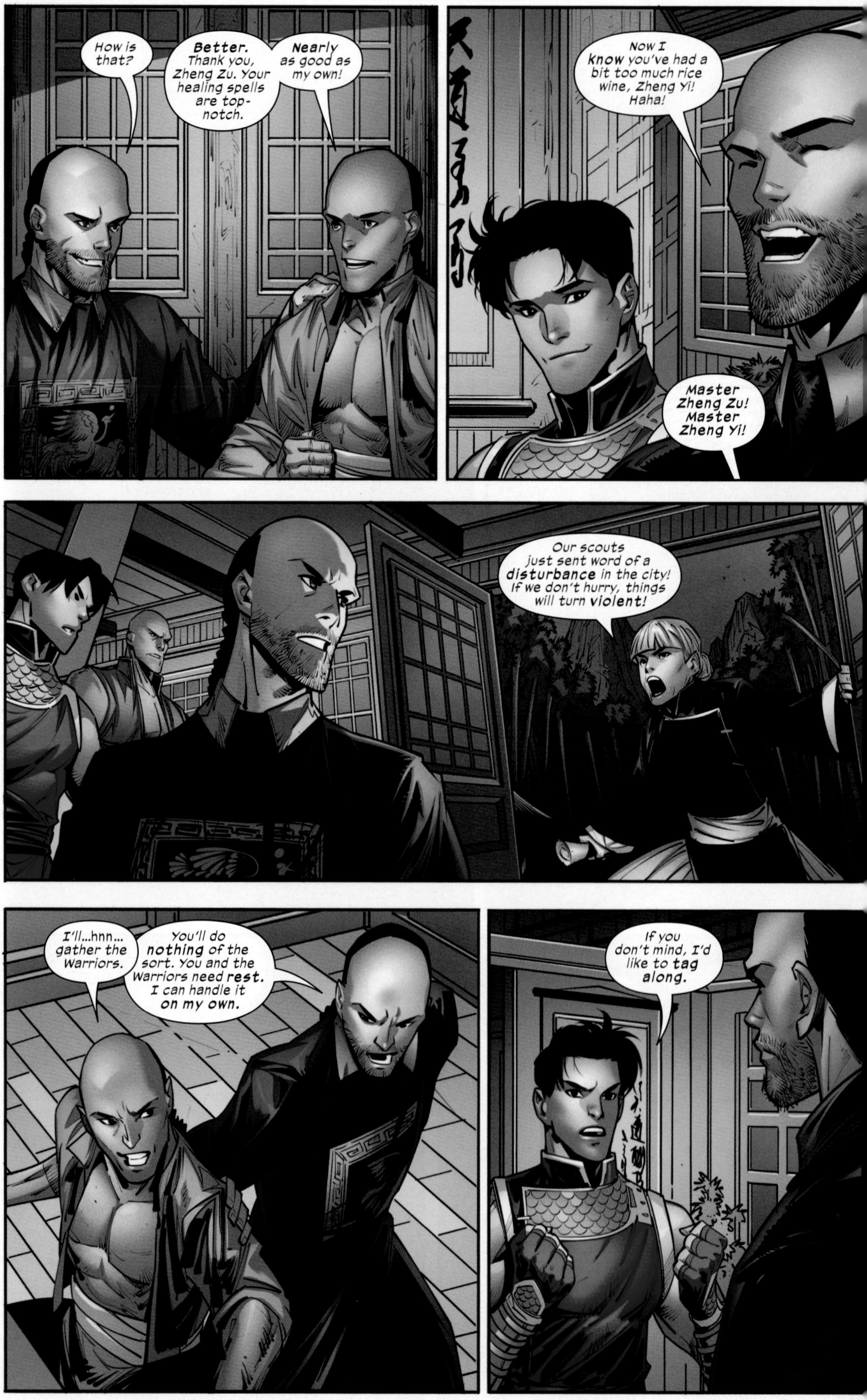
How is that?
Better. Thank you, Zheng Zu. Your healing spells are top-notch.
Nearly as good as my own!
Now I know you've had a bit too much rice wine, Zheng Yi! Haha!
Master Zheng Zu! Master Zheng Yi!
Our scouts just sent word of a disturbance in the city! If we don't hurry, things will turn violent!
I'll...hnn... gather the Warriors.
You'll do nothing of the sort. You and the Warriors need rest. I can handle it on my own.
If you don't mind, I'd like to tag along.

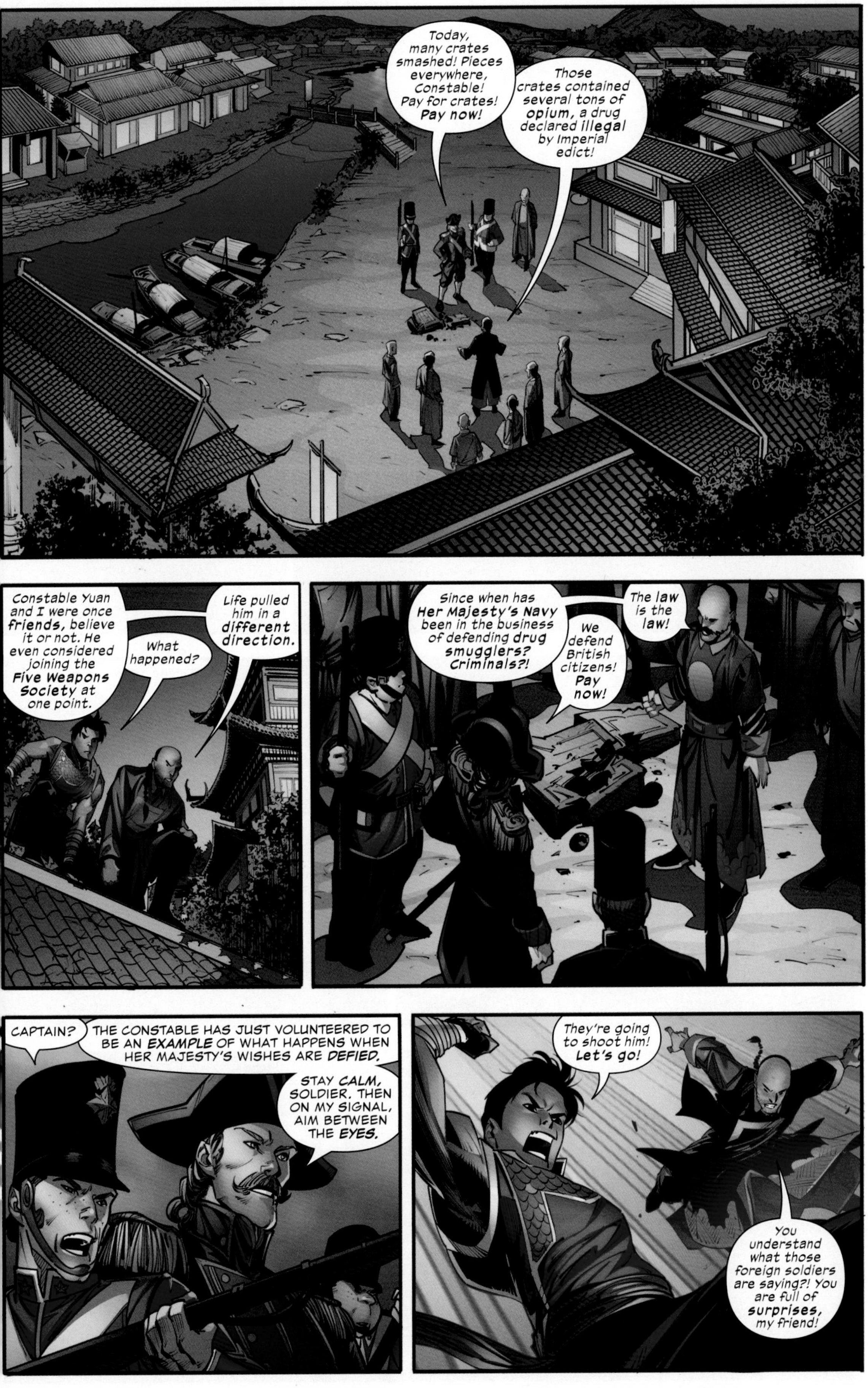

Today, many crates smashed! Pieces everywhere, Constable! Pay for crates! Pay now!
Those crates contained several tons of opium, a drug declared illegal by Imperial edict!
Constable Yuan and I were once friends, believe it or not. He even considered joining the Five Weapons Society at one point.
What happened?
Life pulled him in a different direction.
Since when has Her Majesty's Navy been in the business of defending drug smugglers? Criminals?!
The law is the law!
We defend British citizens! Pay now!
CAPTAIN?
THE CONSTABLE HAS JUST VOLUNTEERED TO BE AN EXAMPLE OF WHAT HAPPENS WHEN HER MAJESTY'S WISHES ARE DEFIED.
STAY CALM, SOLDIER. THEN ON MY SIGNAL, AIM BETWEEN THE EYES.
They're going to shoot him! Let's go!
You understand what those foreign soldiers are saying?! You are full of surprises, my friend!

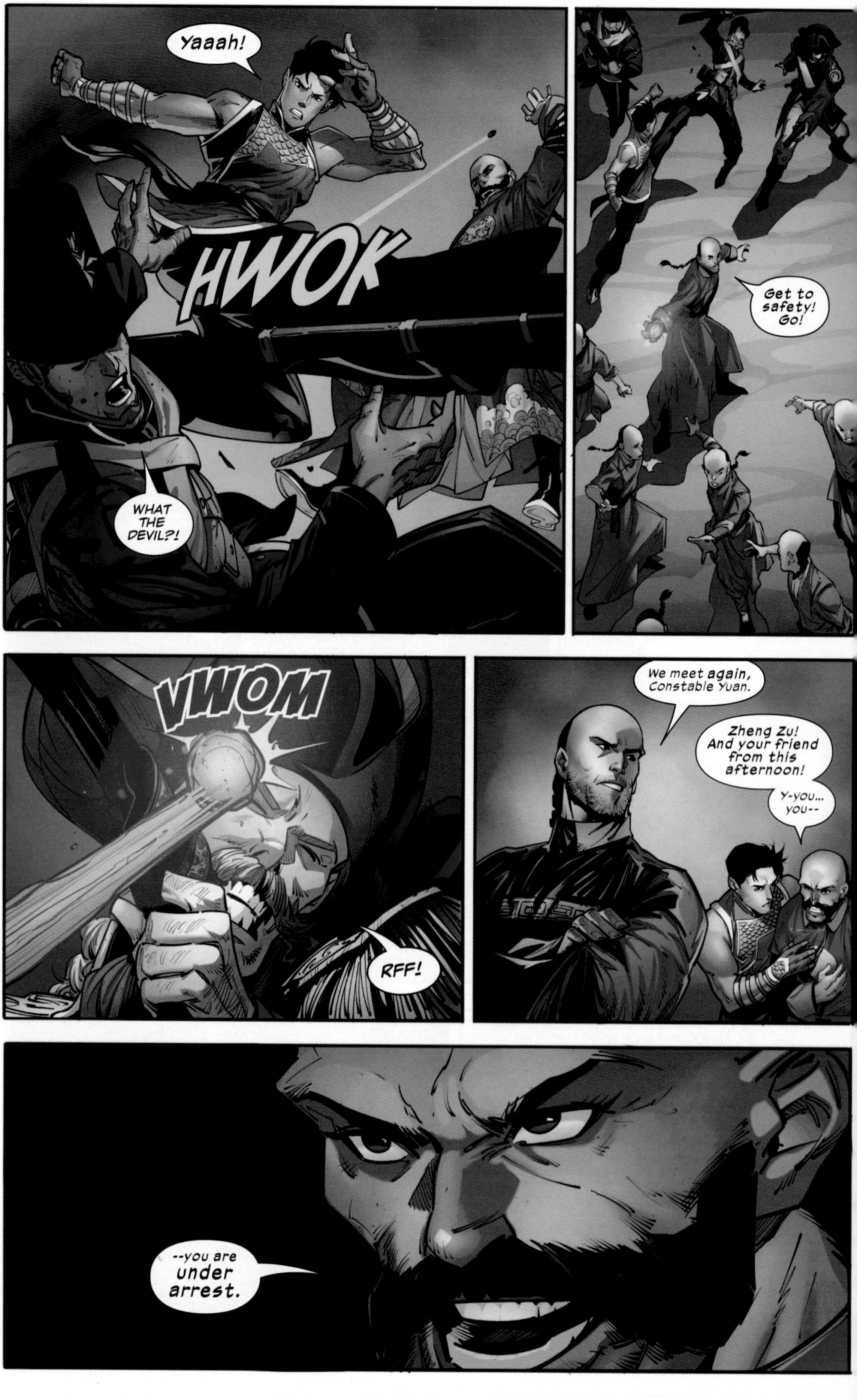
Yaaah!
HWOK
WHAT THE DEVIL?!
Get to safety! Go!
VWOM
RFF!
We meet again, Constable Yuan.
Zheng Zu! And your friend from this afternoon!
Y-you... you--
--you are under arrest.

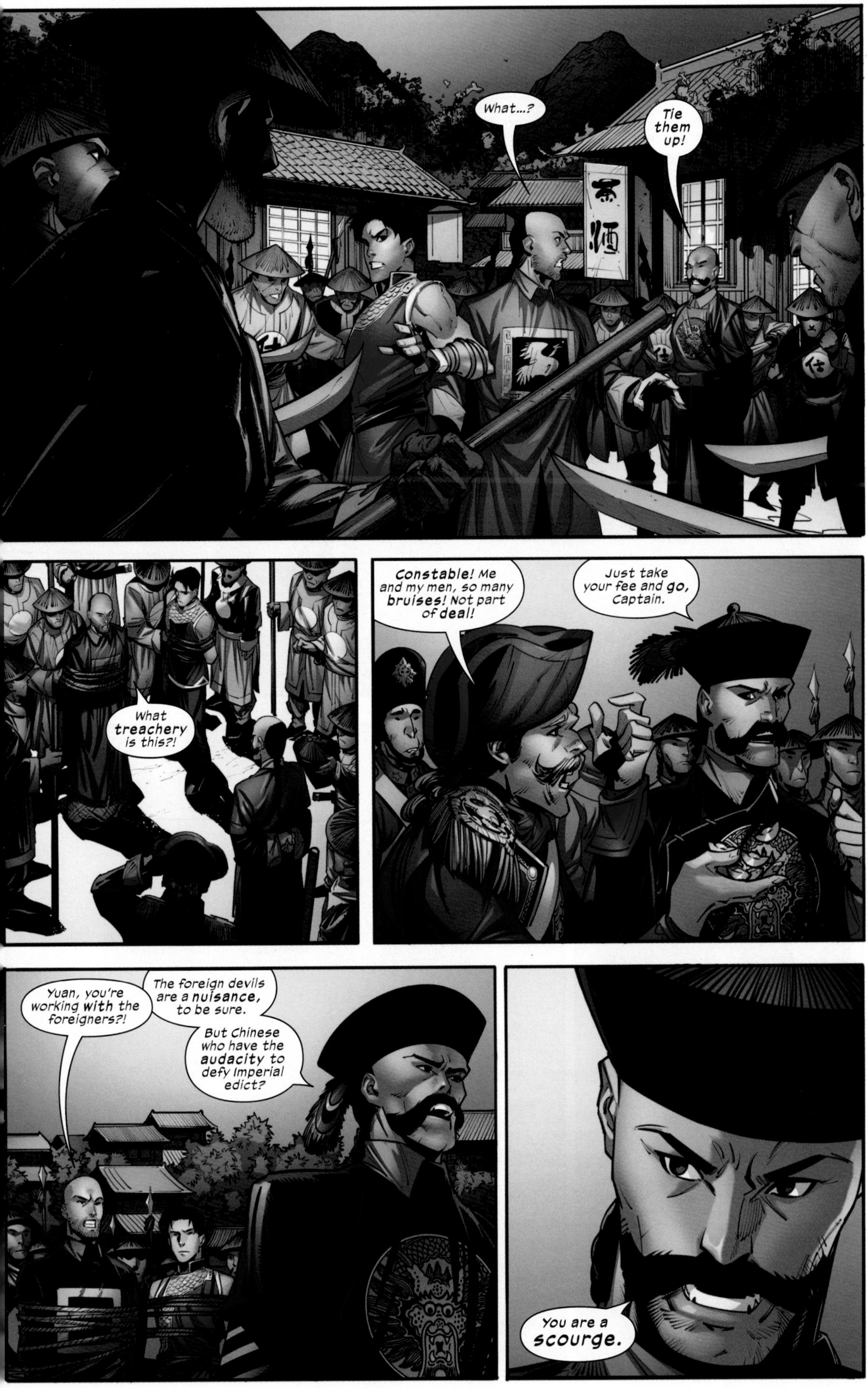

What...?
Tie them up!
What treachery is this?!
Constable! Me and my men, so many bruises! Not part of deal!
Just take your fee and go, Captain.
Yuan, you're working with the foreigners?!
The foreign devils are a nuisance, to be sure.
But Chinese who have the audacity to defy Imperial edict?
You are a scourge.

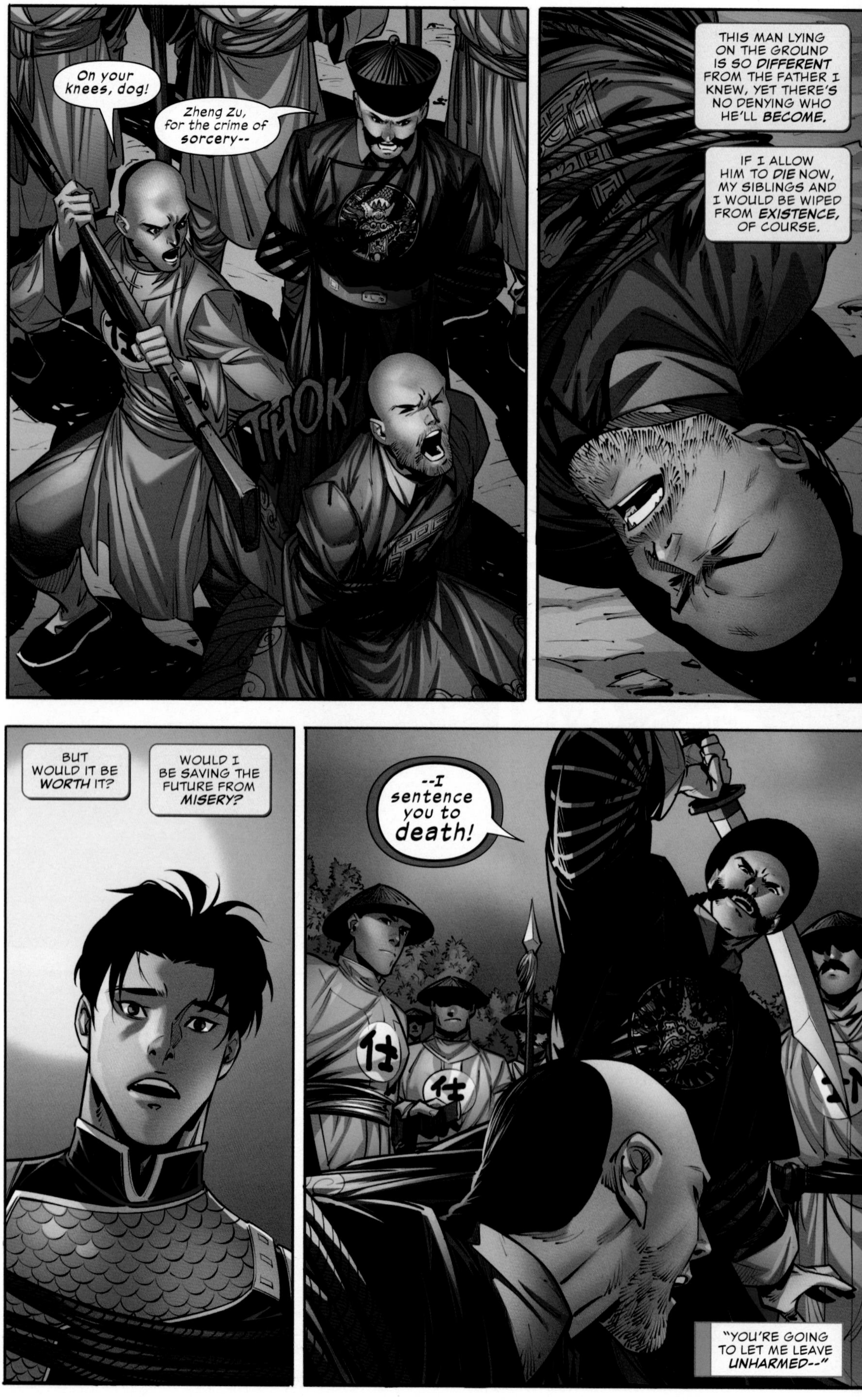
On your knees, dog!
Zheng Zu, for the crime of sorcery--
THOK
THIS MAN LYING ON THE GROUND IS SO DIFFERENT FROM THE FATHER I KNEW, YET THERE'S NO DENYING WHO HE'LL BECOME.
IF I ALLOW HIM TO DIE NOW, MY SIBLINGS AND I WOULD BE WIPED FROM EXISTENCE, OF COURSE.
BUT WOULD IT BE WORTH IT?
WOULD I BE SAVING THE FUTURE FROM MISERY?
--I sentence you to death!
"YOU'RE GOING TO LET ME LEAVE UNHARMED--"

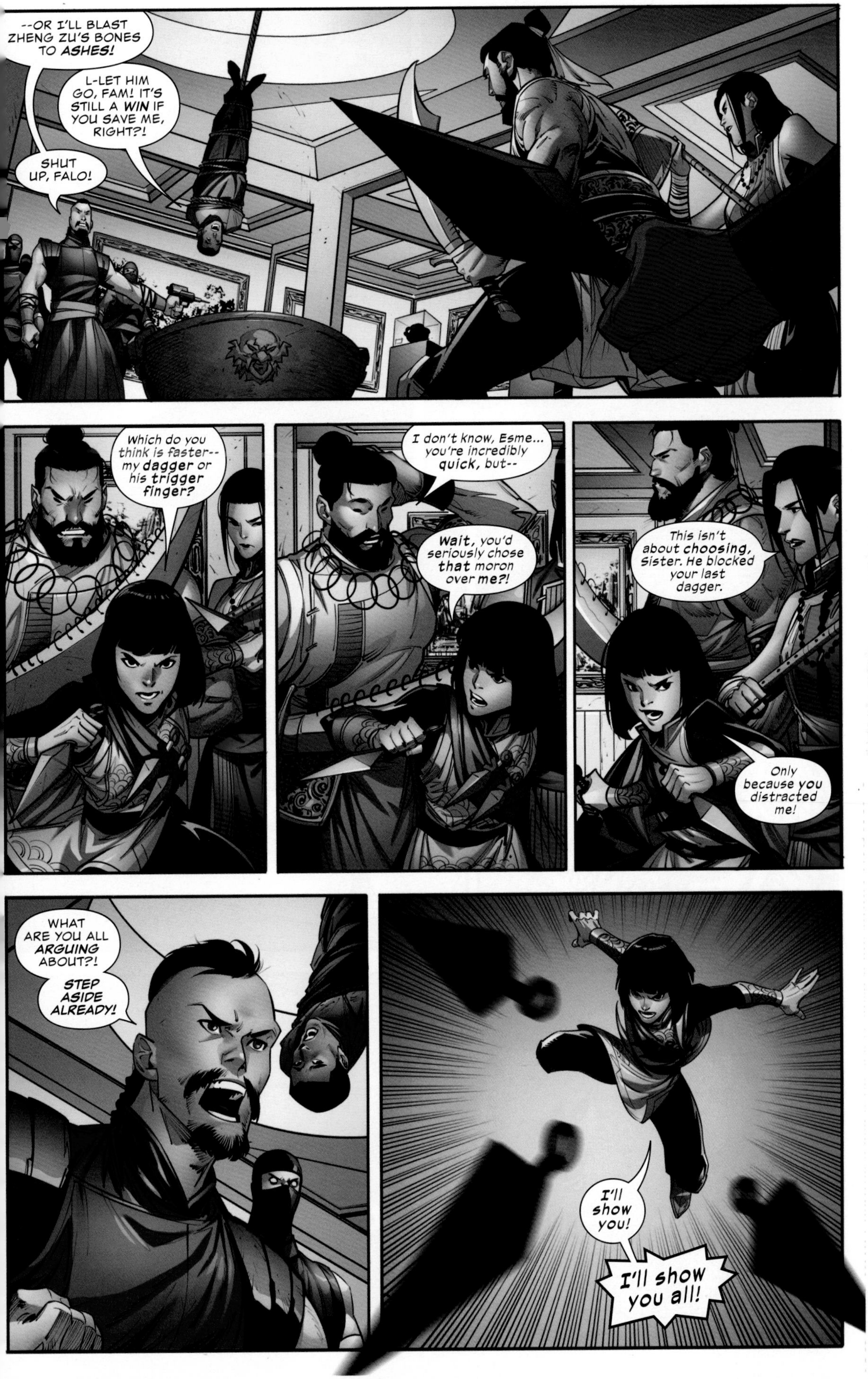
--OR I'LL BLAST ZHENG ZU'S BONES TO ASHES!
L-LET HIM GO, FAM! IT'S STILL A WIN IF YOU SAVE ME, RIGHT?!
SHUT UP, FALO!
Which do you think is faster--my dagger or his trigger finger?
I don't know, Esme... you're incredibly quick, but--
Wait, you'd seriously chose that moron over me?!
This isn't about choosing, Sister. He blocked your last dagger.
Only because you distracted me!
WHAT ARE YOU ALL ARGUING ABOUT?!
STEP ASIDE ALREADY!
I'll show you!
I'll show you all!

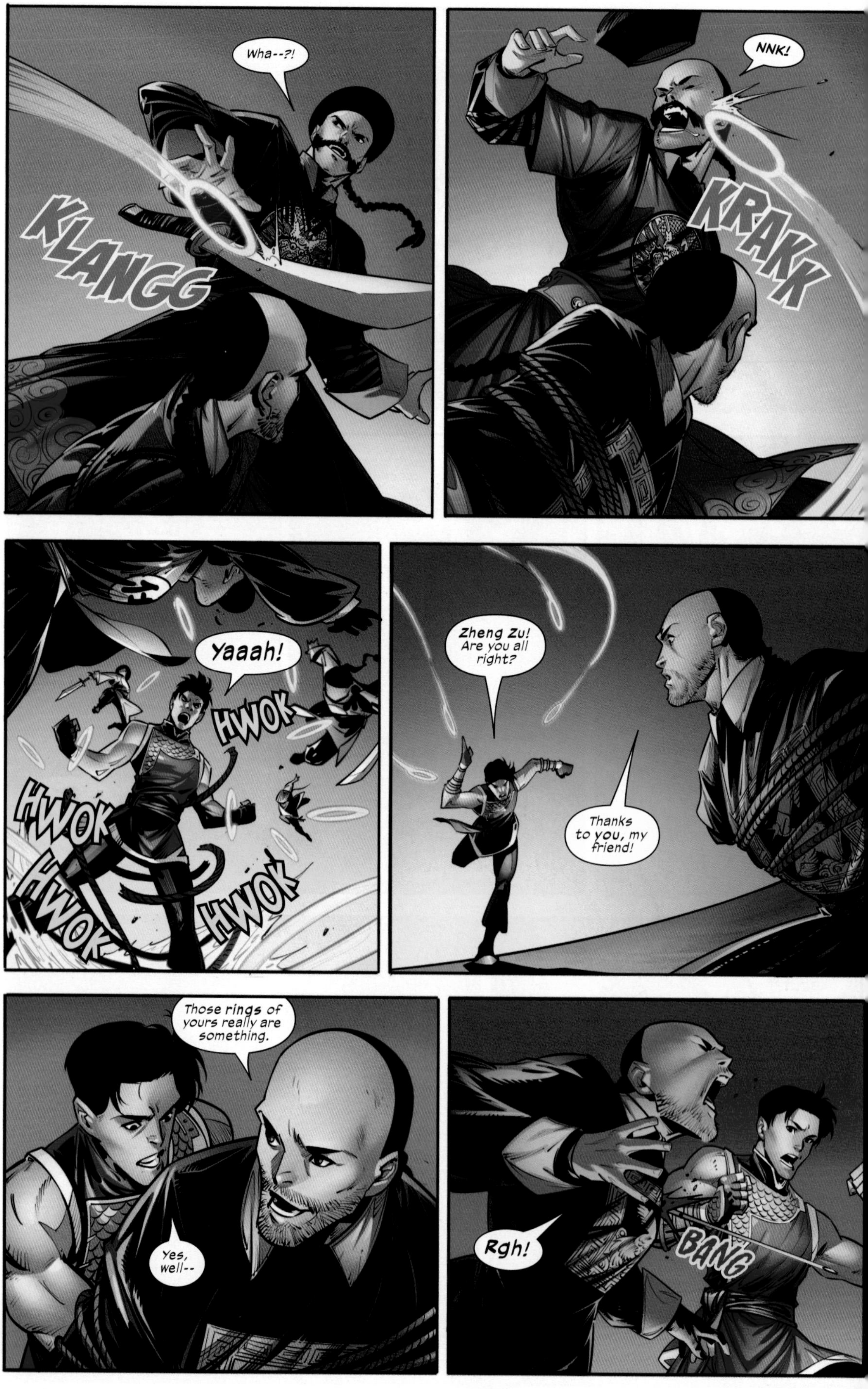
Wha--?!
KLANGG
NNK!
KRAKK
Yaaaah!
HWOK
HWOK
HWOK
HWOK
Zheng Zu! Are you all right?
Thanks to you, my friend!
Those rings of yours really are something.
Yes, well--
Rgh!
BANG

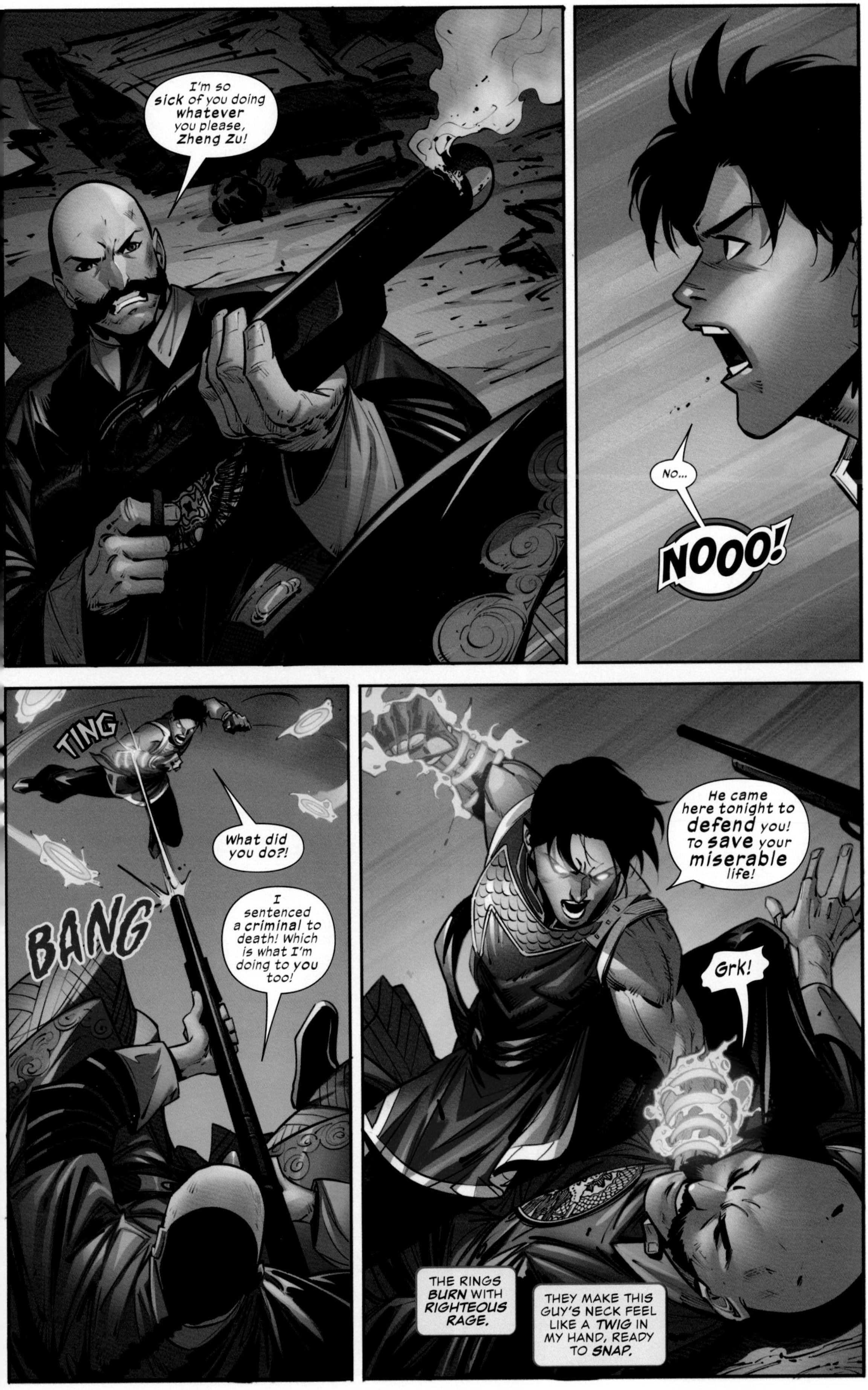
I'm so sick of you doing whatever you please, Zheng Zu!
No...
NOOO!
TING
What did you do?!
BANG
I sentenced a criminal to death! Which is what I'm doing to you too!
He came here tonight to defend you! To save your miserable life!
Grk!
THE RINGS BURN WITH RIGHTEOUS RAGE.
THEY MAKE THIS GUY'S NECK FEEL LIKE A TWIG IN MY HAND, READY TO SNAP.

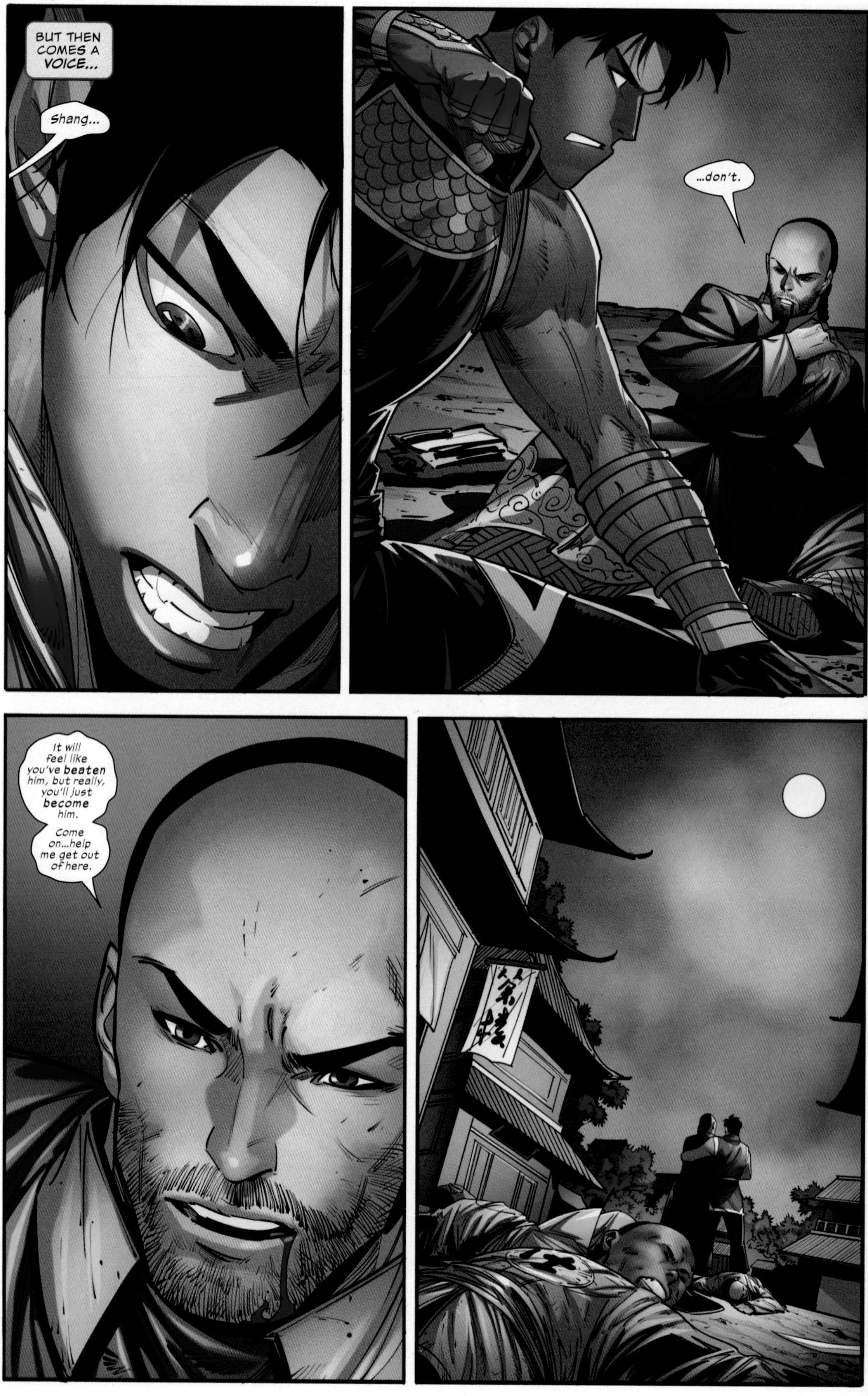
BUT THEN COMES A VOICE...
Shang...
...don't.
It will feel like you've beaten him, but really, you'll just become him.
Come on...help me get out of here.

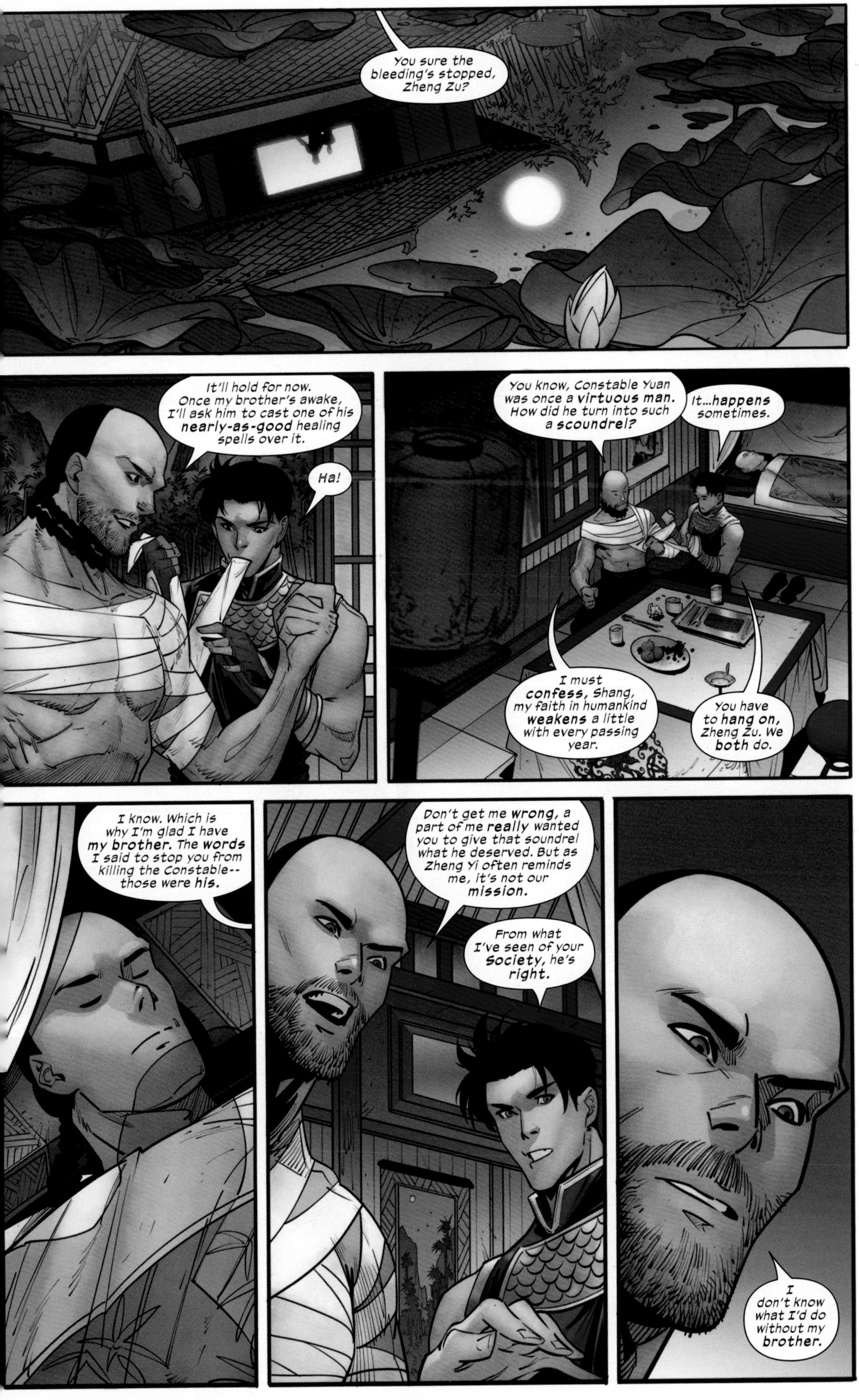

You sure the bleeding's stopped, Zheng Zu?
It'll hold for now. Once my brother's awake, I'll ask him to cast one of his nearly-as-good healing spells over it.
Ha!
You know, Constable Yuan was once a virtuous man. How did he turn into such a scoundrel?
It...happens sometimes.
I must confess, Shang, my faith in humankind weakens a little with every passing year.
You have to hang on, Zheng Zu. We both do.
I know. Which is why I'm glad I have my brother. The words I said to stop you from killing the Constable-- those were his.
Don't get me wrong, a part of me really wanted you to give that soundrel what he deserved. But as Zheng Yi often reminds me, it's not our mission.
From what I've seen of your Society, he's right.
I don't know what I'd do without my brother.

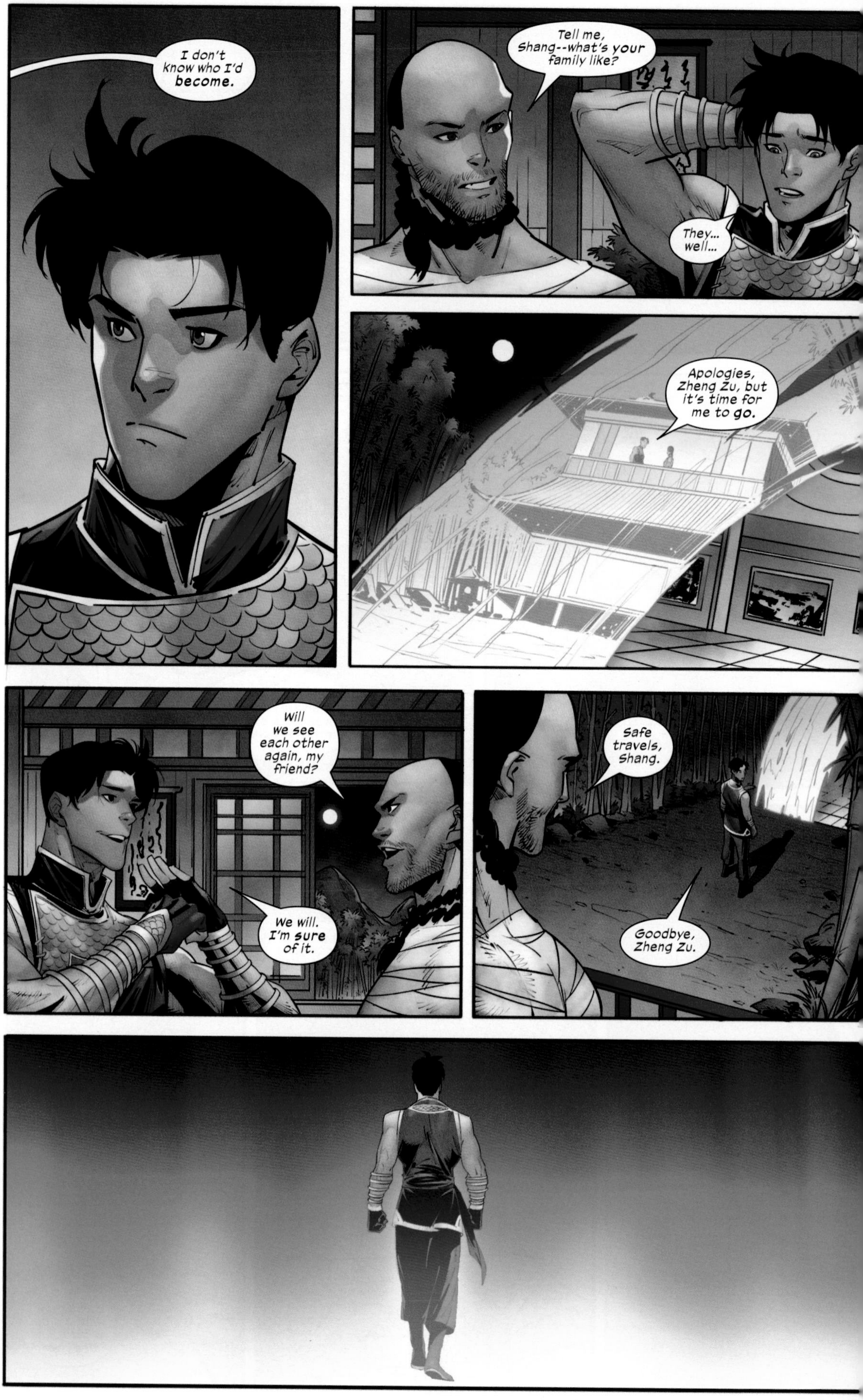
I don't know who I'd become.
Tell me, Shang--what's your family like?
They... well...
Apologies, Zheng Zu, but it's time for me to go.
Will we see each other again, my friend?
We will. I'm sure of it.
Safe travels, Shang.
Goodbye, Zheng Zu.

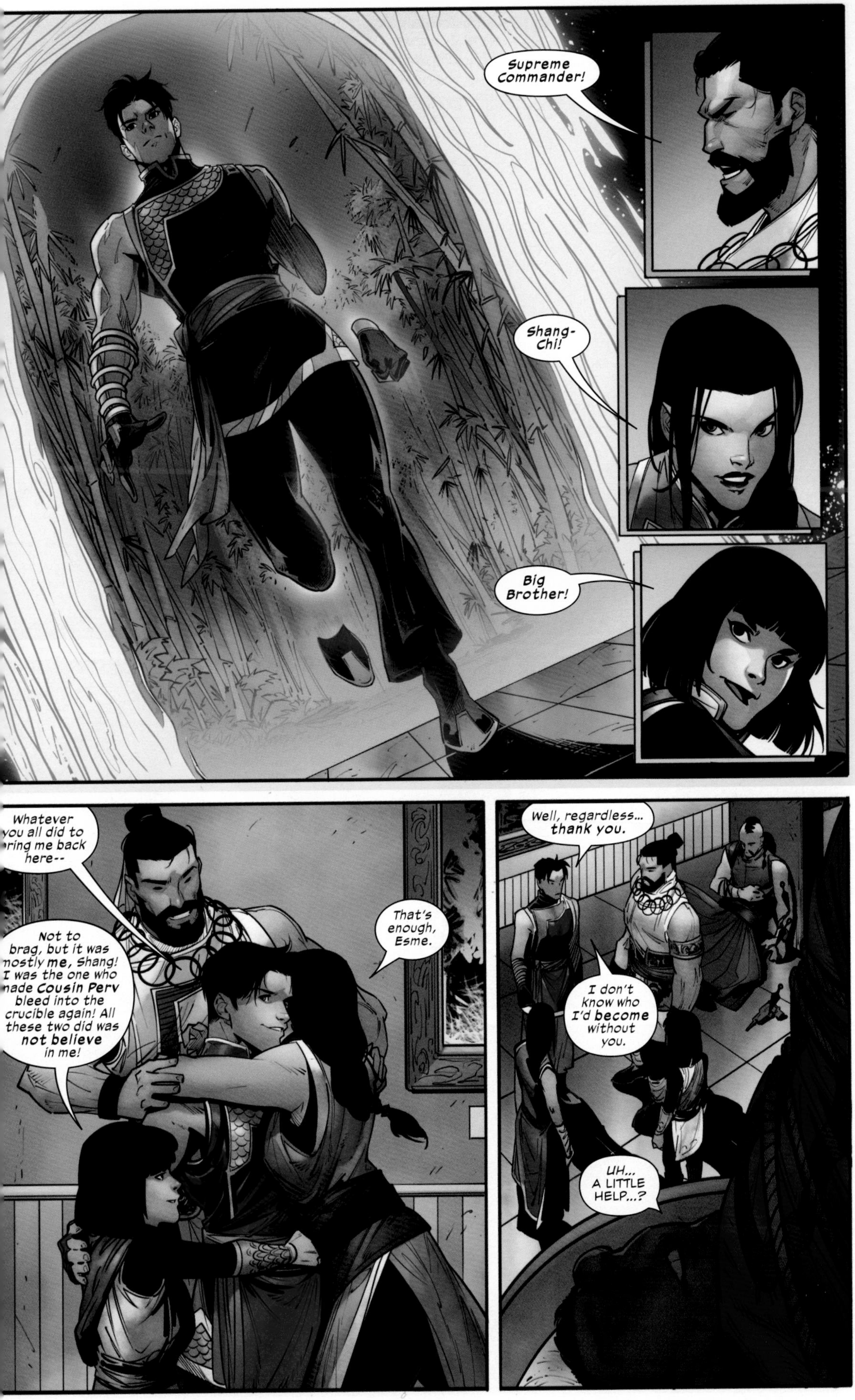

Supreme Commander!
Shang-Chi!
Big Brother!
Whatever you all did to bring me back here--
Not to brag, but it was mostly me, Shang! I was the one who made Cousin Perv bleed into the crucible again! All these two did was not believe in me!
That's enough, Esme.
Well, regardless... thank you.
I don't know who I'd become without you.
UH... A LITTLE HELP...?

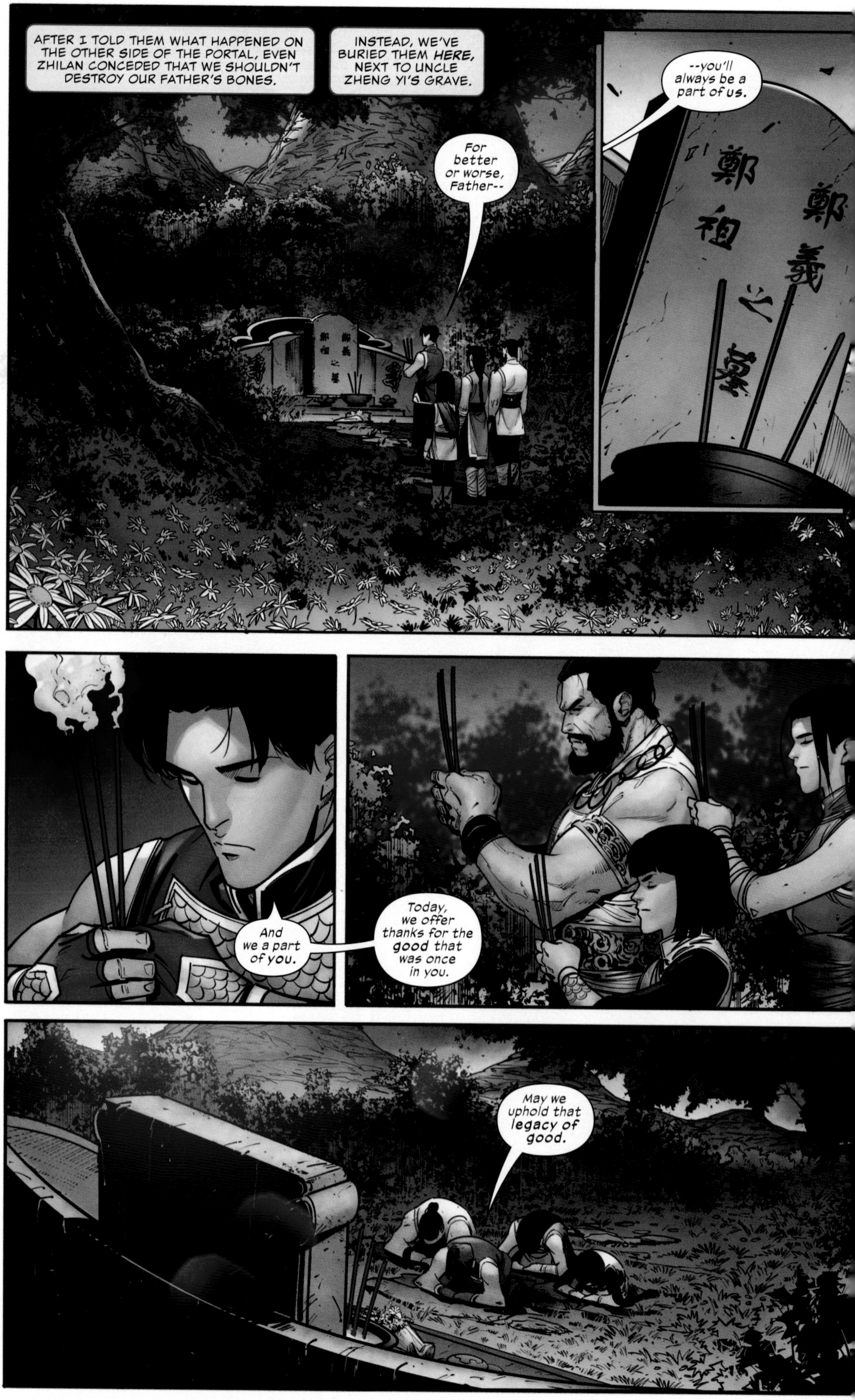
AFTER I TOLD THEM WHAT HAPPENED ON THE OTHER SIDE OF THE PORTAL, EVEN ZHILAN CONCEDED THAT WE SHOULDN'T DESTROY OUR FATHER'S BONES.
INSTEAD, WE'VE BURIED THEM HERE, NEXT TO UNCLE ZHENG YI'S GRAVE.
For better or worse, Father--
--you'll always be a part of us.
鄭祖
鄭義之墓
And we a part of you.
Today, we offer thanks for the good that was once in you.
May we uphold that legacy of good.

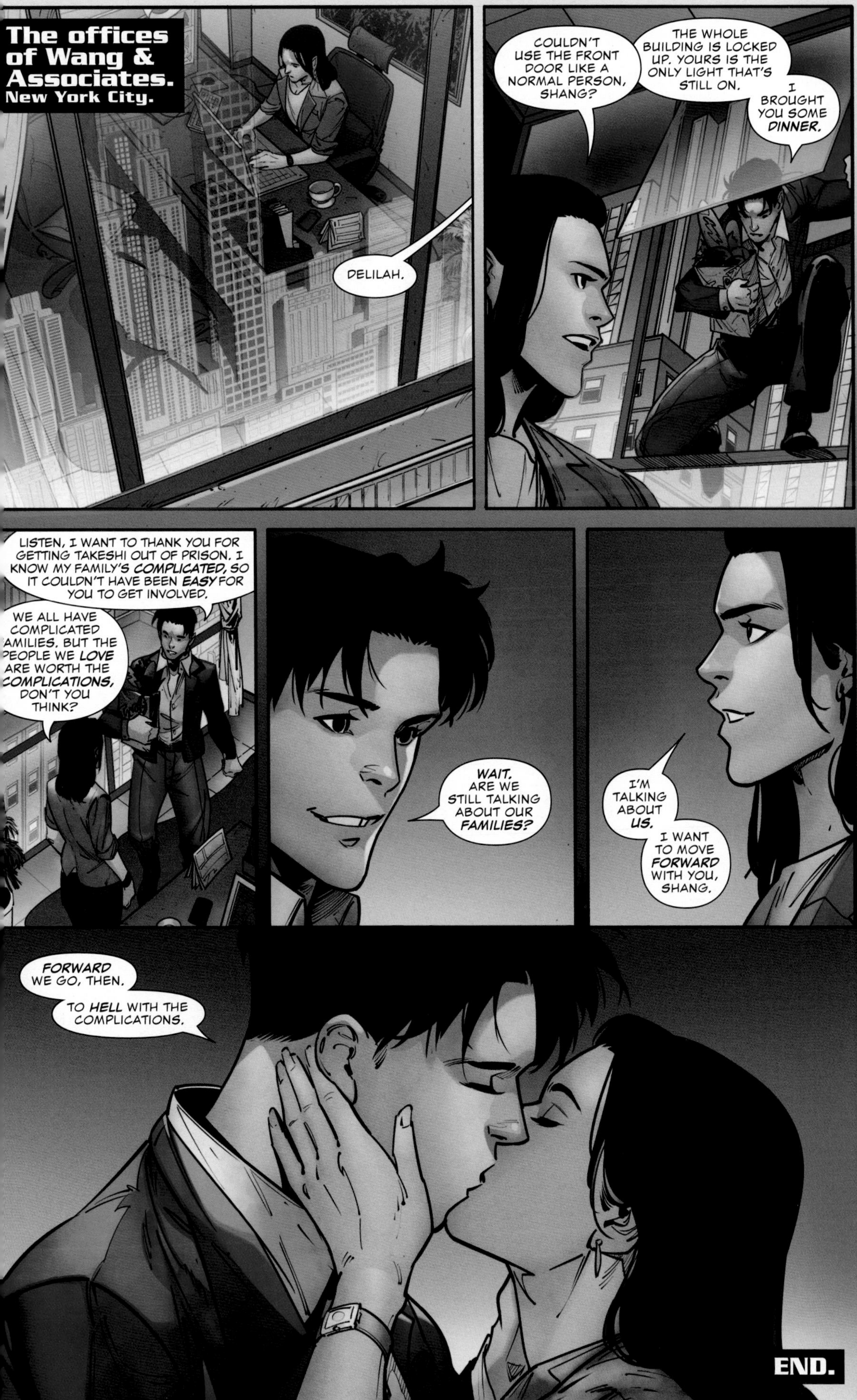
The offices of Wang & Associates. New York City.
DELILAH.
COULDN'T USE THE FRONT DOOR LIKE A NORMAL PERSON, SHANG?
THE WHOLE BUILDING IS LOCKED UP. YOURS IS THE ONLY LIGHT THAT'S STILL ON.
I BROUGHT YOU SOME DINNER.
LISTEN, I WANT TO THANK YOU FOR GETTING TAKESHI OUT OF PRISON. I KNOW MY FAMILY'S COMPLICATED, SO IT COULDN'T HAVE BEEN EASY FOR YOU TO GET INVOLVED.
WE ALL HAVE COMPLICATED AMILIES. BUT THE PEOPLE WE LOVE ARE WORTH THE COMPLICATIONS, DON'T YOU THINK?
WAIT. ARE WE STILL TALKING ABOUT OUR FAMILIES?
I'M TALKING ABOUT US.
I WANT TO MOVE FORWARD WITH YOU, SHANG.
FORWARD WE GO, THEN.
TO HELL WITH THE COMPLICATIONS.
END.

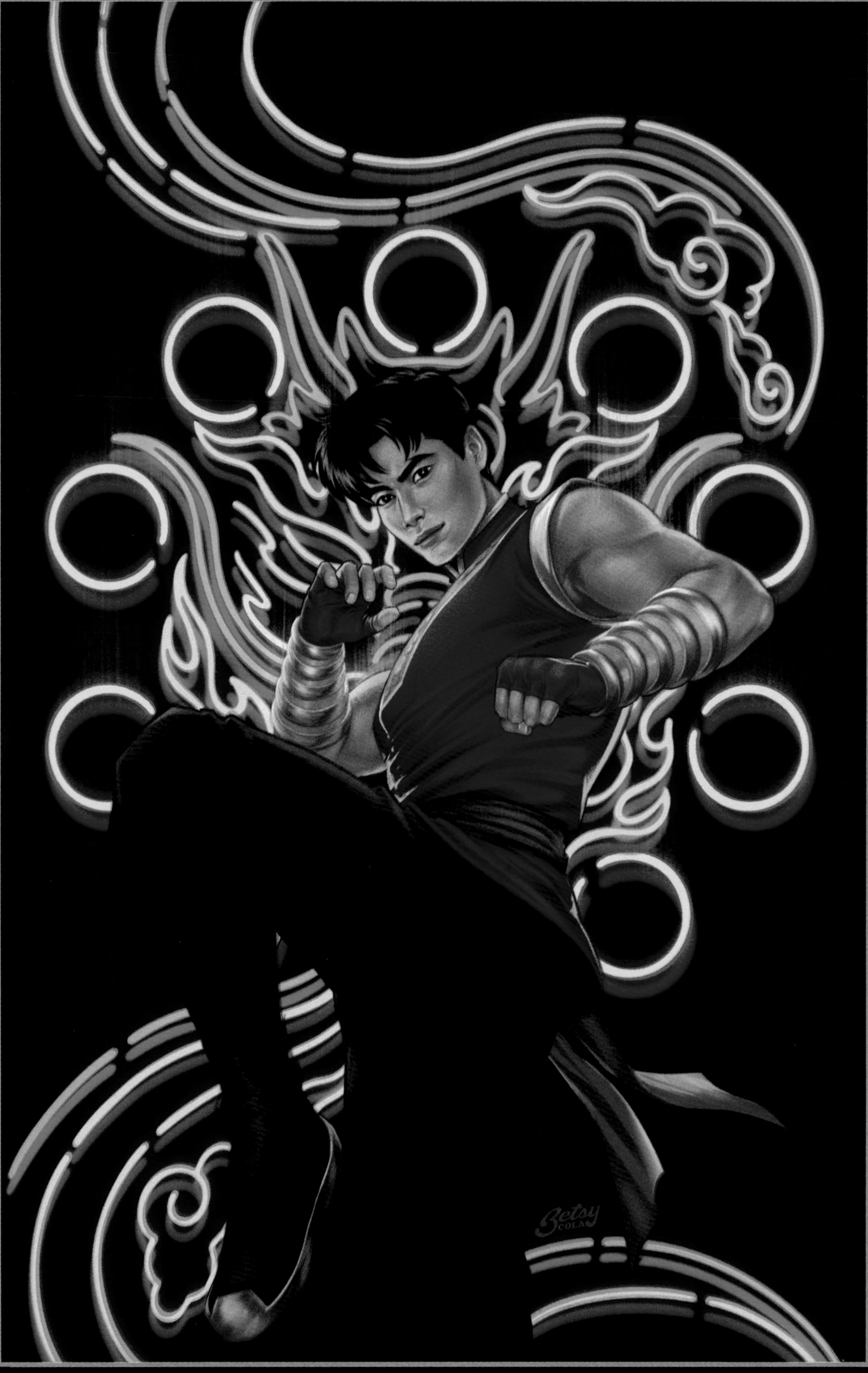
Betsy
COLA

SHANG-CHI AND THE TEN RINGS #2 VARIANT BY
BETSY COLA

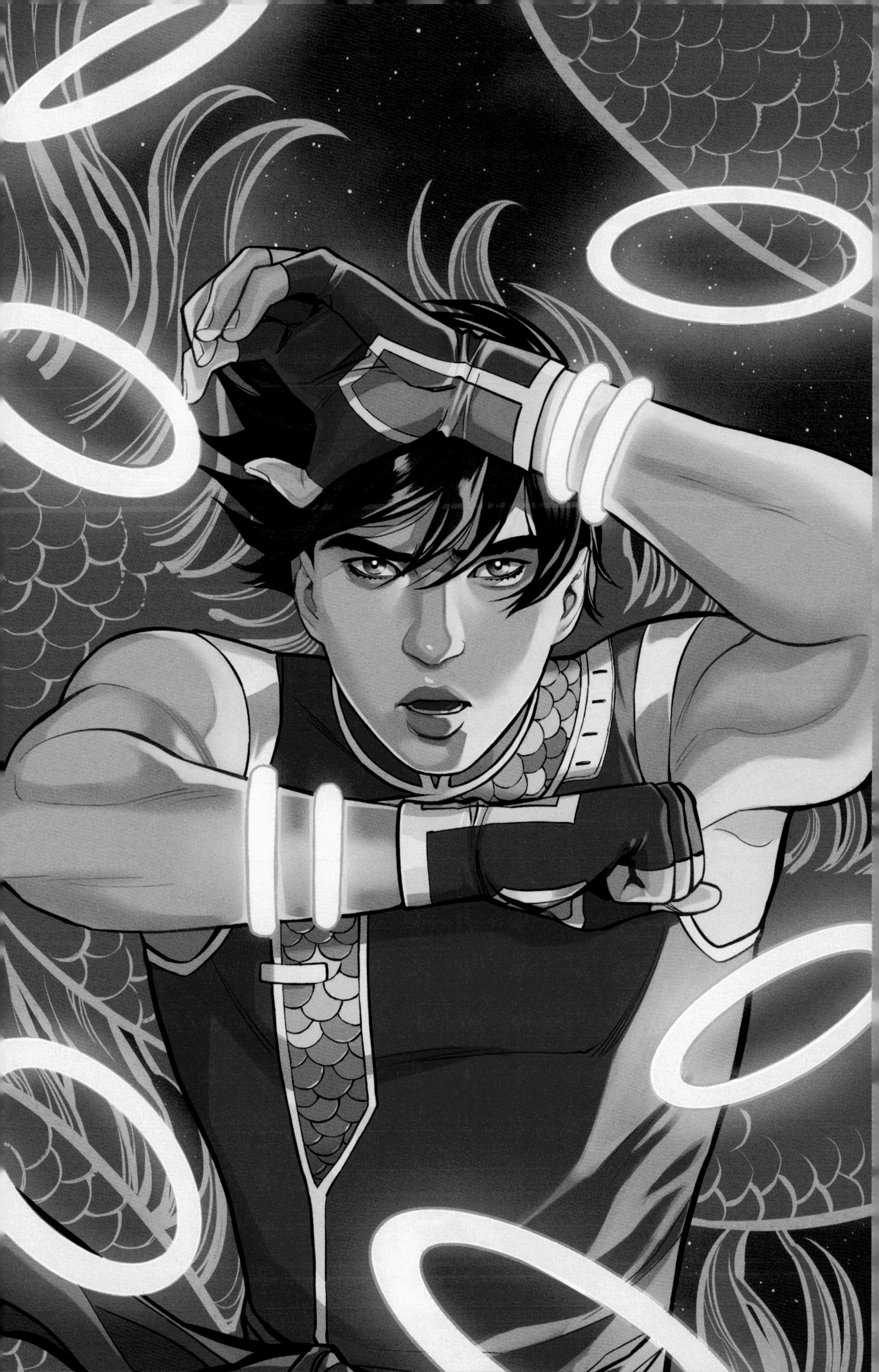

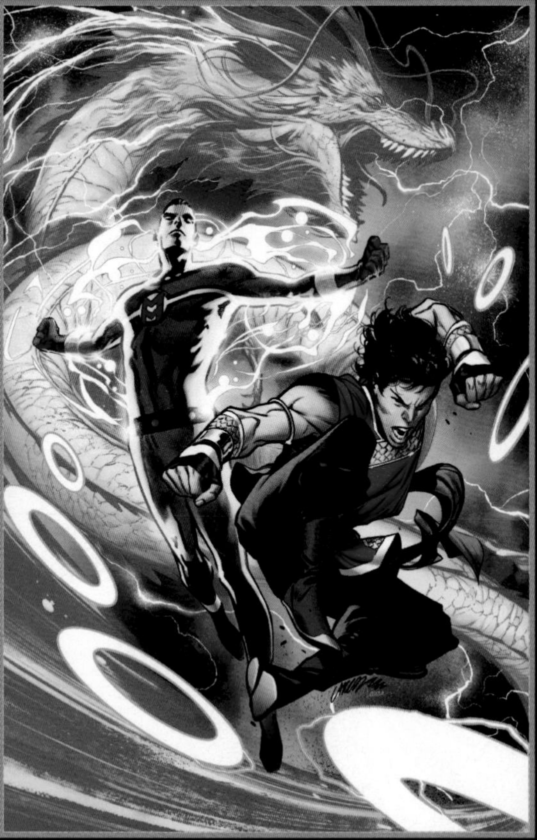

SHANG-CHI AND THE TEN RINGS #3 MIRACLEMAN VARIANT BY
PEPE LARRAZ & LAURA MARTIN

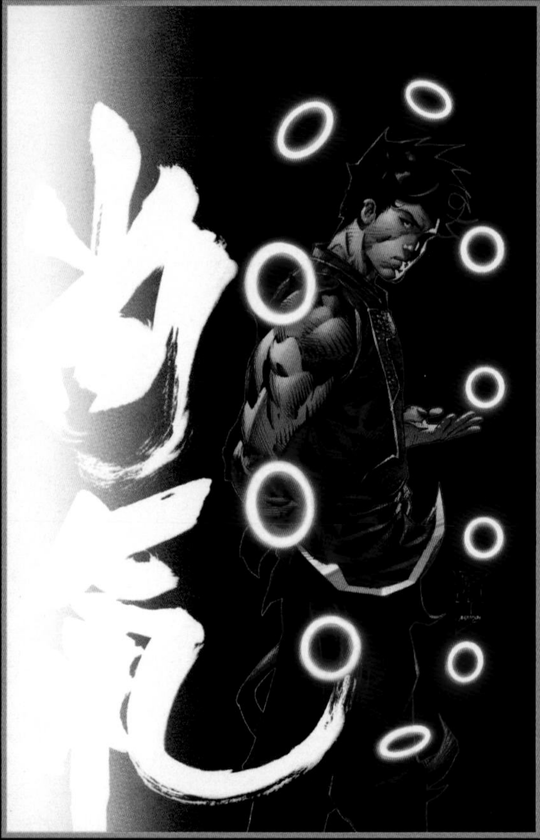

SHANG-CHI AND THE TEN RINGS #4 VARIANT BY
PHILIP TAN & BRAD ANDERSON

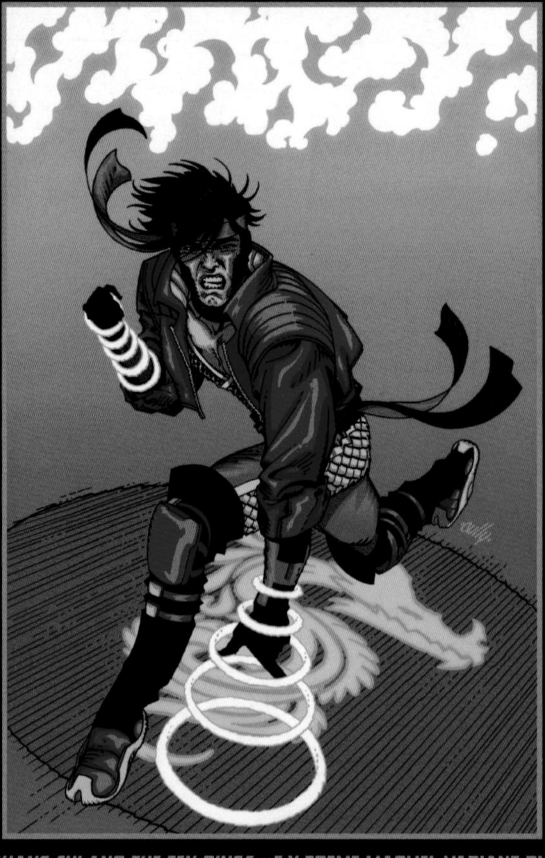

SHANG-CHI AND THE TEN RINGS #5 X-TREME MARVEL VARIANT BY
CULLY HAMNER & JORDIE BELLAIRE

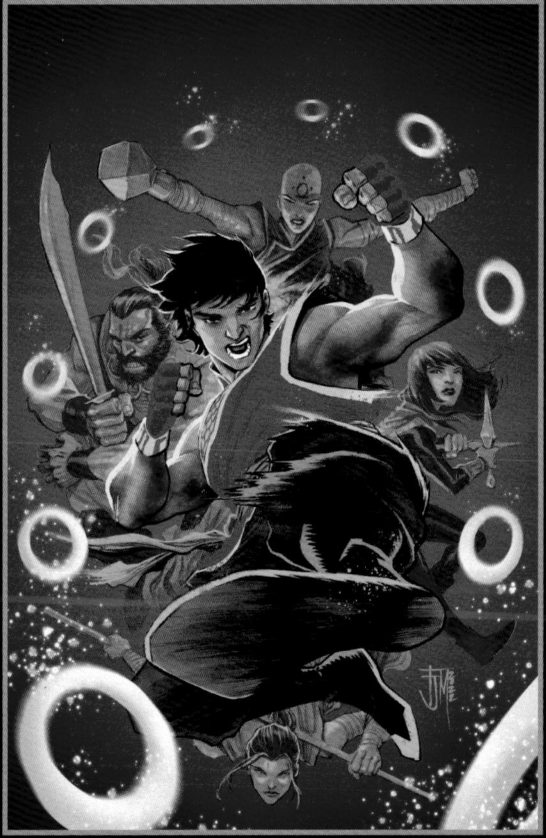

SHANG-CHI AND THE TEN RINGS #6 VARIANT BY
FRANCIS MANAPUL

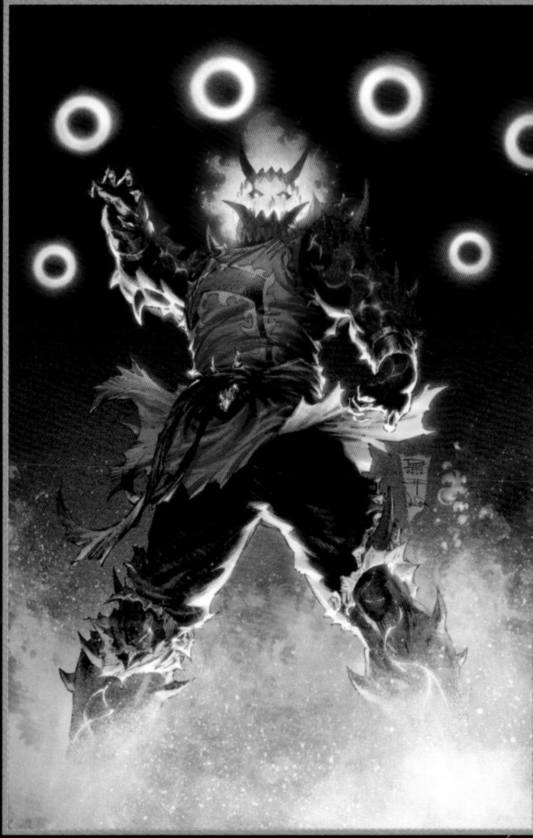

SHANG-CHI AND THE TEN RINGS #6 DEMONIZED VARIANT B
PHILIP TAN & SEBASTIAN CHENG

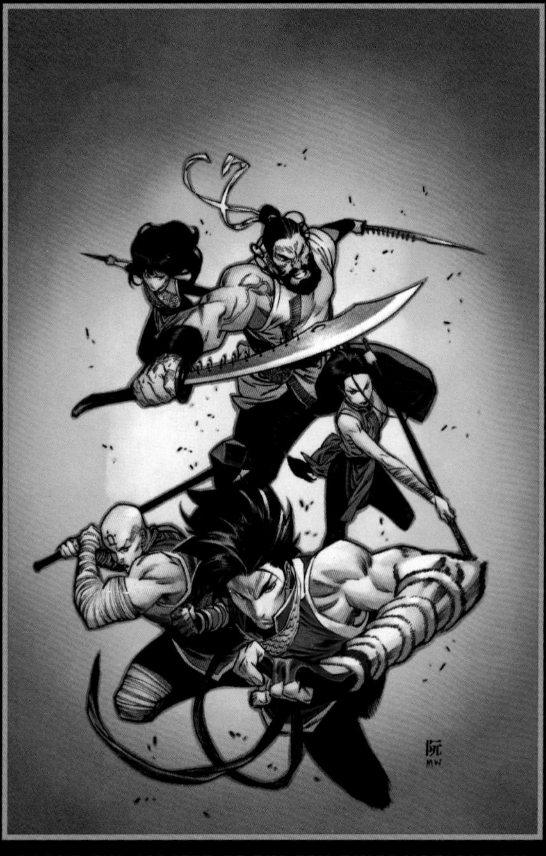

SHANG-CHI: MASTER OF THE TEN RINGS VARIANT BY
DIKE RUAN & MATTHEW WILSON

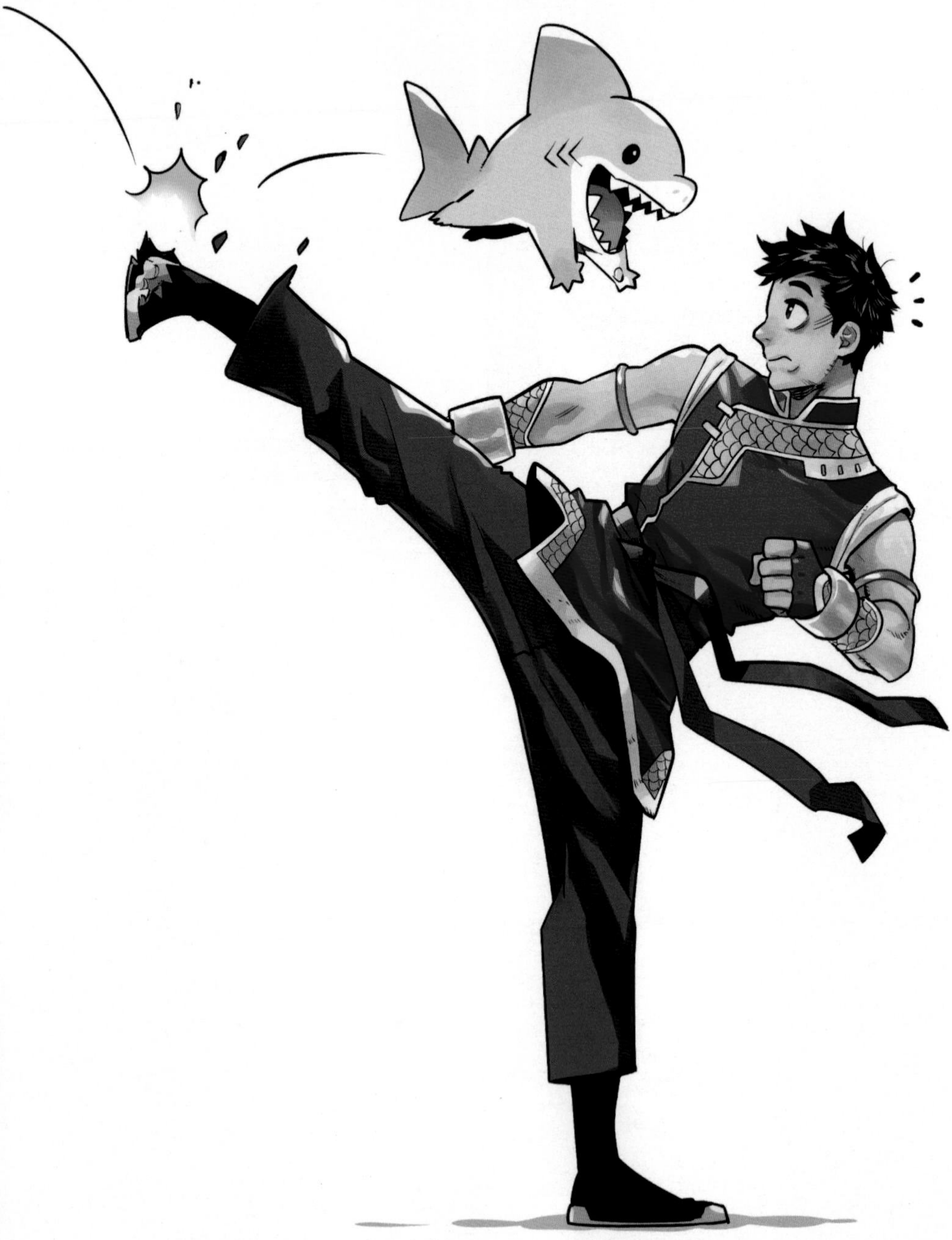